THE INTERNATIONAL TAX REVOLUTION

The International Tax Revolution offers the first comprehensive analysis of the profound changes in international taxation over the past decade, culminating in the landmark October 2021 agreement by over 140 countries to implement a global corporate minimum tax and modify profit allocation and nexus rules for the digital economy. The book provides a historical narrative of how the original International Tax Regime (ITR) crumbled under the pressures of globalization and tax competition between 1980 and 2008, and how the financial crisis of 2008–10 and subsequent cuts to social welfare programs spurred governments to adopt new approaches to taxing multinational corporations. Chapters explore the impact of globalization and tax competition on countries' ability to provide a social safety net for their citizens, and outline how the world has come together to limit such competition, modify the outdated rules, and promote greater equity in the global tax system.

Reuven S. Avi-Yonah is the Irwin I. Cohn Professor of Law and director of the International Tax LLM Program at the University of Michigan. He specializes in corporate and international taxation.

Young Ran (Christine) Kim is Professor of Law at Benjamin N. Cardozo School of Law, Yeshiva University. Her research focuses on international tax, business tax, and taxation in the digital economy.

CAMBRIDGE TAX LAW

Tax law is a growing area of interest. It is included as a subdivision in many areas of study and is a key consideration in business needs throughout the world. Books in this series expose the theoretical underpinning behind the law to shed light on taxation systems, so that the questions to be asked when addressing an issue become clear. These academic books, written by leading scholars, are a central port of call for information on tax law, with content illustrated by case law and legislation. The books will be of interest to those studying law, business, economics, accounting and finance courses.

Series Editor

Professor Peter Harris, Law Faculty, University of Cambridge, Director of the Centre for Tax Law.

Professor Peter Harris brings a wealth of experience to the series. He has taught and presented tax courses at more than a dozen different universities in as many countries and has acted as an external tax consultant for the International Monetary Fund for over twenty years.

The International Tax Revolution

REUVEN S. AVI-YONAH
University of Michigan Law School

YOUNG RAN (CHRISTINE) KIM
Benjamin N. Cardozo School of Law

CAMBRIDGE
UNIVERSITY PRESS

CAMBRIDGE
UNIVERSITY PRESS

Shaftesbury Road, Cambridge CB2 8EA, United Kingdom

One Liberty Plaza, 20th Floor, New York, NY 10006, USA

477 Williamstown Road, Port Melbourne, VIC 3207, Australia

314–321, 3rd Floor, Plot 3, Splendor Forum, Jasola District Centre, New Delhi – 110025, India

103 Penang Road, #05-06/07, Visioncrest Commercial, Singapore 238467

Cambridge University Press is part of Cambridge University Press & Assessment, a department of the University of Cambridge.

We share the University's mission to contribute to society through the pursuit of education, learning and research at the highest international levels of excellence.

www.cambridge.org
Information on this title: www.cambridge.org/9781009331845

DOI: 10.1017/9781009331852

When citing this work, please include a reference to the DOI 10.1017/9781009331852

First published 2025

A catalogue record for this publication is available from the British Library

Library of Congress Cataloging-in-Publication Data
NAMES: Avi-Yonah, Reuven S. (Reuven Shlomo), 1957- author. | Kim, Christine (Writer of International tax revolution), author.
TITLE: The international tax revolution / Reuven S. Avi-Yonah, University of Michigan Law School; Christine Kim, Yeshiva University, New York.
DESCRIPTION: Cambridge, United Kingdom ; New York, NY : Cambridge University Press, 2025. | Includes bibliographical references and index.
IDENTIFIERS: LCCN 2024061369 (print) | LCCN 2024061370 (ebook) | ISBN 9781009331845 (hardback) | ISBN 9781009331821 (hardcover) | ISBN 9781009331852 (epub)
SUBJECTS: LCSH: International business enterprises–Taxation–Law and legislation–History. | Corporations–Taxation–Law and legislation–History. | Electronic commerce–Taxation–Law and legislation. | Double taxation.
CLASSIFICATION: LCC K4475 .A95 2025 (print) | LCC K4475 (ebook) | DDC 343.06/7–dc23/eng/20250111
LC record available at https://lccn.loc.gov/2024061369
LC ebook record available at https://lccn.loc.gov/2024061370

ISBN 978-1-009-33184-5 Hardback

Contents

Abbreviations

ADS	Automated Digital Services
AEoI	Automatic Exchange of Information
ALS	Arm's Length Standard
ATAD	Anti-Tax Avoidance Directive
ATO	Australian Tax Office
ATR	average tax rate
BEAT	Base Erosion and Anti-Abuse Tax
BEPS	Base Erosion and Profit Shifting
BP	Benefits Principle
BVI	British Virgin Islands
CAMT	Corporate Alternative Minimum Tax
CAMTC	Commentaries on the Articles of the Model Tax Convention
CBCR	Country-by-Country Reporting
CCCTB	Common Consolidated Corporate Tax Base
CEN	Capital Export Neutrality
CFA	Committee on Fiscal Affairs
CFB	Consumer-Facing Businesses
CFC	Controlled Foreign Corporation
CIN	Capital Import Neutrality
CIV	Collective Investment Vehicles
CON	Capital Ownership Neutrality
CRS	Common Reporting Standard
CRS	Congressional Research Service
DD	Double Deduction
D/NI	Deduction/No Inclusion
DPT	Diverted Profits Tax
DST	Digital Services Taxes
EATR	Effective Average Tax Rate

EBITDA	Earnings before Interest, Taxes, Depreciation, and Amortization
EC	European Commission
EL	Equalizations Levy
EMTR	Effective Marginal Tax Rate
EoIR	Exchange of Information on Request
ESG	Environmental, Social, and Corporate Governance
ETR	Effective Tax Rate
EU	European Union
FATCA	Foreign Account Tax Compliance Act
FDI	Foreign Direct Investors or Investment
FDII	Foreign Derived Intangible Income
FFI	Foreign Financial Institution
FHTP	Forum on Harmful Tax Practices
FTA	Forum on Tax Administration
FTC	Foreign Tax Credit
GAAR	General Anti-Avoidance Rule
GAFA	Google, Apple, Facebook, and Amazon
GDP	Gross Domestic Product
GILTI	Global Intangible Low-Taxed Income
GLoBE	Global Anti-Base Erosion
IF	Inclusive Framework
IGA	Intergovernmental Agreements
IIR	Income Inclusion Rule
IMF	International Monetary Fund
IRA	Inflation Reduction Act
IRC	Internal Revenue Code
ITC	Investment Tax Credits
ITR	International Tax Regime
LOB	Limitation on Benefits
MAAL	Multinational Anti-Tax Avoidance
MAATM	Multilateral Agreement on Administrative Cooperation in Tax Matters
MAP	Mutual Agreement Procedure
MLI	Multilateral Instrument
MNE	Multinational Enterprises
MTC	Multilateral Tax Convention
OECD	Organisation for Economic Co-operation and Development
OEDT	Obligations to Eliminate Double Taxation
PCOI	Permanent Committee on Investigations (US Senate)
PE	Permanent Establishment
PPT	Principal Purpose Test or Primary Purposes Test

PSI	Permanent Subcommittee on Investigations
QBAI	Qualified Business Asset Investment
QDMTT	Qualified Domestic Minimum Top-Up Tax
QFTB	Qualified Flow Through Tax Benefits
QI	Qualified Intermediary
QRTC	Qualified Refundable Tax Credits
R&D	Research and Development
R&E	Research and Experimentation
SBIE	Substance-Based Income Exclusion
SHIELD	Stopping Harmful Inversions and Ending Low-Tax Developments
STP	Single Tax Principle
STTR	Subject to Tax Rule
TANF	Temporary Assistance for Needy Families
TCJA	Tax Cuts and Jobs Act
TFDE	Task Force on the Digital Economy
TIEA	Tax Information Exchange Agreements
TPG	Transfer Pricing Guidelines
UK	United Kingdom
UN	United Nations
UPE	Ultimate Parent Entity
USTR	United States Trade Representative
UTPR	Undertaxed Profits Rule
VAT	Value Added Tax
VCLT	Vienna Convention on the Law of Treaties
WTO	World Trade Organization

Introduction

The International Tax Revolution, 2008–2023[*]

The past decade has witnessed the creation of a new International Tax Regime (ITR). The original ITR was created a century ago by the League of Nations based on a compromise reached in 1923. Until the 1980s, it functioned well by preventing most instances of double taxation and double non-taxation by allocating cross-border income between home and host jurisdictions.

However, since the advent of globalization in the 1980s and digitalization in the 1990s, the original ITR has ceased to function as intended. The main problem is the increased mobility of capital related to increased intangibility and digitalization, in conjunction with a relaxation of capital controls and increased tax competition.

These developments posed a problem for countries that wished to leave their financial borders open to reap the benefits of globalization. Countries were faced with a difficult choice if they wished to continue to participate in an open, globalized financial economy. They could either refuse to engage in cutthroat tax competition and face the risk of capital fleeing their borders, or they could give in, engage in tax competition, and lose tax revenue as they slashed rates to placate corporations. The outcome was a significant fall in tax revenues that threatened the social safety net of the modern welfare state.

The challenging trilemma faced by countries of open borders in the globalized economy, tax competition among countries, and financially supporting the welfare state became unsustainable following the financial crisis of 2008–09, after which many countries were forced to implement harsh austerity measures. These governments subjected their populations to austerity while parliamentary hearings, leaks, and media reports revealed that rich individuals and large corporations were paying little tax on cross-border income. The result over the past decade has been the creation of a new ITR designed to curb both tax evasion by the rich and tax competition by countries.

[*] This chapter draws heavily from a previous piece written by the first author. Reuven S. Avi-Yonah, *International Taxation, Globalization, and the Economic Digital Divide*, 26 J. INT'L ECON. L. 101 (2023).

The key question going forward is how the new ITR will deal with inter-nation equity – that is, the division of tax revenues among states. Here, we will first provide an overview of the decline and fall of the original ITR from 1980 to 2009, then the creation of the new ITR from 2010 on, and finally the implications of the new ITR for inter-nation equity (especially between developed and developing countries).

I.1 GLOBALIZATION AND THE DECLINE OF THE INTERNATIONAL TAX REGIME, 1980–2009

Before the 1980s, the ITR functioned as an adequate protective device against tax competition, therefore protecting tax revenues and the social safety net. The old ITR was based on two principles: the benefits principle, and the single tax principle. The benefits principle is that active (business) income should be taxed primarily in the *source jurisdiction* and passive (investment) income should be taxed primarily in the *residence jurisdiction*. The single tax principle is that the goal of the ITR is to prevent both double taxation and double non-taxation. Therefore, the secondary taxing jurisdiction (residence for active income and source for passive income) should impose a tax in a situation where the primary taxing jurisdiction does not do so.

Prior to the 1980s, residence jurisdictions were able to impose tax on most passive income because exchange controls made it difficult to invest offshore, and because source jurisdictions imposed withholding taxes on such income. Active income was in turn taxed by source jurisdictions because it was less mobile and Controlled Foreign Corporation (CFC) rules imposed residence-based tax on the income in cases where it was mobile and escaped source-based taxation.

This situation changed in the 1980s and 1990s. Globalization led most countries to relax their exchange controls, and portfolio investments overseas became more common. In addition, starting with the United States in 1984, most members of the Organisation for Economic Co-operation and Development (OECD) unilaterally abolished withholding taxes on outbound interest payments, thereby aiding and abetting tax evasion by residents of other OECD members. For active income, the increased mobility of multinational enterprises (MNEs or multinationals) led source jurisdictions to offer targeted tax holidays, and the fear of tax competition for the headquarters of those MNEs led residence jurisdictions to relax their CFC rules. Neither the residence jurisdiction of the MNEs nor the production jurisdiction typically taxed the MNEs' income on a current basis. The only jurisdiction that was not subject to this sort of tax competition was the *market jurisdiction*. However, after the creation of the internet and the rise of the digital economy in the 1990s, it became possible for MNEs to earn billions in income from market jurisdictions without being subject to tax because they lacked a permanent establishment (PE) in a market.

In the first decade of the twenty-first century, things only got worse. On the passive income front, it became possible to avoid withholding taxes not just on interest (because of unilateral abolition), royalties (because of the tax treaties, which abolish withholding), and capital gains (because of the source rules, which provide for residence taxation) but also on portfolio dividends because of the rise of derivatives, which enabled portfolio investors to receive the economic equivalent of dividends without being subject to withholding taxes. It also became clear that limits on the exchange of financial information meant that, in most cases, *residence jurisdictions* could not effectively tax foreign source portfolio income. In 2005, Joseph Guttentag (the former Treasury Deputy Assistant Secretary for international tax affairs) and the first author estimated that the United States was losing $50 billion a year to such tax evasion, and that most other countries were in worse shape because their shadow economies were larger.[1]

On the active income front, the decade from 1998 to 2008 saw the enactment of Check the Box and Internal Revenue Code (IRC) section 954(c)(6), which cause US tax authorities to become incapable of using the CFC rules to enforce residence-based taxation of US-based multinationals. Deferral, which is categorized as a tax expenditure in the United States, exploded from less than $20 billion in the mid-1990s to the second largest tax expenditure in the US budget, worth $1.348 trillion from 2017 to 2026.[2]

This was justified in the name of preserving the competitiveness of US-based MNEs, but it resulted in shifting of massive amounts of income from the United States to low-taxed jurisdictions. By 2017, US MNEs had close to $3 trillion in profits "trapped" in low-taxed, offshore jurisdictions. Ireland, Luxembourg, and other jurisdictions enacted low-tax regimes designed to attract such active income, as well as the headquarters of multinationals.[3] Over thirty US-based MNEs "inverted" to Ireland and other low-taxed jurisdictions, primarily to reduce their US tax rate on US source income and to enable the distribution of low-taxed foreign-sourced income to shareholders.

Thus, a decade after the OECD first tried to tackle international tax competition, the problem had gotten significantly worse. Both the individual income tax (designed primarily to preserve progressivity) and the corporate income tax (designed primarily to regulate MNEs) were under tremendous pressure. The decline in revenues and the inability of most jurisdictions to raise consumption taxes (because the consumption tax rates were already prohibitively high) placed the social safety net under severe financial pressure. This pressure became too much for the system to bear following the financial crisis of 2008.

1 Reuven S. Avi-Yonah & Joseph Guttentag, *Closing the International Tax Gap*, in BRIDGING THE TAX GAP: ADDRESSING THE CRISIS IN FEDERAL TAX ADMINISTRATION 99 (Max B. Sawicky ed. 2005).

2 US Treasury, *Tax Expenditure Budget* (2017).

3 *See* Edward Kleinbard, *Stateless Income*, 11 FLA. TAX REV. 699 (2011) and Edward Kleinbard, *The Lessons of Stateless Income*, 65 TAX L. REV. 99 (2011).

I.2 THE CREATION OF THE NEW INTERNATIONAL TAX REGIME, 2010–2023

The financial crisis and the Great Recession that followed led to millions losing their jobs and their homes. In Europe, governments reacted to this pressure by imposing harsh austerity measures not seen for some time in these countries. While the Obama administration made no such cuts, the size of the US fiscal stimulus in response to the crisis was limited. While the banks were saved, millions of Americans suffered a decade of slow growth and high unemployment.[4]

The political reaction on both sides of the Atlantic was dramatic. It led to Brexit and the election of right-wing populists across the western world including Donald Trump in the United States. With this new political turn came the prospect of serious limits to globalization in the form of immigration restrictions, tariffs, and exchange controls. The nation state was reasserting itself against globalization, and one of the instruments it used was taxation. In the United States, the focus on taxation was limited to the first couple of years after the crisis because the Republican takeover of the House of Representatives in 2010 meant that no tax measures would be enacted before the 2017 Tax Cuts and Jobs Act (TCJA). In the United States, the "Double Irish Dutch Sandwich," which allows large corporations to shift profits to low- or no-tax jurisdictions, was once featured as a tax avoidance technique in detail in 2010 on the *NBC Nightly News*, but the topic faded thereafter. In contrast to the United States, in Europe, austerity meant a continued political focus on taxing both the rich and MNEs. European taxes became a front-page matter for the period after 2008. Such political momentum brought a series of developments that led to a significant enhancement in the ability of the ITR to capture cross-border income.

On the passive income front, the UBS scandal of 2006–08 led directly to the enactment of the US Foreign Account Tax Compliance Act (FATCA) in 2010. The UBS hearing before the Senate Permanent Committee on Investigations (PSI) revealed that UBS sent bankers directly to the United States to solicit rich individuals to set up shell companies in the Cayman Islands and then reinvest the money through UBS into the United States. UBS claimed that even though it was a "qualified intermediary" (QI) and knew who the real owner of the shell was, it was justified under the QI regulations in relying on a form W8-BEN that stated that the owner of the income was the Caymans shell and that it was foreign.[5]

4 Reuven S. Avi-Yonah & Orli K. Avi-Yonah, *Be Careful What You Wish For? Reducing Inequality in the Twenty-First Century*, 116 Mich. L. Rev. 1001 (2018).

5 Reuven S. Avi-Yonah, *Testimony on Banking Secrecy Practices and Wealthy American Taxpayers*, US House Committee on Ways and Means, Subcommittee on Select Revenue Measures (Mar. 31, 2009); Reuven S. Avi-Yonah, *Testimony for Hearing on Offshore Tax Evasion*, US Senate Finance Committee (May 3, 2007); Reuven S. Avi-Yonah, *Testimony for Hearing on Offshore Transactions*, US Senate Permanent Subcommittee on Investigations (Aug. 1, 2006).

The FATCA imposes a 30 percent withholding tax on the US income of any foreign financial institution (FFI) that knows or has reason to know it holds accounts of US residents or citizens and does not reveal such information to the Internal Revenue Service (IRS). Because FFIs are frequently prohibited from directly revealing financial information to the IRS, the Obama administration negotiated over 100 intergovernmental agreements (IGAs) that enable the FFIs to turn over the information to its own government, which then exchanges it with the IRS under tax treaties and tax information exchange agreements (TIEAs). Many of the IGAs are reciprocal, so that the United States is also obligated (at least on paper) to exchange this same information about foreign residents. This bilateral diplomatic initiative has enabled the United States and other countries to enforce rules against previously shady FFIs.

The IGAs in turn made countries develop a Common Reporting Standard (CRS) for the automatic exchange of financial information. The OECD negotiated a Multilateral Agreement on Administrative Cooperation in Tax Matters (MAATM), which relies on the CRS to provide for automatic exchange without the ability to rely on bank secrecy or dual criminality provisions. Most countries in the world, and all OECD members except the United States, have ratified the MAATM.[6]

It is now much more difficult to evade income taxation due to these new regulations and reporting rules. An evader must worry that, in almost every country, information about her income may be collected and transmitted to her residence jurisdiction. In addition, the evader must worry that the information may be leaked by a whistleblower (as in the Panama Papers and the Paradise Papers). We would estimate that the FATCA alone led to a significant decrease in the international tax gap in the United States, well below the $50 billion estimated in 2005.

On the active income front, there have also been dramatic developments in the last decade. First, there was the OECD Base Erosion and Profit Shifting (BEPS 1.0) project (2013–15), which was led by the G20 and resulted in fifteen action steps designed to enhance both source-based and residence-based taxation of active income. For example, BEPS 1.0 Action 2 bars a deduction for payments to hybrid entities, thereby eliminating the tax avoidance impact of Check the Box.

BEPS 1.0 was introduced in the EU as the Anti-Tax Avoidance Directive II (ATAD II). ATAD II generally came into effect in January 2019 and, requires all EU members to adopt strict CFC rules (generally requiring residence-based taxation if the effective tax rate of the source jurisdiction is below 50 percent of the tax rate in the residence jurisdiction).[7] This measure, in addition to the enactment of BEPS 1.0 Action 2, means that it is now much harder to shift profits artificially out of EU

6 Reuven S. Avi-Yonah, *And Yet It Moves: Taxation and Labor Mobility in the Twenty-First Century*, 67 Tax L. Rev. 169 (2014); Reuven S. Avi-Yonah & Gil Savir, *IGAs vs. MAATM: Has Tax Bilateralism Outlived Its Usefulness?* 66 CCH Global Tax Weekly 11 (Feb. 13, 2014).

7 *See* Council Directive (EU) 2017/952 of May 29, 2017 (ATAD II), applying the anti-hybrid rules to third countries.

member states.[8] Another important measure in BEPS 1.0 and ATAD II is the primary purpose test (PPT), which requires that all tax treaties incorporate language that the treaty will not apply to transactions if the primary purpose of the transaction was tax avoidance.[9]

Until 2017, it could be argued that the United States was falling behind in terms of combating tax avoidance, because it took the position that it was already compliant with BEPS 1.0, rejected the PPT, and did not sign the MAATM. The passage of the 2017 TCJA dramatically changed this. The TCJA includes three measures that significantly increase taxation of US-based as well as foreign-based MNEs: the transition tax, the Global Intangible Low-Taxed Income (GILTI), and the Base Erosion and Anti-Abuse Tax (BEAT). First, the TCJA imposed a one-time, hefty transition tax on $3 trillion of past, accumulated, foreign earnings of US-based MNEs. Second, while the TCJA provided for an exemption for certain future dividends from CFCs to their US parents, this exemption is strictly limited to a deemed 10 percent return on tangible property, which for most US-based MNEs is close to zero (as they rely heavily on intangibles). For any amount that exceeds this deemed return, TCJA imposes a current minimum tax of 10.5 percent (13.125 percent if foreign tax credits are included) on the worldwide earnings of the MNE. Third, the TCJA imposes an alternative minimum tax of 10 percent on both US- and foreign-based MNEs by disregarding interest, royalty, and some other payments from the United States to the related foreign entity.

These developments (BEPS 1.0, ATAD II of the EU, and the TCJA of the United States) resulted in both US-based and foreign MNEs being subjected to significantly higher levels of tax on cross-border active income than they were before 2018.[10]

For example, the structure used by most US-based MNEs before 2017 for their foreign operations was to have a top-level CFC in a low-tax jurisdiction, with lower-tier CFCs in high-tax jurisdictions. The parent would transfer intellectual property to the top-tier CFC via a cost sharing agreement, and the top-tier CFC would, in turn, license the IP to the lower-tier CFCs. The key to this structure under Check the Box was only the top CFC would be treated as a corporation, while all the lower CFCs would be treated as disregarded entities by tax authorities (i.e., treated as branches of the top CFC). While for foreign tax purposes deductible royalties from the lower CFCs to the top CFC would be effective in shifting profits to the low-tax jurisdiction of the top CFC (and not subject to withholding under treaties and EU Directives), for US tax purposes these royalties did not exist and did not trigger a deemed dividend to the US parent.

8 Another measure included in ATAD is a 30 percent of EBITDA limit on interest deductions, similar to IRC 163(j).

9 *See* Reuven S. Avi-Yonah & Gianluca Mazzoni, *BEPS, ATAP and the New Tax Dialogue: A Transatlantic Competition?* 46 INTERTAX 885 (2018).

10 *See* Kimberly A. Clausing, *Profit Shifting before and after the Tax Cuts and Jobs Act*, 73 NAT'L TAX J. 1233 (2020).

This structure does not work anymore due to the new reforms. Under BEPS 1.0 Action 2, as implemented by the EU's ATAD II, the royalties from the lower CFCs to the top CFC are not deductible because they are directed to a hybrid entity. Second, the cost sharing payments from the US parent to the top CFC would be subject to the BEAT minimum tax. Finally, the top CFC as well as all the disregarded entities below would be subject to the GILTI minimum tax (10.5 percent or 13.125 percent with foreign tax credits) on a current basis. The result is US-based MNEs need to restructure their foreign operations and are likely to be subject to a significantly higher worldwide effective tax rate than before 2018, even though both Check the Box and IRC section 954(c)(6) have only been indirectly affected by the TCJA.

Despite these achievements, BEPS 1.0 has some limits. Specifically, no consensus was reached about taxing the digital economy (i.e., primarily the US tech giants). In addition, transfer pricing was not meaningfully reformed. The PE threshold and arm's-length standard (ALS) remained in place despite both being obsolete in a modern, digital economy. In addition, relatively few of the BEPS 1.0 actions were minimum standards that had been adopted by all participants.

The political pressure to do something about BEPS 1.0 in the EU and in the developing world has not subsided, manifesting in the quick rise and fast adoption of digital services taxes (DSTs) and equalizations levies (ELs) designed to bypass the treaty limits on taxing the digital economy. This in turn has led the OECD and G20, working with over 100 countries, to propose BEPS 2.0, which was finalized in principle in October 2021.[11]

BEPS 2.0 consists of two pillars: Pillar One and Pillar Two. Pillar One is designed to address the problem of taxing corporate income at source in accordance with the benefits principle (BP). Pillar One allows source jurisdictions to tax a limited amount of income without regard to the PE and ALS limits, and to tax an additional amount in the market jurisdiction subject to the PE and ALS limits.

The main innovation in Pillar One is Amount A, which represents 25 percent of residual profit (defined as profit more than 10 percent of revenue) of in-scope MNEs (MNEs with revenues over 20 billion euros and a pretax profit margin of 10 percent). Amount A will be allocated to market jurisdictions with nexus (at least 1 million euros in revenue), using a revenue-based allocation key – that is, a single factor sales formula.

Amount A eliminates the two features of the international tax regime that have long been identified as obsolete: The requirement that MNEs have a permanent establishment (PE) in a source jurisdiction and the ALS for calculating the amount of income attributable to the PE. The PE requirement is obsolete in a world in which MNEs can earn billions in a market jurisdiction with no physical presence. The ALS is unworkable for the residual profits of MNEs (defined here as profits

[11] OECD, Statement on a Two-Pillar Solution to Address the Tax Challenges Arising from the Digitalisation of the Economy (Oct. 8, 2021) (the "Statement").

above 10 percent) because there are typically no comparable transactions. In other words, a formula, not the ALS, is the best way to allocate the residual profits. The PE requirement and ALS were both introduced into the international tax regime at an early stage, primarily through the work of Mitchell Carroll in the 1930s. It is time for both to go to make way for reforms that ensure large MNEs like Amazon, Apple, Meta, and Google pay tax in the source country they derive profits from.

Amount A is fully consistent with the benefits principle. It can be argued that a residence country should also get a share as typically the algorithms that underlie the business model were developed there; this is reflected by the fact that 75 percent of the residual profit is not taxed in the market jurisdiction and therefore should be taxed in other jurisdictions based on Pillar Two. The allocation of income to these jurisdictions is based on payroll and tangible assets (depreciation).

Pillar Two directly implements the single tax principle (STP) by ensuring a minimal tax in the residence jurisdiction if the source country tax is insufficient, and, if that is not enough, by ensuring a minimal tax in the source jurisdiction. In addition, residence or source jurisdictions can adopt a Qualified Domestic Minimum Top-Up Tax (QDMTT) to prevent the application of minimum taxes by other jurisdictions. The STP was envisaged in the original League of Nations 1923 report and the tax treaty model from 1927. But the STP was first implemented in the 1960s, and then gradually accepted (with some retreat such as the US portfolio interest exemption in 1984 and Check the Box in 1997) and implemented in BEPS 1.0 (2013–15) and the TCJA's BEAT and GILTI (2017).

Pillar Two consists of the Income Inclusion Rule (IIR), the Undertaxed Profits Rule (UTPR), and the QDMTT. The IIR reflects the ability of residence countries to implement the STP by taxing their MNEs on a residence basis. Since 95 percent of large MNEs are resident in G20 countries, this is expected to be highly effective. The UTPR is designed to enable residual source taxation when residence taxation is ineffective. The QDMTT enables both residence and source jurisdictions to turn off the other rules on domestic income by imposing their own minimum tax. The agreed-upon minimum tax rate of 15 percent is low, but it was the best that could be expected given the size of the coalition of countries. The G20 can be expected to use a higher rate for the IIR. The substance carve-out is unfortunate (since it allows for some double non-taxation in violation of the STP) but it is quite limited.

Together with the CRS regime that implements the STP for individuals, Pillar Two will ensure that the STP will apply to large MNEs as well.

I.3 THE NEW INTERNATIONAL TAX REGIME AND INTER-NATION EQUITY

A key question regarding the new ITR is how it will apply to inter-nation equity. Specifically, how will the new ITR apply to and affect developing countries?

The answer is clear; the new ITR will help developing countries curb massive tax evasion by their rich residents. As documented by recent leaks in the Panama Papers, the Paradise Papers, and the Pandora Papers, rich individuals in the developing world use tax havens to hide their investment income in developed countries from the tax administrations in their home countries. Although it does not go far enough, the CRS should significantly limit this strategy. Despite CRS and MAATM, we do not think the solution can depend entirely on the exchange of information and residence-based taxation rules. There are too many residence countries that would need to cooperate effectively, and there will always be non-cooperative tax havens hoping to attract evaders. But the key point is that portfolio investments are limited to a small number of large jurisdictions. If the United States and the EU could cooperate to reinstitute withholding taxes on interest, a large part of the issue could be solved.[12]

Regarding BEPS 2.0 and the two pillars, the answer is more complicated. Pillar One shifts some of the tax revenue from where goods and services are produced to where they are consumed. This will help large developing countries like China and India but not smaller developing countries that do not have large national markets. However, Pillar One is unlikely to harm developing countries because they will remain able to tax MNEs based on the location of production.

Pillar Two is potentially more problematic because it eliminates the ability of developing countries to engage in tax competition by setting the global minimum corporate tax rate at 15 percent, and by giving primacy to the IIR, which is based on residence. Despite this, developing countries should still be able to tax MNEs based on their local production activities and adopt the QDMTT.

The deeper issue is that Pillar Two limits developing countries' autonomy by restricting their ability to engage in tax competition. The standard advice by economists to small open economies is that they should refrain from taxing foreign investors, because such investors cannot be made to bear the burden of any tax imposed by the capital importing country. This attracts foreign capital and the tax will necessarily be shifted to less mobile factors in the host country, such as labor and/or land, and it is more efficient to tax those factors directly.

While this advice is valid when applied to portfolio investment, it is less valid regarding foreign direct investors (FDI) for two reasons. First, the standard advice does not apply if a foreign tax credit (FTC) is available in the home country of the investor, which frequently would be the case for FDI. Second, the standard advice assumes that the host country is small. Extensive literature on multinationals suggests that typically they exist to earn economic rents (or supernormal returns). The host country is no longer "small" in the economic sense. There is a reason for the investor to be there and not elsewhere. Therefore, any tax imposed on such rents

[12] Reuven S. Avi-Yonah, *What Goes around Comes around: Why the USA Is Responsible for Capital Flight (and What It Can Do about It)*, 13 Haifa L. Rev. 321 (2019).

will not necessarily drive the investor to leave even if it is unable to shift the burden of the tax to less mobile factors.

This argument defending the host country taxation holds in the case of rents that are linked to location specific factors, such as natural resources or a large market. But what if the rents can be earned in many potential locations? In this case, the host country will not be able to tax the rents if the multinational can credibly threaten to go elsewhere. This situation, which is probably the most common, would require coordinated action to enable all host countries to tax the rent earned within their borders. This is precisely what Pillar Two does.

This point relates to another prevalent argument: Host countries need to offer tax incentives to be competitive. Extensive literature has demonstrated that taxes do play a crucial role in determining the location of investment. But these studies emphasize that tax incentives are crucial *given the availability of such incentives elsewhere*. It can be argued that, given the need for tax revenues, developing countries would in general prefer to refrain from granting tax incentives, only if they could be assured that no other developing country would be able to engage in tax competition.

Thus, restricting the ability of developing countries to engage in tax competition does not truly restrict their autonomy, nor does it counter their interests. Whenever competition from other countries drives the tax incentives, eliminating the competition does not hurt the developing country, and may aid its revenue raising efforts (assuming it can attract investment on other grounds, which is typically the case).

* * *

The following chapters will develop these themes in greater detail. Chapter 1 will describe the old ITR as it functioned before the recent globalization. Chapter 2 will show how globalization and digitalization undermined the old ITR in the period between 1980 and 2008. Chapter 3 will discuss the impact of the financial crisis of 2008 and the development of the Common Reporting Standard (CRS) for Automatic Exchange of Information (AEoI). Chapter 4 will evaluate the OECD's Base Erosion and Profit Shifting project (BEPS 1.0). Chapter 5 will discuss Pillar One of BEPS 2.0 (the digital economy), and Chapter 6 will analyze Pillar Two (the global minimum tax). Chapter 7 will discuss where the new ITR might be heading in the future. Chapter 8 concludes by exploring the extent to which the new ITR constitutes a revolution or paradigm shift and what were the origins of the new ITR.

1

The Ancien Régime, 1923–1979*

The old international tax regime was a flawed miracle. It was a miracle, because taxes are the last topic on which one would expect sovereign nations to reach a consensus, since, to some extent, international taxation is a zero-sum game and one country's gain in revenue is another's loss. When income is derived by a resident of one country from sources in another, and both countries have a legitimate claim to tax that income and the ability to enforce that claim, either country will lose revenue by granting the other the primary right to tax that income.

Nevertheless, and contrary to a priori expectations, a coherent international tax regime exists. This regime enjoys near-universal support and underlies the complexities of the international aspects of individual countries' tax systems. This regime was developed since the 1920s, when the League of Nations first undertook to study ways to avoid international double taxation. And it has been embodied in the model tax treaties developed by the OECD and the UN and in the over 3,000 bilateral treaties that are based on those models. The existence of this regime shows that despite each country's claim to sovereignty in tax matters, it is possible to reach an internationally acceptable consensus that will be followed by most of the world's taxing jurisdictions. This international tax regime, based on voluntary consensus, can be regarded as one of the major achievements of twentieth-century international law.

Yet the miracle was flawed. The old regime, or the ancien régime, suffered from significant weaknesses, especially in two areas in which the development of the world economy has made the principles that were agreed upon in the 1920s and 1930s obsolete: the growth of internationally mobile capital markets for portfolio investment and the rise of integrated multinational enterprises (MNEs).[1] Thus, as the twentieth century neared its end, it was time to reexamine the prevailing

* This chapter is built upon a section of the first author's previous paper. Reuven S. Avi-Yonah, *The Structure of International Taxation: A Proposal for Simplification*, 74 Tex. L. Rev. 1301, 1303–16 (1996).

[1] We currently believe there are additional challenges facing the regime, such as international tax competition and tax arbitrage.

international tax regime and to ask whether a new consensus can be reached to remedy its major weaknesses, and to ensure its continued viability in the next century.

1.1 THE STRUCTURE OF INTERNATIONAL TAXATION: THE ACTIVE/PASSIVE DISTINCTION

In 1923, a committee of four economists submitted to the League of Nations a report that, for the first time, set out the basic principles underlying international tax jurisdiction.[2] The report pointed out that an income tax based on ability to pay does not answer the question of whose ability to pay is to be considered in each taxing jurisdiction. To answer this question, the report developed the "doctrine of economic allegiance," which underlies modern discussions of jurisdiction to tax. Fundamentally, the report endorsed two bases for economic allegiance that justify a country's imposition of tax: Where income is produced (or the source jurisdiction), and where it is consumed or saved (or the residence jurisdiction).

The 1923 report also addressed the issue of double taxation and presented the benefits principle: As between the source and residence jurisdictions, which should have the primary claim to tax income produced in the other, and which should have the obligation to prevent double taxation by giving up its claim? On practical grounds, the source jurisdiction has the primary right because it can generally impose its taxes on income deriving from within it first. However, the 1923 report recommended that, in future negotiations between tax jurisdictions, income items should be classified according to whether the primary economic activity giving rise to the income takes place in the source or in the residence country, and the prior right to tax the income be divided accordingly between them.

The benefits principle underlies the development of the current consensus regarding the proper allocation of taxable income among taxing jurisdictions. While the source country is granted the prior right to tax all income and the residence country has the primary obligation to prevent double taxation, this is a concession to the source country's ability to impose taxes first and does not reflect the optimal allocation. Instead, the goal underlying the international tax regime is that *active* business income should be taxed in the country in which it originates (the source country), while *passive* income should be taxed in the country in which the recipient of the income resides (the residence country).

This consensus can best be seen in operation by examining the extensive tax treaty network. Tax treaties reflect the active/passive distinction in two ways. First, they define what constitutes an active business operation in each country (a "permanent

[2] *League of Nations Report on Double Taxation Submitted to the Financial Committee by Professors Bruins, Einaudi, Seligman, and Sir Josiah Stamp*, League of Nations Doc. **E.F.S.** 73 **F.** 19 (1923).

establishment") and give the source country the primary right to tax the profits from that operation. The residence country is required to exempt those profits from tax, at least to the extent they were taxed by the source country, either by exempting foreign source business income or by granting a foreign tax credit. Second, the tax treaties seek to reduce as much as possible the taxes levied by the source country on passive income (such as dividends, interest, and royalties) derived from within it, leaving the right to tax that income to the residence country.

The tax treaties do not completely achieve their goal of dividing the worldwide taxing jurisdiction between source and residence countries along active/passive lines. First, the "permanent establishment" concept reflects a compromise: Not all active business income is taxable primarily in the source country, but only income that is attributable to a permanent establishment, because otherwise international business would be subject to burdensome administrative requirements of filing returns and paying tax in every country in which it has a minimal presence. However, the threshold of what constitutes a permanent establishment is quite low, although it does require physical presence: A single office, or even a single agent with authority to conclude sales, is generally sufficient. Second, the taxation of passive income at source is not completely abolished but is reduced in most treaties to the lowest possible levels. For example, the 1992 OECD Model Income Tax Treaty recommended tax rates of 5–15 percent on dividends, 10 percent on interest, and 0 percent on royalties; the 1996 US Model Income Tax Treaty recommended tax rates of 5–15 percent on dividends, and 0% on interest and royalties. These low withholding tax rates represent a compromise between the desire of source countries to levy some tax on income derived by foreigners from within the country, and the international consensus that such income should be primarily taxed in the residence country. In the absence of a treaty, much higher withholding tax rates may apply; but these rates reflect the fact that in the absence of a treaty the source country has no assurance that the income will in fact be taxed by the residence country, and therefore arrogates to itself the taxes that should be paid to the residence country.

Nevertheless, the distinction between active and passive income is thus a fundamental element of the current regime. Is this a distinction that reflects a real difference? There are three arguments that it does. First, from an economic perspective, one may conceive of the pool of worldwide income as produced by value-adding firms. A firm is a joint venture of persons who invest in it, seeking returns. The value added by each firm is the sum of its undistributed profits, plus the dividends, interest, royalties, and rents which it pays, and which represent different ways of distributing the firm's income among the persons who invest in it. The investment may be in the form of equity capital, debt capital, or tangible and intangible assets, depending on the level and type of risk that the investor is willing to undertake. From this perspective, the taxation of active business income represents the taxation of the profits of the firm, while the taxation of passive income represents the taxation of the division of those profits among investors in the firm. The active/passive distinction in international taxation reflects this economic analysis.

Second, the active/passive distinction reflects to some extent the degree of control exercised over the activity. Active business income is generally derived from economic activities under the taxpayer's direct control. In the international sphere, it is usually linked with foreign direct investment. Passive income, on the other hand, is frequently derived from activities in which the taxpayer has only a very small degree of voting control. Examples would be a small shareholder in a corporation, or a third-party lender whose relationship contains no elements of control. However, passive income (in the sense of distributions of a firm's earnings) may also be earned by persons who control the underlying operations, such as when a controlling shareholder derives dividends or interest from her corporation. This type of passive income (associated with direct investment) is frequently treated differently from passive portfolio income, but under the current consensus it is still taxed primarily in the country of residence of the controlling shareholder, and not in the country where the corporation engages in business. In the following discussion, the term "portfolio income" will be reserved for passive income that is not linked with control.

Third, the active/passive distinction is significant because to a substantial extent it overlaps with the distinction between publicly traded corporations on the one hand, and individuals, close corporations, and other legal entities on the other hand. Much of the world's active income is earned by large, publicly traded corporations, and, in the international context, by MNEs; much of the world's passive income is earned directly by individuals or through close corporations or pass-through entities. We shall discuss the importance of this empirical distinction below.

1.2 IS THE CONSENSUS JUSTIFIED?

If the active/passive distinction reflects some economic reality, why should active income be taxed on a source basis, while passive income is taxed on a residence basis? The 1923 League of Nations report attempted to justify this distinction by means of an analysis of which types of income derive more from activities performed in each jurisdiction. But this type of analysis has been rejected by modern economists, who cast doubt on whether income can meaningfully be said to derive from one source rather than another.[3] Instead, a better understanding of the logic behind the active/passive distinction can be reached if one examines the two extreme

[3] *See, e.g.*, Gary C. Hufbauer, U.S. Taxation of International Income: Blueprint for Reform 98–100 (1992); Hugh I. Ault & David F. Bradford, *Taxing International Income: An Analysis of the U.S. System and Its Economic Premises*, *in* Taxation in the Global Economy 11, 30–31 (Assaf Razin & Joel Slemrod eds., 1990).

alternatives: taxing all income in the country of residence and taxing all income in the country of source.

The 1923 report argued for the abolition of source-based taxation on the ground that it is incompatible with the modern notion of ability to pay. Indeed, since ability to pay is not adequately measured by income from one source, but rather by "all income from whatever source derived," it seems difficult to reconcile source jurisdiction with an income tax based on ability to pay. However, this argument by itself does not explain why the residence jurisdiction should have the sole claim to tax global income. In terms of the taxpayer's economic allegiance, she owes taxes to both residence and source countries. Each contributes to her ability to earn, and therefore each has the right to tax her entire income, which reflects her global ability to pay. However, since this result is impracticable and would result in complete multiple taxation, one sensible route would be to permit each jurisdiction to tax the income derived from within it (i.e., on a source basis), resulting in the taxpayer being taxed on her global income according to her ability to pay. Of course, each of the source jurisdictions may have a different tax rate (including a zero rate), but the fact that a taxpayer may not be taxed or may be taxed at a lower rate in one jurisdiction does not automatically give the residence jurisdiction the residual right to tax that income.

There appear, however, to be several solid grounds for preferring residence over source taxation for individuals. The first is a pragmatic ground: Individuals can only be in one place at any given time. Thus, residence for individuals is a relatively easy concept to establish, and in fact it is possible to set down bright line rules (based, as is the case in the United States, on counting days) for determining fiscal residence of individuals. On the other hand, the establishment of the source of income is a highly problematic endeavor, and in most cases, income will have more than one source. Thus, if one jurisdiction is to be given the primary right to tax individuals, or at least the residual right to tax income that is untaxed at source, the residence jurisdiction is an obvious candidate.

Second, because most individuals have only one residence jurisdiction, and are part of one society, distributional concerns can be effectively addressed only in the country of residence. If the personal income tax is to have a significant redistributive function through progressive rates, it is necessary to include all income (including foreign source income) in the measurement of ability to pay. There may be no horizontal equity problem in taxing differently two equivalently situated taxpayers, only one of whom invests abroad and earns low-taxed income there, if the other has the same choice of investments open to her. There is, however, a significant vertical equity problem in taxing an investor with low domestic and high foreign earnings which are not taxed abroad the same as a person with only low domestic earnings. This problem can be resolved if the residence jurisdiction is allowed to tax on a residual basis only foreign source income that is not taxed abroad (or is taxed at lower effective rates), and allow a credit for foreign taxes, but it is much simpler to address the issue if the residence jurisdiction is given the primary right to tax all income of its residents.

Third, the residence of individuals to some extent overlaps with their political allegiance. In democratic countries, it is considered important for individuals to have a right to participate through their representatives in deciding how much tax they must pay. The converse is even more significant: Democratic legislatures prefer raising taxes on foreigners precisely because they cannot vote. Thus, taxation based on residence is a useful, though far from perfect, proxy for taxation with representation.

Why, then, not follow the path of pure residence-based taxation? There are two major grounds for rejecting this position. The first is that to implement full residence-based taxation, it is necessary either to artificially determine the residence of corporations, which cannot be determined the way the residence of individuals can be, or to impute the earnings of publicly traded MNEs to their shareholders, which is a very complex task and may be administratively impossible.

The second objection to pure residence-based taxation is that it results in too much revenue being collected by developed countries and too little by developing countries. To illustrate this, it is convenient to refer to a stylized model world made up of only three jurisdictions: a developed country (e.g., the United States), a developing country (e.g., India), and a tax haven (e.g., the Caymans). The residents of the United States earn active income from the United States, earn passive income from investments in the United States and in the Caymans, and earn passive income from investments in X, a MNE headquartered in the United States. The residents of India earn active income from India, earn active income from working for X in India, and, in the case of the elite, earn investment income from the United States and the Caymans. X develops products in the United States, manufactures them in India, and sells them in the United States, but its profits are to a large extent channeled to investments in the Caymans.

In this stylized world, if all taxation were based on residence, the United States would receive the taxes from the income of its residents (active and passive), as well as the entire taxes from X, either because X is headquartered there (if corporations are to have a fiscal residence) or because all of X's shareholders are residents of the United States and none are residents of India. India, the developing country, would thus be left only with the taxation of the local income of its residents and with the taxes due on the income of its elite from the United States and the Caymans, which are very difficult for India to collect. This would likely be an insufficient amount of income for India, which would therefore refuse to cooperate in the residence-based system.

The other extreme alternative – taxing all income on a source basis – appears more appealing in this regard. In the simplified world, it would result in the United States collecting taxes on active and passive income from the United States, including X's income from the United States, and India collecting taxes on active and passive income from India, including X's income from India (assuming that X can be effectively taxed on a source basis). In comparison with a regime under which each country has the right to tax passive income of its residents and active income earned within its borders, India would not lose from this arrangement, except for the taxes it forgoes on passive income from the United States and the Caymans, which are difficult for India to collect. Moreover, it would gain to the extent that there is some portfolio income derived by investors from India.

However, as was indicated earlier, pure source-based taxation is also unattractive. It undermines the ability to use the income tax as a redistributive mechanism in the country of residence unless a complicated residual residence-based taxation with a foreign tax credit mechanism is implemented; and it severs the connection between taxation and participation in the political process.

None of these reasons apply with the same forcefulness to active business income as they do to passive income, precisely because much of the active income in the world is earned by MNEs, which do not vote, and which are not residents of a single society.

The taxation of active business income by the source jurisdiction and of passive portfolio income by the residence jurisdiction would appear to address most of the issues identified above. The taxation of passive income on a residence basis is congruent with the need to preserve redistribution and representation for individuals, who earn most of this income (especially if one ignores passive income earned by affiliated corporations). It appears unlikely that source countries would be harmed significantly by giving up source-based taxation of passive income earned by individuals and close corporations. The taxation of active income by the source country is congruent with the need to preserve some source of revenue for the source country, and if most such income is earned by MNEs, the arguments for taxing it on a residence basis do not apply. Thus, it appears that the current international consensus (which is preserved under BEPS) has significant advantages, which should be borne in mind when considering ways to simplify and modernize it.

2

The Decline of the Ancien Régime, 1980–2008*

2.1 TAX COMPETITION: ONE SIDE OF THE TRILEMMA IN GLOBALIZATION

The current age of globalization can be distinguished from the previous one (from 1870 to 1914) by the much higher mobility of capital than labor. In the previous age before immigration restrictions, labor was at least as mobile as capital, and that still applies to the rich but less to others. In the current age, the increased mobility of capital is the result of technological changes (i.e., the ability to move funds electronically) and the relaxation of exchange controls. The mobility of capital has resulted in international tax competition, in which sovereign countries lower their tax rates on income earned by foreigners within their borders to attract both portfolio and direct investment. Tax competition, in turn, threatens to undermine the individual and corporate income taxes, which traditionally have generated the largest share of revenue for modern welfare states.

Developed countries, the only group of countries that contributed to the old regime, have responded in two ways: first, by shifting the tax burden from (mobile) capital to (less mobile) labor; and second, when further increased taxation of labor becomes politically and economically difficult, by reducing the social safety net. Thus, globalization and tax competition lead to a fiscal crisis for countries that wish to continue to provide social insurance to their citizens while demographic factors and the increased income inequality, job insecurity, and income volatility that result from globalization render such social insurance more necessary.

These fiscal crises pressure nations to limit globalization (e.g., by reintroducing exchange controls), an act that risks reducing world welfare. However, if both globalization and social insurance are to be maintained, it is necessary to cut the

* This chapter draws heavily from a previous piece written by the first author: Reuven S. Avi-Yonah, *Globalization, Tax Competition, and the Fiscal Crisis of the Welfare States*, 113 HARV. L. REV. 1573, 1575–651 (2000).

intermediate link by limiting tax competition in a way that is congruent with maintaining the ability of democratic states to determine the desirable size of their government. Such trilemma of balancing (1) economic openness, (2) avoiding tax competition, and (3) securing a social safety net will be further discussed in Chapter 6.

From its inception in the late nineteenth century through the recent rise of payroll taxation, the welfare state has been financed primarily through progressive income taxation. Unlike other forms of taxation (such as consumption or social security taxes), income tax includes income from capital in the tax base, even if that income is saved and not consumed. Because the rich save more than do the poor, a tax that includes income from capital in its base is more progressive than a tax that excludes income from capital (such as a consumption tax or a payroll tax). However, greater capital mobility and international tax competition allow investors to escape taxation easily by shifting capital to low- or no-tax jurisdictions. Consequently, the income tax's progressive effect is significantly weakened.

Two developments have dramatically augmented the ability of both individuals and corporations to earn income overseas free of income taxation since 1980: (1) the effective end of withholding taxation by developed countries and (2) the rise of production tax havens in developing countries. First, since the United States abolished its withholding tax on interest paid to foreigners in 1984, no major capital importing country has been able to impose such a tax for fear of driving mobile capital elsewhere (or increasing the cost of capital for domestic borrowers, including the government itself). As a result, individuals can generally earn investment income free of host country taxation in any of the world's major economies. Second, tax havens with strong bank secrecy laws have made it exceedingly difficult for developed countries – let alone developing countries with their weaker tax administrations – to collect tax on the foreign income of their individual residents in the absence of withholding taxes in the host countries. Thus, cross-border investment income could largely be earned free of either host- or home-country taxation.

When we switch our attention from passive to productive (or active) investment, a similar threat to the taxing capacity of both home and host jurisdictions emerges. After 1980, competition for inbound investment led an increasing number of countries (103 in 1998) to offer tax holidays specifically geared to foreign corporate investors.[1] Given the relative ease with which an integrated multinational corporation can relocate production facilities in response to tax rates, such "production tax havens" enable multinationals to derive most of their income from abroad, free of host-country taxation. Moreover, these multinationals generally manage to escape home-country taxation as well. Most developed countries (including the United

[1] *See* RAYMOND VERNON, IN THE HURRICANE'S EYE: THE TROUBLED PROSPECTS OF MULTINATIONAL ENTERPRISES 32 tbl.2–1 (1998) (citing UNITED NATIONS, INCENTIVES AND FOREIGN DIRECT INVESTMENT 2 tbl.III (1996)).

States) do not dare impose current taxation (or, in some cases, any taxation) on the foreign source business income of their resident multinationals for fear of reducing their multinationals' ability to compete against multinationals of other countries. If they did, new multinationals would choose to become residents of jurisdictions that do not tax such foreign source income. Thus, businesses can earn income abroad largely free of either host- or home-country taxation.

If much of both passive and productive income from capital can escape the tax net, income tax becomes in effect a tax on labor. Several empirical studies have suggested that in some developed countries, the effective tax rate on income from capital approaches zero. Since the early 1980s, when exchange controls were relaxed, nominal tax rates have gone down sharply. As a result, countries that used to rely on the revenues from income tax were forced to increase relatively regressive taxes, such as consumption taxes and payroll taxes, which were the two fastest growing taxes in the member countries of the OECD between 1980 and 2000. Consumption taxes rose from 12 percent of total revenues in 1965 to 18 percent in 1995; and payroll taxes rose from 18 percent to 25 percent over that time. Moreover, during the same period, neither personal nor corporate income tax has grown as a percentage of total revenues (personal income tax accounted for 26 percent of total revenues in 1965 and 27 percent in 1995; corporate income tax, 9 percent and 8 percent, respectively). The total tax revenue as a percentage of GDP in developed countries went up sharply during the same period (from an average of 28 percent in 1965 to almost 40 percent in 1994), and this increase is largely accounted for by the rise of consumption and payroll taxes. Moreover, there is evidence that as an OECD member country's economy becomes more open, its taxes on capital tend to go down while its taxes on labor go up.

At some point, developed countries find themselves politically unable to raise income taxes on labor, consumption taxes, or payroll taxes any further. High income taxes on labor discourage work, high payroll taxes discourage job creation and contribute to unemployment, and high consumption taxes (e.g., on luxury goods) drive consumption overseas. If developed countries are unable to tax income from capital and if alternative taxes are not feasible, their only recourse is to cut the social safety net – a net that is needed more than ever both because of demographic factors and because of the increased income inequality, income volatility, and job insecurity that tend to result from globalization. Thus, globalization leads to a more pressing need for revenues at the same time that it limits governments' ability to collect those revenues.

This dilemma threatens to undercut the social consensus about the value of the welfare state that underlies modern industrialized societies and to create a backlash against globalization that produces so many overall benefits. The previous age of globalization collapsed in the 1920s in the face of just such a backlash. Maintaining the social compact underlying the modern welfare state requires a means of taxing cross-border income from capital at rates that approximate the rates imposed domestically on labor income – that is, it requires a limit on tax competition. However, any such limit must (as both a normative and a practical matter) be balanced against the desire of democratic countries to determine the size of their own public sectors.

2.2 TAX COMPETITION AND THE TAXATION OF CAPITAL

2.2.1 *Taxation of Savings: Portfolio Exemptions and Traditional Tax Havens*

In 1984, the United States unilaterally abolished its withholding tax of 30 percent on foreign residents earning "portfolio interest" income from sources within the United States.[2] "Portfolio interest" was defined to include interest on US government bonds, bonds issued by US corporations (unless the bondholder held a 10 percent or more stake in the shares of the corporation), and interest on US bank accounts and certificates of deposit. This "portfolio interest exemption" is available to any nonresident alien (i.e., any person who is not a US resident for tax purposes) without requiring any certification of identity or proof that the interest income was subject to tax in the investor's country of residence.

The enactment of the portfolio interest exemption resulted from a fortuitous combination of three factors. First, because of the Reagan tax cuts of 1981, which dramatically lowered the US effective tax rate, and the accompanying defense buildup, the US government faced a significant budgetary deficit that could only be financed by borrowing abroad, especially from Japan (which had a large savings surplus). Second, the Japan–US tax treaty imposed a 10 percent withholding tax on interest, unlike most other US tax treaties with developed countries that provide a zero-withholding rate on interest.[3] Third, in 1984, the United States decided to terminate its tax treaty with the Netherlands Antilles, which had a zero-withholding rate on interest and no limitation on benefits to Antilles residents. The Antilles treaty was used by US corporations to borrow abroad without having a withholding tax imposed on the interest by channeling the loans through a Netherlands Antilles finance subsidiary. Thus, the enactment of the portfolio interest exemption was motivated by the desire of both the US government and US multinationals to borrow abroad without having to bear the cost of any withholding tax (which under the circumstances of 1984 was likely to be shifted to the borrower).

The US enactment of the portfolio interest exemption has resulted in a classic "race to the bottom." One after another, all the major economies have abolished their withholding taxes on interest for fear of losing mobile capital flows to the United States. Table 2.1 shows the 1993 withholding rates imposed by EU member countries and the United States on various forms of capital income (interest on bank

2 Internal Revenue Code of 1986, as amended ("I.R.C."), § 871(h).

3 *See* Convention between the United States of America and Japan for the Avoidance of Double Taxation and the Prevention of Fiscal Evasion with Respect to Taxes on Income, July 9, 1972, Japan-U.S., art. XIII, 23 U.S.T. 967, 990.

TABLE 2.1 *Withholding taxes on interest, 1993 (percentage rates)*

Country	Bank accounts	Securities	Dividends
Belgium	0	10	15
Denmark	0	0	15
France	0	0	15
Germany	0	0	15
Greece	10	10	0
Ireland	0	0	0
Italy	10	10	15
Luxembourg	0	0	15
Netherlands	0	0	15
Portugal	15	15	15
Spain	0	0	15
United Kingdom	0	0	15
United States	0	0	30

accounts; interest on securities, specifically government and corporate bonds; and dividends) paid to foreign residents in the absence of a treaty.[4]

As Table 2.1 indicates, most developed countries levy no withholding tax on interest paid to nonresidents on bank deposits and on government and corporate bonds. These nations do levy taxes on dividends, but dividends (unlike interest) are not deductible, and the underlying income has, therefore, already been taxed once. In reality, the discrepancy between interest and dividends may be smaller than the table indicates, for two reasons. First, a significant portion of the return on equity comes in the form of capital gains, which are not subject to source-based taxation in any of the countries included in the table. Second, the withholding tax on dividends is generally easy to avoid for sophisticated investors. For example, a foreign investor can construct a "total return equity swap" in which she receives payments equivalent to dividends from an investment banker in the source country, who in turn hedges by holding the underlying stock and receiving the actual dividends. Most countries do not subject the dividend-equivalent payments to withholding, and the underlying dividends are free from withholding because they are paid to a domestic recipient. This situation has led to calls for a "portfolio dividends exemption."

The standard economic advice to small, open economies is to avoid taxing capital income at its source, because the tax will be shifted forward to the borrowers and result in higher domestic interest rates.[5] However, the countries in Table 2.1 include several large economies (the United States, Germany, and the United Kingdom) in which the tax would not necessarily be shifted forward, but which refrain from

4 *See* Vito Tanzi, TAXATION IN AN INTEGRATING WORLD 130–31 tbl.8–4 (1995).

5 *See, e.g.*, JACOB A. FRENKEL ET AL., INTERNATIONAL TAXATION IN AN INTEGRATED WORLD 203–07, 214–16 (1991).

imposing withholding taxes primarily out of fear that capital would otherwise move swiftly to other locations that do not impose a withholding tax. Thus, the Ruding Committee, writing about the European Community, concluded in 1992 that "recent experience suggests that any attempt by the EC to impose withholding taxes on cross-border interest flows could result in a flight of financial capital to non-EC countries."[6]

The experience of Germany is a case in point: In 1988, Germany introduced a (relatively low) 10 percent withholding tax on interest on bank deposits but had to abolish it within a few months because of the magnitude of capital flight to Luxembourg (over 100 billion DM). In 1991, the German Federal Constitutional Court held that withholding taxes on wages but not on interest violated the constitutional right to equality; and the government, therefore, was obligated to reintroduce the withholding tax on interest but made it inapplicable to nonresidents.[7] "Nonresidents" may, however, be German residents investing through Luxembourg bank accounts and benefiting from the Luxembourg tradition of bank secrecy.[8]

This situation resembles a multiple-player assurance ("stag hunt") game: All developed countries would benefit from reintroducing the withholding tax on interest because they would gain revenue without fear that the capital would be shifted to another developed country. However, no country is willing to be the first one to cooperate by imposing a withholding tax unilaterally; and thus, they all defect (i.e., refrain from imposing the tax) to the detriment of all.

In global terms, this outcome would make no difference if residence jurisdictions were able to tax their residents on foreign source interest (and dividend) income as required by a global personal income tax on all income "from whatever source derived." However, as Joel Slemrod has written, "although it is not *desirable* to tax capital on a source basis, it is not administratively *feasible* to tax capital on a residence basis,"[9] because residence-country fiscal authorities generally had no means of learning about the income that their residents earn abroad. Even in the case of sophisticated tax administrations like the IRS, tax compliance depends decisively on the presence of either withholding at source or information reporting. When neither is available, as in the case of foreign source income, compliance rates drop dramatically from over 90 percent to about 30 percent.[10]

6 Comm'n of the Eur. Cmtys *Report of the Committee of Independent Experts on Company Taxation* 201 (1992) [hereinafter *Ruding Report*].

7 *See* Leif Muten, *International Experience of How Taxes Influence the Movement of Private Capital*, 94 TAX NOTES INT'L 49-17 (Mar. 14, 1994).

8 *See* Suzanne McGee, *Tax Inquiry Turns Grayer in Luxembourg*, WALL ST. J. (July 20, 1999); *Tax Raids: Sleepless Nights in Frankfurt, Again*, ECONOMIST (June 20, 1998).

9 *See* TANZI, *supra* note 4, at 141, 144.

10 *See* General Accounting Office, Tax Administration: Approaches for Improving Independent Contractor Compliance, GAO/GGD-92-108 (July 23, 1992); I.R.S. Publication 1415, tbl.A-54 (July 1988).

In the case of foreign source income, withholding taxes are not imposed for the reasons described above. Even though tax treaties contained an exchange of information procedure, it was vitally flawed in two respects. First, the lack of any uniform worldwide system of tax identification numbers means that most tax administrations are unable to match the information received from their treaty partners with domestic taxpayers. Second, there were no tax treaties with traditional tax havens, and routing the income through a tax haven sufficed to block the exchange of information. For example, if a Mexican national invested in a US bank through a Cayman Islands corporation, the exchange of information article in the US–Mexico tax treaty would not avail the Mexican authorities. The IRS had no way of knowing (given bank secrecy) that the portfolio interest that is paid to the Caymans is beneficially owned by a Mexican resident covered by the treaty.[11]

The result was that much of the income from portfolio investments overseas escaped income taxation by either source or residence countries. Latin American countries provide a prime example: After the enactment of the portfolio interest exemption, about $300 billion fled from Latin American countries to bank accounts and other forms of portfolio investment in the United States.[12] Most of these funds were channeled through tax haven corporations and therefore were not subject to taxation in the country of residence. For all developing countries, various estimates of the magnitude of capital flight in the 1980s average between $15 billion and $60 billion per year.[13] Nor is the problem limited to developing countries: Much of the German portfolio interest exemption benefited German residents who maintain bank accounts in Luxembourg, and much of the US portfolio interest exemption benefited Japanese investors who hold US Treasuries and do not report the income in Japan.[14] It is questionable how much tax even the United States actually collects on portfolio income that its residents earn abroad other than through mutual funds. One estimate puts capital flight from the United States between 1980 and 1982 as high as $250 billion.[15]

Thus, in the absence of withholding taxes or effective information exchange, income from foreign portfolio investments frequently escaped being taxed by any jurisdiction. This immunity from taxation is particularly significant because the

[11] *See generally* Tanzi, *supra* note 4, at 78–89.

[12] *See* Charles E. McLure, Jr., *U.S. Tax Laws and Capital Flight from Latin America*, 20 Inter-American L. Rev. 321 (1989) [hereinafter *Capital Flight from Latin America*].

[13] Chander Kant, Foreign Direct Investment and Capital Flight 21 tbl.3 (Princeton Studies in Int'l Fin. No. 80, 1996).

[14] *See Germans Find Tax Evasion Good Sport*, Fin. Times (London) (June 19, 1999), at 3; Mark Milner, *Dresdner Tax Arrests*, Guardian (London) (Jan. 4, 1996), at 15; Hiroshi Oda, *Japan*, *in* Butterworths International Guide to Money Laundering and Practice 109, 110 (Richard Parlour ed., 1995).

[15] Michael P. Dooley, *Comment on the Definition and Magnitude of Recent Capital Flight*, *in* Capital Flight and Third World Debt 79 (Donald R. Lessard & John Williamson eds., 1987).

flows of portfolio capital across international borders have been growing much faster than either world gross domestic product or foreign direct investment (FDI). It was estimated in the 1990s that international capital flows amount to $1 trillion *a day*; and although this figure is much larger than income from capital, it gives a sense of the magnitudes at stake.[16]

This situation has led knowledgeable observers like Richard Bird to write that "the weakness of international taxation calls into question the viability of the income tax itself … If something is not done to rectify these problems soon, the future of the income tax is bleak."[17] Other commentators have written articles like "Can Capital Income Taxes Survive in Open Economies?" and "Is There a Future for Capital Income Taxation?"[18]

2.2.2 *Taxation of Multinationals: PE, Headquarters, and Production Tax Havens*

There are three types of jurisdictions that could, under pre-BEPS accepted rules, impose a corporate income tax on income from the sale of goods or provision of services across national borders: (1) The demand jurisdiction (where consumption of the goods or services takes place) may impose a tax if, and only if, the goods or services are provided through a "permanent establishment" (PE) (which consist of some physical presence in the demand jurisdiction) or through a subsidiary to the extent of the income attributable thereto. In post-BEPS days, the term "market jurisdiction" is more frequently used for this jurisdiction. (2) The supply jurisdiction (where production of the goods or services takes place) may impose a tax on the income attributable to such production. These two jurisdictions have the right to tax based on source. (3) In addition, a third jurisdiction has a residual right to tax income that is not taxed at source based on being the jurisdiction where the corporation is resident (i.e., where the corporation is incorporated or managed and controlled).

Out of these three jurisdictions, the one most likely to want to tax multinationals on income derived therein, the demand (or market) jurisdiction, did not under pre-BEPS rules have the right to tax such income in an increasing number of cases. The jurisdictions that did have such a right (the supply and corporate residence jurisdictions) are unlikely to want to do so because of tax competition. Thus, income

[16] *See* Peter D. Sutherland, *Sharing the Bounty: Challenges of Globalization*, 148 BANKER 16 (1998); Erik R. Peterson, *Looming Collision of Capitalism?*, 17 WASH. Q. 65 (1994).

[17] Richard Bird, *Shaping a New International Tax Order*, 42 BULL. INT'L FISCAL DOCUMENTATION 292, 303 (1988).

[18] Roger H. Gordon, *Can Capital Income Taxes Survive in Open Economies*, 47 J. FINANCE 1159 (1992); Jack Mintz, *Is There a Future for Capital Income Taxation?* (OECD Working Paper 108, 1992).

earned by multinationals from cross-border transactions is likely, to a significant extent, to escape the income tax altogether.

2.2.2.1 Demand (or Market) Jurisdictions and the Permanent Establishment Threshold

Out of the three jurisdictions that had the right to impose an income tax on multinational enterprises under the old ITR, the one most likely to have a significant corporate tax rate is the demand (or market) jurisdiction because large consumer markets typically have corporate income taxes imposed on foreign as well as domestic corporations. Under the pre-BEPS international tax regime, as embodied in the tax treaty network, a seller is taxable in a demand jurisdiction only if it has a physical presence therein. The physical presence test can be satisfied by either a "permanent establishment" or, in US terms, a "trade or business within the United States." Most often, the physical presence takes the form of a branch or subsidiary of the corporation.

Traditionally, multinationals typically had to establish such a physical presence in demand jurisdictions to gain significant market share or to avoid tariff barriers. However, the tariff barriers disappeared because of the GATT/WTO tariff reductions, and the rise of electronic commerce makes it increasingly feasible to sell large quantities of goods or services into a demand jurisdiction without establishing a physical presence therein. Most authoritative discussions of taxation of electronic commerce conclude that the most common forms of such commerce (a web page or even a server located in a jurisdiction) do not amount to a permanent establishment and thus fall under the taxing threshold of the demand jurisdiction.[19] Therefore, while multinationals currently pay some tax in demand jurisdictions in which they have subsidiaries engaged in distribution, this tax base is rapidly diminishing in the face of technological developments and cannot be relied on in the long run if the permanent establishment threshold remains unchanged.

2.2.2.2 Supply Jurisdictions and Production Tax Havens

Because of the coincidence between production and consumption in the developed world, most supply jurisdictions, no less than (and often the same as) demand jurisdictions, imposed significant income tax rates on both domestic and foreign corporations. However, a crucial development in the last decade or so has been the increasing prevalence of production tax havens. A production tax haven is a jurisdiction that grants a tax holiday to foreign production facilities located therein, but

[19] *See* Office of Tax Policy, Treasury Dep't, Selected Tax Policy Implications of Global Electronic Commerce (1996), *reprinted in* Daily Tax Rep. (BNA), Nov. 22, 1996, at L-1.

still levies an income tax on domestic corporations and individual residents. This type of haven differs from the traditional offshore tax haven, which has no corporate income tax (and sometimes no significant tax at all). This distinction is crucial because it means that a foreign investor in a production tax haven can enjoy the benefits of government services, which the government finances by taxing relatively immobile factors of production such as labor and land, while the investor itself pays little or no corporate income tax.

Tax competition has led to the proliferation of production tax havens. There were by 1998 at least 103 countries that offer special tax concessions to foreign corporations that set up production facilities or administrative facilities within their borders.[20] They include such developed countries as Belgium, Ireland, and Israel, and such developing countries as Malaysia and India. The extent of the tax holiday varies, but in general, the tax haven reduces its statutory tax rate to 10 percent or less for foreign corporations investing in specified types of facilities or areas within the jurisdiction. However, the jurisdiction imposes a higher tax rate of between 30 percent and 40 percent on local corporations, a personal income tax at even higher rates on resident individuals, and a VAT.[21]

Studies by economists have shown that such tax incentives were quite widespread and that investments in such countries were significant. For example, Rosanne Altshuler and T. Scott Newlon studied the 1986 tax returns of US multinationals and report that out of 1,827 foreign subsidiaries (or CFCs) of such multinationals, 659 were in countries with a tax rate below 20 percent.[22] These CFCs had assets of $51 billion and earnings of $5.2 billion in 1986, which represented over 40 percent of the total assets and earnings of all the CFCs. Almost three quarters of US multinationals studied had CFCs in both high- and low-tax jurisdictions.[23] Similarly, James R. Hines and Eric M. Rice documented the extent of US investment in foreign tax havens for 1982.[24] They show that while the havens had only 1.2 percent of world population and 3 percent of world GDP, their share of the foreign operations of US MNEs was 26 percent of assets, 21.4 percent of equity, and 30.6 percent of net income (but only 4.3 percent of employment and 4.2 percent of property, plant, and equipment).[25]

Two specific examples may help to illustrate this phenomenon. Intel Corporation, a top-ten multinational, has operations in more than thirty countries

[20] *See* VERNON, *supra* note 1, tbl.2-1; UNITED NATIONS, *supra* note 1, tbl.III.2.

[21] *Id.*

[22] *See* Rosanne Altshuler & T. Scott Newlon, *The Effects of U.S. Tax Policy on the Income Repatriation Patterns of U.S. Multinational Corporations*, *in* STUDIES IN INTERNATIONAL TAXATION 92, 93 (Alberto Giovannini et al. eds., 1993) [hereinafter *Effects of U.S. Tax Policy*].

[23] *Id.*

[24] *See* James R. Hines & Eric M. Rice, *Fiscal Paradise: Foreign Tax Havens and American Business*, 109 Q. J. ECON. 149 (1994).

[25] *See id.* at tbl.1. The share of net income in the havens is much higher than that reported for continental Europe (14.8 percent), which has 10.7 percent of world population and 34.5 percent of world GDP.

around the globe. The company states: "An Intel chip developed at a design center in Oregon, might be manufactured at a wafer fabrication facility in Ireland, packaged and tested in Malaysia, and then sold to a customer in Australia. Another chip might be designed in Japan, fabricated in Israel, packaged and tested in Arizona, and sold in China." Specifically, outside the United States, Intel has major manufacturing facilities in Puerto Rico, China, Malaysia, the Philippines, Ireland, and Israel – all jurisdictions that grant tax holidays.[26]

This phenomenon is not confined to new-fangled high-tech corporations like Intel. For example, new assembly plants for General Motors cars built since 1990 were in Gravatai, Brazil (Opel cars); Rosario, Argentina (Chevrolet Corsica); Silao, Mexico (Chevrolet Suburban, Silverado); Gliwice, Poland (Opel Astra); Rayong, Thailand (Opel Astra); Jakarta, Indonesia (Opel Blazer, Vectra, Astra); and Shanghai, China (Buicks).[27] Except for Mexico, all these locations are in production tax havens.

The rise of electronic commerce is likely to make it easier to locate production in such production tax havens. The Intel example, involving traditional (i.e., non-digital) goods, is a case in point: Intel's ability to coordinate production across the globe and locate its production facilities in production tax havens like Malaysia is based on modern communication technology including corporate intranets. Where goods can be conveyed in digital form, such as software, it is even easier to locate the entire operation in tax havens: The software can be written anywhere (e.g., in India or Israel where Microsoft has major operations) and transmitted elsewhere over secure corporate intranets. Information services in general have no inherent source, and online pornography, which is still one of the most profitable types of electronic commerce, is run largely from Guyana for both regulatory and tax-related reasons.

Are these corporate decisions about where to locate influenced by the tax regime in the host country? There have been several studies by economists that examined the importance of tax differentials in location decisions. James Hines has summarized ten quantitative studies of US direct investment abroad and ten quantitative studies of foreign direct investment in the United States. He concludes that although taxes are not the only determinant of the location of investments, "[t]he answer that emerges in a variety of contexts and from a variety of approaches is that, in spite of all the other economic and political considerations that are clearly important, taxation exerts a significant effect on the magnitude and location of FDI."[28] Hines estimates that the studies are generally consistent with a −0.5 elasticity of investment with respect to tax rates at the currently prevailing rates. These statistical findings are corroborated by G. Peter Wilson, who interviewed managers

[26] [26] Intel Corporation Form 10K (1998).

[27] *See* Robyn Meredith, *The Brave New World of General Motors*, N. Y. Times (Oct. 26, 1997), at sec. 3, 1.

[28] James R. Hines, *Tax Policy and the Activities of Multinational Corporations*, *in* Fiscal Policy: Lessons from Economic Research 414–15 (Alan J. Auerbach ed., 1997); *see also* James R. Hines, *Lessons from Behavioral Responses to International Taxation*, Nat'l Tax J. 305 (1999).

from nine firms regarding sixty-eight location decisions and concluded that "tax considerations largely dictate location decisions for business activities . . . such as administrative and distribution centers."[29] As for production locations, taxes are an important consideration in the location decision although they rarely dominate the decision process.

Studies have also demonstrated the ability of multinationals to shift profits to low-tax jurisdictions through transfer pricing or otherwise. For example, David Harris and his colleagues concluded based on a sample of 200 US manufacturing firms for 1984–88 that having a subsidiary in Ireland or in the four Asian "dragons" (Taiwan, South Korea, Singapore, and Hong Kong), all jurisdictions offering a tax holiday for foreign investors, is associated with lower US taxes as a fraction of US assets or US sales "in a way that is consistent with tax-motivated income shifting."[30] Hines surveys several studies on the financial behavior of multinationals, including the use of debt and transfer pricing, and concludes that "[t]he evidence indicates that the financial behavior of multinational corporations is quite sensitive to tax considerations, though not completely determined by them . . . In some instances, it may be less valuable to test the standard hypothesis that taxes influence financial behavior than to test the alternative hypothesis that only taxes influence financial behavior."[31]

Some late 1990s studies based on actual data derived from US-based multinationals tend to bolster the view that (a) tax competition among countries has driven effective tax rates down, and (b) US investment abroad has become more sensitive to tax rates. Rosanne Altschuler, Harry Grubert, and Scott Newlon used data from US Treasury corporate tax returns for 1984 and 1992 to assess both questions for manufacturing affiliates of US-based multinationals.[32] Average effective tax rates for CFCs in about sixty countries were calculated based on dividing total income taxes paid by their total earnings and profits (a measure defined by the Internal Revenue Code that approximates "book" income). They found that average effective tax rates in manufacturing fell by more than 15 percent between 1984 and 1992. The statutory tax rates likewise fell by 14 percent, indicating that rate reductions were not compensated for base broadening measures. They also found that the elasticity of investment to tax rate differentials in open economies increased from 1984 to 1992, indicating that the location of real manufacturing capital by manufacturing firms may have become more sensitive to tax rates in this period. This result held when

[29] G. Peter Wilson, *The Role of Taxes in Location and Sourcing Decisions*, *in* Studies in International Taxation 229 (Alberto Giovannini et al., eds., 1993).

[30] David Harris et al., *Income Shifting in U.S. Multinational Corporations*, *in* Studies in International Taxation, *id.* at 277, 301.

[31] Hines, *Tax Policy and the Activities of Multinational Corporations*, *supra* note 28, at 430–31.

[32] *See* Rosanne Altshuler et al., *Has U.S. Investment Abroad Become More Sensitive to Tax Rates?* (Nov. 1997) (unpublished article presented at NBER International Tax Conference no. 6383) [hereinafter *U.S. Investment Abroad*].

countries with populations of less than 1 million, including most traditional tax havens, were excluded from the calculations. The authors conclude that their results are "consistent with increasing international mobility of capital and globalization of production."[33]

A study by Grubert focused directly on the questions whether there is evidence of tax competition and US multinationals response thereto based on US Treasury data for 1984 and 1992.[34] He found that the mean average effective tax rate fell by almost 10 percent from 1984 to 1992, but there was no notable convergence in tax rates. Grubert interprets this as suggesting that there was no tax competition, but this does not follow from the data: It is possible that countries with high tax rates in 1984 reduced them because of competition with countries with low tax rates, but that the low-tax countries responded with further decreases, resulting in a lower average rate overall but no convergence. Significantly, Grubert found that tax reductions were greater in countries with a population of less than 15 million suggesting that small, open economies were more sensitive to capital movements (i.e., countries with less open economies cut their tax rates less). Using firm-level data, Grubert also found that the firms with low foreign tax rates in 1984 had the lowest rates in 1992, suggesting that those firms were highly mobile or more aggressive in their tax planning.

From the point of view of an investing multinational, there is no added cost to investing in a low-tax jurisdiction. This is in contrast to the standard Tieboutian paradigm of tax competition in the state and local context, in which individuals choose jurisdictions based on their preferred level of government services and bear the cost of reduced services if they choose the lower tax jurisdiction. Here, the level of services provided by the host country is fixed before the tax holiday and is based on the revenues that were collected without regard to the tax holiday. Typically, the holiday jurisdiction would try to provide the same level of services with the tax holiday in place, replacing the revenue needed by increasing taxes on relatively immobile factors of production (chiefly land and labor). The tax holiday thus represents a pure windfall to a multinational that can choose among several jurisdictions with similar levels of government services but different tax rates.

2.2.2.3 Corporate Residence Jurisdictions and Headquarters Tax Havens

When the source country refrains from exercising its right to tax (which it commonly does for the reasons described above), the corporate residence jurisdiction can exercise its right to residual taxation. However, before 2010, it was unlikely that

[33] *Id.* at 18.

[34] *See* H. Grubert, *Tax Planning by Companies and Tax Competition by Governments: Is There Evidence of Changes in Behavior?* (Nov. 1997) (unpublished article presented at NBER International Tax Conference).

corporate residence jurisdictions will impose a current tax on the foreign source active business income earned by multinationals whose headquarters are in those jurisdictions (or whose parent corporation is incorporated therein), for fear of driving those multinationals to reincorporate in headquarters tax havens.

Most corporate residence jurisdictions either exempt their multinationals' foreign source active business income from taxation ("exemption") or permit their multinationals to avoid paying tax on the income earned by their foreign subsidiaries until the income is actually repatriated to the parent in the form of dividends or otherwise ("deferral"). For example, under pre-2017 US rules, deferral applied to active business income earned by subsidiaries of US parent corporations abroad. Significantly, deferral did not depend on whether the income was taxed abroad.

Under deferral, a US-based multinational can avoid paying taxes indefinitely on its active foreign source income as long as it does not need to repatriate it. Under the well-known Cary Brown formula, deferral is equivalent to exemption of the yield on the amount deferred.[35] Thus, the income earned on foreign-source profits of US multinationals becomes exempt from US tax. Another way of stating the advantage of deferral is that if deferral lasts long enough, the present value of any tax imposed when the income is eventually repatriated approaches zero.

The obvious solution to this problem would be to repeal deferral, that is, to apply Subpart F (a concept discussed further below) to *all income* rather than limiting it to *Subpart F income* (i.e., generally passive income), as the Kennedy administration originally suggested in 1961. This solution has been repeatedly suggested by various administrations, incorporated in several legislative proposals, and endorsed by academic commentators. But it has never gotten off the ground. In fact, the trend in the 1990s has been in the opposite direction: Internal Revenue Code section 956A, which limited the ability of multinationals to avoid repatriation by imposing current taxation on excess passive assets held abroad, was repealed in 1996; and the extension of Check the Box to foreign entities generally allows US multinationals to elect deferral regardless of the entity's foreign legal status as a corporation or otherwise.

How has deferral been so successfully maintained against all criticism, and why have other jurisdictions maintained an exemption for foreign source active business income? Consider what would happen were the United States to end deferral. Parent corporations of new multinationals, especially in new industries like electronic commerce, would be less likely to be incorporated in the United States. Instead, they would prefer to incorporate in countries that do not tax holding corporations, such as Belgium (although it taxes other corporations quite heavily and even has a classical system like the United States).

35 *See, e.g.*, E. Cary Brown, *Business-Income Taxation and Investment Incentives*, *in* INCOME, EMPLOYMENT AND PUBLIC POLICY: ESSAYS IN HONOR OF ALVIN H. HANSON (Lloyd A. Metzler et al. eds., 1948).

Roger H. Gordon and Jeffrey MacKie-Mason have shown that a firm's decision *whether* to incorporate is significantly affected by tax considerations.[36] Similarly, the decision *where* to incorporate can be influenced by tax considerations. This can be demonstrated in several ways. First, one can consider Wilson's evidence, gleaned from interviews with corporate management, that "tax considerations largely dictate location decisions for ... administrative and distribution centers."[37] Belgium and other jurisdictions that market themselves as "corporate headquarters tax havens" seek to attract just such centers engaged in supervising worldwide manufacturing operations. Like production tax havens, such headquarters tax havens are proliferating because of tax competition.

Second, one can consider industries that are taxed exclusively on a residence basis because taxation at source is considered too difficult or too likely to lead to multiple taxation. Prominent examples include the shipping and commercial insurance industries, which are not subject to source-based income taxation because they do not have permanent establishments and can locate their production in tax havens. In these cases, the corporate residence is frequently also in a tax haven (often Liberia or Panama for shipping, Bermuda for insurance) and therefore no income tax is levied. (Excise taxes are typically levied at source as a minimal but inadequate substitute.)

Third, there is evidence that even the loose US anti-deferral rules may have induced attempts to change corporate residence to avoid them. In 1994, the United States changed its tax rules to impose a tax on publicly traded US corporations that change the residence of their corporate parent to another jurisdiction. This rule was prompted by a well-publicized case of a cosmetics distributor that reincorporated tax-free in the Cayman Islands to avoid application of Subpart F to its future subsidiaries. However, the change did not prevent numerous US multinationals from "inverting", or establishing a new parent in a tax haven, between 1994 and 2017.

Reincorporating in Panama or in the Cayman Islands may be a step most US multinationals would be unwilling to take. But establishing the corporate headquarters and formal corporate residence in Belgium, even when the entrepreneurs are US residents, would seem to carry little business risk. Moreover, the shares of most multinationals are currently traded on several exchanges, diminishing the significance of the country in which the parent is incorporated because the shareholder-protection laws of the trading jurisdiction will typically apply. Although a move may be unlikely for established US corporations like General Motors or even Intel, the major players in new industries have yet to incorporate, and future incorporation decisions may well be influenced by tax considerations.

The Treasury discussion paper on taxation of electronic commerce suggests that because of such considerations, "a review of current residency definitions and

[36] *See* Roger H. Gordon & Jeffrey K. MacKie-Mason, *Tax Distortions to the Choice of Organizational Form*, 55 J. PUB. ECON. 279, 280–81 (1994).

[37] Wilson, *supra* note 29, at 229.

taxation rules may be appropriate."[38] But it is hard to see what definition of corporate residence can be adopted that will avoid these problems. A definition that focuses on the corporation's place of management may prove unworkable because the rise of corporate intranets has eliminated the need for corporate boards to meet in one physical location. A rule that focuses on the residence of shareholders is likewise problematic because (as stated above) the shares of most multinationals now trade on several exchanges, leading to many corporate residences and no clear way to divide the tax base among them. As long as residence jurisdictions compete with each other for the location of corporate headquarters, effective residence-based taxation seems unlikely.

To sum up: Corporate income from cross-border transactions is increasingly unlikely to be taxed in the demand (or market) jurisdiction because of the absence of a permanent establishment. It is also unlikely to be taxed in the supply jurisdiction because production can take place in production tax havens. Finally, taxation by the corporate residence jurisdiction is likewise unlikely, at least on a current basis, because of deferral and headquarters tax havens. Thus, unless the rules of the old ITR were changed, such income was increasingly likely to escape tax altogether.

2.2.3 *Revenue Losses*

The preceding discussion indicates that it is possible to avoid income taxation on cross-border portfolio and direct investment. But how much revenue was lost in this way? This question turns out to be much harder to answer given the present state of the publicly available data.

The 1998 OECD Report on "Harmful Tax Competition: An Emerging Global Issue" argues that tax competition should be curbed primarily to prevent erosion of the revenue bases of OECD member countries.[39] At the very beginning of the chapter containing its recommendations, the OECD Report states, "Governments cannot stand back while their tax bases are eroded through the actions of countries which offer taxpayers ways to exploit tax havens and preferential regimes to reduce the tax that would otherwise be payable to them." Unfortunately, the OECD Report does not contain any numerical data to bolster its claim that tax bases are eroding because of harmful tax competition. Aggregate data on tax collections, reviewed in Section 2.3, do not support the claim: There is no evidence that overall revenue from the personal or corporate income tax in OECD member countries has declined either as a percent of GDP or of total tax revenue from 1965 to 1995. However, these data do not distinguish between income from labor and capital, and

[38] Office of Tax Policy, Treasury Dep't, *supra* note 19, at 1.

[39] OECD, Harmful Tax Competition: An Emerging Global Issue 8, 14 (1998).

it may be that a decline in the tax revenues from taxing capital is masked by a rise in revenues from taxing labor. This hypothesis would be consistent with the findings on changes in the overall tax mix reported in Section 2.3.

In this section, we will present the publicly available data on the revenue effects of tax competition in the 1990s. These data are quite sparse and incomplete, but some of it is quite suggestive.

2.2.3.1 Personal Income Tax

Assessing the revenue losses from tax competition in the personal income tax area is difficult because it involves (illegal) tax evasion rather than (legal) tax avoidance. All developed countries and most developing countries include in taxable income foreign source passive investment income of their individual residents so that not reporting that income is illegal. However, as described above, even developed countries find it difficult to collect the tax on such income in the absence of either withholding or information reporting.

Vito Tanzi and Partho Shome described several methods often used to estimate the magnitude of tax evasion in general.[40] All these methods have their own problems, but they all reach consistently high estimates. For developed countries, the available estimates of the untaxed portion of the economy range from 6 percent to 20 percent of GDP in the United States (in 1980) to 20 percent to 33 percent of GDP for Italy (in 1982). For developing countries, the estimates are as shown in Table 2.2.[41]

However, these numbers include much domestic tax evasion that does not relate to tax competition. Chander Kant has summarized the available data on capital flight using a variety of measures.[42] Given the wide availability of opportunities described above, it is reasonable to assume that most departing capital is invested in countries where it is not subject to taxation at its source. Although Latin America accounts for the largest share of capital flight, virtually all regions of the developing world experience this phenomenon. Estimates of capital flight from all developing countries for the period 1980–88 range from $15 billion to $60 billion per year. The total capital accumulated abroad from Latin America alone was estimated in 1992 at $300 billion. For developed countries, estimates are rare, but Michael P. Dooley estimated capital flight from the United States between 1980 and 1982 at $250 billion.[43]

[40] Vito Tanzi & Partho Shome, Tax Evasion: Causes, Estimation Methods, and Penalties, a Focus on Latin America 13–19 (1993).

[41] *Id.* at 20–22, tbl.3 (recreated by the authors).

[42] Kant, *supra* note 13, at 5–10 (Foreign Direct Investment and Capital Flight 1 (Princeton Studies in Int'l Fin. No. 80, 1996).

[43] Michael Dooley, *Comment*, *in* Capital Flight and Third World Debt 79 (Donald R. Lessard & John Williamson eds., 1987).

TABLE 2.2 *Estimates of revenue losses due to tax evasion (developing countries)*

Country	Revenue loss
Argentina (1989)	50% of GDP
Bolivia (1986)	44% of GNP
Brazil (1989)	50% of GDP
Chile (1986)	14–32% of GNP
Costa Rica (1986)	11% of GNP
Dominican Republic (1986)	14–32% of GNP
Ecuador (1986)	30–32% of GNP
Guatemala (1986)	30–32% of GNP
Honduras (1986)	30–32% of GNP
Mexico (1986)	14–32% of GNP
Peru (1986)	35% of GNP

It seems reasonable to assume that the income from such capital is untaxed by either the source country or the residence country for the reasons discussed above. If so, positing a 10 percent average rate of return and a 50 percent individual tax rate would put the Latin American countries' revenue loss on $300 billion of departed capital at about $15 billion per year. Though significant, this figure is probably far too low because it assumes that the initial capital investment represents after-tax income. If, more realistically, one assumes that the migrating capital was never taxed, the lost revenue from $300 billion held abroad would be an initial $150 billion plus an additional $15 billion per year, assuming the same 50 percent tax rate. The total lost revenue for all developing countries may be as high as twice that amount.

These very high numbers suggest that developing countries could raise significant tax revenues were they able to tax the income that their residents invest abroad. Such revenue gains could be very important: The United Nations (UN) estimated that basic social services (such as universal primary education) could be assured for all developing countries for a mere $30 billion to $40 billion a year.[44] The corresponding numbers for developed countries (such as Germany) could also be quite large, although much smaller as a percentage of total tax revenues. Thus, tax competition seems to lead to significant tax base erosion of the personal income tax, which is still a major – if not the largest – tax base for most developed and developing countries.

2.2.3.2 Corporate Income Tax

Estimating revenue losses from tax competition in the corporate income tax should be easier than in the personal income tax area, because the revenue loss in this

[44] United Nations, World Summit for Social Development (1995) [hereinafter World Summit for Social Development].

category involves legal tax avoidance, rather than illegal tax evasion. Most developed countries exempt or defer taxing the active business income of foreign subsidiaries of "their" MNEs, while developing countries grant explicit tax holidays to those subsidiaries.

Nevertheless, there is little publicly available data on revenue losses resulting from deferral, from exemption by home countries, or from preferential tax regimes in host countries. OECD member countries are the home countries for about 85 percent of the world's MNEs.[45] However, the OECD's data on tax expenditures reveal that no member countries, except for the United States and France, quantify the revenue lost by granting exemption or deferral to the foreign source active business income of their MNEs.[46] The United States estimated its 1997 revenue loss from "deferral of income from controlled foreign corporations" at $2.2 billion, a figure it expects to swell to $3.4 billion by 2003.[47] France estimated the potential revenue gain from taxing its MNEs on their foreign source profit in 1994 at 18 billion French francs (FF) (about $3.3 billion as of December 1994).

These numbers are significant, but they represent only a small portion of all MNEs. However, their true significance for each home country can only be assessed if one compares these figures to other tax expenditures and to the overall budget. For the United States, $3 billion is a small tax expenditure compared to the largest tax expenditure at the time, which amounts to $50 billion and more. It is also a small figure in terms of overall tax receipts from the corporate income tax ($189 billion in 1998). For France, on the other hand, FF 18 billion in 1994 represented the second largest tax expenditure in the budget. It also represented a larger share of total receipts from the corporate tax (FF 119 billion in 1994). These figures may explain why France was one of the OECD member countries most interested in pushing the tax competition issue. It co-chaired the Special Sessions of Tax Competition that drafted the OECD Report which focuses entirely on the corporate tax issue.

Information is sparse also for host countries that grant tax holidays or other preferential regimes targeted at foreigners. The OECD Report on tax competition gives no figures, except that total direct investment by G7 countries in traditional tax havens in the Caribbean and South Pacific increased more than fivefold from 1985 to 1994, to more than $200 billion. This represented a rate of increase well more than the growth of total outbound FDI. If one assumes that the major motivation of such investment in traditional tax havens is avoiding taxation, and therefore that most of the income from the $200 billion escapes the net of existing

[45] *See* United Nations Conference on Trade and Dev., World Investment Report 1999: Foreign Direct Investment and the Challenge of Development 5–6 (1999) [hereinafter World Investment Report].

[46] *See* OECD, Tax Expenditures: Recent Experiences 62 (1996).

[47] *Budget Analytical Perspectives, Chapter 5 – Tax Expenditures*, 98 Worldwide Tax Daily 25, tbl.5-1 (1998).

anti-deferral regimes, this number will represent a significant loss of corporate tax revenue for the G7 countries.

Two member countries of the OECD had preferential tax regimes targeted at foreigners: Ireland and Belgium. Ireland provided a reduced tax rate of about 10 percent to foreign MNEs that establish manufacturing facilities in selected areas (making it a "production tax haven"). Belgium grants near-complete tax relief to "centres de coordination" (making it a "headquarters tax havens"). The estimated revenue loss for Ireland from its reduced tax rate in 1991 and 1992 was 748.9 million Irish pounds (about $1.2 billion). The estimated revenue loss for Belgium from its headquarters tax reduction in 1992 was 46 billion Belgian Francs (about $1.5 billion). These numbers are relatively small, but far from negligible in the budgets of Ireland and Belgium. Ireland's tax expenditure on the production tax haven was the largest such expenditure in its budget for the tax year 1991–92. Belgium's tax expenditure for the headquarters tax haven was the fifth largest expenditure in its 1992 budget.

Tax expenditure figures are of doubtful accuracy, however. In particular, the US figures (which are determined by methods that are relatively sophisticated compared to those used to calculate other countries' expenditures) may be understated because they do not take into account any behavioral changes that shift income overseas, including those caused by such legal changes as amendments to the corporate tax laws. Thus, the $2 billion to $3 billion estimated annual revenue loss from deferral was not an accurate estimate of the revenue that would be lost were Subpart F (the principal US anti-deferral regime) repealed or severely curtailed. In that case, US-based MNEs would presumably shift revenues abroad, resulting in increased tax revenue losses. Nor was the $2 billion to $3 billion figure necessarily even a good estimate of the revenue that could be gained if Subpart F were expanded to cover all income because such an expansion could encourage more MNEs to incorporate outside the United States and further deprive it of tax income.

In addition, the United States lost-revenue estimate did not change (except for adjustments for inflation and other macroeconomic variables) since the 1980s, even though the Treasury data indicate a significant reduction in average effective foreign tax rates. But based on the available data, it appears that the total revenue to be gained from repealing deferral was relatively small (although significant in relation to total US corporate tax revenues from foreign source income). This result changed significantly later in the 2000s.

On the other hand, it should be recalled that the United States has the strictest anti-deferral regime of all OECD member countries and that its corporate tax rate is relatively low. A country like Japan, which has an ineffective anti-deferral regime and a high effective corporate tax rate, is likely to face a much more significant loss from revenue deferral. This greater loss may explain why Japan was at the forefront of the OECD effort to combat harmful tax competition and co-chaired the OECD's Special Sessions of the Committee on Fiscal Affairs.

Thus, the limited available data on revenue losses from tax competition in the corporate income tax area suggest that these losses, although significant, are probably much smaller than the potential losses in the personal income tax area. On the other hand, the revenue losses may vary dramatically from country to country depending on their effective corporate tax rate and the stringency of their anti-deferral rules. Some countries, such as France and Japan, have suffered significant revenue losses from corporate tax competition, even in terms of their overall budget. But became much larger after 1997, as discussed below. In other countries, like the United States, those losses may have been relatively insignificant.

2.3 THE PROBLEM OF TAX COMPETITION FROM A GLOBAL NORMATIVE PERSPECTIVE

We have argued that increased capital mobility, when combined with tax competition, leads to the likelihood that cross-border flows of capital will be taxed more lightly than either domestically invested capital or domestic labor. In this section, we will attempt to evaluate whether this situation is problematic from a global efficiency or equity perspective. We will then attempt to balance those arguments against the right of democratic countries to determine the size of their governments, and to develop a distinction between harmful and acceptable forms of tax competition.

2.3.1 *Efficiency: Global Welfare and Public Choice*

Let us first focus on the economic arguments that have been made in favor of and against tax competition from a welfare economics perspective. The economic analysis of tax competition typically begins with Charles Tiebout's seminal 1956 article "A Pure Theory of Local Expenditures."[48] Tiebout addresses the problem of the provision of public goods in a local government context and shows that, in that situation, the problem of knowing true voter preferences for public goods and avoiding free riders can be resolved. The key to Tiebout's solution is the assumption that individuals can move and face a choice among localities offering fixed but different levels of public services financed through benefits taxes. Tiebout shows that the optimal outcome in terms of satisfying individuals' preferences can be achieved because individuals will sort themselves geographically based on their differing preference levels, paying different levels of benefits taxes, and the final outcome will not be inferior to market-based outcomes for private goods. The implication of Tiebout's analysis is that tax differentials among jurisdictions are positive because they maximize the ability of individuals to satisfy their preferences and, therefore, actions to harmonize tax rates are inefficient.

Tiebout's analysis depends on two crucial assumptions: first, that individuals are completely mobile between taxing jurisdictions; and second, that all taxes are

[48] Charles M. Tiebout, *A Pure Theory of Local Expenditures*, 64 J. POL. ECON. 416 (1956).

benefits taxes and represent payments for goods and services provided by government, rather than taxes based on ability to pay with distributive goals. When either assumption is relaxed, Tiebout's analysis becomes less valid. At the international level, both of Tiebout's assumptions are problematic. As argued above, restrictions on immigration impede individuals' ability to move between countries, and the main form of taxation is an income tax with explicitly distributive goals. Nevertheless, we argue below that Tiebout's analysis retains some validity at the international level for generally applicable corporate tax-rate differentials among countries.

Following Tiebout, extensive public finance literature has focused on tax competition at the local level, concentrating specifically on the types of taxes available to the local jurisdiction. As noted earlier, Tiebout's model assumes that jurisdictions levy only benefits taxes. What happens when distortionary taxes, such as taxes on capital, are used instead of benefits taxes or lump-sum taxes? George Zodrow and Peter Mieszkowski have shown that in such a case, the supply of public services will be less than optimal.[49] They analyzed the supply of such services in a situation in which capital is mobile and the options available to local government are either a non-distorting lump sum tax or a tax on capital (e.g., a property tax). Under such circumstances, if so, communities would levy only the head tax for fear that the tax on capital would drive out investment. However, if the head tax had to be reduced (e.g., for political reasons), the level of public services would fall below the optimal level.

Zodrow and Mieszkowski's analysis has generated several studies that focus on the negative effects of the tax competition that occurs when jurisdictions must tax a mobile factor, such as capital. For example, David Wildasin has reconceptualized the analysis as a fiscal externality: When a jurisdiction raises its taxes on capital, it causes a flow of capital to other jurisdictions that increases their tax revenues. Consequently, the first jurisdiction's desire to avoid the externality will lead to an insufficient supply of government services in that jurisdiction.[50]

Sam Bucovetsky and John Wilson have extended this analysis to situations in which a tax on wages, as well as a tax on capital, is possible. Because labor is relatively immobile, one could argue that taxes on wages would prevent the underprovision of public services that would otherwise result from the fear of driving capital elsewhere; such wage taxes would be like Pigouvian head taxes or Tieboutian benefits taxes. However, Bucovetsky and Wilson show that even with wage taxation, the supply of public services will continue to be inefficiently low because a tax on labor tends to reduce the labor supply in the taxing country. Capital will then flow

49 *See* George R. Zodrow & Peter Mieszkowski, *Pigou, Tiebout, Property Taxation, and the Underprovision of Local Public Goods*, 19 J. URB. ECON. 356, 368–69 (1986).

50 *See* David E. Wildasin, *Interjurisdictional Capital Mobility: Fiscal Externality and a Corrective Subsidy*, 25 J. URB. ECON. 193, 194 (1989).

out of the taxing country, and as a result, wages and labor supplies will rise in other countries, creating the same kind of positive externality as a tax on capital. Notwithstanding this analysis, Bucovetsky and Wilson also show that worldwide taxation of capital, if it were possible, would result in the efficient provision of public goods.

If tax competition is harmful in these ways, why do countries not attempt to coordinate tax policy? A series of studies by Wilson, Bucovetsky, and Ravi Kanbur and Michael Keen address this issue.[51] They show that in a tax competition situation, the residents of smaller regions tend to benefit because small countries perceive capital elasticity to be higher and therefore undercut the larger countries' tax rate. Thus, even if the combined tax revenue from both large and small regions would rise to the optimal level under a system of tax coordination, the residents of the smaller regions would object because they gain more from tax competition. The same political difficulties make restrictions on tax competition in the international setting less likely because smaller countries are more likely to be tax havens.

Thus, although most of the public finance literature has tended to favor restrictions on tax competition from a utilitarian perspective of welfare maximization, a different line of analysis by public finance economists yields opposite results. A fundamental assumption of the studies cited above is that governments are benevolent – that they seek to maximize the utility of their residents. However, as the public choice literature shows, governments may also be conceived as Leviathans that seek to maximize their revenues in their own self-interest without regard for the good of the general citizenry. From that perspective, tax competition may be beneficial because it constrains governments' tendency to grow.

In an influential article, which he wrote while serving as President Reagan's Deputy Assistant Secretary of the Treasury for Tax Policy, Charles McLure makes a forceful statement of the public choice perspective on tax competition.[52] McLure criticizes the literature on tax competition and public finance for assuming that taxes must be levied on mobile capital. If governments can employ benefits taxes and individuals are mobile, the Tiebout analysis indicates that the problem of under-provision of public services will not arise. McLure then argues that at the state and local level, benefits taxes are both feasible and desirable. However, the core of McLure's argument is that because of the Leviathan problem, "tax competition is, on balance, good." It forces governments to be more attentive to the desires of voters.

[51] *See* S. Bucovetsky, *Asymmetric Tax Competition*, 30 J. URB. ECON. 167 (1991); Ravi Kanbur & Michael Keen, *Jeux Sans Frontières: Tax Competition and Tax Coordination When Countries Differ in Size*, 83 AMER. ECON. REV. 877, 883 (1993); John Douglas Wilson, *Tax Competition with Interregional Differences in Factor Endowments*, 21 REGIONAL SCI. & URB. ECON. 423, 424–26 (1991); John Douglas Wilson, *Theories of Tax Competition*, 52 NAT'L TAX J. 269, 278–79 (1999).

[52] Charles E. McLure, *Tax Competition: Is What's Good for the Private Goose Also Good for the Public Gander?*, 39 NAT'L TAX J. 341 (1986).

The first prong of McLure's argument is problematic at the international level, given the limited labor mobility of individuals and the relevance of distributive concerns. However, the Leviathan prong of the argument has proven to be quite influential. Most of the literature addressing this issue considers two questions: First, is either the Leviathan model or the benevolent model an accurate description of governments? Second, if governments are neither completely self-serving nor completely benevolent, what are the implications for tax competition?

On the first question, Wallace E. Oates has studied whether the extent of fiscal decentralization, which enables tax competition to take place, is negatively correlated with the size of the public sector as the Leviathan model suggests. He studied the extent of fiscal decentralization in a sample of forty-three countries (based on IMF data) and in the forty-eight contiguous US states. In both cases, there was no relationship between the degree of decentralization and the size of the public sector; if anything, greater decentralization tended to be correlated with larger government, contrary to the Leviathan hypothesis. Dani Rodrik advances a hypothesis that may explain this last result: More open economies with more tax competition tend to correlate with more extensive social insurance programs because voters demand government insurance against the risks associated with an open economy. Thus, the empirical data are at best inconclusive and do not support the Leviathan model.

Jeremy Edwards and Michael Keen have directly compared the Leviathan and benevolent views of government from the perspective of tax competition.[53] They point out that both of those views are extreme cases of a more plausible model, in which policy makers value both the welfare of their citizens and the surplus they extract from them for their own uses. Using the model developed by Zodrow and Mieszkowski (who assumed a benevolent government), they ask whether tax competition is beneficial if policymakers act to maximize the welfare of citizens, if they act to maximize tax revenues, or if their goals fall somewhere in between. They show that if coordination leads to a small increase in the tax on mobile capital, the policymakers' welfare will unambiguously increase. The welfare of a representative citizen may also increase "if and only if the elasticity of the tax base exceeds the policy-maker's marginal propensity to waste tax revenue." For example, if it is estimated that the elasticity of capital to tax increases is 0.4, then coordination is beneficial as long as government wastes less than 40 percent of the capital tax revenue on bureaucrats rather than using it to benefit citizens. Edwards and Keen also show that the benefits of coordination are greater the higher one estimates the deadweight loss from taxation because coordination makes the tax closer to an unavoidable lump-sum tax. Thus, if the deadweight loss from the tax is thirty cents on the dollar, they calculate that coordination is desirable as long as an increase of

[53] *See* Jeremy Edwards & Michael Keen, *Tax Competition and Leviathan*, 40 Eur. Econ. Rev. 113, 114–15 (1996).

revenues by $1 does not increase socially unproductive public expenditure by more than twenty-three cents.

Applying Edwards and Keen's analysis requires that one define and quantify government waste of tax revenue. However, their analysis indicates that even relatively low estimates of the elasticity of capital to taxation and of the deadweight loss from taxation require a very high estimate of government waste for the Leviathan model to be persuasive.

To sum up, from an efficiency perspective, a persuasive argument can be made that undertaxation of cross-border capital flows is problematic because it leads to deadweight losses. Such losses decrease global welfare and are unlikely (except under extreme assumptions regarding the extent of governmental waste) to be adequately compensated by benefits flowing from increased tax competition.

2.3.2 *Equity: The Tax Mix*

Equity in international taxation has two aspects: inter-individual equity and inter-nation equity. Inter-individual equity considerations determine the proper rate of taxation on cross-border transactions. Inter-nation equity considerations determine the proper division of the tax base among countries. In this section we will concentrate on inter-individual equity because the focus is on the tax rate while inter-nation equity issues will be discussed in Section 2.4.

The traditional inter-individual equity analysis of international taxation is as follows: Suppose individual A earns 100 of income from domestic sources while individual B earns 100 of income from domestic sources and 100 of income from foreign sources. Vertical equity requires taxing B more than A because of his greater income; but if foreign source income is excluded, B and A will be taxed the same. Thus, undertaxation of foreign source income is inconsistent with inter-individual equity.

The problem with this argument, when couched in such general, impersonal terms, is that it tells us nothing about the parties' ability to respond to taxation by shifting the source of their income. Suppose, for example, that A can easily shift her income to a foreign source (e.g., it is interest income) while B's domestic source income is labor income which cannot so easily be moved. In that case, taxing B the same as A is not problematic from an equity perspective because A can easily ensure that she pays less tax than B by shifting the source of her income (or else other people will adjust their investments so that in equilibrium the after-tax returns to A and B will be equal). In that case, as Boris Bittker has shown, the equity violation turns into a violation of efficiency.[54]

[54] *See* Boris I. Bittker, *Equity, Efficiency and Income Tax Theory: Do Misallocations Drive Out Inequities?*, 16 SAN DIEGO L. REV. 735, 738 (1979).

To make the equity argument, a broader framework is needed, which considers the relative mobility of capital and labor. In general, as argued in the Introduction, the present age of globalization can be distinguished from the preceding one (from 1870 to 1914) by the much higher mobility of capital than labor. This is the result of three historical changes that took place between 1914 and 1980: First, during the 1920s extensive restrictions were placed on immigration by all developed countries, so that large movements of labor in response to taxation are very difficult. Second, during the 1980s capital controls were relaxed in all developed and many developing countries so that they do not pose a significant barrier to capital mobility. Finally, technological changes from the development of electronic banking to the rise of the internet have made it easy to transfer funds worldwide at the speed of light. As noted above, it is estimated that international capital movements in the 1990s approximate $1 trillion a day, which exceeds the annual GDP of most countries.

Given these changes and the difficulty of taxing foreign-source income from capital (as explained above), economists have long predicted that the tax base will shift from taxes on capital (the relatively mobile factors) to taxes on labor and land (the relatively immobile factor). Thus, the standard recommendation in the public finance literature for small, open economies is to refrain from levying any taxes on capital because its mobility means that the tax burden will be shifted to domestic labor and land, and it is more efficient to tax those factors directly.

Can we in fact observe such a shift from taxes on capital to taxes on labor? A good place to start would be to consider the "tax mix," that is, the relative percentage of various types of tax in total tax revenues, in OECD member countries from 1965 (i.e., before the relaxation of exchange controls) to 2000. The data for 1965–95 are summarized in Table 2.3.

Based on these data, the following observations can be made. First, the data should be interpreted against an overall tendency for government revenues to grow as a percentage of GDP. This is true not just for OECD member countries (from an unweighted average of 30 percent in 1975–80 to 34.3 percent in 1986–92) but also for most developing countries. This trend has continued in OECD member countries, where in 1994 average government revenues reached 37.6 percent of GDP.

TABLE 2.3 *Structure of taxation in OECD countries, 1965–1995 (percent of total revenue)*

Type of tax	1965	1970	1975	1980	1985	1990	1994	1995
Personal income	26	28	30	31	30	29	27	27
Corporate income	9	9	8	8	8	8	8	8
Social security	18	20	22	22	22	23	25	25
Property	8	7	6	5	5	6	6	5
General consumption	12	14	13	14	16	17	18	18
Other goods and services	26	22	19	18	18	14	15	15

However, the rate of growth has been considerably less steep in the 1980s and early 1990s than in the 1970s. As discussed below, the overall growth in the tax burden can be explained in terms of the growing role of the state in providing social insurance. The slower recent growth can be explained in terms of the state facing political and practical obstacles to raising taxes to maintain further growth in social insurance programs. The growth in overall government revenues means that the 25 percent of total revenues attributed to social security (payroll) taxes in 1995 represents a significantly higher percentage of GDP than the 26 percent of total revenue attributed to "other goods and services" (i.e., excise taxes and tariffs) in 1965.

Second, revenues from both the corporate and personal income taxes tended to be flat as a percentage of total revenues (although rising as total revenues rose). In OECD member countries, revenues from the personal income tax were 26 percent of total tax revenues in 1965 and 27 percent in 1995. Revenues from the corporate income tax in the same years were 9 percent and 8 percent respectively. While in developing countries the corporate income tax is more important than the individual income tax, the same flatness can be observed for those countries as well. Because the income tax taxes both labor and capital, this flatness may mask a trend to shift the tax from capital to labor. The flatness is striking because in OECD member countries tax rates have tended to go down in recent years.

Third, a trend in both OECD member countries and developing countries was the rise in taxes on consumption, which are usually considered as taxes on labor. In OECD member countries, general consumption tax (VAT) revenues have risen from 12 percent of total tax revenues in 1965 to 18 percent in 1995. In developing countries, general consumption taxes rose from 25.5 percent of total tax revenues in 1975–80 to 31.8 percent in 1986–92. Most of this increase can be explained by rises in the tax rate: Owens shows that almost every OECD member country that has a VAT (i.e., all OECD members, except the United States) has raised the standard rate since the tax was introduced.

Fourth, in OECD member countries another trend was the rise in payroll (social security) taxes to fund social insurance programs. Such payroll taxes rose from 18 percent of total tax revenues in 1965 to 25 percent in 1995. In most OECD member countries, more revenue was raised from social security taxes in 1995 than from the income tax. This trend can be explained by the expansion of social insurance programs because of the aging of the population and increases in unemployment benefits, which are discussed below.

The combination of these trends can be summarized as follows: From 1965 to 1995, governments all over the world increased substantially the proportion of GDP that they collected as tax revenues. As revenues from both the individual and corporate income taxes have been generally flat (as a percentage of total revenues) over this period, the increase in total tax revenues was financed by increases in consumption taxes (in all countries) and in payroll taxes (in developed countries). Since both consumption taxes and payroll taxes fall on labor, while income taxes may be imposed on both labor and capital, the data are consistent with the shift from taxing capital to taxing labor that has been predicted theoretically to occur as a consequence of globalization.

These broad data on the tax mix can be supplemented with more specific data on trends in income taxation, which suggest that the effective income tax rate on income from capital may be declining. Effective tax rates can be calculated in three ways. First, using the model developed by Mervyn A. King and Don Fullerton, the effective marginal tax rate (EMTR) can be calculated for a country by using a simulated investment project and assuming certain inflation and interest rates. The EMTR is the difference between the pre- and post-tax rate of return for the marginal investment. Second, a similar model can be used to calculate the effective average tax rate (EATR) which is relevant for a project that earns some economic rent (as most projects financed by multinationals tend to do). The EATR is the difference between the value of the project in the presence and absence of tax in each country. Finally, a different measure of effective tax rates is to attempt to calculate the actual average tax rate (ATR) based on financial data published by firms in their financial accounts. The ATR differs from the EMTR and EATR in that it is based on actual firm-level data and not on hypothetical assumptions, but the quality of the available data varies greatly from country to country.

The advantage of all three methods is that they attempt to calculate effective tax rates and therefore consider both changes in the statutory tax rate and changes in the tax base. Thus, if tax reform leads to a reduction in the statutory rate that is offset by widening the tax base (as most tax reforms in the 1980s in OECD member countries aimed to do), effective tax rates should be unchanged. Lucy Chennells and Rachel Griffith report results from calculating EMTRs, EATRs, and ATRs for a sample of ten OECD member countries over the period 1979 to 1994. They found that domestic EMTRs declined from an average of 21.7 in 1979 to 20.5 in 1994. Domestic EATRs, which are more relevant for foreign direct investment, declined over the same period from 21.7 to 17.9. Finally, ATRs based on actual accounting data for six of the countries (Australia, France, Germany, Japan, the United Kingdom, and the United States) declined from 40 percent in 1985 to 32.6 percent in 1994. Since these calculations are based on corporate income taxes, they can be assumed to fall on income which is mobile relative to labor income.

Further confirmation of this trend for effective corporate tax rates to decline can be found in Harry Grubert's data based on actual tax returns filed by US-based multinationals showing taxes paid by their overseas affiliates. Grubert studied changes in the average effective tax rates in a sample of sixty countries for the period 1984 to 1992 and supplemented it by published financial data for the years after 1992. He found that ATRs fell from 32.9 percent in 1984 to 23 percent in 1992, a decline of almost ten percentage points. Statutory rates also fell but by less than effective tax rates (from 41.2 percent to 33.4 percent). Moreover, the decline in ATRs was largest in countries with a population of less than 15 million, which are likely to be more sensitive to capital flows, and smallest in countries with more restrictions of capital flows. Thus, the data are consistent with the hypothesis that capital mobility may be driving effective rates on income from capital down.

Rodrik has calculated unweighted average effective tax rates on capital and labor for France, Germany, the United States, and the United Kingdom for the period 1970–91. The data indicate that taxes on both capital and labor in those countries went up in tandem from 1970 until about 1981, but since then taxes on capital have gone down while taxes on labor have continued to go up.

Finally, there are a series of studies that used data from national income accounts to calculate tax rates. The advantage of this method is that it uses actual revenues to construct effective tax rates on consumption, capital, and labor separately. Mendoza, Razin, and Tesar calculated tax rates for the G7 countries from 1965 to 1988 and found that while taxes on consumption and capital income tended to be stationary, the tax rate on labor income has followed an increasing trend in all countries. In another study, Mendoza and his colleagues used the same methodology to calculate tax rates for eighteen OECD member countries for the period 1965–91. They then calculated a regression relating those data to a measure of "lagged openness," defined as the sum of imports plus exports divided by total output in the economy for the previous year. They found that taxes on labor respond positively to increases in lagged openness while taxes on capital respond negatively. That is, the more open to capital flows an economy becomes, the more it tends to shift the tax burden from capital to labor consistently with the prediction.

What are the equity implications of these data? Since labor is generally less mobile than capital, a decline in taxes on capital and a rise in taxes on labor will generally involve a shift in tax burden which cannot be offset by income shifting and therefore tends to violate vertical equity. More broadly, since the rich save more than the poor, taxes on labor (consumption and payroll taxes) are generally more regressive (i.e., tax the poor more heavily) than taxes on capital (savings). Thus, a shift in tax burden from capital to labor would tend to render the tax system more regressive. Such a tax system is also less capable of redistributing resources from the rich to the poor. As a result, the overall distribution of income in a society compared to a proportional distribution, which is measured by the Gini coefficient, would tend to become more inequitable (i.e., the Gini coefficient would rise).

2.3.3 *Democracy: Two Types of Tax Competition*

In the preceding two sections we have focused on the ways in which tax competition on income from capital can be harmful: It can lead to an inefficient global allocation of capital, and it can force governments to use relatively regressive forms of taxation and limit their ability to use taxes on capital for redistributive purposes. These efficiency and equity considerations all lead to the conclusion that tax competition should be limited.

However, these considerations need to be balanced against another: Tax competition can reflect the different preferences of citizens in democratic countries for differing sizes of their governments. In fact, the level and type of taxation is one of the most important decisions made by voters in democratic countries, and it provides an image of the kind of society they wish to live in. From a welfare perspective, tax competition is beneficial to the extent it reflects these voter preferences. Thus, it becomes necessary to inquire whether it is possible to distinguish between types of tax competition that are likely to reflect such preferences and those that are less likely to do so. A clear case can be made for limiting the latter type of tax competition; the case for limiting the former type (tax competition that reflects preferences for the desirable size of government) is more problematic.

We can start with the Tiebout model in which tax competition (or at least differences in tax rates among jurisdictions, since Tiebout assumes that these are fixed) is beneficial because it enables citizens to maximize their welfare by voting with their feet. On its face, this model is inapplicable to the problem that lies at the heart of this chapter, that is, how to tax mobile capital in an open economy. The model is inapplicable because on the international level individuals cannot easily choose to move from one country to another and because taxes are used for redistribution as well as payments for government goods and services.

However, the degree to which the Tiebout model is inapplicable can be exaggerated. First, even though citizens cannot move from country to country, in democratic countries they can vote, and given the salience of the tax issue in politics it seems likely that their votes affect the level of government spending. Thus, one can envisage a situation in which the world is divided into jurisdictions with different levels of public spending depending on the wishes of (the majority of) each country's citizens.

Second, the focus in tax competition has been on source-based corporate taxes. These taxes are much closer to the benefits taxes envisaged by Tiebout than is generally recognized. They are not a significant factor in redistribution (in fact, their incidence is both unknown and possibly shifting). Instead, they represent a payment to the source country for the costs it incurs to enable investment by a multinational as well as a way of assuring source countries (and especially developing source countries) an adequate tax base.

This leads to an important distinction: If a multinational corporation invests in a country with a small public sector, it is likely to have to incur more costs or earn lower profits than if the public sector were larger. For example, it may have to invest in training its workers because the government provides inadequate public education, or it may have to build its own transportation systems because the government does not provide adequate infrastructure. In that case, it would be inappropriate to penalize the multinational by taxing it at a higher rate (e.g., its home country rate) to offset the lower taxes levied by the host country. If the multinational faces lower profits, the incentive to locate in the low-tax country would be limited, and therefore the negative effects of tax competition would be limited as well.

But this argument holds true only if the public sector is smaller in general because of a generally applicable tax decrease. If, on the other hand, the government decides to maintain generally high taxes on immobile factors (such as labor and land) but to grant the multinational a targeted tax holiday (or equivalently to subsidize it with targeted expenditures on training and infrastructure), the multinational obtains a windfall. Having made the decision to invest somewhere, it can then choose the location that offers it the best tax and subsidy package with the awareness that because the general level of taxation on domestic labor and land is high it will not have to incur additional costs.

Thus, this line of analysis suggests that a distinction should be made between tax competition in the form of generally applicable tax decreases that reduce the overall size of the public sector and tax decreases (or subsidies) that are limited only to foreign investors. In the former case, the tax reduction represents the wishes of the electorate and does not confer a windfall on foreign investors. In the latter case, the electorate is unlikely to be involved (since tax holidays to foreign investors are rarely the subject of political attention even if they are made public). Moreover, the tax holiday represents a windfall to the multinational since it benefits from a large public sector financed by overall high taxes.

The same distinction can also be made from a Leviathan perspective. Tax competition may be beneficial when it reduces wasteful government spending but only if it reduces the size of government. Overall tax reductions can be beneficial from this perspective especially if mandated by the voters and if they result in smaller governments. Targeted incentives aimed at foreigners are not beneficial because they are typically too small in the aggregate to affect the overall size of government. In fact, targeted tax incentives can themselves be seen as a form of government waste: They enable elected officials to boast about job creation in the short run without engaging in an adequate cost/benefit analysis in terms of lost revenues in the longer run. The costs of targeted tax incentives (in lost revenues and congestion problems) are likely to be less salient politically than the immediate benefits in job creation, especially where unemployment is a central political issue.

Thus, we would suggest that the line between harmful and beneficial tax competition be drawn between general tax reductions that apply to all taxpayers (domestic and foreign) and targeted tax reductions that are granted only to foreign investors. Harmful tax competition should thus include both production and headquarters tax havens since these are typically only granted to foreign multinationals. Harmful tax competition should also include reductions in withholding taxes that are aimed solely at attracting foreign capital unless measures are taken to ensure residence-based taxation. Finally, harmful tax competition also includes traditional offshore tax havens with an overall low or zero tax rate if the tax base is confined almost entirely to foreign investors. Such investors in traditional tax havens have no real business operations in the tax haven and therefore do not suffer a detriment from the small size of the public sector. However, harmful tax competition does not include overall reductions in the tax rate that apply to all taxpayers in a jurisdiction when the tax base includes significant numbers of domestic taxpayers.

It may be objected at this point that the arguments made in the preceding sections against tax competition on efficiency and equity grounds apply to all forms of tax competition and not just to harmful tax competition (as defined above). After all, a generally applicable tax decrease can lead to a large flow of capital from one country to another and result in an inefficient allocation of capital and limit the ability of the home country to redistribute income equitably.

However, as noted above, such considerations need to be balanced against the ability of voters in democratic countries to determine the desirable size of their public sector, even if this has potential adverse consequences for other countries. This is both a normative judgment and a practical one: As the failed attempts to impose minimum tax rates in Europe show, countries would be very reluctant to give up their right to set generally applicable tax rates, which is a core attribute of sovereignty. On the other hand, countries would be more likely to give up their right to target tax incentives at foreigners if the main reason for granting the incentive is fear that otherwise the capital would flow to another country that does grant such incentives. In this kind of an assurance game situation, multilateral action is possible to achieve the best outcome for all concerned.

The distinction proposed here between harmful and beneficial tax competition can be illustrated by two examples drawn from US history. Ronald Reagan was elected president in 1980 based on explicit promises to reduce the size of the federal government and cut taxes. In 1981, these promises were fulfilled through the largest individual and corporate tax decrease in US history. In particular, the adoption of the accelerated cost recovery system and an investment tax credit meant that new capital investment by corporations would be more than expensed, resulting in negative tax rates on normal corporate profits. This, in turn, led to a proliferation of tax shelters for individuals, so that Gordon and Slemrod estimated that in 1983 the United States collected no tax whatsoever on capital income.

The other result of the Economic Recovery Tax Act of 1981, together with the Reagan defense buildup, was a burgeoning budget deficit which was in fact predicted by the Congressional Budget Office. This deficit was financed by a flow of foreign capital into the United States, which at least in part was the direct result of lower tax rates. Sinn has estimated that the ACRS and ITC were responsible for a flow of between $1 trillion and $1.5 trillion into the United States from 1981 to 1984, or 7 percent of the world's capital stock. This influx of foreign capital could have been predicted at the time of enactment since in the absence of an increase in domestic (private) savings and given a decline in aggregate (public and private) savings, additional investment could only be financed from abroad.

Hans Werner Sinn has also argued that the consequences of this inflow were clearly beneficial to the United States and detrimental to the rest of the world:

> The first half of the eighties was characterized by enormous capital imports into the U.S. accompanied by a strong dollar and a high world interest rate level. Most countries suffered from this situation. Europe was driven into the worst recession of the post-war period, and the developing countries were shaken by one debt crisis after another. A number of countries were unable to meet their interest obligations, and a collapse of the world banking system was avoided only by strenuous effort. The U.S. alone seemed to have benefited; despite the high interest rate, it enjoyed a significant consumption and investment boom.[55]

Thus, Sinn would support actions taken by Europe to curb such tax competition by the United States, for example, by taxing its residents on their US source income. But it is highly unlikely that the United States would have agreed to cooperate in such a move (and thus forego the benefits of its tax reduction). Without cooperation from the United States, it is highly unlikely that Europe could have succeeded in taxing its individual residents on their US source income.

Moreover, from a normative perspective the United States could argue that it had no obligation to maintain a larger public sector than its citizens desired and that its citizens were entitled to the tax cuts they voted for, even if they had negative incidental effects on Europe. The primary obligation of the US government is the welfare of US citizens who elect it, not of Europeans.

On the other hand, consider the portfolio interest exemption enacted in 1984 to facilitate financing the same deficit. As described above, this was a targeted provision aimed solely at foreigners. It was not widely discussed and was passed in Congress largely at the behest of the Treasury and US banks. As a provision aimed solely at foreigners, it had a relatively small impact on the overall size of government (it is not even included in the tax expenditure budget). But the results for Latin American countries, which lost $300 billion in capital flight as a direct result of enacting the exemption, have been devastating. In part because of the lack of public exposure, these results were apparently not foreseen by the administration. If they had been, perhaps another way could have been found to reduce the cost of borrowing (e.g., by maintaining the Antilles treaty or renegotiating the treaty with Japan).

2.4 THE COSTS AND BENEFITS OF TAX COMPETITION FROM EACH COUNTRY'S PERSPECTIVE

We discussed the arguments for and against tax competition from a global perspective. However, international tax rules are not designed by an authoritative "world tax organization," but are set by each country separately with its own interests in mind. Thus, in this section, we will attempt to analyze the costs and benefits of tax competition from the perspective of the countries affected by it, turning first to developed welfare states and then to developing and transition economies. Then, we

[55] Hans-Werner Sinn, Capital Income Taxation and Resource Allocation 224–25 (1987).

will attempt to analyze how tax competition affects the division of tax revenues among countries, which relates to the concept of inter-nation equity.

2.4.1 *Developed Countries and the Fiscal Crisis of the Welfare State*

The welfare state, which began over a century ago with Bismarck's social insurance scheme (financed by a comprehensive income tax),[56] faces a severe fiscal crisis. The fundamental problem is an aging population, resulting from the baby boom of 1946–70 and an increasing life span, together with a decreasing number of births. The result is a significant increase in the "dependency ratio," defined as the ratio of the young (to age twenty) and the elderly (above retirement age for public pensions) to the working age population, in almost all OECD member countries. For example, in Japan the dependency ratio will rise from about 40 percent in 1995 to a peak of 60 percent in 2045; in Germany it will rise from 30 percent in 1995 to over 60 percent in 2035. Even in the United States, which has relatively high fertility and immigration rates, the dependency ratio will rise from about 20 percent in 1995 to 40 percent in 2035.[57] In the OECD in general, the percentage of the population over sixty will rise from 18.2 percent in 1990 to 27 percent in 2020 and peaks at 31.2 percent in 2050.[58]

The fiscal implications of this "old age crisis" are profound.[59] The OECD has published fiscal scenarios for its members based on their starting position in 2000, the nature of the demographic changes in each country, and the exposure of their budgets to the effects of aging through existing arrangements for public pensions and public health spending.[60] The results are that by 2030 all the OECD members studied except Ireland will experience a budget deficit ranging from 0.5 percent of GDP in Belgium to 8.8 percent of GDP in Japan[61] (the United States is in about the middle with a deficit of 3.8 percent of GDP). Total expenditures on social insurance programs (including pensions, health, unemployment, and others) in all OECD countries are scheduled to rise from 18.3 percent of GDP in 1990 to 25.5 percent in 2050 with a significantly higher percentage in Japan (27 percent) and Western Europe (33.4 percent of GDP in 2050).[62]

56 *See, e.g.*, Alexander Hicks, Social Democracy and Welfare Capitalism 13 (1999).

57 *See* Deborah Roseveare et al., *Ageing Populations, Pensions Systems and Government Budgets: Simulations for 20 OECD Countries* 27 fig.I (OECD Econ. Dep't Working Paper No. 168, 1996).

58 *See* McLure, *Capital Flight from Latin America*, *supra* note 12, at 3.

59 World Bank, Averting the Old Age Crisis: Policies to Protect the Old and Promote Growth 1 (1994) [hereinafter Averting the Old Age Crisis]; *see also* Estelle James, *Protecting the Old and Promoting Growth: A Defense of Averting the Old Age Crisis* 2 (World Bank Policy Research Dep't Working Paper No. 1570, 1996).

60 *See* Roseveare et al., *supra* note 57, at 5–6.

61 *See id.* at 21 tbl.5.

62 ILO Annual Report (1999), at tbl.3.1. For more data on the old age crisis and its fiscal implications, *see* OECD, New Directions in Health Care Policy 13–19 (1995); OECD, Maintaining Prosperity in an Aging Society 9–27 (1998).

The tax implications of this phenomenon can be analyzed by using "generational accounting." Generational accounting estimates the lifetime net tax rates will have to be on future generations compared with current newborns to finance government expenditures at their current levels (i.e., if no changes are made to government programs)[63]. Net tax rates are taxes paid minus transfers received. For the United States, Laurence J. Kotlikoff estimated that the net tax rate required on future generations will be as high as 84 percent.[64] This 84 percent estimate is impossibly high to practically implement. To equalize lifetime net tax rates of current newborns and future generations from 2006 onward, Kotlikoff estimates that it will be necessary to either (i) increase federal income taxes by 61 percent; (ii) cut transfer payments by 43 percent; or (iii) reduce federal purchases by an astonishing 109 percent.[65] The picture is similar for other countries: The generational imbalance for males, that is, the increase in net tax payments for future generations required to finance future benefits at current rates, ranges from 27 percent in Germany to 446 percent in Italy.[66]

The OECD study concludes that "[w]here major fiscal pressures have been identified ... some policy action will be needed to redress imbalances. Without such action, government dissaving could also lead to significant reductions in national savings in some countries."[67] The policy options identified by the OECD are (i) increasing the workforce through immigration, (ii) increasing taxes or cutting other expenditures, or (iii) cutting health and pension programs.[68] The first option is rejected as unrealistic given the numbers of immigrants required. The second option is likewise rejected because cutting other expenditures by the necessary amount would require, for example, the United States to eliminate all defense spending and Japan to cut twice all spending on general public services and defense. As for raising taxes, "[g]iven concerns about existing overall tax burdens, the option of raising taxes is not considered further."[69] Thus, the third option remains as the only viable alternative.

The conclusion regarding existing burdens from taxes is too broad. The key questions are what types of taxes are involved and in which countries. For the United States, for example, since overall taxation is only about 30 percent of

63 *See The Erosion of the American Dream: Hearing before the House Comm. on the Budget*, 104th Cong. 28–29 (1996) (statement of Laurence J. Kotlikoff, professor of economics, Boston University).

64 *See id.* at 30–31.

65 *See id.* at 32–33 and chart 2.

66 *See* Willi Leibfritz et al., *Ageing Populations, Pension Systems and Government Budgets: How Do They Affect Saving?* 40 tbl.II (OECD Econ. Dep't Working Paper No. 156, 1995).

67 *Id.* at I 7. *See, e.g.*, Theodore P. Seto, *Drafting a Federal Balanced Budget Amendment That Does What It Is Supposed to Do (and No More)*, 106 YALE L.J. 1449, 1463 (1997); Herbert Stein, *The Significance of Budget Deficits, in* A NATION IN DEBT: ECONOMISTS DEBATE THE FEDERAL BUDGET DEFICIT 235, 238–39 (Richard H. Fink & Jack C. High eds., 1987).

68 *See* Leibfritz et al., *supra* note 66, at 18–23.

69 *Id.* at 21.

GDP, there appears theoretically to be considerable scope for raising additional revenues (e.g., through a VAT) before reaching European levels of public expenditure (about 50 percent of GDP). However, in Europe the scope for raising taxes is much more limited.

Value added tax rates in many European countries exceed 20 percent,[70] which is about as high as a consumption tax can practically go before the incentive to consume elsewhere becomes too significant and enforcement costs swallow the additional revenues. Most social insurance is currently funded through payroll taxes, but given the high level of unemployment in Europe, it is counterproductive to raise payroll tax rates even further.[71] In addition, high payroll tax rates may also create inefficient incentives for employers to hire part time or foreign workers whose wages are not subject to the same rates.[72]

This still leaves the option of raising more revenues through the income tax. The impediment to doing so is the risk of exacerbating current distortions in the choice of whether to work or not and whether to save or consume. These concerns are inherent in Europe's current high rates of income tax. However, as discussed above, income from cross-border investments is currently taxed at much lower effective rates than generally applicable ones. Therefore, taxing such income at rates that approximate the rates on domestic investment would both advance world efficiency and equity and raise more revenues to help address the fiscal crisis described above.

This rationale may explain why both the EU and the OECD began, in the 1990s, showing such interest in curbing "harmful tax competition," even though there may be insufficient evidence of actual erosion of the tax base. The potential for erosion certainly exists, and OECD governments are acutely aware that, at least until 2050 or so, they will need every penny they can collect in taxes to sustain the promises they made to the baby boom generation.

Since the need for additional revenues is predictable on demographic grounds, and the potential for tax base began erosion resulting from globalization, it is not surprising that the developed countries are taking actions to shore up the tax base even before any significant erosion has occurred. This analysis will appear to many readers to beg the question: Why should the welfare state not be drastically reduced? Political calculations and voters may coerce governments to maintain existing programs, but from a normative perspective, it is less clear that government should be doling out billions in pensions and health care for the elderly, especially since the private sector can shoulder much of the burden.

70 *See* OECD, CONSUMPTION TAX TRENDS 13 tbl.1.5 (2d ed. 1997) (showing rates at 20 percent or above in ten OECD member countries).

71 *See* OECD, IMPLEMENTING THE OECD JOBS STRATEGY 63–64 (1997); OECD, MAKING WORKPAY: TAXATION, BENEFITS, EMPLOYMENT AND UNEMPLOYMENT 65 (1997); OECD, THE OECD JOBS STUDY: TAXATION, EMPLOYMENT AND UNEMPLOYMENT 68 (1995).

72 *See* Jack M. Mintz, *Is National Tax Policy Viable in the Face of Global Competition?*, 1999 WORLD WIDE TAX DAILY 28–29, 31, available in WL 1999 WTD 128-20.

There are two answers to this question, both of which depend on normative value judgments that may not be shared by everyone. The first one is given by Dani Rodrik: Failing to maintain existing social insurance programs risks causing a political backlash against globalization and a return to 1920s-style protectionism and isolationism.[73] Rodrik points out an empirical relationship between economies becoming more open and increased spending on social insurance programs. Calculating the relationship between openness and the size of government yields an "unmistakable positive association," which is not confined to OECD countries.[74] This relationship lies in the role of social insurance in minimizing exposure to risk. Opening the economy to competition from abroad increases risk to both income and consumption because of increased specialization and the difficulty of diversifying human capital.[75] Theoretically, this could be offset by decreased exposure to domestic risks (e.g., by the ability to invest abroad), but empirically Rodrik shows that for 105 countries, increased openness results in a net absolute increase in risk to both income and to consumption.[76] The risk is expressed in terms of income insecurity (e.g., loss of employment) and income volatility (extreme fluctuations because of more frequent job shifts). The increased risk falls on the less mobile factors in society (primarily unskilled and semi-skilled labor) as suggested by the resulting increased income disparities.[77]

Social insurance programs can reduce such risks. The most direct link is to unemployment insurance, which can cushion against increased risk to income and job volatility resulting from globalization. Pensions and health care can also play a major role in reducing lifetime uncertainty over income which creates an increased willingness to tolerate exposure to external risks.[78]

If social insurance programs are cut because of the fiscal crisis described above, important buffers against the risks inherent in globalization will disappear. Such cuts can give rise to massive social resistance, for example in the French strikes of 1996, which were set off by the need to cut social insurance programs to meet the Maastricht budgetary guidelines for monetary union. It is no accident that as Europe moved toward economic integration in the 1990s, voters in almost all European countries elected center-left governments on a platform of protecting

[73] *See* Dani Rodrik, Has Globalization Gone Too Far? 49–69 (1997) [hereinafter Rodrik, Globalization]. For a critique of Rodrik's approach, *see* Paul B. Stephan, *Book Review*, 18 Nw. J. Int'l L. & Bus. 246 (1997).

[74] Rodrik, Globalization, *supra* note 73, at 52.

[75] *See id.* at 55.

[76] *See id.* at 57.

[77] *See* Peter Gottschalk & Mary Joyce, *The Impact of Technological Change, Deindustrialization, and Internationalization of Trade on Earnings Inequality: An International Perspective*, *in* Poverty, in Equality, and the Future of Social Policy 197, 197–228 (Katherine McFate et al., eds., 1995).

[78] *See* Rodrik, Globalization, *supra* note 73, at 58.

social insurance programs.[79] At the same time, European voters gave increasing power to extreme right-wing parties committed to the fight against globalization.[80] The danger, as Rodrik pointed out, is if social insurance programs are eroded, it could lead to a retreat from the commitment to openness which was championed in the 1980s and early 1990s.[81] Assuming that globalization itself is a positive phenomenon, such an outcome would be unfortunate. The previous retreat from globalization during the 1920s had disastrous consequences and led to a global depression and a world war. More recent developments have only bolstered the strength of this argument.

The second argument in favor of social insurance programs is purely normative. To make it, one needs to distinguish between social insurance and social assistance, both of which are integral parts of the modern welfare state.[82] Social assistance is government aid designed to ensure that every citizen is assured a minimal standard of living. Social insurance, on the other hand, is designed to ensure that citizens who are unable to work because of age, disability, health, or temporary unemployment can replace the income they had while working.[83] Social insurance, unlike social assistance, is connected to employment status and, frequently, to contributions paid by the employee.

This chapter focuses on social insurance rather than social assistance for two reasons. Social insurance is more directly linked to the pressures resulting from globalization since globalization can result in increased income insecurity and employment volatility. In addition, social insurance enjoys far broader acceptance among OECD members than social assistance: All OECD member countries have some form of social insurance programs which are quite popular, while only some OECD members have social assistance programs, and those programs enjoy much less popular support.[84]

Social insurance is popular precisely because in a market economy people may lose their income due to factors beyond their control. Nobody can prevent being too

79 *See Unsocialist Realism*, ECONOMIST (Oct. 3, 1998), at 66; Martin Walker, *Europe's Third Way Labs: Tony Blair's Formula for Reforms Contagious on the Continent*, NEW DEMOCRAT (May/June 1999), at 8.

80 *See* Tony Judt, *The Social Question Redivivus*, FOREIGN AFF. (Sept./Oct. 1997), at 95, 96.

81 *See* RODRIK, GLOBALIZATION, *supra* note 73, at 9; *see also* Dani Rodrik, *Trade, Social Insurance, and the Limits to Globalization* (National Bureau of Econ. Research Working Paper No. 5905, 1997).

82 For the definitions of these terms, *see* JOHN DITCH ET AL., COMPARATIVE SOCIAL ASSISTANCE: LOCALISATION AND DISCRETION (1997), which discusses social assistance systems in Germany, the Netherlands, Sweden, and Switzerland; and TONY EARDLEY ET AL., SOCIAL ASSISTANCE IN OECD COUNTRIES 15 (1996) [hereinafter EARDLEY ET AL., SOCIAL ASSISTANCE].

83 *See* MICHAEL J. GRAETZ & JERRY L. MASHAW, TRUE SECURITY: RETHINKING AMERICAN SOCIAL INSURANCE 27, 28 (1999).

84 *See* EARDLEY ET AL., SOCIAL ASSISTANCE, *supra* note 82, at 12. For a measure of the programs' support in the United States, *see* Virginia P. Reno & Robert B. Friedland, *Strong Support but Low Confidence: What Explains the Contradiction?*, *in* SOCIAL SECURITY IN THE 21ST CENTURY 178, 178–94 (Eric R. Kingson & James H. Schulz eds., 1997).

young or too old, nor is it possible to forestall illness, disability, or unemployment caused by factors beyond one's control. From an ex-ante perspective, we all face a similar likelihood of suffering from disruptions to income: "there but for the grace of God go I." It is not surprising that social insurance programs designed to prevent such risks from threatening a reasonable standard of living are very widespread. As Graetz and Mashaw state, "the social insurance systems of capitalist democracies have a solid claim to represent the greatest triumph of twentieth century domestic public policy ... social insurance ... is a crucial underpinning of a vibrant market economy."[85]

For a lot of social insurance programs, the private market is unable to provide adequate protection. This can occur for a variety of reasons. First, the risk can be too uncertain for private insurance companies to predict. Second, risks can covary in ways that threaten all policyholders at once, such as the demographic changes described above. If the risk cannot be adequately diversified, private insurance may become impossible to obtain. Third, adverse selection may occur if the potential insured know the risks much better than the insurers. This results in high-risk cases being overrepresented in the insurance pool. This could result in high premiums that price out lower- and moderate-risk individuals. Finally, there could be cases of moral hazard when the insured changes their behavior to increase the risk.[86]

Social insurance can, at least theoretically, alleviate these problems through a combination of taxation and regulation. The uncertainty problem can be overcome by paying compensation when the risk materializes and taxing to pay the costs at that point. Covariance of risk can be addressed because governments do not go out of business; they can borrow and then tax to meet their fiscal responsibilities. Adverse selection disappears with a government mandate to insure everybody, and moral hazard can be reduced by effective regulations such as requiring the unemployed to seek work.[87]

Globalization results in increased job insecurity, income volatility, and income disparities that exacerbate, rather than reduce, the need for government social insurance. The risks posed by globalization are inherently uncertain and covarying, falling on large numbers of people at once in an unpredictable pattern. In addition, both adverse selection and moral hazard are inherent in those risks. Insurance companies are typically less able to assess an employee's chances of being displaced

85 Graetz & Mashaw, *supra* note 83, at 4, 8.

86 *See Id.*, at 296–99; Lawrence H. Thompson & Melinda M. Upp, *The Social Insurance Approach and Social Security*, *in* Social Security in the 21st Century, *supra* note 84, at 3, 5. For discussions from a European perspective of the appropriate public/private mix in providing social insurance, *see* OECD, Private Pensions and Public Policy (1992); and Martin Rein & Eskil Wadensjo, *The Emerging Role of Enterprise in Social Policy*, *in* Enterprise and the Welfare State 1, 1–33 (Martin Rein & Eskil Wadensjo eds., 1997).

87 *See* Graetz & Mashaw, *supra* note 83, at 297; OECD, Benefit Systems and Work Incentives 49–50 (1998).

by global competition than the employee (or her employer, who in a typical private market provides the insurance). And moral hazard is the major problem in providing unemployment insurance since the employee can take steps to mitigate or exacerbate the risk.

Unemployment insurance is not the only type of social insurance affected by globalization. The largest social insurance expenditures are for pensions and health care. While these depend, for the most part, on demographic trends that are unrelated to globalization, the risk of inadequate income in old age or upon falling ill depends on the availability of private savings. If employees must save primarily to cover periods of temporary unemployment, they may not have enough left over for temporary or permanent loss of income resulting from disability or old age. Particularly in a system like the United States, in which both pensions and health insurance are tied to permanent full-time employment, there is a direct link between the decline of full time, unionized jobs with benefits due to globalization and the increasing need for government mandated social insurance.[88]

Thus, there is a strong normative basis for the desire of the developed countries to preserve their existing social insurance programs in face of the dual risks posed by demographic realities and globalization. To accomplish this, it is necessary to prevent the erosion of the individual and corporate income tax base as it is the biggest source of revenue in almost all the OECD member countries. In many countries, especially those in Europe, increasing other taxes (i.e., the VAT and payroll taxes) to cover any shortfall in income tax revenues is not a viable alternative for the reasons discussed above.[89] Moreover, since one result of globalization is an increase in income disparity, using the income tax to reduce such disparities through social insurance programs (which themselves have a redistributive aspect) seems particularly appropriate.

Given the extent of the fiscal crisis described above, no amount of change in the income tax is likely to produce sufficient revenues to preserve existing programs unchanged in all OECD member states. In particular, the imposition of effective income taxation on cross-border transactions, as advocated in this book, would not solve the fiscal deficit. Moreover, it is clear that existing programs may need to be changed in ways that are consistent with their normative underpinnings. Means testing should be introduced as a change. European countries are largely already moving in this direction.[90] But there is a strong normative case in favor of ensuring

88 For a strong critique of the US social insurance system, *see* GRAETZ & MASHAW, *supra* note 83, at 26–46. *See also* Michael J. Graetz, *The Troubled Marriage of Retirement Security and Tax Policies*, 135 U. PA. L. REV. 851 (1987); Jeffrey S. Lehman, *To Conceptualize, to Criticize, to Defend, to Improve: Understanding America's Welfare State*, 101 YALE L.J. 685 (1991). For a discussion of the vulnerable position of retirees in the United States and Canada, *see* OECD, THE TRANSITION FROM WORK TO RETIREMENT 119–25 (1995).

89 *See* GRAETZ & MASHAW, *supra* note 83, at 285–87.

90 *See* EARDLEY ET AL., SOCIAL ASSISTANCE, *supra* note 82, at 23. But *see* Eric R. Kingson & James H. Schulz, *Should Social Security Be Means-Tested?*, *in* SOCIAL SECURITY IN THE 21ST CENTURY, *supra* note 84, at 41.

that the income tax base is not eroded by globalization so sufficient revenues to fund social insurance programs can be maintained.

2.4.2 *Developing Countries and Tax Incentives*

The analysis above suggests that it is in the interest of developed countries to prevent tax competition from developing countries to protect their own income tax base. But what about the developing countries? Is it not in their interest to engage in tax competition to attract foreign investors, and would or should they resist any attempt by the developed countries to prevent them from doing so?

Several arguments need to be addressed. First, one might argue that developing countries need the tax revenues less than developed countries because they are not welfare states and are less affected by the fiscal crisis described above. Second, an economic case can be made that developing countries should refrain from taxing any foreign investment. Finally, tax competition may be the only way for developing countries to attract crucially needed foreign investors even if there is a cost involved (i.e., they need the revenues and cannot obtain them otherwise).

2.4.2.1 Do Developing Countries Need the Revenues?

A common misperception is that the fiscal crisis described above is a problem unique to members of the OECD. In fact, as fertility rates go down and health care improves, dependency ratios are expected to increase in other regions as well.[91] Outside the OECD and the transition economies, the dependency ratio was under 10 percent in the 1990s but is projected to rise to just below 30 percent by 2100.[92] Nor is it accurate to say that social insurance programs are unique to the developed world. A study by the International Labour Office shows that total spending on social insurance in Central and Eastern European countries is projected to reach 25.6 percent of GDP by 2050, that is, the same level as in the OECD (25.5 percent). For Example, in Poland and Slovakia, spending is scheduled to exceed 30 percent of GDP.[93] Outside the transition economies direct spending on social insurance is much lower, but other forms of government spending (e.g., government employment) effectively fulfill a social insurance role. In Latin America direct government spending on social insurance is much lower than indirect spending through government employment and procurement programs.[94]

[91] *See, e.g.*, Averting the Old Age Crisis, *supra* note 59, at 303 tbl.3.1.

[92] *See* Charles E. McLure, Jr., *International Considerations in United States Tax Reform, in* Influence of Tax Differentials on International Competitiveness 55 (1990). This statistic excludes Central and Eastern Europe, where the ratios are as high as in Western Europe.

[93] *See* Averting the Old Age Crisis, *supra* note 59, at 142 box 4.7.

[94] *See* K. Subbarao et al., Safety Net Programs and Poverty Reduction: Lessons from Cross-Country Experience 138–44 (1997).

It seems strange to argue that developing countries need tax revenues less than developed countries because they have less developed social insurance programs. If one accepts the case for social insurance, it applies to developing countries with even greater force because of widespread poverty where losing a job can have much direr consequences.[95] Furthermore, the need for revenues in developing countries goes far beyond social insurance. In some developing countries, revenues are needed to ensure the very survival of organized government, as the Russian fiscal crises demonstrated.[96] In other, more stable developing countries, revenues are needed primarily to provide for adequate education (investment in human capital), which many regard as the key to promoting development.[97]

However, one could argue that in many developing countries, government inefficiency and corruption are widespread and that many developing country governments are authoritarian dictatorships, so it may seem misguided to argue that they deserve more revenues. While this is undoubtedly true, it is a far less accurate description of most third world governments now than it was two decades ago. Democracy is more prevalent now than in 1980,[98] and corruption is declining (in part due to recent OECD efforts to combat it, and to constraints imposed by globalization itself).[99] Moreover, this argument seems more relevant to direct aid to developing countries than to designing tax rules. While direct aid can be targeted at those countries whose governments seem able to use it best, it is doubtful that tax rules can be tailored this way.[100] It seems inappropriate to refrain from designing general tax rules that enable all developing countries to raise needed revenues merely because in some cases those revenues may be used for inappropriate ends, such as lining some corrupt official's pockets or enabling a dictator to wage war more effectively. In fact, insofar as the tax rules are directed to foreign investment, those investments are more likely over time to flow to countries with less corruption and more democratic governments.[101]

95 *See* United Nations Human Dev. Programme, *Human Development Report* 1997, at 112 box 6.4 (1997) [hereinafter *Human Development Report*].

96 *See, e.g.*, Andrew Higgins & Mark Whitehouse, *Russia Crisis Deepens as Duma Rejects Premier*, WALLS ST. J., (Sept. 1, 1998), at A10; *Meltdown in Russia*, ECONOMIST (Aug. 29, 1998), at 47.

97 *See, e.g.*, OECD, HUMAN CAPITAL INVESTMENT: AN INTERNATIONAL COMPARISON 8 (1998); Amartya Sen, *Development Thinking at the Beginning of the XXI Century*, *in* ECONOMIC AND SOCIAL DEVELOPMENT INTO THE XXI CENTURY 531, 540–42 (Louis Emmerij ed., 1997).

98 *See* DANI RODRIK, THE NEW GLOBAL ECONOMY AND DEVELOPING COUNTRIES: MAKING OPENNESS WORK 82–100, 105–10 (1999) [hereinafter RODRIK, NEW GLOBAL ECONOMY].

99 *See* SUSAN ROSE-ACKERMAN, CORRUPTION AND GOVERNMENT: CAUSES, CONSEQUENCES, AND REFORM 185–87, 189 (1999).

100 *See* James R. Hines, Jr., *Taxed Avoidance: American Participation in Unsanctioned International Boycotts* (National Bureau of Econ. Research Working Paper No. 6116, 1997); Canute R. Miller, *Third World Views of the Ends and Means of United States Tax Policy*, *in* UNITED STATES TAXATION AND DEVELOPING COUNTRIES 83, 91–102 (Robert Hellawell ed., 1980).

101 *See generally* RODRIK, NEW GLOBAL ECONOMY, *supra* note 98, at 96–99.

2.4.2.2 Should Developing Countries Tax Foreign Investors?

Economists make a more powerful argument in favor of allowing developing countries to engage in tax competition when they argue that, in general, small open economies should refrain from taxing foreign investors.[102] The argument goes as follows: If an economy is small, this means that it must accept worldwide prices (including interest rates) as given. If it is open, foreign investors can choose to invest there or elsewhere. Since foreign investors will not accept an after-tax yield that is lower than the yield available elsewhere (which, by definition, the small economy cannot affect), they cannot be made to bear the burden of any tax imposed by the capital importing country. Therefore, the tax will be shifted to less mobile factors in the host country, such as labor and/or land. In spite of this, it is more efficient to tax those factors directly. Thus, it is argued, a small open economy should only tax domestic labor and land, and (if it can) domestic capital invested either domestically or overseas, but not foreign capital.

This argument seems quite valid as applied to portfolio investment which can earn the worldwide rate of interest free of tax in many locations around the world. The only effective way to tax such portfolio investment is on a residence basis, although as an administrative matter coordinated source-based backup withholding may be needed to enforce the tax. Regarding FDI, the argument is less valid for two reasons.

First, a precondition for the argument is that a foreign tax credit is not available for the tax. If a foreign tax credit is available in the home country of the investor, the investor is unaffected by the host country tax (since it would have to pay it to either the home or host jurisdiction). Thus, if the host country refrains from taxation, it is merely giving away revenue to the home country. This situation is relatively rare for portfolio investment because (as argued above) home countries are rarely able to tax such investment, making the credit irrelevant. However, in the case of direct investment the credit is generally available, and therefore, host countries should not refrain from taxing the investor.[103]

The second argument is even more powerful because it applies even in the absence of a credit (i.e., where the home country grants an exemption or deferral). The analysis above assumes that the host country is small and that the investing MNE can earn similar returns elsewhere. This assumes a competitive market

[102] *See* Assaf Razin & Efraim Sadka, *International Tax Competition and Gains from Tax Harmonization*, 37 ECON. LETTERS 69, 69–70 (1991) [hereinafter Razin & Sadka, *International Tax Competition*].

[103] *See* TIMO VIHERKENTTA, TAX INCENTIVES IN DEVELOPING COUNTRIES AND INTERNATIONAL TAXATION 71–139 (1991). *See* Eric W. Bond & Larry Samuelson, *Strategic Behaviour and the Rules for International Taxation of Capital*, 99 ECON. J. 1099 (1989). *See* Michael J. Graetz & Michael M. O'Hear, *The "Original Intent" of U.S. International Taxation*, 46 DUKE L.J. 1021, 1044–51 (1997).

situation. However, extensive literature on MNEs suggests that typically they exist to earn economic rents, that is, super-normal returns that result from an imperfectly competitive market.[104] In a perfectly competitive market, it typically makes more sense to operate through independent distributors given the transaction costs involved in operating directly in a foreign market. However, where there are rents involved, it makes sense to engage in FDI to keep those rents to oneself.

If an investor earns rents in a country, it is no longer "small" in the economic sense. That is, there is a reason for the investor to be there and not elsewhere. Therefore, any tax imposed on such rents (so long as it is below 100 percent) will not necessarily drive the investor to leave, even if it is unable to shift the burden of the tax to labor or landowners. Thus, the standard advice to host countries (refrain from taxing the foreign investor) does not apply.

This argument holds in the case of rents that are linked to a specific location such as natural resources or a large market. But what if the rents can be earned in many potential locations? For example, assume the rent is a result of possessing a unique intangible (an "ownership" advantage). Such an intangible can be a patent or another form of knowhow (e.g., a manufacturing technique that reduces costs drastically). For the rent to be earned, the MNE must invest somewhere, but there are many available locations. In this case, the host country will not be able to tax the rent if the MNE can credibly threaten to go elsewhere, although once the investment has been made the rent can be taxed.[105] This situation, which is probably the most common,[106] would require coordinated action to enable all host countries to tax the rent earned within their borders.

2.4.2.3 Do Developing Countries Need to Offer Tax Incentives for Investment?

The standard advice given by international institutions like the World Bank and the IMF to developing countries is to refrain from offering tax incentives to foreign investors. For example, the IMF's *Tax Policy Handbook* stated "[t]he IMF maintains a widely held view that tax incentives of all sorts have proved to be largely ineffective, while causing serious distortions and inequities in corporate taxation."[107] In the 1980s an IMF mission to Indonesia successfully advocated the abolition of all tax incentives for foreigners. Similarly, a World Bank study of Central and Eastern Europe recommended eliminating all tax incentives and instead levying a low,

[104] *See* Jean-Fransois Hennart, *The Transaction Cost Theory of the Multinational Enterprise, in* The Nature of the Transnational Firm 81, 81–85 (Christos N. Pitelis & Roger Sugden eds., 1991).

[105] *See* John H. Dunning, Explaining International Production 3 (1988).

[106] *See* Hennart, *supra* note 104, at 96–98.

[107] Janet Stotsky, *Summary of IMF Tax Policy Advice, in* Tax Policy Handbook app. at 279, 282 (Parthasarathi Shome, International Monetary Fund, ed., 1995).

general corporate tax rate on all activities.[108] In attracting foreign investors, it is argued, the country's overall business climate (stable government, well-educated workforce, good infrastructure) is much more important than specific tax incentives.[109]

This view is also widely shared by academics, who argue that tax incentives do little to attract foreign investment. For example, Peter Enrich argues in the US state tax context,

> for as long as states have been racing to outdo each other in the tax breaks they offer, economists and other researchers have been searching for evidence of the influence of states' tax policies on the vitality of their economies. The conclusion from these efforts has been, at best, inconclusive... All the evidence points to a single conclusion: State tax incentives are a thoroughly unproven tool for promoting economic development.[110]

If one accepts this view, then it would be relatively easy to agree with Enrich that constraining the ability of countries to engage in tax competition does them no harm. But, the evidence for the impact of taxation on business location incentives is stronger than Enrich suggests.[111] Even in the state context, recent studies with better methodologies have tended to conclude that taxes do impact business location decisions. In the international context, where tax rates are much higher, the evidence for the impact of taxation is decisive. As Hines and others have shown, taxes play a crucial role in determining investment location decisions, at least when international sites are otherwise equivalent.[112]

Moreover, it is hard to dispute that in some cases tax incentives may have played an important role in improving the welfare of a nation's citizens. The most frequently cited example is Ireland, which was an economic basket case in the early 1980s, but by 1998 Ireland was the fastest growing GDP in Europe with an income per capita exceeding even the UK. This growth was the result of massive foreign

[108] *See* JACK M. MINTZ & THOMAS TSIOPOULOS, CORPORATE INCOME TAXATION AND FOREIGN DIRECT INVESTMENT IN CENTRAL AND EASTERN EUROPE 10 (1992); *see also* OECD, TAXATION AND FOREIGN DIRECT INVESTMENT: THE EXPERIENCE OF THE ECONOMIES IN TRANSITION 30 (1995).

[109] *See* OECD, PROMOTING FOREIGN DIRECT INVESTMENT IN DEVELOPING COUNTRIES 53 (1993); *see also* Jack M. Mintz, *Corporate Tax Holidays and Investment*, 4 WORLD BANK ECON. REV. 81 (1990).

[110] Peter D. Enrich, *Saving the States from Themselves: Commerce Clause Constraints on State Tax Incentives for Business*, 110 HARV. L. REV. 377, 389–92 (1996) (footnotes omitted).

[111] *See, e.g.*, JOHN D. DONAHUE, DISUNITED STATES 92–119, 171–82 (1997).

[112] *See* Eric Bond, *Tax Holidays and Industry Behavior*, 63 REV. ECON. & STAT. 88 (1981); Michael J. Boskin & William G. Gale, *New Results on the Effects of Tax Policy on the International Location of Investment*, *in* THE EFFECTS OF TAXATION ON CAPITAL ACCUMULATION 201 (Martin Feldstein ed., 1987); Hines, *Tax Policy and the Activities of Multinational Corporations*, *supra* note 28.

investment, aided by factors like an educated, English-speaking workforce, and an elaborate system of targeted tax holidays.[113]

How, then, can it be argued that developing countries should not grant tax holidays to foreign investors even if they generally need the revenues if doing so is the only way to attract mobile business? Developing countries can certainly argue that they need the investment, and that the investment would not happen without the tax incentive. For example, a case study has focused on Intel's decision to invest $300 million in Costa Rica.[114] Intel was attracted primarily by non-tax factors, such as political stability, a commitment to economic openness, and an excellent educational system. Costa Rica had not granted any specific tax breaks or other subsidies.[115] But it is also clear that the investment would not have taken place without Cost Rica's general regime of tax holidays for foreign investors given the availability of such holidays in Costa Rica's nearby competitors (principally Mexico).[116]

Several studies of determinants of business location have concluded that the tax incentives are crucial *given the availability of such incentives elsewhere*. For example, the groundbreaking study of Stephen Guisinger and his colleagues concluded that tax incentives are crucial because otherwise the host country could not compete with countries that do engage in this form of tax competition.[117] The definition of competitiveness used by Guisinger was "would a foreign investment project have located in a particular country if that country had eliminated its incentives and disincentives while other countries maintained incentive policies at existing levels."[118] Using that definition, they found that the tax incentives were essential.

However, the crucial assumption made by Guisinger and his colleagues is that such countries have "no opportunity for cooperative agreements limiting incentive policies."[119] The solutions discussed below presuppose precisely such a multilateral mechanism. Thus, it can be argued that given the need for tax revenues, developing countries would, in general, prefer to refrain from granting tax incentives if only they could be assured of their competitiveness.

When they do grant tax incentives, it is precisely because of competition from other developing countries. Thus, Israel gave Intel $600 million under threat that it

[113] *See* OECD, OECD ECONOMIC SURVEYS 1998–1999: IRELAND 52–54 (1999); John Murray Brown, *Ireland: Eve of an Emerald Era*, FINANCIAL TIMES (London) (Sept. 22, 1998), at Survey; Rob Norton, *The Luck of the Irish*, FORTUNE (Oct. 25, 1999), at 194.

[114] *See* DEBORAH SPAR, ATTRACTING HIGH TECHNOLOGY INVESTMENT: INTEL'S COSTA RICAN PLANT (1998).

[115] *See id.* at 8–10.

[116] *See id.* at 12–21.

[117] STEPHEN E. GUISINGER AND ASSOCS., INVESTMENT INCENTIVES AND PERFORMANCE REQUIREMENTS 37–39 (1985).

[118] *Id.* at 39.

[119] *Id.*

would locate its investment in Ireland,[120] and Indonesia recently reintroduced its tax incentives under the strain of the Asian Financial Crisis of 1997–98 and the incentives offered by both Malaysia and Singapore.[121]

Thus, restricting the ability of developing countries to compete in granting tax incentives does not truly restrict their autonomy or counter their interests.[122] That is the case whenever they grant the incentive only for fear of competition from other developing countries. Had they operated without this fear, or in a vacuum, the tax incentives would never have been offered. Whenever competition from other countries drives the tax incentive, eliminating the competition does not hurt the developing country and may aid in raising revenue (assuming it can attract investment on other grounds). If, on the other hand, the tax incentives are not driven by competition, then a country remains free to lower its generally applicable tax rates.

The Irish case illustrates this distinction. Ireland was able to benefit from its tax incentives precisely because it was the only EU member to offer them. Ireland had no real competition given the reality of tariff barriers and the high tax rates maintained by other EU members.[123] But Ireland could have achieved the same result by maintaining a lower general tax rate and has now done so. Its preferential regimes have come under fire from the EU as other EU member states take issue with Ireland engaging in aggressive tax competition.[124] In a typical tax competition scenario, on the other hand, a developing country is competing directly against the preferential regime of another developing country. In that case, lowering the tax rate generally is typically not an option due to the revenue needs of both countries.

Competition limited to foreign investment is feasible, but it still hurts both countries in lost revenues, especially if the incentives cancel each other out. In that case, it would be in the interest of both countries to see the incentives eliminated if a cooperative solution could be found.

In summary, from the perspective of a typical developing country, the revenue loss from granting targeted tax holidays appears unlikely to be adequately offset by the benefits flowing from the investment. The reason for this is that a typical developing country is not competing against every other country in the world for the location of investment. Rather, it is competing against a limited subset of countries with characteristics similar to itself. When a multinational enterprise decides to look for an investment location, it engages in a process of analysis reminiscent of Fernand Braudel's three levels of historical change.[125] It first

[120] *See* Robert Lenzner, *Investing, Not Giving*, FORBES (Dec. 18, 1995), at 106.

[121] *See, e.g., World Watch: Indonesia Seeks to Spur Investment*, WALL ST. J. (Jan. 27, 1999), at A17.

[122] For a similar conclusion in the context of US states, *see* DONAHUE, *supra* note 111, at 115–19; and Enrich, *supra* note 110, at 467.

[123] *See* Gimme Shelter, ECONOMIST (Jan. 29, 2000), at Survey 15, 17.

[124] *See id.* at 16.

[125] *See* FERNAND BRAUDEL, THE MEDITERRANEAN AND THE MEDITERRANEAN WORLD IN THE AGE OF PHILIP II, at xiv (Sian Reynolds trans., Harper Collins Publishers 2d rev. ed. abr. 1992) (1966).

eliminates countries that are unsuitable based on long-term factors, such as geography and climate. Then, it eliminates countries that are unsuitable because of shorter-term factors, such as labor costs, education levels, or political instability. Finally, the multinational conducts an auction among the remaining countries, which focuses on the factors under direct government control, such as tax holidays and other forms of subsidy. In that auction, the developing country is likely to find itself forced to offer subsidies merely because other countries offer them, and not because it would choose to do so based on a cost/benefit analysis of the situation, independent of the specter tax competition.

Two additional points need to be made from a developing country perspective. The first concerns the question of tax incidence. Since the tax competition that is most relevant to developing countries concerns the corporate income tax, it is important to assess the incidence of that tax in evaluating the effects of collection on the welfare of the developing country. Unfortunately, after decades of analysis, no consensus exists on the incidence of the corporate tax. While older studies have tended to conclude that the tax is borne by shareholders or by all capital providers, more recent studies have suggested that the tax is borne to a significant extent by consumers or by labor.[126] Another possibility is that the tax on established corporations was borne by those who were shareholders at the time the tax was imposed or increased, because thereafter it is capitalized into the price of the shares.[127] It is unlikely that this debate will be decided any time soon (in fact, the incidence may be shifting over time, especially as globalization may enable corporations to shift more of the tax burden to labor). However, from the perspective of a developing country, deciding whether to collect taxes from a multinational, three out of the four possible alternatives for incidence (current shareholders or capital providers, old shareholders, and consumers) are largely the residents of other jurisdictions, and therefore from a national welfare perspective, the developing country gains by collecting the tax. Even if some of the tax is shifted to labor in the developing country, it can be argued that as a matter of tax administration it is more efficient (as well as more politically acceptable) to collect the tax from the multinational than to attempt to collect it from the local workers.

Finally, it should be noted that a developing country may want to collect taxes from multinationals even if, in general, it believes that the private sector is more efficient at allocating the resources than the public sector. This is because, in the case of a foreign multinational, the taxes that the developing country fails to collect may be used by the private sector, but in another jurisdiction, and therefore will not benefit the developing country. One possible solution, which is employed by developing countries, is to refrain from taxing multinationals while they reinvest domestically, but tax them upon remittance of the profits abroad. However, such

[126] *See, e.g.*, Joseph A. Pechman, Federal Tax Policy 141–46 (5th ed. 1987).
[127] *See id.* at 144.

taxation of dividends and other forms of remittances are subject to the same tax competition problem discussed above. Thus, overcoming the tax competition problem is, in most cases, in the interest of developing countries, and the question remains how to do so in the face of a lack of coordination and collective action.

2.4.3 *Inter-Nation Equity and the Division of Global Tax Revenues*

Having established that both developed and developing countries need tax revenue, can we decide how to split the available revenue between them? This question relates to the concept of inter-nation equity, which was first developed by Peggy Musgrave. As Musgrave used it, the concept related primarily to the question of entitlement, that is, which country was entitled to the revenue, and was used to defend the prevalent practice of source-based taxation against the preference for residence-based taxation that comes from capital export neutrality.

This formulation of inter-nation equity is vague and does not easily lead to practical recommendations. Even a preference for source-based taxation over residence-based taxation is not meaningful unless one can develop a coherent notion of the source of income. However, most income has multiple sources, and economists have generally concluded that assigning income to a single source is not an accurate exercise (albeit a necessary one for legal and tax purposes).[128] If that is the case, then any generally acceptable sourcing rule is fine from an economic perspective, but a concept of inter-nation equity that is based on sourcing does not give us any guidance in designing such a rule. Inter-nation equity does not really tell us how much income a country "deserves" to tax.

Perhaps some progress can be made if one attempts to relate inter-nation equity to its better known cousin, inter-individual equity. It is widely accepted that redistributive income taxation can be justified by considerations of vertical equity and the declining marginal utility of income.[129] But there appears to be no sound theoretical reason to restrict redistribution to members of any single tax jurisdiction. If there were a world taxing authority, it would be both justified and required to redistribute on a worldwide basis.

Given that there are many taxing jurisdictions, redistribution in practice takes place within countries, and this can be justified on political grounds ("no taxation without representation"). Explicit redistribution among countries is rare especially given the widespread unpopularity of foreign aid. This analysis suggests that in designing international tax rules, it should be a goal to account for the relative wealth and poverty of the countries involved. In federal states, it is common to have

[128] *See, e.g.*, Hugh J. Ault & David F. Bradford, *Taxing International Income: An Analysis of the U.S. System and Its Economic Premises*, *in* Taxation in the Global Economy 11, 30–31 (Assaf Razin & Joel Slemrod eds., 1990).

[129] *See* Louis Kaplow, *Horizontal Equity: Measures in Search of a Principle*, 42 Nat'l Tax J. 139, 144 (1989).

an explicit redistributive mechanism from the richer to the poorer provinces.[130] If there were a world taxing authority, a similar mechanism could be justified to redistribute revenues from richer to poorer countries. This could be done by direct transfers, but also indirectly through tax rates. For example, whenever a transaction took place between two jurisdictions, the poorer one could explicitly be allowed to retain a larger share of the revenue (e.g., in proportion to GDP).[131]

In practice there is no world taxing authority, nor is one likely to be established soon.[132] But some of the current practice of international taxation can be interpreted as reflecting concern for the greater revenue needs of poorer countries. In particular, the widespread acceptance of the right of the source country to levy its tax first and of the imposition of the burden of alleviating double taxation on the residence country reflects in part the position of the poorer (capital importing) countries in the 1920s. This position was accepted by the League of Nations and (subject to certain limits such as the permanent establishment concept) enshrined in the model treaties which are the foundation of the current international tax regime.[133]

Thus, we would argue that the concept of inter-nation equity can be given practical meaning if it is interpreted as embodying explicit distributive goals through the design of international tax rules. More specifically, when a choice is presented between two alternative rules, one of which is progressive and the other regressive for the division of the international tax base among poorer and richer countries, the progressive rule should be explicitly preferred over the regressive one. In the absence of a world tax authority able to redistribute tax revenues and given the paucity of direct international transfers from developed to developing countries, such a concept of inter-nation equity has the best chance of achieving meaningful and effective distributive goals.

The problem of tax competition, as described above, is a good illustration of such a dilemma. The problem has two components: portfolio and direct investment. For portfolio investment, the home country of the invested capital may be either a developed or a developing country while the host country is typically a developed country. For direct investment, the home country of the invested capital is typically a developed country while the host country may be either a developed or a developing country.[134]

Tax competition undermines the ability of both home and host jurisdictions to tax income from cross-border portfolio and direct investments. In each case, it is

[130] *See, e.g.*, Albert J. Radler, *Germany*, *in* COMPARATIVE INCOME TAXATION: A STRUCTURAL ANALYSIS 49, 49 (Hugh J. Ault et al. eds. 1997).

[131] *See* PEGGY BREWER RICHMAN [Musgrave], TAXATION OF FOREIGN INVESTMENT INCOME: AN ECONOMIC ANALYSIS 79 (1963).

[132] *See infra* Chapter 9.

[133] *See* Reuven S. Avi-Yonah, *International Taxation of Electronic Commerce*, 52 TAX L. REV. 507, 534–35 (1997); Reuven S. Avi-Yonah, *The Structure of International Taxation: A Proposal for Simplification*, 74 TEX. L. REV. 1301, 1303–04 (1996); Graetz & O'Hear, *supra* note 103, at 1023.

[134] *See* WORLD INVESTMENT REPORT, *supra* note 45, at 18–24.

possible to design solutions that emphasize either home (residence) or host (source) taxation. For portfolio investment, one could have either a final withholding tax which would accrue to the host jurisdiction or a refundable withholding tax which would be waived upon proof that the income was reported to the home jurisdiction. The first solution would favor host countries, while the second would favor home countries. As the home countries are, on average, poorer than the host countries, inter-nation equity would suggest preferring the second solution over the first one.

Similarly, for direct investment, it is possible to design a regime that allocates corporate tax revenues entirely to the home (residence) country. For example, corporations could be assigned a residence based on the residence of their shareholders and the corporate tax revenues allocated to those countries.[135] Or a form of corporate–shareholder integration could be implemented that eliminates the corporate tax base and allocates all revenues to the home country of the shareholders.[136] Alternatively, the corporate tax could be abolished, and shareholders taxed on their holdings on a mark-to-market basis.[137] All these solutions favor the home over the host country.

On the other hand, solutions to tax competition that seek to maintain the existing preference for host country (source) taxation of direct investment could also be developed. From an inter-nation equity perspective, this solution is to be preferred precisely because in the direct investment context host jurisdictions are poorer than home jurisdictions. If one accepts the need for redistribution in general, taking such distributive considerations into account explicitly in the international tax context would be a significant step forward since almost all the current literature on international taxation omits any discussion of these issues.

In the period after 2010, the financial crisis and such tax considerations led to the international tax revolution, which attempted to create a new ITR based on curbing international tax competition.

[135] *See* Richard L. Doernberg, *Electronic Commerce and International Tax Sharing*, 98 Worldwide Tax Daily 60-43, at 36–38 (1998), available in WL 98 WTD 60-43.

[136] *See* Alberto Giovannini & James R. Hines, Jr., *Capital Flight and Tax Competition: Are There Viable Solutions to Both Problems?*, *in* European Financial Integration 172, 194–95 (Alberto Giovannini & Colin Mayer eds., 1991).

[137] *See* Joseph M. Dodge, *A Combined Mark-to-Market and Pass-Through Corporate-Shareholder Integration Proposal*, 50 Tax L. Rev. 265, 266–67 (1995); Daniel Halperin, *Will Integration Increase Efficiency? – The Old and New View of Dividend Policy*, 47 Tax L. Rev. 645 (1992).

3

The Beginnings of the New Regime, 2008–2013*

3.1 MOMENTUM FOR ENHANCED TRANSPARENCY

The financial crisis of 2008 and the Great Recession that followed have raised anew the problem of how to address a growing inequality within and between countries. Both dimensions of inequality, the intra- and inter-country ones, have increased in this century, and the Great Recession has made both problems worse. The current rise of populism in both the United States and Europe and the vehement reactions to a tide of migrants from poorer to richer countries show how these two problems are intertwined.[1]

Over twenty years ago, the first author examined the challenge that globalization and tax competition pose to the fiscal viability of the post–World War II welfare state.[2] He argued that if tax evasion by rich individuals and tax avoidance by multinational corporations is allowed to undermine the ability of both developed and developing countries to provide adequate social insurance for their citizens, a violent reaction against globalization may ensue that risks ending this current era of opening borders, just like World War I ended the previous era of globalization a century ago. In 2016, we worried that the inadequate response to the Great Recession was leading to the rise of anti-globalization sentiments embodied in the United States by the rise of Bernie Sanders and Donald Trump and in Europe by an even more virulent rejection of the open border policies of the EU.[3]

Following the financial crisis and ensuing austerity, politicians discovered the twin problems of tax evasion and tax avoidance. On the individual tax evasion front,

* This chapter draws heavily from *Evaluating BEPS: A Reconsideration of the Benefits Principle and Proposal for UN Oversight*, 6 Harv. Bus. L. Rev. 185 (2016) (with H. Xu).

1 *See, e.g.*, Peggy Noonan, *Trump, Sanders and the American Rebellion*, WSJ (Feb. 11, 2016), http://on.wsj.com/1QavpWY.

2 Reuven S. Avi-Yonah, *Globalization, Tax Competition, and the Fiscal Crisis of the Welfare State*, 113 HARV. L. REV. 1573 (2000).

3 Noonan, *supra* note 1; *see also Why Is EU Struggling with Migrants and Asylum*, BBC (Mar. 3, 2016), http://www.bbc.com/news/world-europe-24583286.

the response has been driven by the US enactment of the Foreign Account Tax Compliance Act (FATCA) in 2010. This law led to the signing of a series of intergovernmental agreements (IGAs) between the United States and 115 other countries (and counting) for the exchange of tax information. The IGAs led to the developments by the OECD of common reporting standards (CRS) and to the Multilateral Agreement for Administrative Assistance in Tax Matters (MAATM), which has been adopted by over eighty countries (but as of 2025, signed but not ratified by the United States).[4]

An example may be useful to illustrate the tax evasion problem. Sam Wyly was a rich Texas businessman. In 2006, *Forbes* estimated his net worth as $1.1 billion. He and his brother Charles made their money in computers, a steakhouse chain, and Michael's Arts and Crafts, which they bought in 1982 and sold in 2006 to a group of private equity firms, including Bain Capital, for $6 billion. Sam is a major philanthropist: A $10 million gift resulted in the naming of Sam Wyly Hall at the University of Michigan Ross School of Business. He is also an avid Republican. In 2004, Sam Wyly helped finance the "Swift Boat" ad campaign that scuttled John Kerry's bid for the presidency.[5]

4 On FATCA, IGAs, and MAATM, *see, e.g.*, Reuven S. Avi-Yonah & Gil Savir, *IGAs vs. MAATM: Has Tax Bilateralism Outlived Its Usefulness?* SSRN (U. of Mich. Pub. L. Rsch. Paper No. 384; U. of Mich. L. & Econ. Rsch. Paper No. 14-002, Feb. 8, 2014), http://ssrn.com/abstract=2392702 or http://dx.doi.org/10.2139/ssrn.2392702; J. Richard (Dick) Harvey, *Offshore Accounts: Insider's Summary of FATCA and Its Potential Future* (Dec. 1. 2011), 57(3) VILL. L. REV. 471 (2012), Vill. L./Pub. Pol'y Rsch. Paper No. 2011-24, SSRN: http://ssrn.com/abstract=1969123; Itai Grinberg, *Beyond FATCA: An Evolutionary Moment for the International Tax System*, SSRN (Jan. 27, 2012), http://ssrn.com/abstract=1996752 or http://dx.doi.org/10.2139/ssrn.1996752; J. Richard (Dick) Harvey, *FATCA – A Report from the Front Lines (August 1, 2012)*, TAX NOTES 713 (Aug. 6, 2012), Vill. L./Pub. Pol'y Rsch. Paper No. 2013-3001, SSRN: http://ssrn.com/abstract=2122491; Itai Grinberg, *Taxing Capital Income in Emerging Countries: Will FATCA Open the Door? (July 21, 2013)*, 5 WORLD TAX J. 325–67 (2013), Geo. Pub. L. Rsch. Paper No. 13-031, SSRN: http://ssrn.com/abstract=2256587 or http://dx.doi.org/10.2139/ssrn.2256587; Joshua D. Blank & Ruth Mason, *Exporting FATCA* (Feb. 1, 2014), 142 TAX NOTES, 1245 (Mar. 17, 2014), NYU L. and Econ. Rsch. Paper No. 14-05, SSRN: http://ssrn.com/abstract=2389500; Allison Christians, *What You Give and What You Get: Reciprocity under a Model 1 Intergovernmental Agreement on FATCA*, CAYMAN FIN. REV. (Apr. 12, 2013), SSRN: http://ssrn.com/abstract=2292645; Allison Christians, *The Dubious Legal Pedigree of IGAs (and Why It Matters)* (Feb. 11, 2013), 69(6) TAX NOTES INT'L 565 (2013), SSRN: http://ssrn.com/abstract=2280508; Susan C. Morse, *Ask for Help, Uncle Sam: The Future of Global Tax Reporting* (December 14, 2012), 57(3) VILL. L. REV. 529–50 (2012), UC Hastings Rsch. Paper No. 35, SSRN: http://ssrn.com/abstract=1999101; Susan C. Morse, *Why FATCA Intergovernmental Agreements Bind the U.S. Government* (Apr. 15, 2013), 70(3) TAX NOTES INT'L (2013), SSRN: http://ssrn.com/abstract=2252843; Itai Grinberg, *The Battle over Taxing Offshore Accounts (2012)*, 60 UCLA L. REV. 304–83 (2012), SSRN: http://ssrn.com/abstract=2497998.

5 Nate Raymond, *Texas Tycoon Wyly Faces $2 Billion Tax Trial Over Offshore Trusts*, REUTERS (Jan. 5, 2016), http://www.dallasnews.com/business/business-headlines/20150327-once-worth-1-billion-sam-wyly-is-bankrupt-but-still-fighting.ece; http://www.reuters.com/article/us-irs-wyly-idUSKBN0UJ13R20160105.

But Sam Wyly was then bankrupt. In 2006, a hearing of the US Senate Permanent Subcommittee on Investigations (PSI) revealed that Wyly had been evading US tax laws by hiding his money in trusts in the Isle of Man, a notorious tax haven.[6] He began by transferring stock options from his various companies to the trusts, which were managed by Isle of Man trustees. The nominal trust beneficiaries were two foreign charities, but the six Wyly children were contingent beneficiaries, and the trustees understood that at Sam's death the children would become the true beneficiaries and collect the funds.

In the meantime, the trusts were free to exercise the stock options and use the stock for investments, with the understanding that twenty years down the road they would have to make annuity payments to Sam. Sam obtained an opinion from a law firm that this arrangement worked to defer taxes on the income gained from exercising the options until he began receiving annuity payments years later. But the linchpin of the legal opinion was that the offshore trusts were independent actors when in fact Sam exercised total control over the trust assets, secretly using the investment profits to operate businesses and buy real estate, jewelry, and art works in the United States. The Wylys' secret control over their offshore funds was revealed in the PSI hearing. In 2010, the SEC charged Sam Wyly with securities fraud based on his hidden control of the offshore trusts. In 2014, a jury found him liable. To avoid paying a $300 million judgment, he filed for bankruptcy, which triggered a tax assessment for his failing to pay any taxes on hundreds of millions of dollars in offshore income since 1992. He is currently battling the IRS in bankruptcy court over a tax assessment totaling $2.2 billion.

How many Wylys are hiding their money from the IRS, with no PSI hearing to bring their misdeeds to light? We will probably never know. An estimate of the global costs of illegal tax evasion by the economist Gabriel Zucman was $200 billion, but this is probably too low since estimates for the United States alone range from $20 billion to $70 billion.[7] Every time a Swiss banker talks, many billions in US tax evasion are revealed. The recent IRS Offshore Voluntary Disclosure Program netted over $6 billion and counting.[8]

3.2 EXCHANGE OF TAX INFORMATION VIA FATCA, IGAS, AND MAATM[9]

In 2010, the United States revolutionized international taxation of individuals when it enacted FATCA. This was in response to the UBS scandal, which revealed that

6 United States Senate, Permanent Subcommittee on Investigations, Committee on Homeland Security and Governmental Affairs, Tax Haven Abuses: The Enablers, the Tools and Secrecy (2006).

7 Gabriel Zucman, The Hidden Wealth of Nations (Sept. 2015); J. Guttentag & Reuven S. Avi-Yonah, *Closing the International Tax Gap*, *in* Bridging the Tax Gap: Addressing the Crisis in Federal Tax Administration 99 (Max B. Sawicky ed., 2005).

8 *IRS Offshore Voluntary Disclosure Efforts Produce $6.5 Billion; 45,000 Taxpayers Participate*, IRS (June 2014), https://www.irs.gov/pub/irs-news/FS-14-06.pdf.

9 Avi-Yonah & Savir, *supra* note 4.

UBS was aiding and abetting tax evasion by US citizens.[10] In response to these revelations, FATCA imposed a 30 percent withholding tax on the US source income of any "foreign financial institution" that is found not to have shared information on its account holders who are US citizens or residents.[11]

Foreign banks and other financial institutions strongly objected to FATCA for two main reasons. First, the banks claimed it imposed unreasonable compliance costs.[12] The fundamental problem stems from the fact that the United States has since 1861 taxed its citizens living permanently overseas, and as a result, FATCA applies to many such expatriates who have no intention of hiding their income from the IRS (in fact, most of them do not owe any taxes to the United States because of the earned income exclusion of IRC section 911[13] and the foreign tax credit of IRC section 901[14]). The solution to this is to stop taxing citizens living overseas.[15]

The second problem with FATCA was that many foreign countries have taxpayer confidentiality laws that prevent banks from sharing information with the IRS. Under the modern version of Article 26 of the tax treaties and under tax information exchange agreements (TIEAs), such prohibitions should not bar the exchange of information, but many treaties have not been updated to reflect the new norms. Thus, the banks argued that they faced a serious dilemma of either violating the laws of their home country or being subjected to the FATCA penalty.

The US Treasury responded by negotiating a series of IGAs with the governments of various countries with which the United States has either a tax treaty or a TIEA. Under the IGAs, foreign governments are responsible for collecting the necessary information from its banks and transmitting it to the IRS. In return, under some IGAs the United States has agreed to do the same for the foreign government, that is, collect information on its residents who have accounts in US banks and share it with the foreign governments. The difference, of course, is that the United States taxes its citizens living overseas, so it has many more taxpayers with accounts in foreign financial institutions than the foreign country is likely to have in US banks.[16]

It is not clear that the IGAs are permitted under FATCA, since the legislation clearly requires direct submission of the information by the FFIs to the IRS. Nor is it clear that Treasury had the authority to enter IGAs under the tax treaties and

[10] Reuven S. Avi-Yonah, *What Goes around Comes around: Why the US Is Responsible for Capital Flight (and What It Can Do about It)* (U of Mich. Pub. L. Rsch. Paper No. 307, Jan. 23, 2013), SSRN: http://ssrn.com/abstract=2208553.

[11] Internal Revenue Code of 1986, as amended (I.R.C.), § 1471.

[12] Grinberg, *The Battle*, *supra* note 4.

[13] I.R.C. § 911.

[14] I.R.C. § 901 – "Foreign Tax Credit."

[15] Reuven S. Avi-Yonah, *The Case against Taxing Citizens* (U. of Mich. L. & Econ, Empirical Legal Stud. Ctr., Mar. 25, 2010), http://ssrn.com/abstract=1578272.

[16] Reuven S. Avi-Yonah, *The Case against Taxing Citizens*, 58 Tax Notes Int'l 389 (May 3, 2010).

TIEAs.[17] But the main concern about the IGAs is that they enshrine the bilateral model of tax information exchange that has dominated the twentieth century. Unfortunately, there are good reasons to believe this bilateral model does not work, especially when the IGAs are signed with countries like the Cayman Islands,[18] who have no interest in reciprocity and every interest in making the agreement ineffective.

The alternative is MAATM. In response to the fallout of the financial crisis and the outrage it caused, the OECD has proposed the Multilateral Agreement for Administrative Assistance in Tax Matters[19] (MAATM), which has by now over [eighty] signatory countries. The MAATM provides for automatic exchange of information, and because it is multilateral, it appears to overcome the problem of nonreciprocity that bedevils the tax treaties, bilateral TIEAs, and the IGAs.

3.2.1 *The Tax Evasion Problem*

Technological advances have made it easy for both companies and individuals to shift income and capital among countries to reduce their global tax amount by using tax haven jurisdictions. This phenomenon has been recognized by the OECD as a "Harmful Tax Competition."[20] Although the ability of individuals to shift their capital income without being taxed is subject to substantial limitations,[21] the possibility still exists, especially in situations where the taxpayer relies on the lack of information-sharing between different countries around the world[22] by not reporting their income.[23] Ever since the OECD members officially recognized the problem in 1998, a significant effort has been made to force those tax havens to share their information[24] about foreign taxpayers who take advantage of the lack of information exchanges between countries, while enabling the tax havens to enjoy the investment of capital in their jurisdiction.

[17] Christians, *The Dubious Legal Pedigree, supra* note 4.

[18] For list of TIEAs *see* http://www.oecd.org/ctp/harmful/taxinformationexchangeagreementstieas.htm (last accessed Feb. 5, 2014).

[19] Organisation for Economic Cooperation and Development [OECD], *Convention on Mutual Administrative Assistance in Tax Matters* (2011) [hereinafter MAATM], http://www.oecd.org/ctp/exchange-of-tax-information/ENG-Amended-Convention.pdf.

[20] OECD, *Harmful Tax Competition: An Emerging Global Issue* (1998), http://www.oecd-ilibrary.org/(last accessed Feb. 5, 2010) [hereinafter OECD Harmful Tax Competition].

[21] Reuven S. Avi-Yonah, *And Yet It Moves: A Tax Paradigm for the 21st Century* (L. & Econ. Working Paper No. 59, 2013), http://repository.law.umich.edu/law_econ_current/59.

[22] Reuven S. Avi-Yonah, *The OECD Harmful Tax Competition Report: A 10th Anniversary Retrospective* (U. Mich. Program in L. and Econ., Working Paper No. 89, 2008), http://law.bepress.com/umichlwps-olin/art89.

[23] Jane G. Gravelle, *Tax Havens: International Tax Avoidance and Evasion* (Cong. Rsch. Serv., Libr. of Cong., 2009), http://heinonlinebackup.com/hol-cgi-bin/get_pdf.cgi?handle=hein.tera/crstax0642&section=1.

[24] Avi-Yonah & Savir, *supra* note 4, at 3.

The "Tax Justice Network," a nonprofit organization, promotes the recognition that the lack of transparency is a major problem for developed countries, out of which there is usually large flows of capital. In 2002 the Tax Justice Network released a report finding that the amount of equity held offshore by individuals alone was about $11.5 trillion, with a resulting annual loss of about $250 billion in taxes, which "is five times what the World Bank estimated in 2002 was needed to address the UN Millennium Development Goal of halving world poverty by 2015." According to the United Nations Office on Drugs and Crimes, the "hidden" money from criminal activities, corruption, and tax evasion was estimated at between $1 trillion and $1.6 trillion per year.[25] The effect on the US Treasury is also significant.[26] A study conducted by the Congressional Research Service (CRS) indicates that tax evasion by individuals alone through setting up foreign corporations in tax havens results in an estimated yearly loss of $70 billion to the US Treasury.[27]

An important contribution to this discussion is the economist Gabriel Zucman's masterful survey of the origins, importance, and danger of tax havens. *The Hidden Wealth of Nations* is a tremendously important contribution to the current discussion on world's income tax systems. In it, Zucman makes three crucial contributions to the discourse about tax havens. First, he offers a history of how tax havens came to be in the interwar period, and how they became much more important after exchange controls were relaxed in the 1980s.[28] Second, Zucman offers an extensive quantitative evaluation of the importance of tax havens in today's global economy.[29] Finally, Zucman proposes a course of action to address the "scourge" of tax havens.[30]

The most original part of Zucman's book is the second, in which he offers the most comprehensive evaluation to date of the scope of tax havens. Zucman came up with a new way of figuring out how much wealth there is in tax havens by examining the difference between reported financial assets and liabilities in the world's financial centers. His estimates found that around 8 percent of the world's financial wealth is held in tax havens. But this overall number masks the true importance of tax havens, because in developing and emerging countries the percentage can be much higher. Zucman estimates that in Africa the share of financial wealth held offshore is around 30 percent, while in Russia and the Middle East it is above 50 percent.[31]

Zucman estimates that these numbers translate into about $200 billion in lost income tax revenue worldwide.[32] This is a large number, but it is significantly below

[25] UNODC, *Transnational Organized Crime: The Globalized Illegal Economy*, https://www.unodc.org/toc/en/crimes/organized-crime.html.

[26] Avi-Yonah, *supra* note 10, at 13.

[27] Gravelle, *supra* note 23.

[28] Zucman, *supra* note 7.

[29] *Id.* at 34–55.

[30] *Id.* at 75–101.

[31] *Id.* at 34–55.

[32] *Id.* at 53.

some other estimates. For example, Joe Guttentag and the first author estimated in 2005 that the United States alone loses $50 billion a year to illegal evasion in tax havens, based on data from the Boston Consulting Group and Merrill Lynch.[33] This number may be lower now because of the enactment of FATCA, which has had a significant deterrent effect. But as Zucman points out, FATCA has significant built-in loopholes; for example, it can be avoided by using a bank that has no US assets.[34] In any case, Zucman's $200 billion is a useful lower bound, and it is a big enough number to induce political action.

3.2.2 *Lack of Information*

Tax evasion has become a central concern of the major economies around the world. Hand in hand with the double taxation convention, the global finance system has developed agreements for the exchange of information to increase the ability of their tax systems (both civil and criminal) to enforce their rules on sophisticated taxpayers.[35] In particular the OECD has targeted countries whose lack of transparency allows them to function as tax havens.[36]

Just before the financial crisis, the first author argued that the OECD has achieved significant progress in the field of information exchange.[37] However, lack of transparency is still a major problem globally. In our opinion, if some countries continue to provide tax shelters to taxpayers, the OECD may win battles but will lose the war. Our assessment is based on two factors. First, in a competitive financial world, some countries will always be willing to host trillions of dollars to attract investment in their infrastructure.[38] Second is sophisticated internal law, such as exists in the British Virgin Islands (BVI), helps to facilitate tax evasion.[39] As of 2010, the BVI population stood at 29,537. However, more than 400,000 companies were incorporated under BVI law. The assumption of the Congressional Research is the fact that the local laws in the BVI "require no identification of shareholders or directors and require no financial records."[40] Thus, even if the country provides information about its taxpayers, no real useful information can be found,[41] so the taxpayer has no real concerns.

33 Guttentag & Avi-Yonah, *supra* note 7.

34 Zucman, *supra* note 7, at 56–74.

35 Kevin Jestin, *Harmful Mutual Legal Assistance in Tax Matters Recent Trends and Challenge Ahead* (2008), http://visar.csustan.edu/aaba/Jestin2008.pdf.

36 OECD Harmful Tax Competition, *supra* note 20, at 21.

37 Avi-Yonah, *supra* note 2, at 5–7.

38 Dhammika Dharmapala & James R. Hines Jr., *Which Countries Become Tax Havens?* SSRN (May 2009), http://ssrn.com/abstract=952721.

39 Gravelle, *supra* note 23, at 22.

40 *Id.*

41 *Id.*; *see also* Randall Jackson, *Brown Pushes U.K. Tax Havens on OECD Standards*, 54(3) Tax Notes Int'l 180–81 (Apr. 20, 2009).

With the information-exchange problem in mind, the United States started signing bilateral treaties and TIEAs with countries around the world.[42] To create a wide network of information exchange, the United States has over sixty bilateral treaties that include articles dealing with the exchange of information. These treaties usually allow exchange of both civil and criminal information.[43] In addition, where a treaty is not in place, the United States has signed TIEAs with over twenty countries.[44]

There are doubts about the effectiveness of the TIEAs.[45] Between the years 2006 and 2010, 5,111 information requests were exchanged between the United States and other countries.[46] However, only 894 were outgoing requests.[47] Several factors can explain the low number of outgoing requests. First, "as pointed out by Avi-Yonah, most of these agreements were restricted to criminal matters, which are a minor part of the revenues involved and pose difficult issues of evidence."[48] Second is the complexity of the information that the IRS agent is required to provide.[49] A review of the agreements reveals that the IRS must provide a specific taxpayer name to retrieve any information. Moreover, the IRS needs to provide the reason that the taxpayer is under investigation. For instance, the United States signed a TIEA with the Cayman Islands in 2004. According to the TIEA, the United States must provide very specific information to the Cayman Islands to get information about a US taxpayer. As a result, the TIEA system is more of a confirmation tool, rather than discovery tool.[50]

In addition to tax treaties, in 2001 the IRS established the "QI Program."[51] Under the program, a QI, such as a bank, is required to identify the payment, and in some types of investments – where the beneficiary is a US resident or any profit that is subject to withholding[52] – the bank should notify the IRS about the transaction without disclosing the name of the taxpayer.[53] In return, the banks are required to

[42] Chris Horton, *The UBS/IRS Settlement Agreement and Cayman Island Hedge Funds*, 41 U. Miami Inter-Am. L. Rev. 357 (2010).

[43] *See* IRS, *The Tax Gap and International Taxpayers* (Feb. 2008), http://www.irs.gov/irm/part5/irm_05-021-002 (last accessed Dec. 10, 2013).

[44] *Id.*

[45] Gravelle, *supra* note 23, at 22.

[46] United States Government Accountability Office (GAO) Report to the Permanent Subcommittee on Investigations, Committee on Homeland Security and Governmental Affairs, U.S. Senate, *IRS's Information Exchanges with Other Countries Could Be Improved through Better Performance Information* (Sept. 2009), http://www.gao.gov/assets/590/585299.pdf [hereinafter GAO Report].

[47] *Id.*

[48] Gravelle, *supra* note 23, at 22.

[49] GAO Report, *supra* note 46, at 8–11.

[50] Horton, *supra* note 42, at 373.

[51] Susan C. Morse, *Qualified Intermediary or Bust?*, 124 Tax Notes (Aug. 3, 2009), http://ssrn.com/abstract=1444291.

[52] *See* I.R.C. § 862(A), 871(A).

[53] Morse, *supra* note 51.

withhold any tax amount and send the payment to the US Treasury.[54] After the UBS Scheme[55] the effectiveness of the program was questioned.[56] Although the UBS was a QI, instead of discovering the identity of the beneficiary account, they created shell companies for their clients in the Cayman Islands to hide their identities.

However, there has been some progress since 2008. For example, in 2009, after the UBS case, the UBS agreed to disclose about 4,450 American clients suspected of using the bank's offshore services to evade taxes.[57] But this was merely a small fraction of the over 24,000 US accounts the bank admitted to having, and only a small portion of the 4,450 names were prosecuted.[58] FATCA and the IRS' offshore voluntary compliance initiative have had some success as well. But they are inherently limited because (a) they only apply to US residents (including US citizens), with no reciprocity; (b) they can be avoided by putting assets in a bank that has no US assets (hence avoiding FATCA penalty tax exposure) in a jurisdiction that does not comply with MAATM.

3.2.3 *The Revenue Rule and Non-assistance in the Collection of Taxes*

As the world becomes more interconnected, tax collection is becomes more complex. Even if a country has determined the right to tax liabilities of its taxpayers, collection can be a difficult task. If a country is trying to collect tax from a taxpayer is devoid of any assets in the country, there are very few solutions available to that country. Any attempt to collect taxes through another country will be considered a violation of the other country's sovereignty.[59]

Assistance in the collection of taxes has a long history in international and American law. In 1955, in the case of *India v. Taylor*,[60] the government of India sought taxes from a company registered in the United Kingdom but trading in India. The House of Lords held that India cannot enforce its collection through a British court:

> My own opinion is that there is a well-recognized rule, which has been enforced for at least 200 years or thereabouts, under which these courts will not collect the taxes of foreign States for the benefit of the sovereigns of those foreign States; and this is one of those actions which these courts will not entertain.

54 Lynnley Browning, *U.S. Tax Agency to Strengthen Program to Catch Offshore Tax Evasion*, N.Y. Times (July 15, 2008), http://www.nytimes.com/2008/07/15/business/worldbusiness/15iht-15tax.14499852.html.

55 Lynnley Browning, *U.S. Ends Inquiry of UBS over Offshore Tax Evasion*, N.Y. Times (Nov. 16, 2010), http://www.nytimes.com/2010/11/17/business/17tax.html.

56 Gravelle, *supra* note 23, at 22.

57 Lynnley Browning, 14,700 *Disclosed Offshore Accounts*, N.Y. Times (Nov. 17, 2009), http://www.nytimes.com/2009/11/18/business/global/18irs.html.

58 Zach Lowe, *Six Months Later: Still a Good Deal for UBS?*, The Am Law Daily (Aug. 19, 2009), http://amlawdaily.typepad.com/amlawdaily/2009/08/six-months-later-a-good-deal-for-ubs-.html.

59 Jestin, *supra* note 35, at 3.

60 Government of India, Ministry of Finance (Revenue Division) v. Taylor [1955] A.C. 491.

In *United States v. Harden* (1963),[61] the United States District Court for the Southern District of California held for a deficiency of $639,500.15 against the respondent, Mr. Harden, for the years 1945–46. When the United States tried to enforce the judgment, they could not locate any assets of the respondent in US jurisdiction. Therefore, the United States tried to enforce the judgment against the respondent through a Canadian court, claiming that this was an agreement that the Canadian court was required to enforce. The Supreme Court of Canada held that no Canadian court could enforce the revenue laws of another country:

> Similarly, in my opinion, the argument that the claim asserted is simply for the performance of an agreement, made for good consideration, to pay a stated sum of money must also fail. We are concerned not with form but with substance, and if it can properly be said that the respondent made an agreement it was simply an agreement to pay taxes which by the laws of the foreign state she was obligated to pay.

The nonenforcement of foreign public judgments is a taboo in legal history.[62] Although countries may enforce private judgments in fields like torts and contracts, when they are faced with a request to enforce foreign judgments in fields such as criminal, antitrust, and tax, the requests are denied.[63] The result is a decrease in the ability of countries to enforce their laws even when public policy is not an issue.

The reasons for this phenomenon are varied.[64] According to Johnson, Alan, and Lawrence, the efforts by one country to enforce its law within the territory of another may "constitute an extraterritorial intrusion."[65]

Although international tax practice has evolved dramatically in the last few decades,[66] it seems that the cooperation of countries is limited and subject to complex and uncertain processes.

3.2.4 *Article 27 under the OECD Model of the Tax Convention*

In January 2003, the OECD added Article 27 – "The Assistance in the Collection of Taxes." Article 27 lays out the rules for contracting parties who wish to collaborate in collecting taxes within the other state.

61 United States of America v. Esperanza p. Harden [1963] S.C.R. 366; 1963 S.C.R. LEXIS 37.

62 William S. Dodge, *Breaking the Public Law Taboo*, 43 Harv. Int'l L.J. (2002), http://ssrn.com/abstract=316660.

63 *Id.*

64 Alan R. Johnson et al., *Reciprocal Enforcement of Tax Claims through Tax Treaties*, 33 Tax Law. 470 (1979), http://heinonline.org/HOL/LandingPage?collection=journals&handle=hein.journals/txlr33&div=4&id=&page=.

65 *Id.*

66 *See* Reuven S. Avi-Yonah, *International Tax as International Law* 7 (U. Mich. L. Sch. Pub. L. Rsch. Paper 41, Mich. L. & Econ., Rsch. Paper No. 04-007, 2004), http://ssrn.com/abstract=516382 or http://dx.doi.org/10.2139/ssrn.516382. (For the evaluation and the impact of the international law on the practice.)

Under paragraph 1 of the article, a country will aid another country upon a request to collect taxes within the foreign country. According to the Commentaries on the Articles of the Model Tax Convention (CAMTC), paragraph 1 is very flexible and is subject to negotiation among the contracting countries, based on their local law. In addition, according to the CAMTC the article is elective.

The collection of taxes is not limited to the type of taxes covered by Article 2 and, most importantly, can be enforced against people who are not entitled to the benefits derived from the convention.

Paragraph 4 of the Article allows a contracting country to require temporary relief before a final judgment is made against the taxpayer to safeguard future collection. This provision combined with paragraph 6 of the Article is very interesting. According to paragraph 6, the "validity or the amount of a revenue claim of a Contracting State shall not be brought before the courts or administrative bodies of the other Contracting State." An interesting question is whether paragraph 6 should also apply in the case where temporary relief is provided (e.g., seizure), and whether the foreign court has the right to determine whether the request is reasonable based on the evidence. A review of the CAMTC supports the view that any judicial proceeding will take place in the country that asks for assistance in the collection of taxes.

3.2.5 *Article 27 in Bilateral Conventions: The US Treaties in Practice vs. the OECD Model*

The MAATM convention operates at the international level, like other multilateral conventions such as the Geneva Convention. Another traditional way to address tax issues among countries is through bilateral conventions. A quick overview of the US model tax convention of 2006 reveals that there is no reference to assistance in the collection of taxes. Nevertheless, in practice the treaties include an article relating to assistance in collection of taxes in a foreign country.[67]

These provisions appear in two forms:[68] "General Enforcement" and "Limited Enforcement" provisions.[69]

The "general enforcement" provision is found in treaties with Canada, Denmark, France, the Netherlands, and Sweden.[70] A review of paragraph 1 of Article 27 of the convention between the United States and Sweden[71] reveals that the collection assistance applies to any type of tax that is covered by Article 2. Paragraphs 2 and 3 of

67 IRS, *Part 5. Collecting Process*, http://www.irs.gov/irm/part5/irm_05-021-002.html.

68 Johnson et al., *supra* note 64, at 472.

69 *Id.* at 473.

70 IRS, *supra* note 67.

71 *The Avoidance of Double Taxation and the Prevention of Fiscal Evasion with Respect to Taxes on Income Treaty*, Article 27, U.S.–Swed. (Jan. 1, 1996), http://www.irs.gov/pub/irs-trty/sweden.pdf.

Article 27 note that in the event a country files a tax[72] claim against a person's assets in another country, the latter country will enforce the claim as if the liability were in its jurisdiction. Article 27 is a fly in the ointment; paragraph 4 sets out that "the assistance provided by the article shall not be accorded with respect to the citizens, companies, or other entities of the state to which the application is made, except when the enforcement is against a person who enjoyed the convention although he was not entitled to." It's worth noting that the application of Article 27 varies from treaty to treaty. For instance, under the tax convention between the United States and Canada,[73] Article 27 is worded differently than in the agreement with Sweden. Under Article 15[74] of the US–Canada tax convention, the article is not applicable against a Canadian citizen if, at the date of the tax deficiency, the taxpayer was a citizen of Canada.

Since the United States was among the first countries to sign the MAATM convention in 2008, it raises the question of why the United States does not include a uniform version of Article 27 in its income tax convention model. One potential reason is the existence of the TIEA agreements. However, the real answer is hidden in the late 1960s, when a broad collection of provisions was deleted from the US model.[75] Three reasons can explain the withdrawal of the provisions: (1) The IRS performed very limited collections abroad under the five treaties that included "general enforcement" provisions.[76] (2) In our opinion, during the years following World War II, countries were more sensitive to measures that could be expressed as a foothold in their territory.[77] (3) There was the development of independent agreements that are more limited, as described above. As a result, the United States entered a collection provision only where a convention was renegotiated, and assistance of tax collection provisions was included.[78]

"Limited enforcement" is assistance in collection of taxes where a person or entity enjoys the benefits provided by the treaty, even though they are not entitled. As a result, the application of the provision is narrow and limited to very specific

[72] *See* IRM 5.1.8.8.7, *Incoming Mutual Collection Assistance Requests Regarding Mutual Collection Assistance Requests*, http://www.irs.gov/irm/part5/irm_05-001-008r.html (for the procedure of filing a claim).

[73] Treaty Concerning the Avoidance of Double Taxation, U.S.–Canada, Article 15 (Aug. 16, 1987).

[74] Article 15 under the Canadian convention is equivalent to Article 27 under the Swedish convention – "Assistance in Collection."

[75] Anne Van de Vijver, ed., The New US-Belgium Double Tax Treaty: A Belgian and EU Perspective 558 (2009).

[76] *Id.*

[77] *See* Peter Dietsch & Thomas Rixen, eds., Global Tax Governance (2015); Grinberg, *The Battle*, *supra* note 4.

[78] *Id.*

situations, as described above.[79] A "limited enforcement" paragraph can be found under the US–Iceland convention.[80]

> Each of the Contracting States shall endeavor to collect on behalf of the other Contracting State such amounts as may be necessary to ensure that relief granted by the Convention from taxation imposed by that other State does not inure to the benefit of persons not entitled thereto.[81]

A similar approach can be found under the treaties with Luxemburg (1996), Germany (1989), Austria (1996), the UK (2001), or Belgium.[82]

3.2.6 *Multilateral Conventions for Tax Collection Assistance*

Due to a historic problem of tax collection by countries within a foreign country, jurisdiction countries have begun to sign mutual agreements.

The first agreement was signed in the beginning of 1950, as a multilateral convention among the Benelux countries for tax collection assistance.[83] Under the convention, the Benelux countries agreed to enforce the collection of tax in their territory for the foreign country. In 1972, the Nordic convention was signed with similar principles.[84] Following the success of the Nordic convention in 1988, the OECD started to draft a new convention that was intended to break lack of cooperation between the countries in collecting taxes.[85] At first, the success of the convention was very limited, with only a few countries signing the convention.[86] Two decades later, in 2008, the OECD opened the convention on Mutual Administrative Assistance in Tax Matters (MAATM)[87] for signature. In the first two years, about fifty countries signed the MAATM convention. This number has since increased to over eighty signatories. It should be noted that the MAATM convention aims for

79 Johnson et al., *supra* note 64, at 475–76.

80 Treaty Concerning the Avoidance of Double Taxation, U.S.–Iceland. (Oct. 23, 2007), http://www.treasury.gov/resource-center/tax-policy/treaties/Documents/Treaty-Iceland-10-23-2007.pdf [hereinafter "U.S.–Iceland Treaty"].

81 *See Id.*, Par. 5, Article 25; *See also* Van de Vijver, *supra* note 75.

82 Van de Vijver, *supra* note 75.

83 Jestin, *supra* note 35, at 3.

84 *Id.* at 3–4.

85 *Id.* at 4.

86 OECD, *Background Brief: The Convention on Mutual Administrative Assistance in Tax Matters and New Protocol* (June 5, 2012), http://www.oecd.org/ctp/exchange-of-tax-information/backgroundbrieftheconventiononmutualadministrativeassistanceintaxmattersandnewprotocol.htm [hereinafter MAATM *Background*].

87 *See* MAATM, *supra* note 19; *see also* OECD, *Convention on Mutual Administrative Assistance in Tax Matters*, http://www.oecd.org/tax/exchange-of-tax-information/conventiononmutualadministrativeassistanceintaxmatters.htm. (For more information regarding the MAATM.)

major cooperation among countries through the creation of a global network that deals with tax evasion cases, making evasion harder and less profitable.[88]

The model of the MAATM convention is based on a combination of tax exchange provisions and administrative assistance in the collection of taxes. Under the model, countries that have signed the convention enjoy "cross-border tax co-operation including exchange of information, multilateral simultaneous tax examinations, service of documents, and cross-border assistance in tax collection, while imposing extensive safeguards to protect the confidentiality of the information exchanged."[89]

One advantage is the flexibility that the convention offers to countries by reserving the right to provide no information or assistance in the collection of taxes.[90] For example, a country can exclude the collection of taxes in its jurisdiction at the time of signing, at the time of ratification, or later.[91] An illustration of this is Poland's withdrawal of its reservations concerning assistance in collection of taxes when it joined the EU.[92]

3.3 THE TAX EVASION PROBLEM RECONSIDERED

The current situation is therefore as follows: The United States has FATCA and a set of bilateral IGAs, but FATCA has loopholes (most obviously, using a bank with no US source income exposure). The IGAs have come under legal challenge in Canada, but in any case, they depend on actual government cooperation to be fully implemented. The Obama administration won in court on the validity of regulations requiring US banks to collect some information on payments of interest eligible for the portfolio interest exemption,[93] but in the absence of knowledge about the true beneficial owners, it is not clear that this information will be of any use even if exchanged under the IGAs. And foreign governments that have signed IGAs can in many cases be expected to behave like they do under the older TIEAs, by pretending to cooperate but not in practice.

The OECD has Article 27, but this has not been implemented in most treaties, and the United States has generally not included it in its treaties or its model. Nor is it clear that courts are willing to overturn the revenue rule, despite the US Supreme Court's *Pasquantino* decision.[94]

88 Grinberg, *The Battle*, *supra* note 4.

89 MAATM *Background*, *supra* note 86.

90 MAATM, *supra* note 19, Article 30.

91 OECD, *MAATM's flyer* (June 5, 2013), http://www.oecd.org/ctp/exchange-of-tax-information/ENG_Convention_Flyer.pdf.

92 *Id.*; *See also* MAATM, *supra* note 19, Article 30.

93 Fla. Bankers Ass'n v. U.S. Dep't of the Treasury, 799 F.3d 1065 (D.C. Cir. 2015).

94 *See, e.g.*, European Community v. RJR Nabisco, Inc., 424 F.3d 175 (2nd Cir., 2005), limiting the scope of Pasquantino vs. United States, 544 US 349 (2005).

Then there are the problems with MAATM. The two key problems with MAATM are that the United States has not ratified it, so that it may become a huge tax haven for the rest of the world; and second, even a small noncooperating jurisdiction may be able to derail it.

In his book, Zucman acknowledges these problems and proposes several solutions.[95] The most important would be to create a worldwide registry of financial wealth, tracking who owns what in stocks and bonds. This registry would act as a central depository of financial information for governments and international organizations, and it would allow national tax administrations to fight tax evasion by levying taxes on capital income flows and wealth stocks.

Zucman points out that private registries of financial assets already exist, such as the ones maintained by the Depositary Trust Company in the United States and by Clearstream in Luxembourg. His idea is to combine them and enlarge the field of data, and to transfer ownership of the data to the public. "Combined with automatic exchange of information between the banks of all tax havens and foreign tax authorities, a financial register would deal a fatal blow to financial secrecy" (p. 5). But what if some tax havens refuse to cooperate? In that case, Zucman proposes sanctions proportionate to the costs the tax haven imposes on other countries. For example, he suggests that a tariff of 30 percent on goods imported by France, Germany, and Italy from Switzerland would suffice to induce the Swiss to cooperate.

We doubt this would work. Like Piketty's wealth tax, the proposed registry seems to require too much global cooperation among governments to be realistic. Moreover, it seems unlikely that a sanctions regime can be applied to all tax havens at once. Switzerland is an easy target because it is landlocked, so three countries can easily block its exports, but the same solution would be less effective with other nations, such as Singapore. Can we realistically expect every country that imports goods from Singapore or the island havens to cooperate in imposing sanctions?

3.4 THE LIMITS OF THE BEPS PROJECT IN ADDRESSING THE FINANCIAL SECRECY ISSUE

One of the missions of the BEPS project is to ensure transparency while promoting increased certainty and predictability. Action 5 focuses on the transparency of harmful tax practices, particularly in the IP regimes. Action 12 requires taxpayers to disclose their aggressive tax planning arrangements. Action 13 reexamines the transfer pricing documentation.[96] However, despite these reports, the issue of financial secrecy has not received enough attention in the BEPS project.

[95] ZUCMAN, *supra* note 7, 75–101.

[96] OECD, *BEPS 2015 Final Reports* (2015), https://www.oecd.org/tax/beps-2015-final-reports.htm.

Therefore, both bilateral and multilateral actions are needed to address the financial secrecy issue.

Since 2009 the Global Forum on Transparency and Exchange of Information for Tax Purposes has been the key international body working on the implementation of the international standards on tax transparency. The Forum currently has 130 members and 15 international organizations participating as observers. There are two internationally agreed-upon standards on the exchange of information for tax purposes: Exchange of Information on Request (EOIR) and Automatic Exchange of Information (AEOI) Portal. All member jurisdictions have committed to implementing the international standard on EOIR. More than ninety countries and jurisdictions have committed to implementing the new standard on AEOI. Work is currently underway to implement these standards, with the first exchanges occurring on a very ambitious timeline of 2017 and 2018.

The global standard for automatic exchange of financial account information was approved by the OECD Council on July 15, 2014.[97] Under the standard, jurisdictions obtain financial information from their financial institutions and automatically exchange that information with other jurisdictions on an annual basis. It sets out the financial account information to be exchanged, the financial institutions required to report, the different types of accounts and taxpayers covered, as well as common due diligence procedures to be followed by financial institutions.

Although AEOI will enable the discovery of formerly undetected tax evasion, there is a long way to go to eliminate the information asymmetry created or exacerbated by domestic financial secrecy regimes and practices. For instance, as Switzerland is "the old grand-daddy of tax havens,"[98] the surprising demise of Switzerland's legendary banking secrecy regime was not easy to achieve. In our opinion, the demise history deserves further reflection.

As observed by Patrick Emmenegger, Switzerland is structurally dependent on the economic welfare of its largest banks, and Swiss banks are again structurally dependent on access to the US financial market. This advantage along with the tax evasion scandal of UBS during the global financial crisis enabled the United States in compelling Switzerland to make a series of bilateral concessions on banking secrecy. In spring 2012, Switzerland accepted group requests for client files by the United States in cases of administrative assistance. In December 2012, Switzerland had agreed in principle with the United States on how to implement FATCA. These Swiss concessions to the United States once again fueled multilateral efforts by demonstrating the continued need to act on banking secrecy and by providing a focal point for collective action.[99]

97 OECD, *What Is the CRS*, http://www.oecd.org/tax/automatic-exchange/common-reporting-standard/.

98 K. H. Finkelstein, The Tax Haven Guide Book 6 (Big Island Media Corp 1999).

99 Patrick Emmenegger, *Swiss Banking Secrecy and the Problem of International Cooperation in Tax Matters: A Nut Too Hard to Crack?* (Nov. 26, 2015), http://onlinelibrary.wiley.com/doi/10.1111/rego.12106/pdf.

The US successful unilateral action against Swiss banks not only rooted out the barrier for the DOJ and the IRS to acquire the files of American taxpayers from the Swiss banks, but also paved the way for collective action to overcome Switzerland's resistance to international tax cooperation. As a result, Switzerland decided to adopt the Standard for Automatic Exchange of Financial Account Information in 2014.[100]

But the unanswered question is, if the United States withdraws its pressure on the next tax haven to toe the line, what will be the effective strategy to make the multilateral actions sustainable and viable? Patrick Emmenegger's answer is that the international community will likely have to wait for the next "demonstration effect" before new substantial improvements are possible.[101] Although we appreciate his concern about the challenge for the viability of multilateral actions, we don't think the international community has no choice but to wait for the demonstration effect of another legal battle between a powerful residence country and another tax haven. The modernization of international tax governance including the global efforts in fighting against BEPS should neither count on Powerball luck associated with the tax evasion scandal nor count on any single white knight among the victim countries. In contrast, the sustainable multilateral actions should be built upon the rule of law, including, but not confined to, rational core value, coherent institutional arrangements, and effective methodology for achieving voluntary practices on the part of the governments, the financial institutions, and the taxpayers.

In our opinion, public shaming of wrongdoing countries and financial institutions has proved to be an effective solution to ensure the compliance of international tax law, as most nations must care out about the international reputation of their government and financial institutions. To improve the credibility of the blacklist, the peer review process of AEOI Group should be impartial, transparent, and inclusive. Each blacklisted country should have the opportunity to be heard and to explain before the final decision is made by the AEOI group. In addition to the banking secrecy, other financial secrecy regimes including anonymous trusts and foundations, shell companies held by nominal shareholders for anonymous shareholders, need to be regulated from the perspective of international tax law. Examined form the domestic law either in the form of statutes or in the form of decided cases, the private relationships in the structure of anonymous trusts and foundations, shell companies are completely lawful and legal. However, the sole purpose of such legal structures is avoiding taxation created by tax law. While recognizing the private legal relationship

[100] OECD, *Switzerland Takes Important Step to Boost International Cooperation against Tax Evasion* (Nov. 19, 2014), http://www.oecd.org/tax/exchange-of-tax-information/switzerland-takes-important-step-to-boost-international-cooperation-against-tax-evasion.htm.

[101] Emmenegger, *supra* note 99.

based on anonymous structures, we urge the international community to ban the abuse of anonymous structures for illegal BEPS purpose. All nominal owners of the taxable properties for the beneficiary owners should be obligated to report the information to the local tax authority, which share such information with the tax authority in other jurisdictions. Of course, the confidentiality of such information should be well protected from being abused by irrelevant individuals or institutions.

4

The Early Revolution and Its Limits, 2010–2015*

4.1 BASE EROSION AND PROFIT SHIFTING (BEPS) PROJECT

In October 2015, the OECD and the G20 released a series of action steps under the BEPS project.[1] OECD Secretary-General Angel Gurria stated that

> Base erosion and profit shifting affects all countries, not only economically, but also as a matter of trust. BEPS is depriving countries of precious resources to jump-start

* This chapter draws heavily from *Evaluating BEPS: A Reconsideration of the Benefits Principle and Proposal for UN Oversight*, 6 Harv. Bus. L. Rev. 185 (2016) (with H. Xu).

1 On BEPS *see, e.g.*, Hugh J. Ault, *Some Reflections on the OECD and the Sources of International Tax Principles* (July 1, 2013). Reprinted from 70(12) TAX NOTES INT'L 1195 (June 17, 2013), Working Paper of the Max Planck Inst. for Tax L. and Pub. Fin. No. 2013-03, SSRN: http://ssrn.com/abstract=2287834 or http://dx.doi.org/10.2139/ssrn.2287834; Dhammika Dharmapala, *What Do We Know about Base Erosion and Profit Shifting? A Review of the Empirical Literature* (Ill. Pub. L. Rsch. Paper No. 14-23, U. of Chi. Coase-Sandor Inst. for L. & Econ. Rsch. Paper No. 702, Sept. 3, 2014), SSRN: http://ssrn.com/abstract=2373549 or http://dx.doi.org/10.2139/ssrn.2373549; Yariv Brauner, *What the BEPS?* (Mar. 12, 2014), SSRN: http://ssrn.com/abstract=2408034 or http://dx.doi.org/10.2139/ssrn.2408034; Hugh J. Ault et al., *Base Erosion and Profit Shifting: A Roadmap for Reform* (June 1, 2014), 68 BULL. INT'L TAX'N 275 (2014), Bos. Coll. L. Sch. Legal Stud. Rsch. Paper No. 324, SSRN: http://ssrn.com/abstract=2459646; Dhammika Dharmapala, *Base Erosion and Profit Shifting: A Simple Conceptual Framework* (Univ. of Chi. Coase-Sandor Inst. for L. & Econ. Rsch. Paper No. 703, Sept. 25, 2014), SSRN: http://ssrn.com/abstract=2497770; Richard J. Vann, *Policy Forum: The Policy Underpinnings of the BEPS Project – Preserving the International Corporate Income Tax? (August 20, 2014)*, 62(2) CAN. TAX J. 433–41 (2014), Sydney L. Sch. Rsch. Paper No. 14/77, SSRN: http://ssrn.com/abstract=2483619; Daniel Shaviro, *The Crossroads versus the Seesaw: Getting a "Fix" on Recent International Tax Policy Developments* (NYU Sch. of L., Pub. L. Rsch. Paper No. 15-20, NYU L. and Econ. Rsch. Paper No. 15-11, July 1, 2015), SSRN: http://ssrn.com/abstract=2605144 or http://dx.doi.org/10.2139/ssrn.2605144; Adam H. Rosenzweig, *Building a Framework for a Post-BEPS World* (June 24, 2014), 74(12) TAX NOTES INT'L (2014), SSRN: http://ssrn.com/abstract=2463259; Itai Grinberg, *Breaking BEPS: The New International Tax Diplomacy* (Sept. 1, 2015), SSRN: http://ssrn.com/abstract=2652894 or http://dx.doi.org/10.2139/ssrn.2652894.

> growth, tackle the effects of the global economic crisis and create more and better opportunities for all. But beyond this, BEPS has been also eroding the trust of citizens in the fairness of tax systems worldwide. The measures we are presenting today represent the most fundamental changes to international tax rules in almost a century: they will put an end to double non-taxation, facilitate a better alignment of taxation with economic activity and value creation, and when fully implemented, these measures will render BEPS-inspired tax planning structures ineffective.

We do not think Mr. Gurria was justified in his optimism. In our opinion, these efforts are inadequate. The basic problem is that they take as a given the fundamental consensus underlying the international tax regime, also known as the "benefits principle." Under the benefits principle, active (business) income should be taxed primarily at source while passive (investment) income should be taxed primarily at residence.[2] This compromise was reached in 1923 and still serves as the foundation of the international tax regime.[3] It is embedded in over 3,000 bilateral tax treaties and in the domestic laws of the United States and most other countries. Unsurprisingly, it is also reflected in both MAATM and BEPS. FATCA, the IGAs, and MAATM are all attempts to enforce residence-based taxation of passive income, while BEPS is an attempt to improve source-based taxation of active income.[4]

In our opinion, this consensus should be reconsidered considering current realities. The shortcomings of both the MAATM and BEPS are directly related to their reliance on the benefits principle because upholding it requires cooperation by too many jurisdictions.

The original rationale for the benefits principle was that economists in the 1920s believed that active (business) income was earned primarily in the country of source, because that is where business activity took place, while passive (investment) income was earned primarily in the country of residence, because that is where the capital invested was accumulated. Economists no longer believe in the validity of this analysis because most types of income have more than one source.[5]

Nevertheless, the common view (including, until recently, our own) is that the benefits principle still makes sense, because most active income is earned by

[2] On the benefits principle and its origins *see* Reuven S. Avi-Yonah, *The Structure of International Taxation: A Proposal for Simplification*, 74 Texas L. Rev. 1301 (1996); Reuven S. Avi-Yonah, *International Taxation of Electronic Commerce*, 52 Tax L. Rev. 507 (1997); Reuven S. Avi-Yonah, Advanced Introduction to International Tax Law (2015), ch. 1.

[3] Avi-Yonah, *Structure*, *supra* note 2.

[4] On FATCA, IGAs, and MAATM *see, e.g.*, Joshua D. Blank & Ruth Mason, *Exporting FATCA* (Feb. 1, 2014), 142 Tax Notes 1245 (Mar. 17, 2014), SSRN: http://ssrn.com/abstract=2389500. On BEPS *see, e.g.*, Ault, *supra* note 1.

[5] For the consensus view that economic source is a meaningless concept *see, e.g.*, Hugh J. Ault & David P. Bradford, *Taxing International Income: An Analysis of the U.S. System and Its Economic Premises*, *in* Taxation in the Global Economy 11, 30 (Assaf Razin & Joel Slemrod eds., 1990). For a recent defense of source as an economic concept and a critique of the consensus view, *see* Mitchell Kane, A *Defense of Source Rules in International Taxation*, 32 Yale J. on Regul. 311 (2015).

corporations and most passive income is earned by individuals. Since individual residence is meaningful in a way that corporate residence is not, it makes sense to tax individuals on a residence basis and corporations on a source basis. This system broke down in the 1980s. For active income, it could generally not be earned without taxation by source countries, because corporate investments by multinationals were generally immobile and tax competition was limited in scope. The Dupont case (1979)[6] is a good example of the limits of tax planning in the pre-globalization world: It involved a multinational manufacturing goods in the United States and selling them in Europe, and both activities were subject to high levels of taxation. Dupont tried to avoid this result by routing the sales through a Swiss subsidiary, but the US court rejected this attempt, and Subpart F was enacted in part to prevent it from happening again. The underlying assumption behind the Subpart F compromise (1962) was that active income would be taxed at source, and therefore it was not problematic to permit deferral of active income while taxing passive income and base company income currently.[7]

On the passive income front, exchange restrictions limited the ability of individuals to earn passive income overseas, so that the capacity to use tax havens was limited. Martin Feldstein found in 1980 that the overall US savings and investment were the same, suggesting a strong "home bias" and resulting taxing capacity for passive income.[8]

But these constraints started to erode in the 1980s. Multinationals became much more mobile as the focus shifted from heavy manufacturing to services and intangibles. The result was tax competition as multinationals became able to pit one country against another. By 1995, Intel, which builds a new chip factory every other year, was able to boast that tax competition enabled it not to pay any foreign tax as it pitted Israel against Ireland and Mexico against Costa Rica as new plant locations, earning tax holidays in all of them.[9]

On the individual level, the relaxation of exchange controls and the abolition of withholding taxes on interest (beginning with the US portfolio interest exemption in 1982) created a world in which, according to Zucman, an estimated $7 trillion can be routed through tax havens and not declared to residence authorities. The adoption of personal jurisdiction by most countries did little to abate this trend.[10]

6 E. I. du Pont de Nemours and Company v. The United States. United States Court of Claims, 608 F.2d 445 (1979).

7 Reuven S. Avi-Yonah, *Tax Competition and Multinational Competitiveness: The New Balance of Subpart F*, 18 Tax Notes Int'l 1575 (Apr. 19, 1999).

8 Martin Feldstein & Charles Horioka, *Domestic Saving and International Capital Flows*, 90(358) Econ. J. 314–29 (1980), JSTOR 2231790.

9 http://www.intel.com/intel/intelis/sites.htm (last accessed Feb. 1, 1999). *See* Intel Corp., *Annual Report Pursuant to Section 13 or 15(d) of the Securities Exchange Act of 1934 for the Fiscal Year Ended December 26, 1998 (Form 10-K)*, File No. 0-6217, at 5, http://www.sec.gov/Archives/edgar/data/50863/0001047469-99-011450.txt [hereinafter Intel 10-K].

10 Gabriel Zucman, The Hidden Wealth of Nations (Sept. 2015); J. Guttentag & Reuven S. Avi-Yonah, *Closing the International Tax Gap*, *in* Bridging the Tax Gap: Addressing the Crisis in Federal Tax Administration 99 (Max B. Sawicky ed., 2005).

The result has been that by the early twenty-first century most cross-border income is untaxed. In the case of multinationals, this is because the source jurisdiction either lacks the authority to tax because it is easy to avoid the required physical presence in the source country;[11] or because source jurisdictions grant tax holidays to multinationals. Residence jurisdictions do not tax active income currently for fear that multinationals will establish their headquarters elsewhere, as the current US inversion saga confirms.[12] In the case of individuals, exchange of information has not proven effective in deterring tax evasion via offshore secrecy jurisdictions, and no withholding taxes are levied by source jurisdictions.

Two recent examples can be used to illustrate the problem of tax avoidance on cross-border income:

> The previous chapter addressed illegal tax evasion by individual taxpayers. Corporations are another story, because what they are doing is legal tax avoidance, and therefore can be better quantified. As of the end of 2015, US multinationals had over $2 trillion in offshore profits in low-taxed jurisdictions.[13] This amount, which translates to about $700 billion in US taxes avoided, is mostly income that was economically earned in the US and shifted offshore to jurisdictions like Singapore, Ireland, or Luxembourg, which have effective tax rates in the single digits.

How did the multinationals do it? A couple of examples can suffice. Apple, Inc. is the world's largest company by market capitalization. Most of its billions in profits relate to intellectual property developed at its headquarters in Cupertino, California. But for tax purposes, most of the profit is booked in its Irish subsidiaries – let's call them Apple Ireland.

Some of the profit shifting is achieved through a "cost sharing agreement." Cost sharing is a concept developed in IRS regulations in the 1980s, but which became more significant due to the increasing importance of intellectual property. The idea behind cost sharing is this: When a US multinational begins a new research project (e.g., a search for a drug to treat a certain disease), it can agree to share the costs of development with its offshore subsidiaries. Then, if the project is successful, the parties share the profits in the same proportions. For example, if Apple Ireland contributed 80 percent of the costs of developing the iPhone 6, it would get 80 percent of the profit. Importantly, none of the actual work is done by Apple Ireland. Apple just gives Apple Ireland the money and Apple Ireland pays it back as its contribution to the research costs.

Why would the IRS regulations permit this? Because if the research failed, then the taxpayer would lose its ability to deduct the costs sent offshore. The more of the cost sent offshore, the more deductions would be at risk. So, the IRS thought there was a natural limit to taxpayer willingness to share costs with offshore affiliates.

[11] *See* Avi-Yonah, Advanced Introduction, *supra* note 2.

[12] *See* Daniel Shaviro, *The Rising Tax-Electivity of U.S. Corporate Residence*, 64 Tax L. Rev. 377 (2011); Reuven S. Avi-Yonah & Omri Y. Marian, *Inversions and Competitiveness: Reflections in the Wake of Pfizer-Allergan*, 41 Int'l Tax J. 39 (2015).

[13] Citizens for Tax Justice, *Held Offshore: A Comparison of International Tax Proposals* (July 14, 2015), https://ctj.org/2-1-trillion-in-corporate-profits-held-offshore-a-comparison-of-international-tax-proposals/.

That analysis may have been true for Big Pharma, which usually waits to enter cost sharing with an offshore affiliate until a drug has passed its initial trials and is well on its way to a patent, and then battles the IRS over valuation issues at the time the cost sharing agreement was executed. But the same analysis makes no sense for Apple, since if there is anything certain in business, it is that a new version of the iPhone will sell.

There is another trick involved in Apple Ireland's profitability. Another portion of its profits derive from countries where Apple sells the iPhones. Apple Ireland licenses the right to use Apple's brand and intellectual property to Apple affiliates in other countries. Those affiliates in turn pay Apple Ireland hefty royalties, which operate to shift the sales profits gained in those countries to Ireland.

Before 1997, such a scheme would not have worked, because the royalties received by Apple Ireland would have triggered a tax in the United States under so-called Subpart F. But in 1997 the Clinton administration adopted a rule called "Check the Box." Under Check the Box, Apple Ireland can treat all its foreign affiliates as if they did not exist as separate entities for US tax purposes and treat the money they paid to Apple Ireland as income earned in Ireland. The result is that for US tax purposes there are no royalties and no US tax triggered by them because Apple Ireland treats the money as its own sales income.

The Obama administration came in promising to repeal Check the Box; this was the biggest international revenue raiser in the first Obama budget. But by November 2009 the administration recanted under pressure from the multinationals. Subsequently, President Obama signed into law a five-year extension of a provision (first enacted by a Republican Congress as a "temporary" measure in 2006) that enshrines Check the Box in the tax law.

Finally, the Senate hearing revealed two Irish-specific tricks used by Apple. Ireland has a tax rate of 12.5 percent, far below the US rate of 35 percent. But Apple did not want to pay even 12.5 percent. Its solution was ingenious: For US tax purposes, Apple Ireland is treated as an Irish company because it is incorporated in Ireland, so it is not taxed by the United States. But for Irish tax purposes, Apple Ireland was a tax resident of the United States. As a result, Apple Ireland claimed it was a tax resident nowhere. On top of that, it negotiated a sweetheart tax deal with Ireland for its Irish income that resulted in it paying a tax rate of less than 2 percent.

These types of tricks are used by most US multinationals. If the primary driver of value of a US multinational is intellectual property developed in the United States, the Apple scheme can simply be replicated.

But what if the value derives from more traditional, tangible items? Some US multinationals do pay higher taxes (e.g., the car companies). But others try to avoid tax. Caterpillar, Inc. is a good example.[14]

Caterpillar does not make a lot of money on the heavy equipment it manufactures. But it makes a bundle on replacement parts, because once you buy a

[14] Homeland Security & Governmental Affairs, *Caterpillar's Offshore Tax Strategy* (2014), http://www.hsgac.senate.gov/subcommittees/investigations/hearings/caterpillars-offshore-tax-strategy.

Caterpillar bulldozer, you will need parts, which you can obtain only from Caterpillar at a huge markup. Caterpillar prides itself on its ability to deliver parts within twenty-four hours anywhere in the world, including the Arctic tundra (where its equipment is used in mineral extraction).

Before 1998, Caterpillar bought the parts from unrelated manufacturers and stored them at its warehouse in Morton, Illinois. When a dealer requested a part for a customer overseas, Caterpillar "sold" (but did not actually ship) the part to a Swiss subsidiary which in turn sold the part to the unrelated dealer.

The problem, according to accounting firm PricewaterhouseCoopers (PwC), was that Caterpillar's sale of the part to its Swiss subsidiary triggered US tax. Much better, PwC said, would be if the parts were sold by the manufacturer directly to the Swiss subsidiary which could then sell it to the dealer. Fine, said Caterpillar, but we do not want to change our operations. So, in exchange for $60 million in fees, PwC came up with a way to lower Caterpillar's US tax without changing its operations. PwC's solution was for the manufacturers to bill the Swiss subsidiary for the parts but continue to ship them to the Illinois warehouse which continued to transport them to Caterpillar's foreign customers. If the parts were shipped overseas, they were deemed to have been "owned" by the Swiss subsidiary, and PwC devised a virtual inventory to track even those the parts that were indistinguishably commingled in the warehouse. The result was that Caterpillar continued to run its parts business from the United States but declared 85 percent or more of the parts profits in Switzerland.

The IRS has challenged this billing arrangement, which resulted in shifting some $2.4 billion in Caterpillar profits from the United States to Switzerland. A Grand Jury has issued subpoenas under a criminal investigation for tax fraud.

But the disturbing fact is that the whole story would not have come to light but for a whistleblower, who alerted both PSI and the IRS. And while Caterpillar is facing a court challenge, in most cases of corporate tax avoidance, like Apple, the IRS' hands are tied because what Apple did may have been legal under the US tax code.

The problem with this situation is that in the absence of taxation of cross-border flows, the progressive income tax cannot be maintained, because it is easier for the wealthy to earn cross-border income. The result has been a worldwide shift to taxing consumption rather than income. But consumption taxes are regressive and cannot reach the unconsumed income of the rich.[15] And without progressive taxation, it will not be possible to maintain the public's commitment to social insurance that is globalization's main defense against growing inequality. While both the MAATM

[15] On the shift to consumption taxes *see* Avi-Yonah, *supra* note 7; on the inability of consumption taxes to reach the unconsumed income of the rich *see* Reuven S. Avi-Yonah, *Why Tax the Rich? Efficiency, Equity, and Progressive Taxation (Review of Slemrod, Does Atlas Shrug? The Economic Consequences of Taxing the Rich)*, 111 YALE L. J. 1391 (2002); Reuven S. Avi-Yonah, *Risk, Rents and Regressivity: Why the United States Needs Both an Income Tax and a VAT*, 105 TAX NOTES 1651 (Dec. 20, 2004).

and the BEPS projects are helpful, neither is likely to solve the underlying issues described above. In both cases the problem is that too many countries need to cooperate for the regime to be effective. In the case of MAATM, every tax haven has to sign on because otherwise all the funds can be routed through the non-cooperating haven. We are far from there, and the United States has not implemented MAATM (it has implemented FATCA, but that applies only for US residents and can be avoided by using financial institutions with no US presence).

In the case of BEPS, the project only addresses artificial profit shifting, not tax competition, and it only applies to the OECD and G20, not to the many source countries outside these two organizations. Thus, it is likely that multinationals can avoid BEPS by sourcing income in countries that are not subject to it.

Fundamentally, if the income tax is to be preserved in the twenty-first century, multilateral solutions are needed. Both MAATM and BEPS are such solutions, but they are hampered by the focus on residence jurisdictions for passive income and source jurisdictions for active income. There are too many residence jurisdictions in the first case, since every country has rich people, and too many source jurisdictions in the second since multinationals operate globally.

Thus, in our opinion it is time to reevaluate the benefits principle.[16] Most of the current issues can be solved if we taxed passive income primarily at source and active income primarily at residence. For passive income, the number of source jurisdictions is much smaller than residence jurisdictions. Because most individuals are relatively risk averse, portfolio investment flows overwhelmingly to a small number of countries – the United States, the EU, and Japan. Even the BRICS mostly attract portfolio investment through mutual funds that are relatively easy to tax. Thus, if the "big three" can coordinate to reinstate a withholding tax on interest, dividends, and royalties flowing from them, most of the problem of taxing passive income can be solved. Crucially, money cannot stay in tax havens and earn decent rates of return, so the cooperation of tax havens is not needed, unlike in the case of the MAATM.

For active income, about 90 percent of large multinationals are headquartered in the G20, and none of those countries have a tax rate below 20 percent, so if they taxed their multinationals currently on a coordinated basis and restricted the ability to move out, most of the problem would be resolved. We would therefore suggest that we reconsider the benefits principle in light of the reality of globalization. We should tax passive income primarily at source and active income primarily at residence.

Importantly, like under current rules, this does not preclude the alternative. Once passive income is taxed at source, taxpayers may be able to credit the tax upon declaring it to their residence country. And once active income is taxed at residence, a credit can be given to source country taxes if the source country responds to the

[16] For the contrary view defending the current validity of the benefits principle and source-based taxation *see, e.g.*, Kane, *supra* note 5.

limitation of tax competition by reimposing its tax. But the key is that the income has already been taxed, so that no double non-taxation ensues even if taxpayers do not declare the income (in the case of passive income, where the residence rate may be higher) or source countries choose not to tax in the case of active income.

4.2 THE LIMITS OF THE BEPS PROJECT

On October 5, 2015, two years after announcing the action plan, the OECD and G20 released the final BEPS package of thirteen reports, which covers the fifteen actions.

The BEPS package represents the first substantial renovation of the international tax standards in almost a century.[17] The BEPS package is an unprecedented turning point in the history of international tax law. Its mission is to align the location of taxable profits with the location of economic activities and value creation. Some generally accepted principles of international tax law, including the single tax principle, the Benefit Principle, the antidiscrimination principle, and the transparency principle, have been incorporated into the project.

Despite considerable progress, there are many shortcomings with the BEPS project due to the short two-year framework. Hence, the BEPS project is not the destination of international tax law reform. Rather, it is merely the first step toward the modernization of global tax governance.

4.2.1 *New Shoes on the Old Road: An Old Approach for the New Destination*

The primary problem with the BEPS project is that although the new goal has been redefined, new principles and new rules have not been established for achieving, and the old principles have been strengthened by a patch-up of current rules.

The core principle of international tax law is the single tax principle, which requires the eradication of both double taxation and double non-taxation.[18] Unfortunately, both governments and MNES have been active in fighting against double taxation and have ignored another danger of double non-taxation.

Based on the single tax principle, the mission of the BEPS project is to prevent and eliminate double non-taxation. As the G20 leaders pointed out the new principle, "profits should be taxed where economic activities deriving the profits are performed and where value is created."[19] The new direction of international tax

[17] OECD, *Explanatory Statement*, OECD/G20 Base Erosion and Profit Shifting Project, OECD (2015), p. 5, www.oecd.org/tax/beps-explanatory-statement-2015.pdf.

[18] Ault, *supra* note 1; Reuven S. Avi-Yonah, *Who Invented the Single Tax Principle? An Essay on the History of US Treaty Policy*, 59 N.Y.L. Sch. L. Rev. 305 (2015); Reuven S. Avi-Yonah, *Full Circle? The Single Tax Principle, BEPS, and the New US Model* (U. of Mich. Pub. L. Rsch. Paper No. 480; U. of Mich. L. & Econ. Rsch. Paper No. 15-019, Oct. 13, 2015), SSRN: http://ssrn.com/abstract=2673463 or http://dx.doi.org/10.2139/ssrn.2673463.

[19] Tax Annex to the St Petersburg Declaration (Sept. 2013).

law reform in the context of BEPS project is to safeguard the single tax principle by fighting against the BEPS.

It is well known that the old international tax regime, including its rules and underlying principles, is one of the primary causes of BEPS project. The ideal roadmap for the BEPS project is supposed to replace the old principles with a new principle, and to redesign the rules based on the requirement of the new principle.

Unfortunately, many old principles of international tax law were preserved in the final BEPS package. The mixture of new principles and old principles has substantially compromised the value of the reforms and made the legal reform of international tax look more like a patch-up of existing rules and principles. The reason is obvious. On one hand, it is practically impossible to abolish or even reconsider the dysfunctional current rules, which have been favored by some large countries and MNEs. On the other hand, it is mandatory to change the current rules to some extent, because of the emerging political pressure against BEPS schemes. Given the short two-year time horizon for serious in-depth research, debate, and negotiation, given the strong tradition and influential interest groups desires to keep the continuity of old principles, given the global voice for closing up the BEPS opportunities, the architects of the BEPS project have no choice but to patch up some loopholes of current rules, instead of a pure fundamental restructuring of the current regime.[20]

As a result, a wholesale reform of the current international tax regime did not happen, and genuine new rules guided by the new principles have not been formulated. Moreover, the patch-up work has produced many more complex, discretionary, uncertain, costly, and, in many cases, contradictory rules.[21] There are two possible negative consequences. First, it is difficult to translate all the new rules into reality. Second, even if the BEPS project is implemented as outlined and promised in the book, it is still possible for the creation of either new BEPS opportunities on the part of MNEs, or arbitrariness on the part of tax authorities.

In addition to adhering to the independent entity principle and rejection of the new principle of single unitary entity, the BEPS project is also silent on the basic concepts of residence and source, and where profit should be considered earned. As the existing rules based on the old principles have been strengthened, and new rules based on the new principle have not been established, the BEPS project is not so revolutionary and fundamental as it appears at first sight.

The ironic fact is that the patch-up of current rules in the BEPS project was made in the name of a new mission and new principle. However, because of the inconsistencies and conflicts between the new principle and old principles, the new

[20] Ault, *supra* note 1.

[21] See detailed discussion below, and the report card prepared by the BEPS Monitoring Group, *Overall Evaluation of the G20/OECD Base Erosion and Profit Shifting (BEPS) Project* (2015) https://bepsmonitoringgroup.wordpress.com/2015/10/05/overall-evaluation/ [hereinafter BEPS Monitoring Group Report].

principle of international tax law has been compromised or undermined by the strengthened current rules based on old principles. Without the support of a new principle and new rules, it is very challenging to achieve the new destination of aligning the taxation of MNE profits with economic activity.

4.2.2 *The Survival and Continuity of Notional and Illusionary Independent Entity Principle and Arm's-Length Principle*

The traditional international tax law is designed and interpreted based on the assumption that the various constituent entities or members of an MNE group are independent of each other and conduct transactions with each other at arm's length.[22]

While criticizing the independent entity theory as a fundamental flaw of the existing rules, the BEPS Monitoring Group identified a new, but implied, approach in the G20 mandate to treat the corporate group of an MNE as a single firm and ensure that its tax base is attributed according to its real activities in each country.[23] This means that the new destination of taxing MNEs "where economic activities take place and value is created" is unlikely to be achieved without treating the MNE group as a single firm.

We also support the single unitary entity principle.[24] In our view, the G20 mandate could be interpreted as a new direction, which requires all the BEPS actions to serve the purpose of taxing MNEs where economic activities take place and value is created in the most efficient manner. Guided by the brand-new view, the principle of single unitary entity and the basic concepts of residence and source need to be established as the cornerstones to support the design, interpretation, and implementation of BEPS package.

Unfortunately, the BEPS project refused to make the implied principle explicit. Consequently, the BEPS project fails to provide a coherent and comprehensive approach and instead proposes a patch-up of existing rules, making them even more contradictory and complex.[25]

22 Reuven S. Avi-Yonah, *The Rise and Fall of Arm's Length: A Study in the Evolution of U.S. International Taxation*, 15 Va. Tax Rev. 89 (1995); Reuven S. Avi-Yonah, *Between Formulary Apportionment and the OECD Guidelines: A Proposal for Reconciliation*, 2 World Tax J. 3 (2010); Reuven S. Avi-Yonah & I. Benshalom, *Formulary Apportionment – Myths and Prospects*, 3 World Tax J. 371 (2011).

23 BEPS Monitoring Group Report, *supra* note 21.

24 For a detailed proposal with legislative language *see* Reuven S. Avi-Yonah et al., *Allocating Business Profits for Tax Purposes: A Proposal to Adopt a Formulary Profit Split*, 9 Fla. Tax Rev. 497 (2009); Reuven S. Avi-Yonah, *A Proposal for Unitary Taxation and Formulary Apportionment to Tax Multinational Enterprises*, *in* Global Tax Governance 289 (Peter Dietsch & Thomas Rixen eds., 2016).

25 BEPS Monitoring Group Report, *supra* note 21.

Our view is that virtually all the new rules of the BEPS package are still built on the notional principle of independent entity.[26] By its very nature, the untouchable principle of the arm's-length principle ultimately derives from the root of independent entity theory. Additionally, many other flawed rules, including weak CFC rules and territorial and deferral systems, are also indirectly but closely connected with the independent entity principle.

The orthodoxy of independent entity taxation has two basic assumptions. First, the members of the MNE group are regarded as equal, separate, and independent legal entities. Namely, the members of MNE group are reasonable legal entities. From the perspective of corporate law, the fiction of an independent entity in the context of a corporate group derives from the orthodoxy of shareholders' limited liability and the corporate independent status as legal persons in the traditional corporate law. Second, the contracts between the related parties in the corporate group are freely negotiated at arm's length, and the terms of the contract are fair and reasonable dealings.[27] In short, both the entities and the transactions in the corporate group are reasonable, therefore legal and moral.

However, the two assumptions do not make sense, and they do not really exist in reality. The multinational corporate group operates more like a single, unitary entity or enterprise rather than separate independent entities. This is done through the controlling power of the parent corporation.

As traditional international tax law stubbornly insists on the old concept of independent entity, the MNEs have been encouraged to incorporate dozens and even hundreds of affiliates all over the world to undertake aggressive BEPS schemes.[28] The more subsidiaries or members in the MNE family, the stronger the parent corporation will be in reducing the overall transaction cost and advance the profitability of the group.

The reason for this is very simple. All the commercial activities of the subsidiaries and affiliates are under direct or indirect control from the parent corporation. Therefore, the profits or benefits could be unlimited by separate, but coordinated, operations of business under the uniform controlling power. On the other hand, the principle of independent entity could better protect the MNEs from unlimited risks and liabilities of group members toward bona fide third parties, including the tax authorities. Therefore, the legal risks and liabilities of a corporate group are limited by law, because there is no joint and several liability between and among the group members unless otherwise agreed to by the corporate group members.

Because of the controlling power of the parent corporation on the top of the pyramid of the complicated corporate structure, like a smart spider on the center of grand network of corporate groups, it is unlikely to find real arm's-length transaction

26 *See* BEPS Action Plan 8–10.

27 *See* Avi-Yonah et al., *supra* note 24.

28 *Id.*

in the reality.[29] In fact, the related-party contracts within the corporate group are always concluded without seriously free, competitive, and transparent bargaining and negotiations.

If the BEPS project is designed on the principle of single unitary entity, the BEPS countermeasure will be much simpler and more effective, as intergroup transactions will be disregarded, and the profit or tax base will be attributed to its real activities which generate the profit and create the value in the jurisdictions.

Unfortunately, many actions of the BEPS project, including, but not confined to, Action 2 on hybrid mismatches, Action 7 on PE, and Actions 8–10 on transferring pricing, heavily rely on the legal fictions of independent entity and arm's-length transaction.[30]

4.2.3 *The Survival and Continuity of the Problematic Benefit Principle*

The OECD declared that the goal of BEPS package is "to tackle BEPS structures by comprehensively addressing their root causes rather than merely the symptoms. Once the measures are implemented, many schemes facilitating double non-taxation will be curtailed."[31] We do not believe all the root causes have been addressed as in our opinion, one of the root causes is the traditional benefit principle, which has guided the allocation of global profits in the past few decades and has created many BEPS opportunities.

Unfortunately, the BEPS project failed to replace the benefit principle. Instead, it was still designed based on residence jurisdictions for passive income and source jurisdictions for active income.

As articulated in this chapter, our view is that BEPS concerns will be more effectively solved if passive income is primarily taxed at source and active income is primarily taxed at residence. This new philosophy will help to build a new international tax framework, which will benefit both developed countries and developing countries. Moreover, the conflicts between the domestic demand for tax revenue and domestic policy to attract foreign direct investment will be better balanced, and the MNEs and domestic firms will be offered a level playing field. As Mindy Herzfeld observed, "attempts at coordination cannot be successful unless there is agreement on an underlying set of principles for allocating the revenue of global citizens (including natural persons and legal entities). A more rigorous effort to develop such a clear and agreed-upon set of principles which rests on economic, philosophic, and fairness grounds is needed."[32]

[29] For a detailed exposition of the case law demonstrating this repeated failure, *see* Avi-Yonah, *Rise and Fall*, *supra* note 22.

[30] *See* BEPS Monitoring Group Report, *supra* note 21.

[31] OECD, *supra* note 17.

[32] Mindy Herzfeld, *The Limits of Tax Coordination*, Working draft (Oct. 11, 2015).

4.2.4 *Limited Inclusiveness and Multilateralism*

Global challenges need global solutions. BEPS, as a global concern, is made possible by uncoordinated tax rules at domestic and international levels. Therefore, global solutions need to be based on inclusive and multilateral global governance. This means each country should be offered equal opportunities and equal weight to shape the outcome of the reforms.

Despite the OECD's/G20's efforts to get many non-member countries and NGOs to participate in the development of the BEPS package, the inclusiveness and multilateralism of the BEPS project is limited for several reasons.

First, it is an undisputed fact that major OECD countries dominate the formulation of the BEPS package in the process of discussions and negotiations. As OECD countries are all developed countries, it is inevitable that the BEPS project is mainly a result of compromise between the rich countries. For instance, weak measures on CFCs, interest deductibility, and innovation box schemes are favored, particularly strongly by the UK.[33]

Second, although over sixty countries were directly involved in the process of the BEPS project, this only accounts for less than one-third of 193 UN members. As MNEs have their taxable presence around the globe, including in the nonparticipating countries, the effectiveness of the BEPS project is very limited. The tax competitions between participating countries and nonparticipating countries will continue. The race to the bottom and the unilateral actions taken by any jurisdiction could hurt all the countries in the world.

Third, although some developing countries were consulted for the BEPS project, it does not necessarily mean that their core proposals were finally accepted by the BEPS package. As observed by independent commentators, some key OECD countries opposed and succeeded in blocking the institutional reform proposal from developing countries at the third International Conference on "Financing for Development."[34]

Fourth, less influential participating countries and more than 120 nonparticipating counties might be hurt because of negative spillover arising from the implementation of the BEPS project in the future. They are weak not only because of their limited influence in the renovation of the current rules, but also because of their limited experience and resources to enforce the BEPS actions.

Fifth, the process of public debate and consulting was relatively insufficient. The BEPS Monitoring Group, an active tax justice advocate, complains that they have been vastly outnumbered by the army of paid tax advisers and representatives of multinational enterprises.[35] Although stakeholder interest, including invaluable

33 BEPS Monitoring Group Report, *supra* note 21, at p.3.

34 *Id.*

35 *Id.*

interactions with business and civil society, saw more than 12,000 pages of comments received on the twenty-three discussion drafts published and discussed at eleven public consultations,[36] it is unknown to what extent these valuable proposals have been adopted by the BEPS package. More importantly, detailed reasons for rejecting different proposals have not been published.

Given the fact that it is impossible to guarantee that countries and stakeholders really had the equal opportunity to influence and shape the outcome of the BEPS package on equal footing, OECD and/or G20 are not the truly global platforms for comprehensive reform of international tax law. To transform the current BEPS project into truly global, coherent, coordinated, and inclusive actions, the UN should undertake the leadership in the next stage of international tax law reform.

4.2.5 *The Limits of Action 1*

Digital economy has greatly expanded the platform of commerce and reduced the cost of business transactions. However, the digital economy has seriously exacerbated BEPS risks. That is why the tax challenges of the digital economy were listed as the first top priority on the agenda of the BEPS project.

To effectively address BEPS concerns in the context of the digital economy, the Action Plan of 2013 established the Task Force on the Digital Economy (TFDE), a subsidiary body of the Committee on Fiscal Affairs (CFA). TFDE's core mission is to identify the main difficulties that the digital economy poses for the application of existing international tax rules and to develop detailed options to address these difficulties.[37]

The Action 1 report analyzed BEPS risks exacerbated from the digital economy and the expected impact of the measures developed across the BEPS project. Rules and implementation mechanisms have been developed to help collect value added tax (VAT) based on the country where the consumer is in the case of cross-border B2C transactions. These measures are intended to level the playing field between domestic and foreign suppliers and facilitate the efficient collection of VAT due on these transactions. Technical options to deal with the broader tax challenges raised by the digital economy such as nexus and data have been discussed and analyzed.[38]

The TFDE identified certain specific issues generated by the key features of the digital economy that warrant attention from a tax perspective. They include ensuring that core activities cannot inappropriately benefit from the exception from permanent establishment (PE) status, and that artificial arrangements relating to sales of goods and services cannot be used to avoid PE status; the importance of intangibles, the use of data, and the spread of global value chains, and their impact

36 OECD, *supra* note 17.

37 OECD, *Action Plan on Base Erosion and Profit Shifting*, OECD (2013), pp. 14–15.

38 OECD, *supra* note 17, at p. 13.

on transfer pricing; and addressing opportunities for tax planning by businesses engaged in VAT-exempt activities.

Although Action 1 considered several options to address the broader tax challenges raised by the digital economy, including a new nexus in the form of significant economic presence, none of these options were recommended at this stage. However, the OECD and G20 countries have agreed to monitor developments, and, based on the future monitoring work, make a determination as to whether further work on the options discussed and analyzed should be carried out. This determination should be based on a broad look at the ability of existing international tax standards to deal with the tax challenges raised by developments in the digital economy.[39]

The Action 1 report was unable to propose all the necessary solutions to the BEPS concerns in the digital economy for the following two reasons. The first reason is that although the digital economy has exacerbated BEPS risks, it has not generated genuinely unique BEPS issues. Almost every BEPS issue is directly or indirectly relevant to digital economy. Almost every BEPS issue is interconnected with each other in the digital economy. Therefore, it would be challenging and unwise for the TFDE to produce unique measures in parallel with other measures of the BEPS project.

The second reason is that the staggered time frame of the BEPS project made it impossible for TFDE to foresee the impact of the future BEPS package in advance. For the same reason, it is difficult for TFDE to evaluate the ultimate scope of the more systemic tax challenges in nexus, data, and characterization, and potential options to address them. However, the limits of the Action 1 report could be overcome by continuing research on the broader tax challenges of the digital economy, and by proposing detailed and viable options to address those challenges. On the one hand, TFDE needs to assist the implementation of other BEPS actions, such as Action 3 on CFC rules, Action 7 on artificial avoidance of PE, and Actions 8–10 on transfer pricing. On the other hand, TFDE should update the Action 1 report based on the experience, performance, and outcomes of the BEPS project to maintain its relevance and the effectiveness of future proposed reforms.

A supplementary report reflecting the outcomes of the continuing work was finalized in December 2015.[40] We doubt whether the intended outcomes of the BEPS project would be available for assessment, given the fact that the implementation of the fifteen actions is a lengthy process domestically and internationally. In our opinion, the Action 1 report should be updated regularly based on the changing business models of the digital economy.

[39] *Id.* at p. 8.

[40] OECD, *Addressing the Tax Challenges of the Digital Economy*, OECD/G20 Base Erosion and Profit Shifting Project (OECD Publishing, 2014), p. 21, http://dx.doi.org/10.1787/9789264218789-en; OECD, Countering Harmful Tax Practices More Effectively, Taking ...

4.2.6 *The Limits of Action 2*

The goal of utilizing hybrid mismatch arrangements is to achieve unintended double non-taxation or long-term tax deferral by, for instance, creating two deductions for one borrowing, generating deductions without corresponding income inclusions, or misusing foreign tax credits and participation exemption regimes. Country rules that allow taxpayers to choose the tax treatment of certain domestic and foreign entities facilitate hybrid mismatches. While it may be difficult to determine which country has lost tax revenue, because the laws of each country involved have been followed, the result is under taxation, which harms competition, economic efficiency, transparency, and fairness.[41]

To establish international coherence of corporate income taxation, the mission of Action 2 is to develop model treaty provisions regarding the design of domestic rules to neutralize the effect of hybrid instruments and entities. The Action 2 report identifies a common approach which will facilitate the convergence of national practices through domestic law and treaty rules to neutralize the effects of hybrid mismatch arrangements.

The domestic law recommendations target deduction/no inclusion (D/NI) mismatches and double deduction (DD) mismatches. The Action 2 report encourages domestic laws to deny a dividend exemption in respect to payments that are deductible in the country of residence of the payer, and to prevent taxpayers from using hybrid transfers to duplicate credits for source-country withholding tax. To avoid double taxation and to ensure that the mismatch is eliminated even when a jurisdiction has not adopted the rules, the recommended rules are divided into a primary response and a defensive rule. The defensive rule only applies where there is no hybrid mismatch rule in the other jurisdiction, or the rule is not applied to the entity or arrangement.[42] The Action 2 report also proposes the OECD Model Tax Convention including a new provision to ensure that an entity which is a hybrid entity under the tax laws of two treaty countries is eligible for treaty benefits in appropriate circumstances but that treaty benefits are not allowed for income that neither treaty country treats as income of one of its residents.

These recommendations will help prevent double non-taxation by eliminating the tax benefits of mismatches and put an end to costly multiple deductions for a single expense, deductions in one country without corresponding taxation in another, and the generation of multiple foreign tax credits for one amount of foreign tax paid. By neutralizing these mismatches, but not otherwise interfering with the use of such instruments or entities, the rules will inhibit the use of these

[41] OECD, *supra* note 37, p. 15.

[42] OECD, *Neutralizing the Effects of Hybrid Mismatch Arrangements*, OECD/G20 Base Erosion and Profit Shifting Project (OECD Publishing, 2014), p. 12, http://dx.doi.org/10.1787/9789264218819-en.

arrangements as a tool for BEPS without adversely impacting cross-border trade and investment.[43]

The solutions of Action 2 are soft recommendations, instead of minimum standards. Although countries have agreed to a general direction in neutralizing the effects of hybrid mismatches, it is difficult to achieve the agreements on minimum standards at this stage. As a result, the Action 2 must choose a common approach to encourage countries to converge over time through domestic law and bilateral treaties.

However, it is not clear how long it will take the countries to converge in a harmonized way, because changes of domestic law are up to the free choice of sovereign states, based on the consideration of complex factors including different legal traditions. Some jurisdictions might wish to continue to treat a certain instrument as indebtedness, while others continue to treat it as equity. For similar reasons, some jurisdictions will continue to treat certain hybrid entities and reverse hybrid entities as fiscally transparent conduits, while others will continue to treat them as separately taxable entities.

If a few countries are slow in the convergence process, the whole process of convergence will be delayed. Although countries may argue that their own measures are consistent with the direction of the BEPS project, the real consequences might depart from the direction originally decided by the BEPS project. Even worse, it is possible that a few jurisdictions will return to the race to the bottom and engage in aggressive tax competition through hybrid mismatches. In this event, the original direction of neutralizing the effects of hybrid mismatch arrangements might be compromised in certain jurisdictions.

We propose that the international community replace the common approach by global minimum standards soon. To better coordinate Action 2 with other relevant Actions, on interest expense deduction limitations, CFC rules, and treaty shopping, the latter actions should be also upgraded to minimum standards.

4.2.7 *The Limits of Action 3*

Many MNEs set up affiliated nonresident taxpayers, and route income of a resident enterprise through the nonresident affiliate. Although the OECD has not done significant work on controlled foreign company (CFC) rules in the past, thirty countries participating in the BEPS project, including the United States, introduced CFC rules and other anti-deferral rules to address the BEPS concerns.[44] While CFC rules lead to inclusion in the residence country of the ultimate parent, they

[43] OECD, *supra* note 17, at p. 13.

[44] Joint Committee on Taxation, *Background, Summary, and Implications of the OECD/G20 Base Erosion and Profit Shifting Project* (JCX-139-15) (Nov. 30, 2015), p. 18.

also have positive spillover effects in source countries because taxpayers have much less of an incentive to shift profits into a third, low-tax jurisdiction.[45]

As the CFC rules in many countries do not always counter BEPS in a comprehensive manner, the Action 3 aims at upgrading CFC rules. The report sets out recommendations in the form of building blocks for effective CFC rules, while recognizing the policy objectives of these rules vary among jurisdictions. The six building blocks include definition of a CFC, CFC exemptions and threshold requirements, definition of income, computation of income, attribution of income and prevention, and elimination of double taxation.[46]

Action 3 also identifies the challenges to existing CFC rules posed by mobile income such as that from intellectual property, services, and digital transactions, and allows jurisdictions to reflect on appropriate policies in this regard.[47]

The recommendations of Action 3 are not minimum standards. They provide flexibility to implement CFC rules and set out design options that could be implemented to be compliant with European Union law. However, they are designed to ensure that jurisdictions that choose to implement them will have rules that effectively prevent taxpayers from shifting income into foreign subsidiaries.

The Action 3 reforms should serve as a backstop to transfer pricing and other rules. Unfortunately, the CFC rules in Action 3 are weak. The building blocks are soft, weak recommendations based on best practices, instead of hard minimum standards.

The reason for the weak CFC rules could be explained by the stubborn insistence on tax incentives by some OECD countries, in particular the UK. According to the BEPS Monitoring Group, the UK and other countries "belie their assertions that they wish to see effective solutions to the problem of taxation of MNEs."[48]

It is very difficult to expect that the Action 3 will effectively reduce incentives for MNEs to abuse the system of exemption or deferral of tax on foreign income, and to shift income from operating affiliates in source jurisdictions to the tax havens. Moreover, it is also likely for the race to the bottom to continue to attract the headquarters of MNEs. Traditional tax havens will feel free to continue their behaviors, while other countries will be motivated to adopt low effective tax rates on foreign income or exempting such income altogether to attract foreign direct capital.

Although the compromise is inevitable in the process of developing Action 3, the OECD and the G20 should seek a win–win solution by maximizing the common denominator of international tax. We urge the international community to strength the weak CFC rules of Action 3, and to adopt full-inclusion CFC rules in the future, and replace the recommendations with minimum standards.

45 OECD, *supra* note 37, p. 16.
46 Joint Committee on Taxation, *supra* note 44, pp. 15–16.
47 OECD, *supra* note 17, at pp. 13–14.
48 BEPS Monitoring Group Report, *supra* note 21

4.2.8 The Limits of Action 4

The mission of Action 4 is to develop recommendations regarding best practices in the design of rules to prevent base erosion using interest expense, for example using related-party and third-party debt to achieve excessive interest deductions or to finance the production of exempt or deferred income, and other financial payments that are economically equivalent to interest payments.

The Action 4 report recommended an approach based on a fixed ratio rule, which limits an entity's net deductions for interest to a percentage of its earnings before interest, taxes, depreciation, and amortization (EBITDA), as measured under relevant tax principles. The recommended approach includes a "corridor" of possible ratios of between 10 percent and 30 percent for adoption by countries. Action 4 also includes factors that countries should consider in setting their fixed ratio within the corridor. A worldwide group ratio rule that allows an entity to exceed this limit in certain circumstances may supplement this approach.[49]

Action 4 was expected to ensure that an entity's net interest deductions are directly linked to the taxable income generated by its economic activities and foster increased coordination of national rules in this space.

As lower transaction cost and more business opportunities are the core features of the corporate group, it is extremely abnormal for the interest deductions to be greater in aggregate than each corporate group's consolidated interest costs to third parties. Theoretically speaking, if the interest cost of intragroup loans is unreasonably higher than the loans from third parties, the group and its members would reduce the interest loans.

While in theory this may make sense, firms have not operated in such a way. One of the pressure areas for the BEPS concerns is that intragroup debt usually exceeds the firm's overall borrowing from third parties, and the interest deductibility is excessive.[50] Therefore, the limitation of deductions of interest should be strong enough to root out BEPS opportunities.

Unfortunately, the Action 4 Report is not minimum standards. Its goal is to facilitate the convergence of domestic rules in interest deductibility. Therefore, its success is entirely dependent upon voluntary coordination between through new domestic rules. If the progress of implementation and operation of the recommendations is not satisfactory, the effectiveness of this Action will be compromised. It is very challenging for the jurisdictions to address excessive deductible payments and address competitiveness considerations at the same time, without having appropriate interest expense limitations lead to double taxation.

49 Joint Committee on Taxation, *supra* note 44, 16.

50 Jennifer Blouin et al., *Thin Capitalization Rules and Multinational Firm Capital Structure* (Jan. 2014), https://www.imf.org/external/pubs/ft/wp/2014/wp1412.pdf.

More problematic is the substance of Action 4, which prioritizes an interest deduction cap within a suggested band of 10–30 percent, with the option of using apportioned consolidated interest costs if they are higher. Such a recommendation is not as powerful and strong as anticipated.[51] The formula of a fixed cap does not match best with every sector and firm. That is why the Action 4 report recognizes the need to develop suitable and specific rules that address BEPS risks in banking and insurance industries. Although it does make sense to respect the specific features of banking and insurance industries, other industries might also claim the special treatments from the BEPS project. It is not realistic to design the specific rules for every firm, industry, or sector.

Before the proposal of a fixed cap was adopted, there were also other better proposals.[52] For instance, based on the doctrine of unitary entity, a proposal suggested apportionment of the MNE group's consolidated interest expenses based on EBITDA, figures for which are readily available. However, the initial proposals have been watered down to recommendations prioritizing a fixed cap.[53]

We strongly urge that the bottom line of international tax law reform is that interest deductions may not be greater in aggregate than each corporate group's consolidated interest costs to third parties.

The recommendations in Action 4 do not prohibit the countries from seeking better alternative solutions for effective control of interest deductibility. If the countries really have no other choice but to follow the default recommendation of a fixed cap on deductions, they should use the lowest limit to deter aggressive interest deductions by MNEs. In fact, even the lowest limit still falls in the range of unrelated loans.[54] Of course, coordination is always important to prevent the MNEs from defeating all the countries by abusing the different rules around the world.

4.2.9 *The Limits of Action 5*

Harmful tax practices, especially preferential regimes together with a lack of transparency in connection with certain rulings, have been widely used by MNEs for artificial profit shifting. Responding to this, the BEPS report calls for proposals to develop "solutions to counter harmful regimes more effectively, taking into account factors such as transparency and substance." In furtherance of this, the mission of Action 5 revamps the work on harmful tax practices with a priority on improving transparency, including compulsory spontaneous exchange on rulings related to preferential regimes, and on requiring substantial activity for any preferential

[51] *See* BEPS Monitoring Group Report, *supra* note 21, Action 4.
[52] *Id.*
[53] *Id.*
[54] *Id.*

regime.[55] The Action 5 report sets out a minimum standard based on an agreed-upon methodology to assess whether there is substantial activity in a preferential regime. In the context of IP regimes such as patent boxes, consensus has been reached on using the "nexus" approach.

This approach uses expenditures in the country as a proxy for substantial activity and ensures that taxpayers benefiting from these regimes did in fact engage in R&D and incurred actual expenditures on such activities. The same principle can also be applied to other preferential regimes so that such regimes would be found to require substantial activities where they grant benefits to a taxpayer.[56] To improve the transparency of preference regimes, a framework has been agreed upon for mandatory spontaneous exchange of information on rulings that could give rise to possible BEPS concerns.

The harmful tax practices proliferating in many countries are a clear example of race to the bottom. Such practices have triggered numerous BEPS opportunities. Hence, Action 5 is designed to effectively reverse the history of this, which damages all countries, including the jurisdiction engaging in harmful tax competition.

Different from the Actions 2–4, Action 5 sets out a minimum standard in terms of substance and transparency that include the results of the application of the elaborated substantial activity and transparency factors to several preferential regimes. Unfortunately, Action 5 is still very weak.

First, the effectiveness of the implementation of Action 5 is still voluntary. Irrational developed and developing countries could still engage in harmful practices, in the name of national competitiveness or attracting international capital.

Second, although the work of the Forum on Harmful Tax Practices (FHTP) will be refocused to develop more effective solutions, no penalty could be imposed by the FHTP. In fact, all forty-three preferential regimes reviewed by the FHTP were inconsistent with the nexus approach.[57] However, there is no effective penalty against violators. It is nearly impossible for all countries to voluntarily and simultaneously bring their IP regimes into compliance with the nexus approach.

Third, the application of the broad and general principles of "nexus" and "substance" to innovation boxes might create different and divergent standards in different countries. The consideration of national competitiveness or specific domestic political and economic circumstances might lead to new forms of harmful tax preference regimes.

Fourth, some developed countries have set bad examples for developing countries in fighting against the harmful practices. As observed by the BEPS Monitoring Group, the UK's strong defense of its patent box introduced in 2012 resulted in a

[55] OECD, *supra* note 37, p. 17.

[56] *Id.* at p. 14.

[57] Joint Committee on Taxation, *supra* note 44, p. 21. This document can also be found on the Joint Committee on Taxation website at www.jct.gov.

compromise agreed with Germany, based on a "modified nexus approach," and a transition to the new standard by 2021; other countries quickly announced that they would introduce their own schemes (Ireland, Italy, Switzerland), and business pressures have led to proposals elsewhere also (Germany, the United States).[58]

As the harmful tax practices always end up hurting every country, we urge the international community to abandon the voluntary self-policing model, and to establish a mandatory monitoring model based on transparency, accountability, condemnation, and even economic sanctions. Harmful tax practices are unjustified and immoral. They are against the core values of international tax law. Therefore, it is inadequate, and even inappropriate, to require countries to conduct cost/benefit analyses of the harmful incentives. In fact, many countries still attempt to acquire the limited selfish benefit at the price of negative spillovers on the other countries. The harmful tax practices themselves have demonstrated the failure of voluntary self-policing approaches.

Of course, all countries should be encouraged to behave themselves in terms of higher standards of transparency, monitoring, review, and accountability of tax incentives. If a country really wants to win the trust from the global community, it must take the firm initiative in this regard. To activate the monitoring function of FHTP, the mechanism of transparent investigation, impartial peer review, reasonable reward, and adequate sanction will be indispensable.

4.2.10 *The Limits of Action 6*

As treaty abuse, especially treaty-shopping, may give rise to double non-taxation, treaty abuse is one of the most important sources of BEPS concerns. Although the Commentary on Article 1 of the OECD Model Tax Convention before 2015 clearly included several provisions to address situations of treaty abuse, tighter treaty anti-abuse clauses coupled with the exercise of taxing rights under domestic laws are expected to repair source.

The Action 6 report includes a minimum standard on preventing and new rules that provide safeguards to prevent treaty abuse while still offering a certain degree of flexibility. The new treaty anti-abuse rules first address treaty shopping, which involves strategies through which a person who is not a resident of a state attempts to obtain the benefits of a tax treaty concluded by that state. Other changes to the OECD Model Tax Convention have been agreed to, to ensure that treaties do not inadvertently prevent the application of domestic anti-abuse rules. A clarification that tax treaties are not intended to be used to generate double non-taxation is provided through a reformulation of the title and preamble of the Model Tax Convention. The report also contains policy considerations to be considered when

[58] BEPS Monitoring Group Report, *supra* note 21.

entering tax treaties with certain low- or no-tax jurisdictions.[59] The three-part approach is adopted by the Action 6 report to counter treaty abuse.

First, countries would include in treaties a clear statement that tax evasion, avoidance, or treaty shopping is not condoned by the treaty countries. Second, a specific anti-abuse rule of limitation-on-benefits (LOB) will be included in the OECD Model treaty, to ensure that there is a sufficient connection between the entity and the country of residence. Third, a more general anti-abuse rule, based on the principal purposes of transactions or arrangements (the principal purposes test, or PPT), will be included in the OECD Model treaty, to address situations not caught under the LOB rule.[60]

Although the three-part approach adopted by the Action 6 will help counter treaty abuse, both the LOB article and the PPT provision have their own advantages and issues.

Although the PPT provision is general enough to cover all the treaty shopping schemes, its interpretation and application heavily depend on discretionary decisions of the tax authorities or the courts,[61] and, while the LOB article is easily understood and applied, a proliferation of treaty-specific varieties of LOB articles would lead to over complexity in the treaties or domestic legislation.

Therefore, the success of the PPT article relies on the individual country's competence, expertise, and resources, especially the useful information relevant to the treaty shopping behaviors. Unfortunately, many developing countries do not have the necessary capacity and information to make the best use of the PPT provision. To offer useful guidance and reference to the developing countries, we urge the OECD/G20 to publish all the latest cases and rulings on the PPT article on a regular basis.

To sharpen the competence of developing countries in applying the anti-abuse clauses, spontaneous, systematic exchange of information between treaty partners should be established to ascertain the prerequisites for the taxpayer to enjoy treaty benefits. Of course, a more ambitious, global, spontaneous, comprehensive, and systematic platform for exchange of BEPS data between and among all jurisdictions should be created in the future. Country-by-Country Reporting (CbCR) is one of the important parts of this data bank.

Although the countries may vary substantially from each other in terms of the legislation framework, judicial interpretation tools, and administrative ability, all countries involved should do their best in endorsing the minimum standard of protection against treaty shopping. In this way, the model treaty provisions included in the Action 6 report will be better adapted to the specificities of individual states and the circumstances of the negotiation of bilateral conventions. To reduce the

59 OECD, *supra* note 17, at pp. 14–15.

60 Joint Committee on Taxation, *supra* note 44, at p. 21.

61 BEPS Monitoring Group Report, *supra* note 21.

treaty renegotiation cost and to prevent the emergence of new treaty shopping platforms, a clear and effective anti-abuse provision should be incorporated as the core article of the proposed multilateral convention.

Finally, another important issue is the policy considerations relevant to treaty entitlement of collective investment vehicles (CIVs) and non-CIV funds.[62] The OECD will continue to evaluate issues related to entitlement to treaty benefits by certain types of investment funds by early 2016.[63] But it is challenging to achieve a satisfied consensus on some key issues, as there are different definitions of CIV in different jurisdictions. Furthermore, CIV may be organized in different forms, including partnerships, agreements, trusts, or incorporated entities.

4.2.11 *The Limits of Action 7*

Current tax treaties "generally provide that the business profits of a foreign enterprise are taxable in a State only to the extent that the enterprise has in that State a permanent establishment (PE) to which the profits are attributable." Stemming from this, the definition of PE included in tax treaties is crucial in determining whether a nonresident enterprise must pay income tax in another state. However, in many countries, the interpretation of the treaty rules on agency-PE allows contracts for the sale of goods belonging to a foreign enterprise to be negotiated and concluded in a country by the sales force of a local subsidiary of that foreign enterprise without the profits from these sales being taxable to the same extent as they would be if the sales were made by a distributor. In many cases, this encouraged MNEs to replace arrangements under which the local subsidiary traditionally acted as a distributor by "commissionaire arrangements" which shifted profits out of the country where the sales take place without a substantive change in the functions performed in that country. Similarly, MNEs may artificially fragment their operations among multiple group entities to qualify for the exceptions to PE status.[64]

To address techniques used to inappropriately avoid the tax nexus, including through the replacement of distributors with commissionaire arrangements or through the artificial fragmentation of business activities, Action 7 developed changes to the definition of PE in Article 5 of the OECD Model Tax Convention, which is widely used as the basis for negotiating tax treaties.

A person who acts exclusively or almost exclusively on behalf of one or more closely related enterprises is not considered an independent agent. The exceptions from creating a fixed place of business for specific activities (such as storage, display,

[62] OECD, *Preventing the Granting of Treaty Benefits in Inappropriate Circumstances, OECD/G20 Base Erosion and Profit Shifting Project* (OECD Publishing, 2014), p. 20, http://dx.doi.org/10.1787/9789264219120-en.

[63] Joint Committee on Taxation, *supra* note 44, at p. 22.

[64] OECD, *supra* note 37, at p. 19.

or delivery of goods) apply only if the overall activity of the fixed place or business is of a preparatory or auxiliary character.[65]

Although Action 7 developed changes to the definition of PE in Article 5 of the OECD Model Tax Convention, the changes are not substantially innovative. This is because the definition of taxable presence still rests on the obsolete PE concept, which requires physical presence for a period of six or twelve months in relation to the activity generating the profit attributable to it. Both the traditional PE definition and the proposed changes in Action 7 are based on the independent entity principle. Without disconnecting the taxable presence and the independent entity principle, it is unlikely to make groundbreaking progress in changing the definition of PE.

Action 7 only targets abuse of the PE definition, instead of rewriting the definition of PE itself, which itself causes many issues. However, not all forms of abuse are covered in this Action. The anti-fragmentation rule in Action 7 is only applicable to artificial fragmentation of sales functions, but not to the artificial fragmentation of non-sales-related functions. This means that MNEs will be free to continue fragmentations of non-sales-related functions, and attribute higher profits to tax havens. According to the findings of the BEPS Monitoring Group, the proposals of Action 7 could only affect some MNEs, such as those engaged in internet-based selling, and which own warehouses in the country of sales. However, the proposals would not deal with sales of immaterial products, or services, so they would affect physical, but not electronic, books and DVDs, but not streaming services. This will greatly undercut the effectiveness of the reforms, especially as the direction of goods and the economy continues to trend away from physical products and toward intangibles. In fact, the MNEs have already restructured their production chains to separate basic manufacturing, which can be allocated a "routine" profit, from functions such as R&D or design, which may be considered high-value-adding and can be located where they will be lightly taxed.[66]

Even the rules against artificial fragmentation of sales functions have loopholes. For instance, although an entity will be deemed to have a PE, if activities can be said to be "preparatory or auxiliary" to sales, the terms "preparatory or auxiliary" are not clearly defined.

Different jurisdictions may have different definitions of the agent. In European civil law jurisdictions, a commissionaire acts in their own name for the account of a principal, but no relationship is created between the customer and the principal. As a commissionaire is not generally viewed as a dependent agent by virtue of the commissionaire status, the activities and place of business of a commissionaire are not attributed to the principal in civil law jurisdictions. However, such an arrangement could create agency in common law countries. Therefore, the anti-fragmentation

[65] Joint Committee on Taxation, *supra* note 44, at p. 23.
[66] BEPS Monitoring Group Report, *supra* note 21.

rule should adopt a functional approach, which should be compatible with the different legal traditions of agency law in different countries.

According to the Action 7 report, follow-up works will be undertaken to provide additional guidance on profit attribution to the PEs resulting from the proposed changes, and to incorporate the proposed changes into the Model Tax Convention.[67] For the latter work, additional clarification on the new treaty wording should be provided, any unintended consequences of the changes should be addressed, and the BEPS issue related to the global trading of financial products should be considered.

We urge that the limited scope of the anti-fragmentation rule will be expanded to cover all the schemes of abuse of the PE definition. If possible, the continuing work should also reconsider the fundamental weakness of the "functionally separate entity" approach and reorient the future reform of anti-fragmentation based on the single and unitary entity principle.

4.2.12 *The Limits of Actions 8–10*

A major BEPS concern is transfer pricing. Transfer pricing rules, which are set out in Article 9 of tax treaties based on the OECD and UN Model Tax Conventions and the Transfer Pricing Guidelines (TPG), are used to determine, using the arm's-length principle, the price for transactions within an MNE group. Transfer pricing rules serve to allocate income earned by a multinational enterprise among those countries in which the company does business. However, the existing transfer pricing rules fail to properly price and efficiently allocate the income of MNEs among jurisdictions. Some MNEs have been able to use those rules to separate income from the economic activities that produce the income and to shift it into low-tax environments. This most often results from transfers of intangibles and other mobile assets for less than full value, the over capitalization of low-taxed group companies, and from contractual allocations of risk to low-tax environments in transactions that would be unlikely to occur between unrelated parties.[68]

As special measures, either within or beyond the arm's-length principle, may be required with respect to intangible assets, risk, and over capitalization to address these flaws, the mission of Actions 8–10 is to assure that transfer pricing outcomes are in line with value creation.[69] The existing standards in this area have been clarified and strengthened, including guidance on the arm's-length principle, and an approach to ensure the appropriate pricing of hard-to-value intangibles has been agreed upon within the arm's-length principle.

67 OECD, *supra* note 17, at p. 8.

68 OECD, *supra* note 37, at pp. 19–20.

69 *Id.* at p. 20.

As misallocation of the profits generated by valuable intangibles has heavily contributed to BEPS concerns, Action 8 aims at developing rules to prevent BEPS by moving intangibles among group members. This involves adopting a broad and clearly delineated definition of intangibles, ensuring that profits associated with the transfer and use of intangibles are appropriately allocated in accordance with value creation; developing transfer pricing rules or special measures for transfers of hard-to-value intangibles; and updating the guidance on cost contribution arrangements. Action 8 looks at transfer pricing issues relating to controlled transactions involving intangibles, since they are often hard to value. To assure the appropriate pricing of hard-to-value intangibles, Action 8 has devised an additional tool for countries to address the use of information asymmetry between taxpayers and tax authorities to undervalue intragroup transfers of intangibles.

Action 9 aims at developing rules to prevent BEPS by transferring risks among, or allocating excessive capital to, group members. This involves adopting transfer pricing rules or special measures to ensure that inappropriate returns will not accrue to an entity solely. Under Action 9, contractual allocations of risk are respected only when they are supported by actual decision-making.

Action 10 focuses on other high-risk transactions and aims at developing rules to prevent BEPS by engaging in transactions which would not, or would only very rarely, occur between third parties. This action adopted transfer pricing rules or special measures to clarify the circumstances in which transactions can be recharacterized; clarify the application of transfer pricing methods, in particular profit splits, in the context of global value chains; and provide protection against common types of base eroding payments, such as management fees and head office expenses. Action 10 deals with the scope for addressing profit allocations resulting from controlled transactions which are not commercially rational, the scope for targeting the use of transfer pricing methods in a way which results in diverting profits from the most economically important activities of the MNE group, and the use of certain type of payments between members of the MNE group (such as management fees and head office expenses) to erode the tax base in the absence of alignment with the value creation.

The combined report contains revised guidance which ensures that transfer pricing rules secure outcomes that better align operational profits with the actual economic activities which generate them. The report also contains guidance on transactions involving cross-border commodity transactions and on low value-adding intragroup services. As those two areas were identified as of critical importance by developing countries, the guidance will be supplemented with further work mandated by the G20 Development Working Group, which will provide knowledge, best practices, and tools for developing countries to price commodity transactions for transfer pricing purposes and to prevent the erosion of their tax bases through common types of base-eroding payments.[70] Actions 8–10 are the most important

[70] OECD, *supra* note 17, at pp. 15–16.

part of the BEPS project in addressing related-party transactions of MNEs. Of course, the transfer pricing documentation requirements in Action 13 are also closely relevant to these actions. The proposals on transfer pricing have made extensive revisions to the OECD Transfer Pricing Guidelines, which will further strengthen the discretionary power for tax authorities to adjust them. Many proposals take the form of international standards, which could have some direct effects as international "soft law." Although the goal is laudable, the approach of Actions 8–10 is very problematic. The solutions still focus on patching up the dysfunctional rules built on the arm's-length principle, which again is rooted in the principle of the separate independent entity. According to the arm's-length principle, all intragroup transactions are supposed to be rational and reasonable as commercial transactions between unrelated parties in comparable economic circumstances.

To implement the arm's-length principle, Actions 8–10 made transfer pricing rules more sophisticated and complex, to authorize tax authorities to recharacterize the related-party transactions within the MNE group. To find the available comparables, the tax authorities are required to make careful, informed judgments in good faith based on the subjective analysis of detailed facts and circumstances relevant to the functions, assets, and risks undertaken by different group members located in different jurisdictions.

As the approach of Actions 8–10 is inevitably subjective and discretionary, the real effect of the attribution of the tax base of MNEs will rely on the negotiation between MNEs and tax authorities. To avoid under taxation, tax authorities will tend to maximize their discretionary power of recharacterizing, which might lead to strong opposition from the MNE taxpayers. For the similar reasoning, to avoid over-taxation, MNEs might upgrade their aggressive BEPS schemes. As a result, both enforcement and compliance costs will be increased, and more disputes will be created.[71] Moreover, as the subjective judgment will be made independently and separately by different national authorities, different jurisdictions might make conflicting recharacterization conclusions on the same intragroup transaction.

The complicated and uncertain approach of recharacterizing intragroup transactions is most challenging for developing countries, as they do not have the necessary resources and expertise to administer the revised version of the Transfer Pricing Guidelines. It is also very costly or even impossible for developed countries to search for precise and genuine comparables to apply the arm's-length principle. Although the G20 Development Working Group promised to help the developing countries to deal with the problem of lack of comparables,[72] it is not clear whether a simple, effective win–win solution on pricing method will be made available anytime soon. We don't wish to see any one-sided solutions, including purely subjective discretion favored by tax authorities, or purely notational transfer pricing method favored by MNEs.

[71] *See* Avi-Yonah, *Rise and Fall*, *supra* note 22, for examples.

[72] *See* BEPS Monitoring Group Report, *supra* note 21.

As indicated earlier, the principle of the separate independent entity and the arm's-length principle are at most legal fictions which do not actually exist in the commercial reality. In fact, even the terms of transactions between independent and unrelated parties are not necessarily fair and reasonable as two parties are rarely equal in negotiating power. As the comparability analysis is not practical and feasible as anticipated, we propose the formulary apportionment system based on the single unitary entity principle. In other words, MNE groups will be treated as a single and unitary entity, and all intragroup transactions will be disregarded. Compared with the approach of separate entity, this route will be simpler, direct, and effective in addressing the BEPS concerns arising from intragroup related-party transactions. The OECD has already noticed the proposed alternative income allocation systems, including formula-based systems. Unfortunately, the OECD refused to replace the current transfer pricing system. The reason is not the flaw of the proposed alternatives, but the familiarity with the current approach and the reluctance to switch to new approach by launching ambitious reforms. In the words of the OECD, "the importance of concerted action and the practical difficulties associated with agreeing to and implementing the details of a new system consistently across all countries mean that, rather than seeking to the best course is to directly address the flaws in the current system, in particular with respect to returns related to intangible assets, risk and over-capitalization."[73]

As early as 2013, the OECD claimed that "there is consensus among governments that moving to a system of formulary apportionment of profits is not a viable way forward; it is also unclear that the behavioral changes companies might adopt in response to the use of a formula would lead to approach."[74]

Although the United States and other states stubbornly defended and insisted on the dysfunctional arm's-length principle for transfer pricing adjustments, there is no credible evidence to indicate that the thirty-four OECD members have reached a clear and concrete agreement on unanimously opposing the system of formulary apportionment of profits based on the single entity principle. Moreover, there are no findings to indicate that the single entity approach has more weaknesses and less strengths compared to the separate entity approach.[75] To offer easy, certain, clear, and predictable solutions to the BEPS concerns arising from transfer pricing, formulary apportionment methods should be adopted, and the allocation of assets, payroll, sales, and other factors needs to be restructured and weighted. This will better allocate the tax base of MNE according to the location where economic activities and value creation take place. To make the formulary apportionment approach successful and sustainable, the principle of separate independent entity needs to be replaced by the principle of single unitary entity.

73 OECD, *supra* note 37, at p. 20.

74 *Id.* at p. 14.

75 *See* Avi-Yonah et al., *supra* note 24, for the economic arguments.

4.2.13 *The Limits of Action 11*

As "significant data limitations severely constrain economic analyses of the scale and economic impact of BEPS," improving the availability and analysis methodologies of data on BEPS is critical for the implementation of the BEPS project. The original title of Action 11 was "Establish methodologies to collect and analyze data on BEPS and the actions to address it." This action aims at "developing recommendations regarding indicators of the scale and economic impact of BEPS and ensuring that tools are available to monitor and evaluate the effectiveness and economic impact of the actions taken to address BEPS on an ongoing basis."

The Action 11 report adjusted the title to "Measuring and Monitoring BEPS." This report defines BEPS as relating to "arrangements that achieve no or low taxation by shifting profits away from the jurisdictions where the activities creating those profits take place or by exploiting gaps in the interaction of domestic tax rules where corporate income is not taxed at all."[76] The report has constructed a dashboard of six BEPS indicators, including the concentration of foreign direct investment (FDI) relative to GDP; high profit rates of low-taxed affiliates of top global MNEs; high profit rates of MNE affiliates in lower-tax locations; effective tax rates of large MNE affiliates relative to non-MNE entities with similar characteristics; concentration of royalty receipts relative to research and development spending; and interest expense to income ratios of MNE affiliates in countries with above-average statutory tax rates.

The research also finds significant non-fiscal economic distortions arising from BEPS and proposes recommendations for taking better advantage of available tax data and improving analyses to support the monitoring of BEPS in the future, including through analytical tools to assist countries to evaluate the fiscal effects of BEPS and impact of BEPS. Going forward, enhancing the economic analysis and monitoring of BEPS will require countries to improve the collection, compilation, and analysis of data.[77]

Although the final report of Action 11 conducted an in-depth research on measuring and monitoring BEPS and offered recommendations on collecting and disseminating data to facilitate analysis of BEPS, there are some weaknesses which clearly need to be improved.

For example, this report emphasizes that analysis of BEPS should not rely on any one indicator and requires that the indicators should be viewed collectively to determine the scale and scope of BEPS. It is impossible for each of the six indicators to have equal weight in each jurisdiction. Unfortunately, this report has not offered a reliable formula of differentiating the separate weights of the six indicators suitable for the jurisdictions.

[76] OECD, *Measuring and Monitoring BEPS* (Sept. 16, 2014), p. 42.

[77] OECD, *supra* note 17, at p. 16.

This report offers recommendations concerning data collection and dissemination to facilitate the analysis of BEPS for participating countries, and proposes to collect new data under Actions 5, 12, and 13. However, this report has not proposed to publish the CbCRs worldwide, in order to make the transfer pricing information available to all the countries and the public.

We live in a society heavily reliant and integrated with the use of big data. Unfortunately, this report has not offered satisfactory big data solutions for the countries to use in a digital society. We believe that it is necessary to develop and deploy a global BEPS data bank as the basic platform for collecting, exchanging, disseminating, and analyzing of BEPS information all over the world.

4.2.14 *The Limits of Action 12*

The availability of timely, targeted, and comprehensive information on aggressive tax planning strategies is extremely essential to enable governments to quickly identify risk areas. However, such information is often unavailable to tax administrations. While audits remain a key source of relevant information, they suffer from several constraints as tools for the early detection of aggressive tax planning threats.

The mission of Action 12 is to require taxpayers to disclose their aggressive tax planning arrangements by developing recommendations for mandatory disclosure rules for aggressive or abusive transactions, arrangements, or structures, taking into consideration the administrative costs for tax authorities and businesses.

The Action 12 report provides a framework for countries to design and improve a regime that guarantees early information on aggressive or abusive tax planning schemes. The recommendations provide the necessary flexibility to balance a country's need for better and more timely information with the compliance burdens for taxpayers. It also sets out specific best practice recommendations for rules targeting international tax schemes, as well as for the development and implementation of more effective information exchange and cooperation between tax administrations.[78]

The purpose of Action 12 report is to enable the governments to have early access to information, and to quickly respond to systemic tax risks through informed risk assessment, audits, or changes to legislation or tax policies.

However, the recommendations for taxpayers to disclose their aggressive tax planning arrangements are, once again, not minimum standards. Countries are free to decide whether to introduce mandatory disclosure regimes. Currently, only seven countries[79] have mandatory disclosure regime in their domestic legislation.

As the recommendations are not mandatory, it is easy for the MNEs to avoid the mandatory requirements in certain jurisdictions by incorporation in another

[78] *Id.* at p. 16.

[79] Ireland, Israel, Korea, Portugal, South Africa, the UK, and the United States.

jurisdiction without such requirements. It is also possible for the jurisdictions to refuse to adopt a mandatory disclosure regime, thereby precipitating more harmful competition to the benefit of MNEs at the expense of tax authorities and the single tax principle.

In our opinion, mandatory disclosure rules should be mandated in each jurisdiction, and the liabilities for violations of the disclosure rules should be designed and enforced in a fair and transparent manner.

4.2.15 *The Limits of Action 13*

A key issue in the administration of transfer pricing rules is the asymmetry of information between taxpayers and tax administrations, which could undermine the administration of the arm's-length principle and enhance opportunities for BEPS.

In many countries, tax administrations do not have the whole picture of a taxpayer's global value chain. Divergences between approaches to transfer pricing documentation requirements could also increase the compliance costs for businesses. In this respect, it is important that adequate information about the relevant functions performed by other members of the MNE group in respect of intragroup services and other transactions is made available to the tax authorities.[80]

Although MNEs demand transparency of tax law administration, they are reluctant to be transparent themselves. BEPS strategies will be difficult for MNEs to implement in a transparent international tax environment. Improved and better-coordinated transfer pricing documentation is vital to the reliable quality of information provided to tax administrations.

Therefore, it is urgent to develop rules regarding transfer pricing documentation to enhance transparency for tax administration, taking into consideration the compliance costs for businesses. The MNEs should provide all relevant governments with needed information on their global allocation of the income, economic activity, and taxes paid among countries according to a common template.[81]

The Action 13 report contains a three-tiered approach to transfer pricing documentation, including minimum standards for CbCR.

First, the guidance on transfer pricing documentation requires MNEs to provide tax administrations with high-level information regarding their global business operations and transfer pricing policies in a "master file" that is to be available to all relevant tax administrations.

Second, it requires that detailed transactional transfer pricing documentation be provided in a "local file" specific to each country, identifying material related-party transactions, the amounts involved in those transactions, and the company's analysis of the transfer pricing determinations they have made about those transactions.

80 OECD, *supra* note 37, at pp. 22–23.
81 *Id.* at p. 23.

Third, large MNEs are required to file a CbCR annually that will provide, for each tax jurisdiction in which they do business, the amount of revenue, profit before income tax and income tax paid and accrued, and other indicators of economic activities. The large MNEs refer to those with annual consolidated group revenue equal to or exceeding EUR 750 million. CbCRs should be filed in the ultimate parent entity's jurisdiction and shared automatically through government-to-government exchanges of information. In limited circumstances, secondary mechanisms, including local filing, can be used as a backup. An agreed implementation plan will ensure that information is provided to the tax administration in a timely manner, that confidentiality of the reported information is preserved, and that the CbCRs are used appropriately.[82]

It is recommended that the first CbCRs be required to be filed for MNEs' fiscal years starting from January 1, 2016.[83] Of course, some jurisdictions may need time to transform the reporting system into their domestic legislation.

For the first time, the three documentation tiers will require taxpayers to disclose consistent transfer pricing positions and will provide tax administrations with useful information of the entire picture of MNE operation, and enable them to assess transfer pricing risks, to make determinations about whether, where, when, and how audit resources can most effectively be deployed. By ensuring a consistent approach to transfer pricing documentation across countries, and by limiting the need for multiple filings of CbCRs through making use of information exchange among tax administrations, MNEs will also see the benefits in terms of a more limited compliance burden.[84] In fact, anticipation of this reporting system has already begun to discourage aggressive tax planning.[85]

The annual CbCR is the most important measure in Action 13 to ensure the minimum transparency of transfer pricing. However, there are some limits to it.

First, the threshold of EUR 750 million of annual consolidated group revenue is unreasonably high for the major MNEs in developing countries, although this threshold is tailor made for the need of developed countries. Such threshold will exclude many large MNEs from the CbCR requirement and deprive developing countries of the access to the information of MNEs below the threshold. In fact, many large MNEs have annual consolidated group revenue less than EUR 750 million. Some large MNEs will be motivated enough to manipulate their group revenue to a level of less than EUR 750 million. In our opinion, all MNEs should be subject to the CbCR requirement.

Second, all the transfer pricing documents are only required to be submitted to the tax authorities, but not to the public and civil society organizations. It seems that

[82] OECD, *supra* note 17, at p. 17.
[83] *Id*. at 6.
[84] *Id*. at 17.
[85] *Id*. at 6–7.

the philosophy of this institutional arrangement is to preserve the confidentiality of the information and to ensure the appropriate use by the government. However, commercial confidentiality is not strong enough to defeat the right of the public to information of BEPS. The relevant stakeholders and the public need to have access to the MNEs' transfer pricing documentation. The reason is very simple: BEPS could hurt other taxpayers and stakeholders in relevant jurisdictions. We believe that the BEPS concerns will be more effectively addressed with the active and informed participation of the stakeholders and the public based on disclosed transfer pricing. Under the public pressure and support, the domestic legislatures and tax authorities will be more diligent and competent in tackling the BEPS issues. Of course, a high level of transparency will also benefit the MNEs, as it will significantly reduce compliance burden, and will improve their public image of credibility in terms of BEPS concerns.

Third, the CbCRs are only required to file with the tax authority of the MNE's ultimate parent entity's jurisdiction, instead of all the tax authorities of the jurisdictions where the MNEs have taxable business presences. To ensure rapid availability of CbCRs, we urge the CbCRs to be shared automatically and simultaneously between and among all the interested jurisdictions which have good reason to believe the existence of taxable presences by MNEs. Of course, if the MNEs' transfer pricing documentation is made available to the public, the double standards will be totally rooted out.

Fourth, although the content of the CbCRs covers the major issues of transfer pricing, it is difficult to exhaust all the data needed by tax authorities to assess the BEPS concerns arising from transfer pricing. Therefore, necessary data should be added into the CbCRs on a regular basis.

4.2.16 *The Limits of Action 14*

The Action 14 report set forth a minimum standard with respect to the resolution of treaty-related disputes. There is a strong political commitment to the effective and timely resolution of disputes through the mutual agreement procedure (MAP). The Forum on Tax Administration (FTA) will continue its efforts to improve MAP through its recently established MAP Forum.

To minimize and control the uncertain outcomes and to remove double taxation as an obstacle to cross-border trade and investment, it is necessary to develop solutions to address obstacles that prevent countries from solving treaty-related disputes under the MAP, including the absence of arbitration provisions in most treaties and the fact that access to MAP and arbitration may be denied in certain cases.[86]

[86] OECD, *supra* note 37, at p. 23.

The commitment also includes the establishment of an effective monitoring mechanism to ensure the minimum standard is met and countries make further progress to rapidly resolve disputes. In addition, a large group of countries have committed to quickly adopt mandatory and binding arbitration in their bilateral tax treaties.[87] Rapid implementation of this commitment will be achieved through the inclusion of arbitration as an optional provision in the multilateral instrument that was developed to implement the BEPS treaty-related measures.[88]

The MAP is the ideal win–win platform to effectively resolve treaty-related disputes between two countries. However, the MAP does not always work effectively, because any party in the dispute could block the MAP unilaterally and Action 14 has not offered remedies for the unilateral deadlock of MAP.

Mandatory arbitration is the suitable remedy for the MAP deadlock. However, Action 14 has not proposed the minimum standard of mandatory arbitration. At most, this action encourages the inclusion of arbitration as an optional provision in the multilateral instruments.

It is important to note that mandatory binding arbitration should be supported by clear and predictable substantive rules, due process of law, and impartial and competent arbitrators.[89] Without effective and fair implementation, countries will not accept arbitration that they may deem to be unfair or wrong. In our opinion, each party may freely appoint one arbitrator to achieve fairness and buy in from the countries in the dispute. If the two parties are unable to collaborate in choosing the chief arbitrator, the arbitration body itself may appoint the chief arbitrator.

4.2.17 *The Limits of Action 15*

The success of the BEPS project depends on swift implementation of the measures. Some actions of the BEPS project have resulted in recommendations regarding domestic law provisions, as well as in changes to the Commentary to the OECD Model Tax Convention and the Transfer Pricing Guidelines. However, changes to the OECD Model Tax Convention are not directly effective without amendments to bilateral tax treaties. It would be very time-consuming and impractical to amend the more than 3,000 bilateral treaties currently in existence on a treaty-by-treaty basis. The Action 15 report explores the technical feasibility of a multilateral instrument to implement the BEPS treaty-related measures and amend bilateral tax treaties across the board. It concludes that a multilateral instrument is desirable and feasible, and that negotiations for such an instrument should be convened quickly. Based on this analysis, a mandate has been developed for an ad hoc group, open to the participation of all countries, to develop the multilateral instrument and

87 OECD, *supra* note 17, at p. 17.

88 *Id.* at 7.

89 The model would be arbitration under the Bilateral Investment Treaties, such as NAFTA.

open it for signature in 2016. So far, about ninety countries are participating in the work.[90]

The goal of Action 15 is to streamline the implementation of the tax treaty-related BEPS measures by drafting a multilateral instrument.[91] Although this action represents a significant step toward multilateralism, the proposed instrument has not been provided for debate. To make the multilateral instrument coherent, inclusive, and feasible, the developing process should be open and transparent. Namely, the negotiations should be published, all relevant stakeholders should be heard, and public debate should be meaningful.

However, participation in developing the multilateral instrument is voluntary, and participating countries are not obligated to sign it.[92] This liberal approach intends to encourage more countries to participate in the development process. However, it is uncertain how many countries will sign it in the end. If the participating countries are obligated to sign the multilateral instrument, many countries will be not interested in participation. This dilemma reflects inadequate multilateralism represented by the OECD. Therefore, we believe that UN is the most qualified international body to develop a universally binding multilateral instrument to address BEPS.

4.3 RECONSIDERING THE INTERNATIONAL TAX REGIME: A MULTILATERAL SOLUTION

It is time to reevaluate the benefits principle. Most of the current issues can be solved by taxing passive income primarily at source and active income primarily at residence.

For passive income, the number of source jurisdictions is much smaller than residence jurisdictions. As most individuals are relatively risk averse, portfolio investment flows overwhelmingly to a small number of countries – the United States, the EU, and Japan. Even the BRICS mostly attract portfolio investment through mutual funds that are relatively easy to tax.[93] Thus, if the "big three" can coordinate to reinstate a withholding tax on interest, dividends, and royalties flowing from them, the passive income taxation problem can be solved. Crucially, money cannot stay in tax havens and earn decent rates of return, as investments in the United States offer better returns than investments in, for example, the Cayman Islands, so the

[90] OECD, *supra* note 17, at p. 18.

[91] OECD, *Developing a Multilateral Instrument to Modify Bilateral Tax Treaties*, OECD/G20 Base Erosion and Profit Shifting Project (OECD Publishing, 2014), p. 10, http://dx.doi.org/10.1787/9789264219250-en.

[92] Joint Committee on Taxation, *supra* note 44, at p. 32.

[93] Reuven S. Avi-Yonah & Gil Savir, *IGAs vs. MAATM: Has Tax Bilateralism Outlived Its Usefulness?* (U of Mich. Pub. L. Rsch. Paper No. 384; U. of Mich. L. & Econ. Rsch Paper No. 14-002, Feb. 8, 2014), SSRN: http://ssrn.com/abstract=2392702.

cooperation of tax havens is not needed. This would take care of the Sam Wyly problem, because all the income of the trusts would be currently taxed where it is invested.

For active income, about 90 percent of large multinationals are headquartered in the G20, and none of those countries have a tax rate below 20 percent, so if they taxed their multinationals currently on a coordinated basis and restricted the ability to move, most of the problem would be resolved. This would take care of the Apple and Caterpillar problems, because all their offshore income would be subject to current US taxation.

There are three common critiques of the above approach. First, it is said that it violates certain economic neutrality norms and is therefore less efficient compared to territoriality (i.e., each country only taxing the income of the multinational earned within it).[94] Second, adopting the proposed global approach is said to harm the competitive position of any given country's multinationals.[95] Third, adopting the proposed approach will, it is said, provide an incentive for multinationals to shift their residence to tax havens.[96]

4.3.1 *Neutrality*

There are three types of neutrality arguments that apply to cross-border investment. The two traditional ones are capital export neutrality (CEN) and capital import neutrality (CIN). CEN requires neutrality in the location of investment between the residence and source jurisdictions, and therefore supports taxing multinationals on a global basis. CIN requires neutrality between two different investors in a third jurisdiction (which is assumed to impose no tax) and therefore requires territoriality if the other jurisdiction taxes on a territorial basis.[97]

It is often said that CEN and CIN are mutually incompatible in a world with different tax rates, and therefore a choice must be made.[98] Traditionally, CEN was regarded as more important than CIN because investment locations were shown to be more sensitive to tax rates than the rate of savings, and CIN was considered to affect the rate of savings in each resident jurisdiction. But in the current environment, where the tax rates of most OECD countries have converged, it is possible to

94 Mihir A. Desai & James R. Hines Jr., *Evaluating International Tax Reform* (Harvard NOM Working Paper No. 03-48, July 2003), SSRN: http://ssrn.com/abstract=425943 or http://dx.doi.org/10.2139/ssrn.425943.

95 *See, e.g.*, National Foreign Trade Council, Inc., *The NFTC Foreign Income Project: International Tax Policy for the 21st Century*, 18 Tax Notes Int'l 1375 (1999).

96 Daniel Shaviro, *The David R. Tillinghast Lecture: The Rising Tax-Electivity of U.S. Corporate Residence* (NYU L. and Econ. Rsch. Paper No. 10-45; NYU Sch. of L., Pub. L. Rsch. Paper No. 10-72, Oct. 1, 2010), SSRN: http://ssrn.com/abstract=1683642.

97 Thomas Horst, A *Note on Optimal Taxation of International Investment Income*, 94 Quart. J. Econ. 793 (1980).

98 *Id.*

achieve both CEN and CIN simultaneously. A new variant of the neutrality argument is capital ownership neutrality (CON), which focuses on the multinational itself and not on its investors.[99] It is said that multinationals exist because of ownership advantages that render them more efficient than their competitors. If one multinational is subject to a higher effective tax rate than a competitor because of global taxation, then it may be forced to forego an investment in a third country even if it is the more efficient one. But if the proposed solution is adopted on a multilateral basis, then all likely competitors will be taxed in the same way and CON can be preserved as well.

4.3.2 *Competitiveness*

Historically, the main argument against adopting the Kennedy proposal and similar unilateral proposals is that they would put US-based multinationals at a competitive disadvantage because multinationals from other countries are not subject to the same type of rule.[100] The first author has always found this argument less than persuasive for several reasons: It is not clear that competitiveness is a meaningful economic concept, or that the United States as a country should care about the competitiveness of multinationals resident in it (as opposed to the competitiveness of the US economy as a whole or of its population); the same argument was made in 1961, where US-based multinationals clearly dominated the globe, unlike in more recent years where their position has become less dominant; there is no evidence that current US rules, which deviate from the global norm of territoriality and impose tax on some foreign source income of US-based multinationals, have injured those multinationals in any significant way.[101] In fact, empirical studies suggest that EU-based multinationals and US-based multinationals pay similar effective tax rates, even though the former benefit from territoriality and the latter do not.[102] But even if competitiveness is a valid argument (and it clearly carries weight among politicians),[103] if a multilateral approach is adopted, it loses its force. About 90 percent of large multinationals are residents in G20 countries, and the others are mostly resident in large developing countries that may also be willing to join a multilateral

[99] Mihir A. Desai & James R. Hines, Jr., *Evaluating International Tax Reform*, 56 Nat'l Tax J. 487 (2003) at 502.

[100] Revenue Act of 1962. Hearings on H.R. 10650 before the Senate Committee on Finance, 87th Cong., 2d Sess. 560–61, 725–26 (1962) (statements by W. Slowinski and R. Landolt); Gary Clyde Hufbauer & Ariel Assa, US Taxation of Foreign Income 1–21 (2007).

[101] Reuven S. Avi-Yonah & Nicola Sartori, *International Taxation and Competitiveness: Foreword*, 65 Tax L. Rev. 313 (2012).

[102] Reuven S. Avi-Yonah & Yaron Lahav, *The Effective Tax Rate of the Largest US and EU Multinationals* (U of Mich. L. & Econ., Empirical Legal Stud. Ctr. Paper No. 11-015; U. of Mich. Pub. L. Working Paper No. 255, Oct. 25, 2011), SSRN: http://ssrn.com/abstract=1949226 or http://dx.doi.org/10.2139/ssrn.1949226.

[103] *See, e.g.*, http://www.hsgac.senate.gov/subcommittees/investigations/hearings/impact-of-the-us-tax-code-on-the-market-for-corporate-control-and-jobs.

approach. Under these circumstances, there will be no competitive disadvantage to any resident country that adopts the global approach unless it stems from its domestic corporate tax rate. As suggested above, the United States was an outlier in this regard because its pre-TCJA corporate tax rate of 35 percent is significantly above the G20 average.[104] In the context of adopting such a reform, the United States can, and should, reduce its rate on a revenue neutral basis.

4.3.3 *Corporate Expatriations*

The last argument against taxing multinationals on a global basis is that the tax can be avoided by shifting the residence of the multinational to a jurisdiction that does not impose such a tax. In fact, before 2017 there was another wave of "inversions," or corporate expatriations, out of the United States because of the high US corporate tax rate.[105]

This argument assumes that there are other jurisdictions that the multinational can move to. If all G20 countries adopt the proposal, most of the likely destinations disappear. There are good business reasons why the headquarters of almost all multinationals are in G20 countries, and those reasons will mitigate the advantage of moving to a non G20 country.

A move to a tax haven may be possible if residence is defined as place of incorporation. But, as suggested above, corporate residence should be defined as the location of the corporate headquarters, and those are much less likely to be movable to tax havens because corporate management is not likely to want to relocate there and other facilities that usually follow the headquarters location, such as research and development, cannot easily be moved there. For the same reasons, it is unlikely that new multinationals can be founded in tax havens outside the G20 countries.[106]

Thus, it seems that none of the common arguments against taxing multinationals on a current basis are valid if one assumes that this approach can be adopted on a multilateral basis.

4.3.4 *Can the Proposal Be Adopted?*

By this point, we hope the reader will be convinced that current taxation of all multinationals on a global basis is the preferred approach, and if such taxation can

104 OECD, *Statutory Corporate Income Tax Rate*, https://stats.oecd.org/Index.aspx?DataSetCode=TABLE_II1 (last accessed Aug. 13, 2023).

105 On inversions *see* Avi-Yonah & Marian, *supra* note 12; Reuven S. Avi-Yonah, *Reflections on the "New Wave" Inversions and Notice 2014-52*, 145 Tax Notes 95 (Oct. 6, 2014); 76 Tax Notes Int'l 63 (Oct. 6, 2014); Reuven S. Avi-Yonah, *For Haven's Sake: Reflections on Inversion Transactions*, 95 Tax Notes 1793 (June 17, 2002); 27 Tax Notes Int'l 225 (July 8, 2002); Proceedings of the National Tax Association 95th Annual Conference 287 (2002).

106 *See* Reuven S. Avi-Yonah & Joel Slemrod, eds., Taxation and Migration (2015).

be adopted on a multilateral basis, then all the usual arguments against its unilateral adoption by any country disappear.[107]

To assess whether multilateral action is possible, it is first necessary to establish the interests of the parties involved. Tax competition for FDI typically involves an MNE deciding which countries are possible investment locations from a non-tax point of view, that is, considering location, infrastructure, education, political stability, and other factors considered to be standard economic, social, and business factors. Once the MNE has established a list of plausible countries, it then approaches these countries and asks what they would be willing to offer it in return for the investment. The countries then engage in a bidding war to grant tax reductions, culminating in the winner receiving the investment. Frequently, more than one country can get the investment. This encourages and frequently leads to countries engaging in a race to the bottom to attract the MNE, to the detriment of themselves and their competition. Without multilateral action and coordination on tax policy, countries get trapped in a prisoner's dilemma where they are incentivized to give in to the wishes of the prospective MNE.

Under these circumstances the investment would be made in any case, whether the tax incentive is granted or not. The tax incentives are therefore a pure windfall for the MNE. If the countries could find a way to coordinate their approaches, they would still get the investment but without the tax cost.

Thus, it is in the interest of most countries to coordinate their approaches to prevent this type of tax competition. The same rationale obtains for capital exporting jurisdictions like the G20. They would prefer to tax their MNEs on a current basis but are constrained from doing so because of the competitiveness and expatriation concerns outlined above.

In our opinion all G20 member countries would benefit from a multilateral approach. Capital-exporting countries could obtain revenues from their MNEs without concerns about harming their competitiveness or MNEs migrating to other G20 countries. Capital-importing countries could obtain FDI without concern that if they do not grant tax holidays the investment would end up in other countries. In the latter case, if all G20 countries were on board, the limits on tax competition would apply outside the G20 as well since almost all MNEs are based in these countries. Countries outside the G20 would have no incentive to grant tax holidays against their own interests if the income were taxed in the residence country of the MNE, since in that case there would be no benefit to the MNE from the tax holiday.

In addition, if the proposal above were adopted, this would also help alleviate the current opposition by MNEs and some countries to country-by-country reporting standards, which is necessary to properly enforce the BEPS project and combat BEPS schemes. Since MNEs would obtain credit for taxes levied by source countries

107 The multilateral approach was adopted in pillar 1 of BEPS 2.0, discussed in the next chapter, but it is unlikely to be implemented given the opposition of the US.

under the proposal, they should be less hostile to country-by-country reporting, which is designed to aid source countries in collecting their fair share of taxes.

While the interest of countries are aligned, there has yet to be unified coordination on this front. In our opinion, it is primarily because of lobbying by the MNEs themselves. They are the primary beneficiaries from the status quo, and they have successfully lobbied both countries and the OECD against meaningful reform.[108]

A useful contrast is to examine a case in which the countries and MNEs were aligned. Prior to 1977, there were no domestic limits on MNEs paying bribes overseas to obtain contracts from corrupt government officials. In 1977, following several scandals, the United States enacted the Foreign Corrupt Practices Act, which imposed criminal sanctions on bribes by US-based MNEs and their executives. Predictably, US MNEs complained that this ban put them at a competitive disadvantage, especially when other countries like Germany permitted foreign bribes to be deducted for domestic tax purposes.

Somewhat surprisingly, the outcome was not relaxation of the US law. Instead, the Clinton administration successfully pushed the OECD to adopt the same provisions as part of a binding, multilateral treaty, which eliminated the competitive disadvantage issue.[109]

The key reason for this success is that not only were the interests of the countries aligned; the MNEs did not like paying bribes either and therefore lobbied in favor of the provision. This will not be the case for tax, where the MNEs are already pushing back against the OECD BEPS project. However, there have been instances in the past where resistance by MNEs has been overcome by the alignment and coordination of countries and governments.

4.3.5 *Constructive Unilateralism*

In the case of corporate tax avoidance, if multilateralism is not possible, we think the best way forward is unilateral US action. The precedent is the adoption of the CFC rules, which proves that such action can be both possible and effective in pushing other countries to adopt similar rules.

Before 1961, no country taxed the foreign source income of subsidiaries of its multinationals, because residence countries believed they lacked both source and residence jurisdiction over foreign source income of foreign corporations. However, in 1961 the Kennedy administration proposed taxing all income of CFCs by using a deemed dividend mechanism from the Foreign Personal Holding Company (FPHC) rules.[110]

[108] *See* BEPS Monitoring Group Report, *supra* note 21.

[109] OECD, *Convention on Combating Bribery of Foreign Public Officials in International Business Transactions*, http://www.oecd.org/corruption/oecdantibriberyconvention.htm.

[110] Reuven S. Avi-Yonah, *The Deemed Dividend Problem*, 4 J. TAX'N GLOB. TRANSACTIONS 33 (2004), *also in* Proceedings of the National Tax Association Annual Meeting (2004).

While this proposal was rejected, the resulting compromise (Subpart F, 1962) aimed at taxing income of CFCs that was unlikely to be taxed by source countries either because it was mobile and could be earned anywhere (passive income) or because it was structured to be earned in low-tax jurisdictions (base company income).

Initially, the adoption of Subpart F seemed to have put US-based multinationals at a competitive disadvantage, because no other country had such rules. But gradually this picture changed. The United States was followed by Germany (1972), Canada (1975), Japan (1978), France (1980), the United Kingdom (1984), New Zealand (1988), Australia (1990), Sweden (1990), Norway (1992), Denmark (1995), Finland (1995), Indonesia (1995), Portugal (1995), Spain (1995), Hungary (1997), Mexico (1997), South Africa (1997), South Korea (1997), Argentina (1999), Brazil (2000), Italy (2000), Estonia (2000), Israel (2003), Turkey (2006), and China (2008). Many other countries, such as India, are considering adopting such rules. As a result, most of our trading partners now have CFC rules. Moreover, the later adopters improved on the US policy in two key ways. First, they rejected the deemed dividend mechanism, which can lead to many unforeseen complications, in favor of taxing the shareholders on a pass-through basis. Second, they explicitly incorporated the effective foreign tax rate into the determination whether a CFC will be subject to current tax. This is better than the US rule that is based solely on the type of income, because after 1980 it became quite easy to earn active income that is not subject to tax.[111]

The result is that the CFCs of EU-based multinationals are currently subject to tax at similar or higher rates than US-based ones,[112] despite the non-taxation of dividends from active income under territoriality. This is a classic example of constructive unilateralism. The United States led and others followed; the result is that most multinationals are subject to similar effective tax rates, with no competitive disadvantage or advantage.[113]

Unfortunately, in the United States, Subpart F has been critically undermined by the adoption of Check the Box and the CFC-to-CFC exception, resulting in $2 trillion of low-taxed accumulated earnings offshore by US multinationals.[114] This cannot happen in other countries with tougher CFC rules and is a major reason why, despite rampant tax competition, most OECD members did not see the sharp drops in overall corporate tax revenues that are seen in developing countries.

The main argument in favor of territoriality (i.e., exempting dividends paid by US CFCs from tax upon receipt by their parents) is the lock-out problem. About $2 trillion in low-taxed foreign source income are in CFCs that cannot repatriate them because of the 35 percent tax on repatriations and the absence of foreign tax

[111] *See* Reuven S. Avi-Yonah, *Globalization, Tax Competition, and the Fiscal Crisis of the Welfare States*, 113 HARV. L. REV. 1573, 1575–651 (2000).

[112] *See* Avi-Yonah & Lahav, *supra* note 102.

[113] *Id.*

[114] Kimberly A. Clausing, *The Effect of Profit Shifting on the Corporate Tax Base*, TAX NOTES (Jan. 25, 2016), www.taxnotes.com (last accessed July 6, 2023).

credits.[115] We know this is a problem because of the effectiveness of the 2004–05 amnesty and because of various attempts by multinationals to avoid the rule (via inversions, "killer Bs," short-term loans, etc.).

We would argue that this is a good opportunity for "constructive unilateralism." No G20 country has a corporate tax rate below 20 percent. If we reduced the corporate tax to, say, 28 percent, and at the same time abolished deferral, the likely response by other G20 members like Germany or France would be to follow suit. They need the extra revenue more than we do, and concerns about competitiveness would be alleviated by the US move, like they were in the original CFC context. It should be remembered that the other G20 have more effective CFC rules than we do, and those CFC rules already act as a de facto worldwide system with a minimum tax: If the foreign tax is below a set level (e.g., 25 percent in Germany or 20 percent in Japan), the CFC rules kick in to tax the income. The result is that there is much less lockout because most low-taxed foreign income is taxed by the CFC rules. The change to a worldwide system would be much less radical than usually envisaged. Therefore, for both the UK and Japan there was no significant increase in repatriations after they adopted territoriality in 2009.[116]

Both the Obama administration and Camp propose that the US not adopt a minimum, but a lower, tax on foreign source income for competitiveness reasons. Obama suggests a 28 percent corporate tax on domestic profits and a 19 percent tax on foreign income, while Camp proposed lower rates at a 25 percent tax on domestic profits and a 12.5–15 percent tax on foreign income.

The problem, of course, is that such a gap would still encourage US-based MNEs to shift profits overseas, with no repatriation tax to deter them. For now, we would suggest taxing all income at the same rate, and if that rate must be lower, so be it. If it is above 20 percent, we do not think we will be outside G20 norms, and a rate in the 20–25 percent range will not put our MNEs at a significant competitive disadvantage given the effective minimum tax imposed by the CFC rules of our trading partners.

It is impossible to predict what will happen, but the history described above suggests that there is a good chance that other G20 countries will follow if we abolish deferral at a lower rate. And if that happens, all the usual objections to worldwide taxation (competitiveness, inversions, and the various neutralities) lose their force. We do not think there is a significant risk involved in this move, and the potential upside is quite large.

4.4 CONCLUSION

The benefits principle should be reconsidered considering the reality of globalization. We should tax passive income primarily at source and active income

[115] *Id.*

[116] Stephen E. Shay et al., *Territoriality in Search of Principles and Revenue: Camp and Enzi (October 14, 2013)*. 141 *Tax Notes* 173; 72 Tax Notes Int'l 155, SSRN: http://ssrn.com/abstract=2340615.

primarily at residence. This will enable the large economies to address both individual tax evasion and corporate tax avoidance. Our tax system is built around voluntary cooperation; if most Americans refused to cooperate, the IRS could not force them to do so. As the Greek experience has demonstrated,[117] once a culture of tax avoidance or nonpayment is established, it is very hard to change. We need to do something about both evasion and avoidance before it is too late and becomes a radically more serious and costly problem, both fiscally and culturally.

The following chapters will discuss the developments since 2017, which have, to some extent, revived a multilateral approach along the lines suggested above. Together, the two pillars of BEPS 2.0 radically transform the international tax regime in ways that may indeed be called an "international tax revolution."

[117] Heather Stewart, *Greece's Tax Revenues Collapse as Debt Crisis Continues*, The Guardian (Aug. 6, 2015) http://www.theguardian.com/world/2015/aug/06/greece-tax-revenues-collapse-debt-crisis-continues-euro.

5

The New Regime and the Digital Economy, 2016–2023*

On October 8, 2021, 136 countries signed on to the Organisation for Economic Co-operation and Development (OECD) Base Erosion and Profit Shifting (BEPS) statement (the Statement) for reforming international corporate taxation in the digitalized economy.[1] There are now more than 140 signatories, including not only the OECD/G20 members, but also most developing countries.[2] Directed toward bringing the international tax regime into the twenty-first century, the global tax deal is the culmination of over a decade of work and diplomacy. However, the outcome is still dependent on plan specifics in upcoming discussions and national implementation legislations. The existing international tax regime was developed during the 1920s and 1930s for a brick-and-mortar world. This outdated system has been unable to address two key problems in today's global, digitalized world. First, multinational enterprises are currently only obligated to pay corporate income tax in foreign market countries (or source countries) where they have a physical presence, such as an office or factory. Because tech giants such as Google, Facebook, and Amazon are now able to generate revenue from market countries entirely online, without ever establishing a physical presence, they can avoid paying sufficient taxes to those market countries. Second, multinational enterprises also avoid taxes in residence countries by shifting profits to subsidiaries in low-tax jurisdictions. The intangible nature of modern assets such as trademarks, software, and other intellectual property allows multinationals to shift earnings and profits away from the higher-tax residence countries where their headquarters are located. The OECD estimates that the resulting corporate tax avoidance costs $100 billion to

* This chapter draws heavily from a previous work by authors. Reuven S. Avi-Yonah et al., *A New Framework for Digital Taxation*, 63 Harv. Int'l L.J. 279 (2022).

[1] OECD, *Statement on a Two-Pillar Solution to Address the Tax Challenges Arising from the Digtialisation of the Economy*, OECD/G20 Base Erosion and Profit Shifting Project (2021) [hereinafter Statement].

[2] OECD, *International Collaboration to End Tax Avoidance*, http://www.oecd.org/tax/beps/ (last accessed July 17, 2023).

$240 billion annually, which amounts to 4–10 percent of global corporate tax revenue.[3]

The global tax deal, as articulated in the Statement announced in October 2021, addresses today's tax challenges with two pillars that are distinct from each other. To solve the problem of market country taxation in the global, digitalized world, Pillar One modifies existing profit allocation and nexus rules. Pillar One allocates part of a multinational's residual profits to market jurisdictions even if the multinational has no physical presence in those market countries.[4] Pillar Two aims to curtail profit shifting and tax base erosion by leveling the playing field with a 15 percent global minimum tax.[5] This chapter examines the details of this monumental new tax framework and critically assesses its mixed prospects of success. It offers guidelines for US international tax policy and highlights alternative proposals for global policymakers to consider.[6]

Pillar One of the Statement features new taxing right, namely, Amount A. Amount A eliminates the physical presence requirement and, by allocating part of a multinational's residual profits to market countries based on a formula, permits those countries to tax the multinational. Incorporating a proposal of the Biden administration, the Statement limits the application of Amount A to multinational enterprises with global revenue above €20 billion and profitability above 10 percent (i.e., profit before tax divided by revenue). For a multinational within scope, a new special-purpose nexus rule permits allocation of Amount A to market countries when the company derives at least €1 million in revenue from that jurisdiction. But the information revealed so far envisages far-reaching changes to the international tax regime by partially abandoning the arm's-length principle and the physical presence requirement to provide greater taxing rights to market countries. Pillar One must be implemented by a multilateral tax treaty coming into but this requires ratification by the United States, which is unlikely to happen anytime soon.

Pillar Two envisages the implementation of a global minimum tax levied on multinational enterprises that meet a threshold of €750 million in revenue – regardless of the jurisdiction where the multinationals are headquartered or operate. If a subsidiary's income is taxed below the minimum tax rate, which is currently proposed at 15 percent, the parent entity will be required to include such income as parent company income and pay the difference in additional taxes to its residence country. If the residence country has not enacted this rule, either the affiliated entity's deduction would be denied, or an equivalent adjustment would be made. Pillar Two will therefore result in the single tax principle or full taxation. Because

[3] OECD, *OECD/G20 Inclusive Framework on BEPS*, 5th Meeting of the Inclusive Framework in Lima, Peru (June 27–28, 2018) [hereinafter OECD, IF Flyer].

[4] Reuven S. Avi-Yonah et al., *A New Framework for Digital Taxation*, 63 Harv. Int'l L.J. 402 (2022) , section I.B.1.

[5] *Id.* at section I.B.2.

[6] Pillar One depends on a multilateral convention (MLC) that cannot come into effect without ratification by the United States.

Pillar Two may be implemented by individual countries through domestic legislation, a formal treaty agreement is not required. The OECD expects that it will be implemented by 2023. As Pillar Two is examined in Chapter 6, this chapter will not discuss it in detail.

However, the successful enactment of Pillar One concerning digital taxation is in peril. First, Pillar One requires a multilateral treaty for global implementation, which is expected to amend articles on physical presence and business profits of all existing bilateral tax treaties. It would be logistically and politically challenging to bring more than 140 countries on board to the multilateral treaty. Furthermore, in the United States, it would be very hard to get this through the Senate for ratification. Even if the United States relies on an executive agreement, it would be challenging to obtain majority support in Congress and would invite many legal issues relating to treaty overrides by executive agreements, which is largely uncharted legal territory.

Second, countries may be unwilling to relinquish an established tax instrument, the Digital Services Taxes (DSTs). DSTs have been unilaterally developed and implemented over the past couple of years by countries seeking to tax the digital service activities of the world's tech giants. DSTs are currently in effect in the United Kingdom, France, and fifteen other countries. The European Union (EU) has proposed a similar tax for its entire twenty-seven-member bloc. These DSTs are imposed on companies' gross revenue, as opposed to net income, at relatively low rates. Because the tax is assessed on gross revenue, US companies are unable to utilize the foreign income tax credit to offset this tax from their US tax liabilities. DSTs are imposed on the provision of digital services, regardless of whether they are provided for free (like Google and Facebook) or for payment (like Amazon and Netflix). They have been criticized as discriminatory toward US tech giants, and the July 2021 Inclusive Framework Statement called for the removal of unilateral DSTs in exchange for the new Pillar One tax regime.

However, the EU had announced that it intended to implement its own digital levy in 2023,[7] but the European Commission has not proposed such an instrument yet. The United Nations has added special provisions for income from automated digital services (ADS) to Article 12B of the UN Model Tax Convention.[8]

The continued use and further enactment of DSTs by individual countries and governing entities presents a perilous obstacle to the successful implementation of the Pillar One tax regime. A previous attempt, the OECD Base Erosion and Profit Shifting Project (BEPS 1.0), failed because the United States resisted what it felt

7 Eur. Comm'n, A *Fair & Competitive Digital Economy – Digital Levy*, https://ec.europa.eu/info/law/better-regulation/have-your-say/initiatives/12836-A-fair-&-competitive-digital-economy-digital-levy_en [https://perma.cc/7KS2-ZXE8] [hereinafter *EU Digital Levy*].

8 Comm'n of Experts on Int'l Cooperation in Tax Matters, Twenty-Second Session, Item 3(i) of the Provisional Agenda, Tax Consequences of the Digitalized Economy – Issues of Relevance for Developing Countries, U.N. Doc. E/C.18/2021/CRP.1 (Apr. 6, 2021) [hereinafter U.N. Proposal].

were discriminatory taxes against its tech industry.[9] Ironically perhaps, it was the very failure of the BEPS 1.0 tax proposal that served as a catalyst for individual countries to begin imposing new digital taxes unilaterally.

We argue that the claim that DSTs represent discriminatory taxation against US tech giants is baseless, even ironic. US tech giants dominate the world market in digital services and the primary reason that they are more predominantly affected by DSTs is because they have no real foreign competition. If Alibaba or Tencent become a truly global digital service provider, they would instantly be subject to the same DSTs. Furthermore, DSTs cannot be dismissed solely because they are unilateral. Sovereign countries cannot be prevented from imposing taxes on income that they can show has been derived from their jurisdiction. The unilateral move to implement a DST is not contrary to the "first bite at the apple" rule of international taxation, whereby source countries have primacy in taxation because source comes before residence in time.[10] The United States has carried out unilateral moves in international tax for decades, without seeking or awaiting consent from any other country.[11] Demonizing DSTs simply because they are "unilateral" is unjustified.

Moreover, the US response to the DSTs has been particularly unsettling. The United States Trade Representative (USTR) adopted trade sanctions on France (currently suspended due to the pending global negotiations) and is threatening to adopt similar sanctions against other countries implementing DSTs. However, the USTR investigation report on France's DST contains many biases and exaggerations that directly influenced its conclusion that France's DST is discriminatory. This chapter scrutinizes the USTR report, unpacks its notable errors, and focuses on its selective bias and revenue threshold analysis.[12] More importantly, the chapter asserts that tariffs are inefficient, regressive, and cause a net harm to economies by raising costs for companies and consumers. The renewed interest of the United States in tariffs in the Trump administration is troubling.[13]

To demonstrate this point and build a case against retaliatory tariffs, the chapter conducts the first empirical analysis of the DST tariff imposed on the import of French sparkling wine.[14] The US sparkling wine importers were chosen by the USTR as "sacrificial companies" to protect Google, Apple, Facebook, and Amazon (GAFA), arguably harmed by France's enactment of DST. The DST tariff increased

9 *See generally* OECD, Addressing the Tax Challenges of the Digital Economy, Action 1 – 2015 Final Report (2015) [hereinafter OECD, Action 1] (describing the implementation of Action 1).

10 Reuven S. Avi-Yonah & Gianluca Mazzoni, *Taking the First Bite: Who Should Tax Apple's $187 Billion in Ireland?* 3–4 (Univ. Mich. L. & Econ., Working Paper No. 16-033, 2017).

11 Examples include foreign tax credits, controlled foreign corporations, and denying treaty benefits to hybrid entities. *See* Reuven S. Avi-Yonah, *Constructive Unilateralism: U.S. Leadership and International Taxation* 2–9 (U. Mich. Pub. L.& Legal Theory Rsch. Paper Ser., Paper No. 463, 2015), https://papers.ssrn.com/sol3/papers.cfm?abstract_id=2622868.

12 Avi-Yonah et al., *supra* note 4, section III.A.2.

13 Kimberly Clausing, *The Progressive Case against Protectionism*, 98 Foreign Aff. 109, 115 (2019).

14 Avi-Yonah et al., *supra* note 4, section III.A.4.

the costs to importers and thus reduced their profit margins, creating negative effects to the sacrificial companies that were mostly small and medium in size. Worse yet, this chapter reveals that the DST retaliatory tariffs have neither caused financial harm to the French wine industry nor have pressured France to discard its DST, therefore failing to accomplish their intended objectives.

Built upon this discussion, we offer policy criteria for digital taxation.[15] Reflecting the tax challenges in the digital economy, any policy proposal should be able to overcome the outdated physical presence nexus and fairly allocate the appropriate tax revenue to market countries. Furthermore, an effective policy proposal should be free from any indicia of discrimination toward companies based on their nationality. Finally, a policy proposal needs to be administrable by both tax administrations and taxpayers alike. A simple, targeted approach may in fact work better and more efficiently than an ambitious, comprehensive approach that inevitably invites political compromises.

This chapter next details two compatible digital taxation proposals: a multilateral solution and a unilateral measure. First, we endorse Article 12B of the UN Model Tax Convention for income from automated digital services (ADS).[16] This multilateral proposal eliminates the physical presence requirement only for certain digital services, defined as automated digital services. Market countries can tax income from automated digital services on a "gross basis" at a modest rate (3 or 4 percent) with an option to the taxpayer to pay tax on a "net basis." The UN approach is a much more simplified approach compared to Pillar One. It reflects the needs of many developing countries with limited administrative capacity. Hence, it seems that the UN approach can serve as a simple, reliable, and efficient method to upgrade income taxation for the digital economy, while also identifying issues that can be improved.

Second, as a unilateral measure, we propose a new data excise tax inspired by several existing proposals.[17] The tax base would be calculated by the volume of collected data, measured in gigabytes. It would only apply to for-profit data collectors, with a safe harbor threshold rule to prevent taxation of individual users and small businesses. Because the proposed tax would not be measured in gross revenue or profits, it would likely avoid the suspicion currently directed at DSTs and accusations that it is a disguised income tax or discriminatory tax based on the nationality of the businesses. As an excise tax, it would be easy to administer, and could be implemented either independently by a market jurisdiction or together with a multilateral solution. The proposed digital excise tax could serve as a model for foreign countries as well as the EU, which is preparing to implement a new digital levy. As an excise tax, it is also a potential option that states and localities could adopt.

15 *Id.*, section IV.A.

16 *Id.*, section IV.B.

17 *Id.*, section IV.C.

The multilateral and unilateral proposals are compatible with each other so that policymakers may adopt them individually or collectively. In addition, the diversified designs provide more options for policymakers with different propensities; the multilateral measure is based on an income tax regime, whereas the unilateral proposal is an excise tax, which is a subcategory of consumption tax. Such diversified designs may provide more options to a wide array of policymakers.

5.1 THE EVOLUTION OF DIGITAL TAX REFORM PROPOSALS

This section describes the history of international tax reform proposals to deal with the tax challenges in the global, digitalized economy in the twenty-first century. It starts with the BEPS 1.0 project in the first half of the 2010s, which failed to achieve complete success due to the project's limitation in digital taxation, which in turn stimulated market countries to adopt unilateral tax measures. In response, the global community launched the BEPS 2.0 project, consisting of the two pillars, producing the Statement in October 2021. Section 5.3 provides for a critical assessment of its results.

5.1.1 *BEPS 1.0 and the Rise of Digital Services Taxes (DSTs)*

Over the past decade, a revolution has begun in international taxation. International taxation rules were developed in the 1920s and 1930s.[18] They have been criticized as being outdated – for example, by requiring physical presence for nexus – and as vulnerable to tax competition, tax base erosion, and profit shifting. Countries that had previously been content to live with such outdated rules came to a collective understanding after the financial crisis of 2008–10 that the rules must be changed.

Under political pressure, the G20, comprising the twenty largest economies in the world, forced the OECD to begin redrafting the ground rules of international taxation. The result was the Base Erosion and Profit Shifting (BEPS) project – BEPS 1.0 – which from 2013 to 2015 advanced fifteen actions designed to counter multinational corporations' ability to engage in tax avoidance through profit shifting and other accounting measures.[19] In 2015, OECD Secretary General Angel Gurria declared that

> The measures we are presenting today represent the most fundamental changes to international tax rules in almost a century: they will put an end to double non-taxation, facilitate a better alignment of taxation with economic activity and value

[18] Michael J. Graetz & Michael M. O'Hear, *The "Original Intent" of U.S. International Taxation*, 46 Duke L.J. 1021, 1023–24 (1997).

[19] OECD, *BEPS Actions*, , https://www.oecd.org/tax/beps/beps-actions/ [https://perma.cc/T5PW-GSCV].

creation, and when fully implemented, these measures will render BEPS-inspired tax planning structures ineffective.[20]

This declaration was overly optimistic: The G20 and OECD failed to reach a consensus on several issues, the most critical of which was Action 1, addressing the digital economy.[21] While France and other EU members pushed for changes to existing "permanent establishment" (PE) tax rules – that is, the physical presence requirement for tax nexus – to enable more source-based taxation of profits from the digital economy, the United States resisted any attempts that would impose additional taxation on its tech giants, such as Amazon, Apple, Facebook, Google, and Netflix.[22]

Given the failure to achieve consensus in the OECD or a multilateral, international system of taxation, countries unilaterally started to adopt their own measures. The pioneer was the United Kingdom, which in 2015 adopted a diverted profits tax (DPT), which taxed the tech giants on the profits of the "avoided PE" that would have been subject to taxation if the permanent establishment rules were different.[23] The United Kingdom was followed by Australia, which adopted the "Netflix tax,"[24] and India, which adopted the first "digital services tax,"[25] a tax on the provision of digital services as well as the use of local consumer data to sell targeted advertising (thus applying to the business models of Amazon, Facebook, and Google). France then adopted its own DST, which was followed by fifteen other jurisdictions passing various iterations of a DST.[26] A broad, multilateral tax in the form of a digital levy implemented across the entire twenty-seven-member EU bloc was also

20 OECD, *OECD Presents Outputs of OECD/G20 BEPS Project for Discussion at G20 Finance Ministers Meeting* (May 5, 2015), https://www.oecd.org/tax/oecd-presents-outputs-of-oecd-g20-beps-project-for-discussion-at-g20-finance-ministers-meeting.htm [https://perma.cc/PV7F-9SXR].

21 OECD, Action 1, *supra* note 8.

22 Ruth Mason, *The Transformation of International Tax*, 114 Am. J. Int'l L. 353, 397–98 (2020); *U.S. Sees Unilateral Taxes on Web Giants as "Discriminatory": Treasury Official*, Reuters (Mar. 12, 2019, 5:09 AM), https://reuters.com/article/us-usa-tax-harter-idUSKBN1QT1CT [https://perma.cc/NLP5-SQQ6].

23 Finance Act 2020, c. 39-72 (UK); Stephanie Soong Johnston, *U.K. Digital Services Tax Becomes Law, Stoking Trade Tensions*, Tax Notes Today Int'l (July 23, 2020), https://www.taxnotes.com/tax-notes-international/digital-economy/uk-digital-services-tax-becomes-law-stoking-trade-tensions/2020/07/27/2crds?highlight=Stephanie%20Soong%20Johnston%2C%20U.K.%20Digital%20Services%20Tax%20Becomes%20Law%2C%20Stoking%20Trade%20Tensions [https://perma.cc/33MX-47FD].

24 Tax and Superannuation Laws Amendment (2016 Measures No. 1) Act 2016 (Austl.); *see also* Lance Cunningham & Meera Pillai, *Insight: 2019 Australian "Election" Budget-Significant International Tax Measures*, Bloomberg Tax (Apr. 22, 2019, 12:53 AM), https://news.bloombergtax.com/transfer-pricing/insight-2019-australian-election-budget-measures-of-international-significance?context=search&index=8 [https://perma.cc/L6N8-EBJ4].

25 The Finance Act, 2016 (India).

26 *See, e.g.*, Liz Alderman, *France Moves to Tax Tech Giants, Stoking Fight with White House*, N.Y. Times (July 11, 2019), https://www.nytimes.com/2019/07/11/business/france-digital-tax-tech-giants.html [https://perma.cc/W939-G5JS].

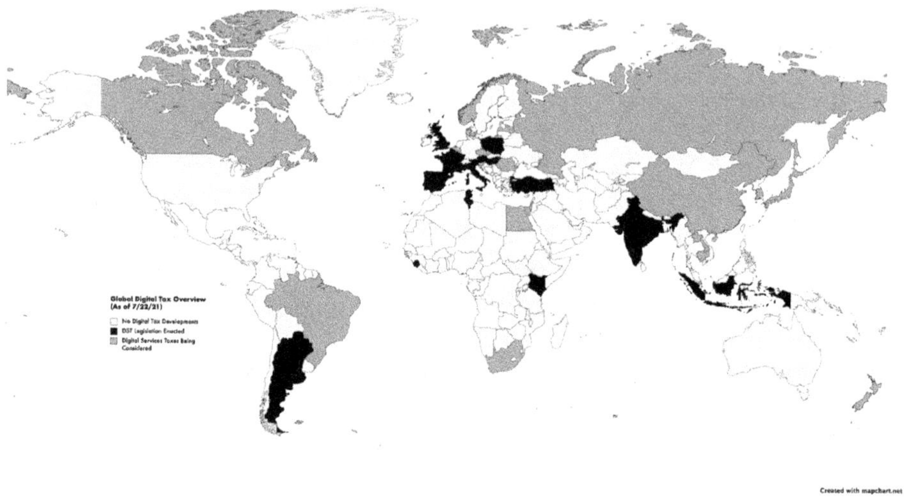

FIGURE 5.1 Countries enacted or proposed DSTs
Figure is created by the author based on the data released by KPMG. KPMG, Taxation of the Digitalized Economy 5 (July 22, 2021), https://tax.kpmg.us/content/dam/tax/en/pdfs/2021/digitalized-economy-taxation-developments-summary.pdf.

proposed.[27] DSTs are widespread (as shown in Figure 5.1) and are now considered the status quo in international tax, as Michael Graetz of Columbia Law School commented in 2019.[28]

The United States responded to the implementation of unilateral DSTs by adopting trade sanctions against France – which are currently suspended pending OECD negotiations – and threatening to do the same to other jurisdictions.[29] More detailed analysis of DSTs, the US response of tariffs, and a potential trade war is discussed in this chapter.

5.2 THE GLOBAL TAX DEAL STATEMENT AS BEPS 2.0

The G20 and the OECD responded to these developments in 2018 by beginning work on BEPS 2.0. Notably, the BEPS 2.0 project has expanded the discussion group to include both developed and developing countries, because the international tax reform consisting of two pillars would only succeed if they were supported by the global community. As a result, over 140 jurisdictions are now

[27] *Proposal for a Council Directive Laying Down Rules Relating to the Corporate Taxation of a Significant Digital Presence*, COM (2018) 147 final (Mar. 21, 2018).

[28] Michael Graetz, Professor of Tax Law, Columbia Law School, Speech at the 2019 USCIB/OECD International Tax Conference (June 3, 2019).

[29] Press Release, United States Trade Representative, *USTR Announces Initiation of Section 301 Investigation into France's Digital Services Tax* (July 10, 2019), https://ustr.gov/about-us/policy-offices/press-office/press-releases/2019/july/ustr-announces-initiation-section-301 [https://perma.cc/58C7-GFMU].

participating in the OECD/G20 Inclusive Framework on BEPS 2.0 toward the development of consensus-based, long-term solutions.[30]

BEPS 2.0 consists of two pillars.[31] Pillar One concerns modifying profit allocation and nexus rules.[32] It aims to allocate a part of corporations' residual profits to market countries even if the corporation has no physical presence in those countries.[33] Pillar Two's provisions are a direct extension of the "global intangible low-taxed income" (GILTI) and "base erosion and anti-abuse tax" (BEAT), enacted as part of the US Tax Cuts and Jobs Act (TCJA) of 2017.[34] It aims to introduce a global minimum tax to level the playing field.[35] Several rounds of proposals have been circulated, but this subsection will discuss the three most important developments: (1) the Report on Pillar One Blueprint (hereinafter Pillar One Blueprint),[36] (2) the US proposals by the Biden administration,[37] and (3) the Statement on a Two-Pillar Solution to Address the Tax Challenges Arising from the Digitalization of the Economy (the Statement), released in October 2021. The Trump administration has proposed levying punitive tariffs and retaliatory tax measures on countries that adopt DSTs or the UTPR, with unclear consequences for the world trade system.[38]

5.2.1 *Pillar One for the Digital Economy*

At the start of the BEPS 2.0 discussion, Pillar One aimed to offer new nexus and profit allocation rules for the digital economy. It recognized that, especially with digital platforms where participation of users in market countries is important, the allocation of taxing rights with respect to business profits could no longer be determined solely by physical presence.[39] The new rules developed through BEPS 2.0 are based on net basis taxation to avoid double taxation and be as simple as possible.[40]

However, after several rounds of proposals for discussion and the release of the Pillar One Blueprint, Pillar One no longer solely targets the digital economy,

30 OECD, IF Flyer, *supra* note 3.

31 *See* OECD, Tax Challenges Arising from Digitalisation – Interim Report 2018 (2018); *see also* OECD, Addressing the Tax Challenges of the Digitalisation of the Economy – Policy Note (2019); OECD, Public Consultation Document, Secretariat Proposal for a "Unified Approach" under Pillar One (2019).

32 OECD, Tax Challenges Arising from Digitalisation – Report on Pillar One Blueprint 3 (2020) [hereinafter OECD, Pillar One Blueprint].

33 *Id.* at 8.

34 OECD, Tax Challenges Arising from Digitalisation – Report on Pillar Two Blueprint (2020) [hereinafter OECD, Pillar Two Blueprint].

35 *Id.* at 3.

36 OECD, Pillar One Blueprint, *supra* note 31.

37 U.S. Department of the Treasury, Presentation by the United States to the Steering Group of the Inclusive Framework Meeting (Apr. 8, 2021).

38 Statement, *supra* note 1.

39 Young Ran (Christine) Kim, *Digital Services Tax: A Cross-Border Variation of the Consumption Tax Debate*, 72 ALA. L. REV. 131, 155–58 (2020).

40 OECD, Pillar One Blueprint, *supra* note 31, at 10.

especially digital platforms where the new tax challenges were significant. It rather targets any business sector that meets its revenue threshold and profitability, even if the business is not part of the digital sector.[41] This is especially odd considering that the title of the Statement still declares that its purpose is "to address the tax challenges arising from the digitalization of the economy."[42] We suggest that the initial focus of Pillar One, which is the digital economy, ought to be emphasized. Below are the key developments of Pillar One.

5.2.2 *Pillar One Blueprint*

The Pillar One Blueprint, released in October 2020, is the first comprehensive proposal to expand the taxing rights of market countries. The new concepts revealed in the Blueprint, called Amounts A and B, were devised for this purpose. Amount A focuses on the new taxing right of market countries by eliminating physical presence requirements,[43] whereas Amount B allocates certain amounts of fixed returns arising from marketing and distribution activities to market countries where businesses have physical presence. In addition to these two concepts, the other goals of Pillar One are to significantly improve tax certainty and dispute resolution mechanisms, and to have relevant unilateral measures (such as DSTs) removed.[44] Below are the key design elements of Amount A, which have shown the most dramatic development in the subsequent negotiations.

Scope: Amount A applies only to consumer-facing businesses (CFB) and businesses performing automated digital services (ADS). A CFB is "a business that supplies goods or services, directly or indirectly, that are of a type commonly sold to consumers, and/or licenses or otherwise exploits intangible property that is connected to the supply of such goods and services."[45] The Blueprint does not offer examples, but Chanel (supplying luxury goods), Starbucks (supplying branded foods and refreshments), Johnson & Johnson (supplying pharmaceuticals), and Mercedes-Benz (supplying automobiles) would be included.[46]

An ADS is a service that is either: (i) on the positive list, such as online advertising services, online search engines, social media platforms, and digital content services; or (ii) is automated (that is, once the system is set up the provision of the service to a particular user requires minimal human involvement on the part of the service

[41] *See, e.g.*, Comment from Katherine Amos, Louise Weingrod & Kris Bodson, Johnson & Johnson, to OECD Centre for Tax Policy and Administration on OECD Tax Challenges Arising from Digitalisation – Report on the Pillar One Blueprint 2–3 (Dec. 14, 2020) (on file with authors).

[42] Statement, *supra* note 1.

[43] OECD, Pillar One Blueprint, *supra* note 31, at 8.

[44] *Id.* at 15–17.

[45] *Id.* at 39.

[46] *See* Glenn DeSouza, *Blueprint on Pillar One – What's New and Important*, BLOOMBERG TAX (Nov. 3, 2020, 3:00 AM), https://news.bloombergtax.com/transfer-pricing/blueprint-on-pillar-one-whats-new-and-important [https://perma.cc/VCZ3-EYYF].

provider), digital (i.e., provided over the internet or an electronic network), and not on the negative list.

Revenue Threshold: Amount A applies to businesses only if they meet a global and local revenue threshold. The specific amounts of these thresholds have not been finalized, with little information provided except for a comment stating that "there may be little advantage in using a threshold below the current €750 million threshold . . . ."[47] At that threshold, an estimated 2,300 multinational enterprise groups would be within the scope of Amount A.[48] The local in-scope revenue threshold is considered to exclude largely domestic businesses.

Nexus: The new nexus rule identifies which market jurisdictions qualify for Amount A without considering the business's physical presence. The Amount A nexus will be recognized if local revenue from in-scope businesses exceeds a certain amount.[49] However, a specific amount has not yet been proposed.

Profit Allocation: The Pillar One Blueprint lays out a three-step process for calculating the quantum of Amount A.[50]

1. Calculate the amount of "residual profit," defined as profit that exceeds a profitability threshold (i.e., pre-tax profit divided by revenue). This amount is subject to profit allocation.
2. Multiply a "reallocation percentage" to residual profit. This amount is reallocated mostly from residence countries to market countries because physical presence requirement is eliminated.
3. If there are multiple market countries, an "allocation key" based on local in-scope revenues applies to divide Amount A among eligible jurisdictions.

5.2.2.1 US Comprehensive Scoping Proposal

During the Trump administration, the United States was not supportive of Pillar One, just as it opposed Action 1 of BEPS 1.0, because it considered the new tax regime to be discriminatory against US tech giants, putting them at a competitive disadvantage.[51] Furthermore, the United States would lose revenue due to the expected revenue reallocation. US resistance to Pillar One was best epitomized by its safe harbor proposal, essentially making the tax regime elective.[52] The global

47 *Id.* at 62.
48 U.S. Department of the Treasury, *supra* note 36, at 11.
49 OECD, Pillar One Blueprint, *supra* note 31, at 65.
50 *Id.* at 120.
51 Channing Flynn & Jennifer Cooper, *BEPS Action 1 – Where Are We?*, INT'L TAX REV. (Oct. 26, 2017), http://www.internationaltaxreview.com/Article/3762337/BEPS-Action-1Where-are-we.html [https://perma.cc/2RWJ-375W].
52 Andrea Shalal et al., *U.S. Drops "Safe Harbor" Demand, Raising Hopes for Global Tax Deal*, REUTERS (Feb. 26, 2021, 11:16 AM), https://www.reuters.com/article/us-g20-usa-oecd/u-s-drops-safe-harbor-demand-raising-hopes-for-global-tax-deal-idUSKBN2AQ2E6 [https://perma.cc/4ARA-6JGT].

community has criticized this attitude as harmful to the effectiveness of the proposal.[53]

However, the Biden administration appears to be more sympathetic to the global effort, as shown by its decision to offer an alternative plan called the "comprehensive scoping proposal," and to withdraw the Trump administration's safe harbor proposal.[54] The comprehensive scoping proposal uses quantitative criteria based on revenues and profit margins to identify the world's largest and most profitable multinational groups, regardless of industry classification or business model.[55] Assuming that the profitability threshold is fixed at 10 percent, the US proposal drastically cuts the number of businesses within scope from 780 to 100 or fewer.[56]

The comprehensive scoping approach has significant merits because it simplifies the business line segmentation in the Pillar One Blueprint. This segmentation is considered "the most complicated and difficult building block" of Pillar One.[57] However, some major market players have criticized the arbitrariness of the cutoff, which would only include 100 multinational enterprises, regardless of the type of business. Non-digital multinationals, like Johnson & Johnson, have argued that they would be included in the top 100 multinationals. Yet there is no reason for them to be subjected to the Pillar One regime, because the misalignment between value creation and taxation does not occur in their type of business.[58] The purpose of Pillar One is to recognize a new tax nexus for digital businesses that do not have any physical presence in market countries and to reallocate the profits to market countries accordingly. Therefore, requiring non-digital companies with physical presence in major market countries to comply with the new regime would waste time and money.

5.2.3 *The Global Tax Deal Statement*

On July 1, 2021, the Inclusive Framework (IF) Statement was released as a preview of the global tax deal,[59] followed by the final Statement released on October 8, 2021. The global tax deal was supported by 137 countries and jurisdictions by that time,

[53] *US Suggests Safe Harbour Regime for OECD Pillar One Proposal*, TAX J. (Dec. 11, 2019), https://www.taxjournal.com/articles/us-suggests-safe-harbour-regime-for-oecd-pillar-one-proposal [https://perma.cc/TW46-CQ4G].

[54] Stephanie Soong Johnston, *U.S. Offers Key to Unlock Scope Issue in Global Tax Reform Talks*, 102 TAX NOTES INT'L 147 (2021).

[55] U.S. Department of the Treasury, *supra* note 36, at 12.

[56] *Id.* at 11.

[57] *Id.* at 18.

[58] *See, e.g.*, Johnson & Johnson Comments on OECD Tax Challenges Arising from Digitalisation – Report on the Pillar One Blueprint 2 (2020); Michael J. Graetz, *A Major Simplification of the OECD's Pillar 1 Proposal*, 101 TAX NOTES INT'L 199, 203 (2021) (criticizing that the exclusion of financial services is likely political).

[59] Statement, *supra* note 1.

and their support represents more than 90 percent of global GDP.[60] The noticeable difference in the Statement from the previously released Pillar One Blueprint was the scope of Amount A. The Statement abandons the industry-based approach, and instead adopts a quantitative approach based on the gross revenue and profitability of businesses. Although its language differs from that of the US comprehensive scoping proposal, the result effectively follows the US proposal by drastically cutting the number of in-scope businesses from 780 to seventy-eight of the world's largest companies.[61] Amount A will be implemented by a multilateral instrument (treaty) that is expected to be developed and opened for signature in 2022 and be effective in 2023.[62]

Scope:[63] A multinational is within the scope of Amount A if its global turnover exceeds €20 billion, and its profitability exceeds 10 percent. Profitability is determined by dividing pretax profit by revenue. Pillar One is to be reviewed seven years after it takes effect. If its implementation is found to be successful, the turnover threshold will be reduced to €10 billion.

The Statement excludes extractives (nonrenewable resources such as petroleum and minerals) and regulated financial services (banking, insurance, and asset management).

Nexus:[64] A market jurisdiction has nexus when an in-scope business derives at least €1 million in revenue from that jurisdiction. For a smaller jurisdiction (those with a GDP of less than €40 billion), the nexus threshold is €250,000.

Profit Allocation (Quantum):[65] Twenty-five percent of the residual profit of an in-scope business will be allocated to market jurisdictions with nexus, whereby residual profit is defined as profit more than 10 percent of revenue. A revenue-based allocation key will determine the specific allocation.

Revenue Sourcing:[66] The source rules determine when revenues of an in-scope business arise in, and thus are sourced to, the end market jurisdictions – that is, the place where goods and services are used or consumed. The OECD has subsequently released the Draft Model Rules for detailed source rules concerning specific categories of transactions. Notably, revenue is sourced on a transaction-by-transaction basis, and all revenues must be sourced using reliable indicators.[67]

60 *Id.*; OECD, *130 Countries and Jurisdictions Join Bold New Framework for International Tax Reform* (July 1, 2021), https://www.oecd.org/newsroom/130-countries-and-jurisdictions-join-bold-new-framework-for-international-tax-reform.htm [https://perma.cc/3AVR-NYAC] [hereinafter OECD, *Press Release*].

61 U.S. Department of the Treasury, *supra* note 36, at 11; Michael Devereux & Martin Simmler, *Who Will Pay Amount A?*, EconPol Pol'y Brief, Oxford Univ. Ctr. Bus. Tax'n, 3 (2021).

62 Statement, *supra* note 1, at 3.

63 *Id.* at 1.

64 *Id.*; OECD, *Pillar One – Amount A: Draft Model Rules for Nexus and Revenue Sourcing*, Organization for Economic Co-operation and Development 5 (2022) [hereinafter OECD, *Draft Model Rules*].

65 OECD, *Draft Model Rules*, *supra* note 63, at 2.

66 Statement, *supra* note 1, at 2.

67 *Id.* at 6.

TABLE 5.1 *Key differences between the Pillar One Blueprint and the Statement*

	Pillar One Blueprint	Statement
Scope	Automated digital services (ADS) and consumer-facing business (CFB)	Global turnover > €20 billion; profitability >10%; excludes extractives and regulated financial services
Nexus	Based on local revenue from in-scope; specific amount not proposed	Revenue of in-scope business from jurisdiction > €1 million (€250,000 for smaller jurisdictions)
Profit Allocation/ Quantum	Three-step calculation; specific ratio or threshold not proposed	25 percent of residual profit; revenue-based allocation key
Revenue Sourcing	Sourced to end-market jurisdictions where goods or services are used or consumed. Source rules to be developed for specific categories of transactions	The same; the Draft Model Rules proposing that revenue is sourced on a transaction-by-transaction basis
Tax Base	Determined by reference to financial accounting income; loss carryforward	The same; segmentation to occur only in exceptional circumstances, in which disclosed segments meet the scope rules
Elimination of Double Taxation	Exemptions or credits	The same; safe harbor for marketing and distribution profits to be developed
Amount B	Standardize arm's-length principle to in-country baseline marketing and distribution activities	To be simplified and streamlined by the end of 2022
Tax Certainty	Mandatory and binding dispute prevention and resolution mechanisms for Amount A–related issues	Elective for certain developing countries

5.2.4 *Pillar Two for Global Minimum Tax*

Pillar Two builds on the TCJA's GILTI and BEAT taxes in implementing the single tax principle,[68] where multinational enterprises that meet the €750 million revenue threshold are subject to a global minimum tax regardless of the jurisdiction in which they are headquartered or operating.[69] Pillar Two consists of (1) two interlocking domestic rules requiring income inclusion (Income Inclusion Rule, or IIR) and denial of deduction

68 Lilian V. Faulhaber, *Taxing Tech: The Future of Digital Taxation*, 39 VA. TAX REV. 145, 175 (2019).

69 Statement, *supra* note 1, at 3–5.

(Undertaxed Profits Rule, or UTPR), together referred to the Global anti-Base Erosion (GLoBE) rules, and (2) a treaty-based rule (Subject to Tax Rule, or STTR).[70]

The Income Inclusion Rule requires the residence country of multinationals to impose a top-up tax on a parent entity at a minimum rate (15 percent) if the source country where the parent entity's subsidiary operates imposes a tax below such a minimum rate on the subsidiary's income. If the residence country does not impose such a minimum tax, the subsidiary's deduction for payment to the parent entity would be denied or an equivalent adjustment would be required, as per the UTPR, to the extent the low tax income of a subsidiary is not subject to tax under an IIR. For example, suppose that a subsidiary in the source country earns $100 of income and the source country imposes tax at 10 percent, which is below the 15 percent global minimum tax rate. Then the residence country of the subsidiary's parent entity would include the $100 with the parent's income and impose tax at a rate that is equal to the difference between the global minimum rate and the 10 percent tax rate the subsidiary paid on the $100 in its low-tax jurisdiction. Suppose further that the subsidiary pays the $100 to the parent in a deductible form, such as royalty. If the residence country does not have the IIR, the subsidiary's deduction for the $100 royalty profit will be denied; or other measures can be taken to increase the subsidiary's tax rate to 15%.

The Subject to Tax Rule, on the other hand, is a standalone treaty rule and specifically targets intercompany payments that exploit treaties to shift profits to low-tax jurisdictions.[71] Therefore, this rule applies to certain categories of payments that present a greater risk of base erosion, such as interest and royalties.[72] For example, suppose that a subsidiary in the source country pays $100 of royalty to a parent, and the parent's $100 of royalty income is subject to a nominal tax rate below the minimum rate (currently suggested at 7.5–9 percent) in the residence country. Then, the source country is allowed to impose a withholding tax on the royalty payment at a rate that is equal to the difference between the minimum rate provided for under the STTR and the nominal tax rate.[73]

The Pillar Two tax regime is quite complex, and much work still needs to be done to determine the details.[74] However, Pillar Two is expected to reduce profit shifting by multinationals. If enough large economies agree to implement Pillar Two, there will be no incentive for companies to put their businesses in low-tax jurisdictions.

In short, Pillar One is a reform to strengthen source-based taxation. It is the most effective way to eliminate profit shifting and tax competition given the location of customers. Pillar Two takes a different approach by strengthening residence-based

70 OECD, Pillar Two Blueprint, *supra* note 33, ¶ 8.

71 *Id.* ¶ 566.

72 *Id.* ¶ 568.

73 *Id.* ¶ 650.

74 *See, e.g.*, Avi-Yonah et al., *supra* note 4; Reuven S. Avi-Yonah, *The New International Tax Framework: Evolution or Revolution?*, 25 Am. Soc. Int'l L. 1 (2021).

taxation. Firms would no longer have incentive to change their place of residence or location of headquarters.

5.3 PROBLEMS OF THE PROPOSED GLOBAL DEAL

The world seems to agree that the OECD's tax reform plan is an overdue and necessary update for the digital age.[75] On July 11, 2021, finance ministers from the G20 announced the G20's endorsement of the OECD's changes to international tax rules.[76] As of November 4, 2021, 137 out of 141 IF member countries and jurisdictions have agreed to the two-pillar proposal for reforming the international tax system.[77] The response from world leaders, journalists, tax organizations, business leaders, and public interest groups has remained overwhelmingly positive. According to US Treasury Secretary Janet Yellen, there is growing consensus that the OECD plan is the right path to establishing a tax regime that is fair for all.[78]

However, the EU and other proponents of the global tax deal must first address several major obstacles to the global tax deal. Crucially, many sensitive and substantive issues regarding Pillar One have been deferred to a potential multilateral instrument, which is unlikely to come into effect because it requires US ratification. It is less likely that the supportive press coverage would continue as more specific details of the tax plan are negotiated, and compromises must inevitably be made. The following are some of the key problems of the proposed global deal.

5.3.1 *An Agreement, Not a Solution*

The Statement is an eight-page document discussing both pillars, whereas the combined Blueprint for both pillars is about 500 pages long. Section I.B introduces only the key elements of both documents, but the Statement, especially with regard to Pillar One, is no more than a general statement that leaves details to be determined in a future multilateral instrument that will be developed later in 2022. There have been major developments since the Blueprint, such as the dramatic change in the scope of Amount A. The Pillar One Blueprint was criticized as a compromise of too many previous proposals, for being too complex, and for deviating from the original tax problem of the digital, global economy. Given that

[75] *OECD Sees Global Minimum Accord Improving Tax System: Cormann*, BLOOMBERG TV (July 8, 2021), https://www.bloomberg.com/news/videos/2021-07-08/oecd-sees-global-minimum-accord-improving-tax-system-cormann-video [https://perma.cc/E4JE-LFGA].

[76] Natalie Olivo, *New Global Tax Rules May Face Old Treaties, Other Hurdles*, LAW360 (July 12, 2021), https://www.law360.com/tax-authority/articles/1402215/new-global-tax-rules-may-face-old-treaties-other-hurdles.

[77] Statement, *supra* note 1, at 1.

[78] Christopher Condon, *G-20 Finance Chiefs Back Tax Deal and Vow to Clear Hurdles*, BLOOMBERG (July 10, 2021), https://www.bloomberg.com/news/articles/2021-07-10/yellen-optimistic-congress-will-back-part-of-global-tax-deal [https://perma.cc/9D7V-XLDJ].

the Statement makes yet another major shift, it needs to provide a policy explanation for doing so. However, the Statement is silent on the reason for the change, not to mention its implications for tax authorities and taxpayers, inviting our critical assessment.

The general nature of the Statement may reflect a political and diplomatic desire to encourage as many countries as possible to join in. However, if the world reaches an agreement on the Statement only because it dodges sensitive issues, it can hardly be considered a long-awaited solution for international tax reform. Such an agreement would be a mere political event to boast a nominal achievement to domestic constituents and would only invite more discord among the IF member states. As details of the plan are negotiated and compromises inevitably made, support from the member states and the press is likely to wane. The following sections identify and discuss grounds for discord.

5.3.2 *Logistical and Political Challenges of Pillar One*

Pillar One will be implemented by a multilateral instrument – a treaty – that was expected to be signed later in 2024 and take effect in 2025, but that did not happen.[79] However, multilateral instruments and the tax treaty ratification process are plagued by various challenges, such as achieving consensus between more than 140 jurisdictions, reconciling the distinct rules and political realities of each country's legal system, and overcoming logistical challenges to implementation and adherence.

Achieving consensus among the global community has proved to be a challenge in the past. For example, international negotiations regarding the BEPS 1.0 project were ongoing for nearly eight years without consensus as to how the international tax regime should change.[80] There are relatively few successful multilateral tax conventions, and those that do exist are typically smaller in scope and have fewer party signatories.[81]

The immense logistical challenges of implementing a multilateral tax agreement between more than 140 jurisdictions are exacerbated by the reality that the OECD international tax plan would control relationships between countries that may not have relationships governed by existing bilateral treaties.[82] This raises complex

[79] Statement, *supra* note 1, at 3.

[80] Gary B. Wilcox & Warren Payne, *Hitching Biden's Corporate Tax Proposals to the Global Tax Bandwagon*, TAX NOTES (June 21, 2021), https://www.taxnotes.com/tax-notes-today-federal/corporate-taxation/hitching-bidens-corporate-tax-proposals-global-tax-bandwagon/2021/06/21/76lr5 [https://perma.cc/DX96-L4LK].

[81] Mary C. Bennett, *Contemplating a Multilateral Convention to Implement OECD Pillars 1 and 2*, TAX NOTES (June 16, 2021), https://www.taxnotes.com/tax-notes-today-international/base-erosion-and-profit-shifting-beps/contemplating-multilateral-convention-implement-oecd-pillars-1-and-2/2021/06/16/76k35?highlight=ratification%20challenges%20multilateral%20treaties#sec-1 [https://perma.cc/RG98-BAV7].

[82] *See id.*

concerns related to binding dispute resolution, introducing another element of political tension among some in the global community.

In addition, even after consensus is reached, it takes time for each country to ratify treaty amendments. In the case of the 2015 BEPS 1.0 tax treaty amendment, many countries took months or years to sign the multilateral instrument, and others, including the United States, have never ratified it.[83]

Furthermore, political realities in the United States illustrate the complexities of ratifying a multilateral tax instrument. There is little likelihood that the US Congress will pass the global tax deal in a single bill, increasing the difficulty of ratification in the US Senate. Additionally, the United States has yet to ratify the 2015 BEPS tax treaty amendments,[84] indicating that despite executive intent to comply with international agreements, it is not always possible under the constraints of the US legal system.

The Pillar One multilateral treaty will alter US bilateral treaties with other countries, and therefore will need to be ratified by two-thirds of the US Senate.[85] However, getting seventeen Republicans to support a treaty measure that many view as penalizing US companies may be a nonstarter in the current economic and political climate.[86] Senate approval of the Pillar One treaty in any form will almost certainly require the inclusion of a ban on all current and future DSTs, including the proposed EU digital levy.[87]

Pillar Two, on the other hand, is generally compatible with existing tax treaties and the GLoBE rules, the main part of Pillar Two, and can likely be implemented through amendments to domestic tax legislation.[88] However, the Biden administration's attempt to use the reconciliation process, which only requires a majority vote, to push through changes related to Pillar Two's tax reform plan in the Build Back Better Act and negotiate with the Senate on Pillar One at a later time, was not

[83] For a graphic indicating the length of time, see (@DanNeidle), TWITTER (July 2, 2021), https://web.archive.org/web/20210702095624/https://twitter.com/DanNeidle/status/1410900061740011521.

[84] OECD, *Signatories and Parties to the Multilateral Convention to Implement Tax Treaty Related Measures to Prevent Base Erosion and Profit Shifting*, BEPS Multilateral Instrument (2021) (showing that the United States is not listed as a signatory).

[85] Lilian Faulhaber, *Will the OECD Plan Fix International Taxation?*, LAW360 (July 7, 2021), https://www.law360.com/articles/1400693 [https://perma.cc/W539-67UV].

[86] Mindy Herzfeld, *Pushing Pillar 1 Past Congress*, TAX NOTES (July 19, 2021), https://www.taxnotes.com/tax-notes-today-federal/fundamental-tax-system-structure/pushing-pillar-1-past-congress/2021/07/19/76vyv?highlight=base%20erosion [https://perma.cc/P4YW-B94D].

[87] Stephanie Soong Johnston, *Crapo and Brady Urge Yellen to Push for Immediate End to DSTs*, TAX NOTES (July 12, 2021), https://www.taxnotes.com/tax-notes-today-federal/fundamental-tax-system-structure/pushing-pillar-1-past-congress/2021/07/19/76vyv [https://perma.cc/2RWX-GMST]; Theodoric Meyer & Jacqueline Alemany, *BBB Negotiations Stall in the Senate, Could Drag into Next Year*, WASH. POST (Dec. 17, 2021), https://www.washingtonpost.com/politics/2021/12/17/bbb-negotiations-stall-senate-could-drag-into-next-year/ [https://perma.cc/EB8B-ZYLR].

[88] Faulhaber, *supra* note 84.

successful.[89] Furthermore, a potential treaty override issue is expected as to the Pillar One implementation, which is discussed further in Section 4.1.

The OECD global tax reform has the public support and momentum to take it over the finish line. However, the piecemeal implementation of the plan likely to happen in the United States means that good faith and trust between the United States and the EU will unfortunately be required if the plan is to be fully implemented. If the EU and United Kingdom make the good faith gesture of abandoning the digital tax levy and immediately repealing their DSTs, there might be at least a possibility that the US Senate would ratify Pillar One, and that the OECD tax plan would be fully implemented throughout much of the world. However, if the EU continues to claim that a digital levy is not a digital tax, and the EU member states engage in brinkmanship with the United States regarding DST repeal, the US Senate will likely reject or decline to vote on Pillar One, and there will be only partial worldwide implementation of the OECD plan.

5.3.3 *Repeal of Existing DSTs and Potential Digital Levy*

The reality of delayed US passage of Pillar One adds further murkiness to the issue of the EU digital tax levy and the unilateral DSTs currently enacted by several countries. Pillar One could be in jeopardy if the EU moves forward with its digital tax levy and its individual members drag their feet in repealing their unilateral DSTs.

Many commentators expect that countries that currently have or propose DSTs – for example, France, Canada, Italy, and India – may be reluctant to repeal them, at least until the United States implements Pillar One.[90] In fact, the United States has entered into individual agreements with the United Kingdom, France, Italy, Spain, and Austria that resulted in these countries retaining their digital taxes for now. If the OECD-brokered global overhaul were implemented by 2023, the countries will offer a credit to refund any taxes collected more than what corporations would pay under the global tax deal, but that did not happen.[91] This means that the five major advanced economies will preserve DSTs if the global tax deal eventually fails, and that taxpayers must deal with DSTs for the time being. In that case, the world might have partial implementation of the two-pillar tax plan. Also, if DSTs are still in

[89] Stephanie Soong Johnston, *U.S. Reconciliation Bill May Have Global Minimum Tax Provisions*, Tax Notes (July 12, 2021), https://www.taxnotes.com/tax-notes-today-international/politics-taxation/us-reconciliation-bill-may-have-global-minimum-tax-provisions/2021/07/07/76rh7 [https://perma.cc/AYY5-TPJ5].

[90] Natalie Olivo, *Digital Taxes May Linger After Global Deal, Panelists Say*, Law360 (July 14, 2021), https://www.law360.com/tax-authority/articles/1402957/digital-taxes-may-linger-after-global-deal-panelists-say- [https://perma.cc/G9UG-LQ9J].

[91] *Id.*

place, the United States may end up imposing punitive tariffs again, the ramifications of which are discussed later in this chapter.

Furthermore, the EU is preparing a new digital levy, asserting that it will be compatible with the two-pillar proposal.[92] If the EU goes forward with a digital levy after the global tax deal is finalized, it is likely that the United States will reject Pillar One.[93]

Despite the Statement's mandate to repeal DSTs and refrain from introducing others in the future, US lawmakers remain skeptical. Two top Republican senators sent a letter to Treasury Secretary Yellen on July 8, 2021, asserting that Congress will not support an OECD tax reform deal unless it protects the US economy, including the instant repeal of DSTs. In 2025, the Trump administration formally announced its opposition to the global tax deal and that it will study the imposition of tariffs and other retaliatory measures in response to DSTs and the UTPR.[94]

5.3.4 *Revenue Competition from Benefits of Tax Reform*

The need to reform the century-old international tax system and the revenue benefits resulting from such reform have been the main drivers behind over 140 jurisdictions agreeing to the proposed global tax reform plan. It is estimated that Pillar One, the new nexus and profit allocation rules, will reallocate profits of $100 billion to market countries annually.[95] Most states joining the global tax deal would likely see a revenue increase as a result of Pillar One.[96] Simultaneously, Pillar Two, with its global minimum corporate income tax of 15 percent, is expected to generate approximately $150 billion in additional global tax revenues each year.[97] Hence, from a global perspective, the global tax reform will benefit the world.[98] The IMF, representing an additional fifty-one countries, also backs the plan.[99]

However, individual countries' interests may not exactly align with the collective benefits. Each country would like to secure net revenue gain rather than loss.

[92] *EU Digital Levy*, *supra* note 6.

[93] Elodie Lamer, *Growing Unease in EU Over Global Tax Deal's Next Steps*, TAX NOTES (July 12, 2021), https://www.taxnotes.com/tax-notes-today-international/corporate-taxation/growing-unease-eu-over-global-tax-deals-next-steps/2021/07/12/76rz4?highlight=OECD [perma link].

[94] Letter from Mike Crapo and Kevin Brady, U.S. Senators, to Janet Yellen, U.S. Treasury Secretary (July 8, 2021).

[95] OECD, *Press Release*, *supra* note 59.

[96] Robert Goulder, *The Cost of Change: Pillar 1 Reduced to the Back of a Napkin*, 103 TAX NOTES 111 (July 1, 2021), https://www.taxnotes.com/tax-notes-today-international/international-taxation/cost-change-pillar-1-reduced-back-napkin/2021/07/06/76qdb?highlight=Global%20Minimum%20TaX [perma link].

[97] *Id.*

[98] William Horobin, *Global Tax Overhaul Endorsed by 130 Nations as Deal Gets Closer*, BLOOMBERG (July 1, 2021), https://www.bloomberg.com/news/articles/2021-07-01/global-tax-overhaul-endorsed-by-130-nations-as-deal-gets-closer [https://perma.cc/DUU2-MXGQ].

[99] Eric Martin, *IMF Sees Room to Simplify Global Tax Deal to Boost Participation*, BLOOMBERG (July 10, 2021), https://www.bloomberg.com/news/articles/2021-07-10/imf-sees-room-to-simplify-global-tax-deal-to-boost-participation [https://perma.cc/JM8S-Y7FR].

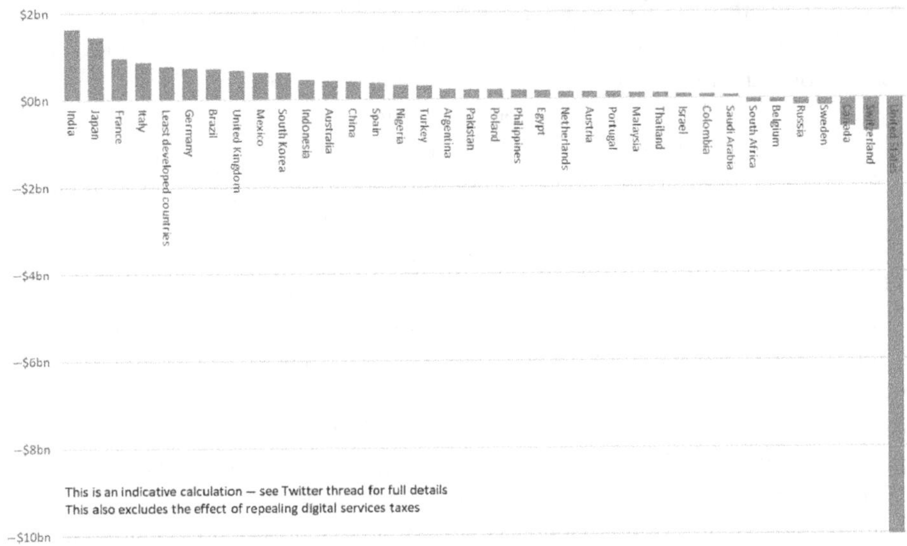

FIGURE 5.2 Approximate net revenue gain from Pillar One
Dan Neidle (@DanNeidle), TWITTER (June 16, 2021, 6:40 AM), https://web.archive.org/web/20210616124055/https://twitter.com/DanNeidle/status/1405143274403270662 (underlying data available at https://github.com/DanNeidle/pillar_one).

Figure 5.2 shows a preliminary, backof-a-napkin estimate based on calculations completed by Dan Neidle, a Clifford Chance tax attorney from London. Countries like the United Kingdom and China would essentially break even under Pillar One's profit reallocation regime after factoring in the cost of crediting. Notably, the United States will experience the greatest loss under Pillar One's profit reallocation regime: $10.3 billion each year despite a revenue increase of $12.6 billion. This estimation may be obvious considering that the US corporate community disproportionately consists of in-scope taxpayers, namely, tech companies. The question thus arises as to why the United States would go along with Pillar One unless there is a quid pro quo, namely, other countries repealing DSTs and adopting Pillar Two.

On the contrary, Treasury Secretary Yellen contended that Pillar One would be revenue-neutral for the United States.[100] To reconcile Secretary Yellen's statement with Neidle's calculations, tax commentator Robert Goulder explores the idea that Yellen made different assumptions regarding foreign tax credits, or that she meant the operation of Pillars One and Two jointly would create a revenue-neutral result for the United States.[101] Another interpretation may be that acceptance of Pillar One

[100] *See* Letter from Janet Yellen, U.S. Treasury Secretary, to Mike Crapo, U.S. Senator (June 4, 2021).

[101] Goulder, *supra* note 95; Robert Goulder, *The Cost of Change, Part II: Rethinking U.S. Exposure to Pillar 1*, TAX NOTES (July 20, 2021), https://www.taxnotes.com/tax-notes-international/tax-avoidance-and-evasion/cost-change-part-ii-rethinking-us-exposure-pillar-1/2021/07/19/76vqp.

by other countries with the mandate that they repeal DSTs and reduce discrimination against US multinationals may offset losses under Pillar One. Nonetheless, these are all speculations, and the US government has not disclosed its own calculation.

Putting aside the revenue competition among countries, let us turn to the taxpayers. Who will be liable for the new tax under the tax reform? In other words, is Pillar One free from the criticism that it is discriminatory against US tech giants? A calculation focusing on the composition of Pillar One's Amount A implies that the answer is no. Michael Devereux and Martin Simmler of Oxford University indicate that the extent of Pillar One will only apply to seventy-eight of the world's 500 largest companies.[102] The aggregate Amount A allocation for the seventy-eight companies subject to Pillar One is approximately $87 billion.[103] Strikingly, 64 percent of Amount A profits will come from companies headquartered in the United States.[104] Contrast this with the fact that the United States only comprises 20–25 percent of world GDP.[105] Furthermore, around 45 percent of the aggregate Amount A allocation will come from technology companies, with approximately 32 percent coming from Apple, Microsoft, Alphabet, Intel, and Facebook.[106] Consequently, the discrimination issue may persist under the Pillar One regime.

5.4 HOW SHOULD THE UNITED STATES RESPOND?

DSTs offer a possible action guide at both the international and domestic levels. Section 5.4.1 explains various legal issues that the United States might face if it uses executive agreements to implement Pillar One while bypassing the treaty ratification in Senate. Section 5.4.2 then suggests severing the two-pillar proposals to at least save Pillar Two and the global minimum tax. Section 5.4.3 suggests avoiding a global trade war even if Pillar One fails and DSTs survive, by offering a case study on France's DST.

5.4.1 *The Inherent Difficulty with Treaty Override*

Section 3.2 expects that the Pillar One tax regime will have difficulty passing Congress.

The United States may not expect to implement Pillar One as a multilateral tax treaty as proposed by the OECD because, without Republican support, In the future it would be impossible to get two thirds of the votes in the Senate. The United States may try a congressional–executive agreement with a majority vote in both houses,

[102] Devereux & Simmler, *supra* note 60.
[103] *Id.* at 1.
[104] *Id.* at 4.
[105] The World Bank, *GDP (Current US$)* (July 30, 2021), https://data.worldbank.org/indicator/NY.GDP.MKTP.CD [https://perma.cc/SQ53-T429].
[106] Devereux & Simmler, *supra* note 60, at 1.

but that still needs to be an override of Articles 5 (permanent establishment), 7 (business profits), and 9 (associated enterprises) of the existing bilateral tax treaties.

Unfortunately, use of "treaty override" to implement Pillar One in the United States is a double-edged sword for proponents of international tax law.[107] While enactment by the United States is essential for the effectiveness of Pillar One, the foundation of international law would be weakened with each treaty override.[108]

5.4.1.1 Overview of Treaty Overrides

DEFINITION In 1989, the OECD issued its report on "Tax Treaty Override."[109] It defined a "treaty override" as a "situation where the domestic legislation of a State overrules provisions of either a single treaty or all treaties hitherto having had effect in that State," and recommended states to "avoid enacting legislation which is intended to have effects in clear contradiction to international treaty obligations."[110] However, such a traditional definition would be too narrow to explain a more recent phenomenon in international law. The expected executive agreement to implement Pillar One is a good example. If the United States implements the Pillar One tax regime by an executive agreement, that will override existing bilateral tax treaties. Will it also be a "treaty override"? Another definition that better encompasses the ways in which an override can occur describes a treaty override as "when a contracting state [to a treaty] intentionally applies domestic law or regulation to accomplish specifically what a treaty forbids."[111] According to this definition, executive agreements that contradict the existing tax treaties would be considered treaty overrides as well.

MONIST/DUALIST DISTINCTION The possibility of a treaty override is also state specific. It depends on the specific constitutional system and the legal mechanisms

[107] *See generally* C. De Pietro, *Tax Treaty Override and the Need for Coordination between Legal Systems: Safeguarding the Effectiveness of International Law*, 7 WORLD TAX J. 73 (2015); Craig Elliffe, *Preventing Unacceptable Tax Treaty Overrides*, 1 BRIT. TAX REV. 38 (2022); Rebecca M. Kysar, *Interpreting Tax Treaties*, 101 IOWA L. REV 1387, 1397–404 (2016); OECD, *Recommendation of the Council Concerning Tax Treaty Override*, OECD/LEGAL/0253 (Oct. 2, 1989), https://legalinstruments.oecd.org/en/instruments/OECD-LEGAL-0253 [hereinafter OECD 1989 Report]; Georg Kofler, *Legislative Tax Treaty Overrides in Austrian, German, and EU Law*, 67 BRIT. TAX REV. 64 (2022); Nicola Sartori, *Tax Treaty Override and Pacta Sunt Servanda: The Italian Perspective*, 1 BRIT. TAX REV. 94 (2022).

[108] OECD 1989 Report, *supra* note 106, at 4; *see* Reuven S. Avi-Yonah, *Sunt Pacta Servanda? The Problem of Tax Treaty Overrides*, BRIT. TAX REV. (2022) (manuscript at 8) (on file with authors). *See generally* RICHARD E. ANDERSEN, ANALYSIS OF UNITED STATES INCOME TAX TREATIES (2010); Nicolas M. Traut, *Tax Treaty Overrides and Friendliness towards International Law: A Comparative Approach to Put the Later-Intime-Rule to the Test*, 48 CAP. U. L. REV. 403, 411–12 (2020); KLAUS VOGEL, TAX TREATIES AND DOMESTIC LAW (2006).

[109] OECD 1989 Report, *supra* note 106.

[110] *Id.*

[111] Richard L. Doernberg, *Overriding Tax Treaties: The U.S. Perspective*, 9 EMORY INT'L L. REV. 71, 74 (1995).

in each country. States that legally permit treaty overrides are labeled dualist states and those that do not are labeled monist States.[112]

In many countries, treaties (including tax treaties) have a legal status superior to that of ordinary domestic laws (e.g., France, Italy, the Netherlands).[113] These countries are considered monist states. The monist view sees both international and domestic law as intrinsically part of the legal system, and international law becomes automatically a part of the domestic legal system. This means that a treaty which is validly executed in the international legal sense automatically takes full legal effect within domestic law. Subsequent general domestic tax legislation would not normally override a treaty.[114]

However, some countries like the United States and the United Kingdom view domestic legislation and international treaties as separate regimes of law.[115] International law (the treaty) regulates the relationship between sovereign states, but domestic law regulates legal matters relevant to that country.[116] These so-called dualist states only apply treaty provisions to domestic law when they are expressly incorporated into domestic legislation.[117]

The United States is noted by many scholars as being the classic example of a dualist overriding state.[118] The US Constitution lays out that "[l]aws of the United States which shall be made in pursuance thereof; and all treaties made, or which shall be made, under the authority of the United States, shall be the supreme law of the land."[119] This Supremacy Clause was intended to ensure the supremacy of both US federal laws and treaties to state laws and was one of the major innovations in the Constitution.[120] Accordingly, when treaties and state law conflict, treaties trump. However, the Constitution is less clear about the relationship between federal laws and treaties. Despite the lack of clarity in the Constitution, the US Supreme Court has established the principle of lex posterior, meaning that the later law prevails. In other words, the US system operates on the notion that the most recent expression of the sovereign is the governing law.[121] This mechanism has allowed the United States to override several international treaties.

[112] Elliffe, *supra* note 106, at 4; De Pietro, *supra* note 106, at 85–87; Sachin Sachdeva, *Tax Treaty Overrides: A Comparative Study of the Monist and the Dualist Approaches*, 41 INTERTAX 180 (2013).

[113] Avi-Yonah, *supra* note 107, at 6–7.

[114] *Id.* at 6–7.

[115] Elliffe, *supra* note 106, at 5–6; De Pietro, *supra* note 106, at 85–87; Sachdeva, *supra* note 111.

[116] Sachdeva, *supra* note 111.

[117] *Id.*

[118] *See* Vienna Convention on the Law of Treaties, May 23, 1969, 1155 U.N.T.S. 331 [hereinafter VCLT]; *see, e.g.*, Avi-Yonah, *supra* note 107, at 11.

[119] U.S. Const. Article VI, cl. 2.

[120] Reuven S. Avi-Yonah & Brett Wells, *The Beat and Treaty Overrides: A Brief Response to Rosenbloom and Shaheen*, 7 (Univ. Mich. L. & Econ., Working Paper No. 157, 2018).

[121] *Id.*

WHEN HAS AN OVERRIDE OCCURRED? An important distinction to note with treaty override is that unlike the termination of a treaty, a treaty override unilaterally changes provisions in a treaty for one party but keeps the treaty in effect.

There are two ways that a treaty override can take place. First are explicit overrides, where the legislative intent to override a specific treaty is clear.[122] This usually comes with an explicit statement.[123] Second, implicit overrides are more challenging for courts to decipher. In these cases, it largely comes down to interpretation.[124] For example, "[r]ecently, the issue of implicit treaty overrides has become 'hot' again because of the debate over whether some provisions of the [TCJA] were an override."[125]

Accordingly, given that treaty overrides can occur both explicitly and implicitly, it is unclear in many dualist states exactly when an override has occurred and whether the legislature must be explicit about it or not.[126] To add some clarity, the OECD has put out two examples for the discussion to build on in its 1989 Report.

Example 1 is a straightforward case of a material breach of the treaty, in which a state introduces a new withholding tax on interest or royalties when these should be exempt from source-based taxation under the treaty. The OECD 1989 Report states that "[t]he breach being a material one, the treaty partners of State A would be justified in terminating their tax treaty relationship with State A. However, termination could do even more harm economically and endanger the possibility of finding an acceptable solution in the future."[127] However, it is hard to find an actual example on which this scenario is based, and thus, this example is not helpful to clarify the situation when an override has occurred.

Example 2 is a more realistic one: State B taxes capital gains from the sale of real property, but under its tax treaties is precluded from taxing capital gains on sales of stock. Taxpayers interpose a State B corporation between themselves and the real property and sell the shares in the corporation instead. State B legislates that the sale of the stock is deemed to be a sale of the real property for purposes of its treaties.[128] This example is based on the US Foreign Investors in Real Property Tax Act of 1980, which explicitly overrode Article 13 (capital gains) of most US tax treaties to impose a tax on the sale of shares in US real property holding companies.[129] In short, there is no guidance that helps clarify the implicit overrides.

[122] *See* Avi-Yonah, *supra* note 107, at 7; Traut, *supra* note 107.
[123] *See* Avi-Yonah, *supra* note 107, at 7; Traut, *supra* note 107; Omri Marian, *Unilateral Responses to Tax Treaty Abuse: A Functional Approach*, 41 Brook. J. Int'l L. 1157 (2016).
[124] *See, e.g.*, Kofler, *supra* note 106.
[125] Avi-Yonah, *supra* note 107, at 14.
[126] *See* Kysar, *supra* note 106, at 1397–404.
[127] OECD 1989 Report, *supra* note 106, at 9.
[128] *Id.* at 9–10.
[129] Avi-Yonah, *supra* note 107, at 9–10; 26 U.S.C. § 897 (2018).

INTERNATIONAL LAW ON TREATY OVERRIDES It is commonly recognized that if a state overrides a treaty, it is a violation of international law according to the Vienna Convention on the Law of Treaties (VCLT).[130] This is true even in countries that have not formally ratified the VCLT, as the VCLT is considered customary international law even in countries such as the United States.[131] To elaborate, Article 26 of the VCLT articulates the pacta sunt servanda principle.[132] It states that "[e]very treaty in force is binding upon the parties to it and must be performed by them in good faith."[133] Moreover, Article 27 adds that "[a] party may not invoke the provisions of its internal law as justification for its failure to perform a treaty."[134] Combining these two articles, "it is clear that treaty overrides constitute a violation of international law."[135]

This interpretation has been confirmed by the OECD, which strongly condemns any treaty overrides: "The OECD Report [also] clarifies that such treaty overrides violate international law (citing the VCLT), although they may still be binding as a matter of domestic law."[136] In addition, the OECD Report specifically stated that "[t]he certainty that tax treaties bring to international tax matters has, in the past few years been called into question, and to some extent undermined, by the tendency in certain countries for domestic legislation to be passed or proposed which may override provisions of tax treaties."[137]

However, in the event of an override, there are few remedies for foreign countries other than termination of the entire treaty, which is a rarely taken step.[138] In the event of a tax treaty dispute, it can only be adjudicated and remedied if both countries agree to submit the dispute to the International Court of Justice.[139] As a result, dualist countries such as the United States are unlikely to end their policy of treaty overrides through domestic legislation.

IMPLEMENTATION IN OTHER JURISDICTIONS As discussed in section II.B and the Statement, Pillar One is intended to be implemented through a multilateral treaty.[140] The multilateral treaty "will be developed to introduce a multilateral

[130] *See, e.g.*, Avi-Yonah, *supra* note 107, at 6–7.
[131] *Id.* at 7.
[132] VCLT, *supra* note 117, Article 26; *see also* Avi-Yonah, *supra* note 107, at 7; Craig Macfarlane Elliffe, *The Lesser of Two Evils: Double Tax Treaty Override or Treaty Abuse?*, 1 BRIT. TAX REV. 62, 70 (2016).
[133] VCLT, *supra* note 117, Articles 26, 27; *see also* Elliffe, *supra* note 131, at 71; Traut, *supra* note 107, at 411–12.
[134] VCLT, *supra* note 117, Article 27.
[135] Avi-Yonah, *supra* note 107, at 8; *see also* OECD 1989 Report, *supra* note 106, at 4.
[136] Avi-Yonah, *supra* note 107, at 9; *see* OECD 1989 Report, *supra* note 106, at 4.
[137] OECD 1989 Report, *supra* note 106, at 2; *see* Avi-Yonah, *supra* note 107, at 8. *See generally* Richard E. ANDERSEN, *supra* note 107; Traut, *supra* note 107, at 411–12; VOGEL, *supra* note 107.
[138] Avi-Yonah, *supra* note 107, at 9–10.
[139] Elliffe, *supra* note 131, at 15.
[140] Statement, *supra* note 1, at 3.

framework for all jurisdictions that join, regardless of whether a tax treaty currently exists between those jurisdictions."[141]

Given this intended strategy, it is unlikely that there will be many major obstacles, outside of the United States, for implementing the global tax deal. Most OECD member countries signed the multilateral instrument for BEPS 1.0, except for the United States, and it proved a success not only for implementing new tax policy but for how treaties in general might be implemented in other areas of international law. However, it is still useful to investigate how implementation in other OECD countries would work, as well.

COMMON LAW COUNTRIES Common law countries tend to be dualist states. These states include: the United Kingdom, Australia, New Zealand, Canada, Israel, India, and South Africa.[142] In each of these countries, Pillar One can only take domestic legal effect after additional domestic legislation is adopted by the respective parliaments.[143] In other words, when these states sign the multilateral treaty, the international obligations associated with Pillar One will be in effect, but additional steps are required on the domestic front to implement Pillar One. The OECD and the Inclusive Framework, however, mandated the Task Force on the Digital Economy to develop model rules by early 2022 as a reference for domestic legislation if members to the multilateral treaty "need to make changes to domestic law to implement the new taxing rights over Amount A ... [to] facilitate consistency in the approach taken by jurisdictions and to support domestic implementation consistent with the agreed timelines and their domestic legislative procedures."[144] In addition, "the model rules will be supplemented by commentary that describes the purpose and operation of the rules."[145] Therefore, implementation in each of these states should be smooth.

CONTINENTAL EUROPEAN/CIVIL LAW JURISDICTIONS Most Continental European states and most civil law jurisdictions are monist states, making implementation through the multilateral treaty streamlined in these jurisdictions. Prominent examples include Belgium, France, Greece, Luxembourg, the Netherlands, Russia, and Spain.[146] In the EU, the analysis of implementation is slightly different, but any involvement by the EU would only make implementation within the European block more likely.

141 *Id.*

142 David Sloss, *Domestic Application of Treaties*, *in* THE OXFORD GUIDE TO TREATIES 3 (Duncan B. Hollis ed., 2012).

143 *Id.*

144 Statement, *supra* note 1, at 7.

145 *Id.*

146 *See* Sachdeva, *supra* note 111.

In fact, on December 22, 2021, the EU Commission (Commission) published a legislative proposal for a directive to implement the rules of Pillar Two[147] and, in 2022, the Council of the EU agreed upon the directive. The directive is thus a binding instrument ensuring the implementation of Pillar Two by all twenty-seven EU member states.

The question now is whether there will also be a directive to implement Pillar One. This would seem entirely unnecessary if there is a multilateral treaty, as proposed by the OECD, but the EU Commission has indicated that they may propose such a directive anyway.[148] This may be helpful in the case there is an unresolved conflict between the multilateral treaty and any given bilateral tax treaties. In such a case, a directive could create an umbrella treaty override for all member states. Therefore, based on these developments, it seems likely that Pillar One will be implemented smoothly in most monist jurisdictions, especially within the European block.

5.4.1.2 Implementing Pillar One from the US Perspective

Given the current international legal climate and the rules regarding treaty overrides, what are the ways in which the United States might implement Pillar One and what are the consequences of a particular path? As mentioned, the United States would also have to override several bilateral tax treaties to implement Pillar One. What are the options, assuming a future US administration would like to implement Pillar One?

WAYS TREATIES ARE IMPLEMENTED Implementation analysis in the United States, and override analysis in this case, are somewhat complicated. As discussed above, there are different types of international agreements the United States makes from a domestic perspective, even though the obligation is all the same from an international perspective. Therefore, determining the domestic status of an international agreement requires looking at the type of agreement the United States is entering. The United States distinguishes between three types of international agreements: (1) treaties, (2) executive agreements, and (3) non-legal agreements, which involve the making of so-called "political commitments" (which are less relevant in this Chapter).[149]

[147] Eur. Comm'n, *Proposal for a Council Directive Laying Down Rules to Prevent the Misuse of Shell Entities for Tax Purposes and Amending Directive 2011/16/EU*, COM (2021) 565 final (Dec. 22, 2021).

[148] Charlotte Kies, *Agreement on Pillar One and Pillar Two Global Tax Reform*, LOYENS & LOEFF (Oct. 11, 2021), https://www.loyensloeff.com/lu/en/news/articles-and-newsflashes/agreement-on-pillar-one-and-pillar-two-global-tax-reform-n23713/ [https://perma.cc/M6MJ-WYAU].

[149] Curtis A. Bradley & Jack L. Goldsmith, *Presidential Control over International Law*, 131 HARV. L. REV. 1201, 1207–09 (2018); CONG. RSCH. SERV., COMM. OF FOREIGN RELS., TREATIES AND OTHER INTERNATIONAL AGREEMENTS: THE ROLE OF THE UNITED STATES SENATE 4 (2001) [hereinafter TREATIES AND OTHER INTERNATIONAL AGREEMENTS].

Treaties Under US law, "a treaty is an agreement negotiated and signed by a member of the executive branch that enters into force if it is approved by a two-thirds majority of the Senate and is subsequently ratified by the President."[150] The Treaty Clause – Article II, section 2, clause 2 of the Constitution – vests the power to make treaties in the President, acting with the "advice and consent" of the Senate. There is much debate about exactly what "advice" and "consent" mean, but the "advice" aspect has generally come to require the President to consult with the Senate during the treaty negotiation process before the Senate votes with its final "consent."[151] Moreover, under established US practice, the President cannot ratify a treaty unless the President accepts the Senate's conditions.[152] In other words, the Constitution allocates primary responsibility for entering treaties to the executive branch, but Congress also plays an essential role in the process.

In addition, treaties can be self-executing or non-self-executing. A self-executing treaty may be enforced in the courts without prior legislation by Congress, whereas a non-self-executing treaty may not be enforced in the courts without prior legislative "implementation."[153] Self-executing treaties, for example, have a status equal to federal statute, superior to US state law, and inferior to the Constitution. Courts generally have understood treaties that are not self-executing to have limited status domestically; rather, the legislation or regulations implementing these agreements are controlling.

US tax treaties have been regarded as self-executing since the first treaty (with France) was ratified in 1932, but there is debate regarding whether they should not be self-executing.[154] In addition, section 894(a) of the Internal Revenue Code requires that "[t]he provisions of this title shall be applied to any taxpayer with due regard to any treaty obligation of the United States which applies to such taxpayer,"[155] which, many scholars argue, indicates that legislation is not required to bring tax treaties into force.[156]

[150] Stephen P. Mulligan, Cong. Rsch. Serv., RL32528, International Law and Agreements: Their Effect upon U.S. Law 3 (2018); *see also* Restatement (Third) of Foreign Relations Law of the United States, § 101 (1987) [hereinafter Third Restatement].

[151] Mulligan, *supra* note 149, at 3; *see also* Louis Henkin, Foreign Affairs and the U.S. Constitution 177 (2d ed. 1996; Arthur Bestor, *"Advice" from the Very Beginning, "Consent" When the End Is Achieved*, 83 Am. J. Int'l L. 718, 726 (1989).

[152] Mulligan, *supra* note 149; United States v. Stuart, 489 U.S. 353, 374–75 (1989) (Scalia, J., concurring).

[153] *See* Carlos Manuel Vazquez, *The Four Doctrines of Self-Executing Treaties*, 89 Am. J. Int'l L. 695, 695 (1995).

[154] *See generally* Reuven S. Avi-Yonah, *Tax Treaties, the Constitution, and the Noncompulsory Payment Rule* (Univ. Mich. L. & Econ., Working Paper No. 178, 2021).

[155] 26 U.S.C. § 894(a) (2021).

[156] Columbia Marine Servs., Inc. v. Reffet Ltd., 861 F.2d 18 (2d Cir. 1988); Michael P. Van Alstine, *Federal Common Law in the Age of Treaties*, 89 Cornell L. Rev. 892, 923 (2004).

Executive Agreements Most international agreements that the United States enters are not treaties, but executive agreements – "agreements entered into by the executive branch that are not submitted to the Senate for its advice and consent."[157] These agreements can be categorized into three subcategories based on the source of the President's authority to conclude the agreement.[158]

First are *congressional–executive agreements.* The constitutionality of congressional–executive agreements is well settled.[159] Essentially, they are different from treaties, where only Senate approval is required, in that "both houses of Congress are involved in the authorizing process for congressional–executive agreements."[160] In other words, both houses of Congress are involved in passing a statute implementing the provisions of the international agreement that was made by the President/executive with prior approval from Congress.[161]

Second are *agreements made pursuant to treaties*. These are agreements made in harmony with existing treaties. These types of agreements are also well established as constitutional,[162] "though controversy occasionally arises as to whether a particular treaty actually authorizes the Executive to conclude an agreement in question."[163] Because the Supremacy Clause includes treaties among the sources of the "supreme Law of the Land,"[164] the power to enter into an agreement required or contemplated by the treaty lies within the President's executive function.[165]

Third are *sole executive agreements*. These are agreements when the President acts without any approval from Congress. The agreements rely on neither treaty nor congressional authority to provide their legal basis but are instead based on the executive authority of the President outlined in the Constitution.[166] "The Constitution may confer limited authority upon the President to promulgate such agreements on the basis of his foreign affairs power."[167] One prominent example that the Supreme Court has recognized is the Presidential power to conclude *sole executive agreements* in the context of settling claims with foreign nations.

157 Mulligan, *supra* note 149, at 6.

158 *Id.*

159 Third Restatement, *supra* note 149, at §303(2).

160 Mulligan, *supra* note 149, at 7.

161 Treaties and Other International Agreements, *supra* note 148, at 5.

162 *See* Third Restatement, *supra* note 149, § 303(3); Treaties and Other International Agreements, *supra* note 148, at 86; *see also* Wilson v. Girard, 354 U.S. 524, 528–29 (1957) (giving effect to an executive agreement defining jurisdiction over US forces in Japan that was concluded pursuant to a treaty).

163 Mulligan, *supra* note 149, at 7; *see also* Treaties and Other International Agreements, *supra* note 148, at 86–87, n.117.

164 U.S. Const. Article VI, § 2.

165 Mulligan, *supra* note 149, at 7.

166 *See, e.g.*, Am. Ins. Ass'n v. Garamendi, 539 U.S. 396, 415 (2003); United States v. Belmont, 301 U.S. 324, 330 (1937).

167 Mulligan, *supra* note 149, at 7–8; *see also* Treaties and Other International Agreements, *supra* note 148, at 5 (citing U.S. Const. Article II, § 1 (executive power), § 2 (commander in chief power, treaty power), § 3 (receiving ambassadors)).

Conversely, if the President acts under authority that he does not have, or his constitutional authority over the subject matter is unclear, "a reviewing court may consider Congress's position in determining whether the agreement is legitimate."[168] In the Court's analysis of such cases, when "Congress has given its implicit approval to the President entering the agreement, or is silent on the matter, it is more likely that the agreement will be deemed valid."[169]

In sum, both treaty implementation and treaty override could occur through domestic legislation, ratification through the Senate, or through an executive agreement, depending on the President's constitutional authority. These aspects make the US system both unique and complicated for discussing treaty implementation and treaty overrides.

PILLAR ONE: EXECUTIVE AGREEMENT? There has been long-standing scholarly debate over whether certain types of international agreements may only be entered into as treaties, subject to the advice and consent of the Senate, or whether a congressional–executive agreement may serve as a constitutionally permissible alternative.[170] In the scholarly debates, "[a] central legal question … concerns whether the U.S. federal government, acting pursuant to a treaty, may regulate matters that could not be reached by a statute enacted by Congress pursuant to its enumerated powers under Article I of the Constitution."[171] Moreover, it appears that tradition also plays a role in determining which direction implementation goes.

Bringing this discussion into the context of Pillar One, tax agreements have traditionally been implemented as self-executing *treaties*.[172] Therefore, based on current scholarly and political debates, implementing Pillar One and overriding other bilateral tax treaties via another mechanism, like a congressional–executive act, would be highly irregular and raise constitutional questions.

There is concern surrounding the feasibility of implementing Pillar One, however, given that treaties require Senate ratification with a two-thirds majority. With and Republican opposition to Pillar One, implementing Pillar One in the current political climate seems difficult, if not impossible. The Biden Treasury, recognizing

[168] Mulligan, *supra* note 149, at 8; *see, e.g.*, Dames & Moore v. Regan, 453 U.S. 654, 686 (1981).

[169] Mulligan, *supra* note 149, at 8.

[170] *Compare* Bradford C. Clark, *Domesticating Sole Executive Agreements*, 93 VA. L. REV. 1573, 1661 (2007), Laurence H. Tribe, *Taking Text and Structure Seriously: Reflections on Free-Form Method in Constitutional Interpretation*, 108 HARV. L. REV. 1221, 1249–67 (1995), *and* John C. Yoo, *Laws as Treaties?: The Constitutionality of Congressional–Executive Agreements*, 99 MICH. L. REV. 757, 852 (2001), *with* Third Restatement, *supra* note149, § 303 n.8, HENKIN, *supra* note 150, at 217, Oona A. Hathaway, *Treaties' End: The Past, Present, and Future of International Lawmaking in the United States*, 117 YALE L.J. 1236, 1244 (2008), and Bruce Ackerman & David Golove, *Is NAFTA Constitutional?*, 108 HARV. L. REV. 799, 861–96 (1995).

[171] Mulligan, *supra* note 149, at 9.

[172] *See, e.g.*, *United States Income Tax Treaties – A to Z*, IRS, https://www.irs.gov/businesses/international-businesses/united-states-income-tax-treaties-a-to-z [https://perma.cc/G6TF-LYNG].

the current political obstacles, commented on this issue on behalf of the administration in October 2021, suggesting it might push to implement Pillar One by other means.[173] Yellen specifically noted at a Senate Banking Committee hearing that the administration is considering alternative means for significantly modifying existing bilateral tax treaties that would bypass Senate approval.[174] Yellen said that implementing Pillar One via a treaty "would be one way" to do it, but there are also "a number of ways" it could be implemented.[175] Expanding on the potential direction of the Treasury, another Treasury official stated that implementation "could occur through several means, such as through an Article II treaty, congressional–executive agreement or through legislation overriding the existing treaties."[176]

As indicated, perhaps in the future the executive could implement the treaty via a congressional-executive agreement, which would only require a simple majority in the House and the Senate. Furthermore, several members of the Senate Foreign Relations and Finance Committees sent letters to the Treasury expressing their concern about these discussions. In one letter dated October 8, 2021, the Senators stated that the changes brought by Pillar One would be a fundamental change in taxing rights [and] would require provisions within all of the US existing bilateral tax treaties to be modified or overridden. Each of these bilateral tax treaties was approved in the same manner – by a two-thirds vote of the Senate. Sweeping changes to modify these treaties and alter long-established protocols under these agreements must be processed through the same constitutionally mandated process. Bypassing this process to override our bilateral tax treaties would irreparably erode the exclusive treaty authority the Constitution provides to the Senate.[177]

In addition, the Senators stated that they were not aware of any prior congressional approval to make such an agreement, and they had not been involved in any steps of the Pillar One negotiation process.[178]

[173] Letter from Mike Crapo, James E. Risch & Pat Toomey, U.S. Senators, to Janet Yellen, U.S. Treasury Secretary (Oct. 8, 2021) [hereinafter Letter Oct. 8]; Letter from U.S. Senators to Janet Yellen, U.S. Treasury Secretary (Dec. 22, 2021) [hereinafter Letter Dec. 22]; *see also* Senate Office of Mike Crapo, *Finance Republicans Demand Treasury Analysis of OECD Agreement* (Dec. 22, 2021), https://www.crapo.senate.gov/media/newsreleases/finance-republicans-demand-treasury-analysis-of-oecd-agreement [https://perma.cc/J73G-A28S]; Senate Office of Rob Portman, *Portman, Senate Finance Republicans Demand Treasury Analysis of OECD Agreement* (Dec. 23, 2021), https://www.portman.senate.gov/newsroom/press-releases/portman-senate-finance-republicans-demand-treasury-analysis-oecd-agreement [https://perma.cc/V2SC-LC2D].

[174] Letter Oct. 8, *supra* note 172.

[175] *Id.*

[176] *Id.*

[177] *Id.*; Letter Dec. 22, *supra* note 172; *see also* Senate Office of Mike Crapo, *supra* note 172; Senate Office of Rob Portman, *supra* note 172.

[178] Senate Office of Rob Portman, *supra* note 172.

5.4.1.3 Analysis/Conclusion

These responses from Senators raise questions regarding the treaty implementation process in the United States, but there are no clear answers. The only real plausible alternative to treaty ratification would be a congressional–executive agreement. The Constitution likely does not give the President sole power to implement a tax treaty, and no existing treaties would give the President the power to unilaterally implement such a substantive tax overhaul. Furthermore, Pillar One is not simply a "political commitment" to improve the international tax regime but requires a number of serious changes to the tax code. Based on this analysis, pursuing a congressional–executive agreement as an alternative method of implementation looks more like a political calculation than a legal determination.

If a future administration does try to implement Pillar One with a congressional–executive agreement, there are two major political considerations that must be considered. First, implementing Pillar One through a congressional–executive agreement would be a break from precedent. This would be the first time a substantive tax treaty would be implemented outside of the formal treaty ratification process. The administration needs to determine if implementing Pillar One and overriding existing bilateral treaties via alternative means is worth the benefits of the global tax deal despite likely domestic political backlash. The backlash could make it harder to implement other international agreements in the future.

Second, it is uncertain whether a congressional–executive agreement is a practical alternative. Furthermore, if the President moves forward with overriding existing bilateral treaties and implementing Pillar One via a congressional–executive agreement, given the lex posterior rule and the letters from conservative members of the Senate, bypassing the traditional treaty process would likely put Pillar One on precarious ground. If a future administration does not work in a bipartisan fashion now, there would be little to stop conservatives from passing legislation that overrides Pillar One the next time the Republican Party controls Congress. In addition, all signs indicate that Republicans would not be concerned with overriding Pillar One, despite the US international obligations.

We are skeptical about the successful implementation of Pillar One by the United States and we are sympathetic about the government's frustration over the treaty ratification process, which has been unfruitful for over a decade. Yet, if an executive agreement is used to bypass the treaty ratification process, there may be doubts as to the legality of this implementation method. Unfortunately, we cannot find a way to resolve this dilemma when it comes to Pillar One. However, there may still be guidelines or alternatives if we are willing to curb our commitment to Pillar One. The remainder of this chapter offers some ideas.

5.4.2 *Sever the Two Pillars*

One objective of the OECD is to adopt both Pillars One and Two as a packaged deal. Both pillars address the tax challenges in the digitalized economy and combat base erosion and profit shifting by multinationals. However, Pillars One and Two are conceptually distinct from each other – Pillar One strengthens source-based taxation, whereas Pillar Two reinforces residence-based taxation. Unlike what the United States argues, there is no logical reason to treat the two pillars as "linked by more than just politics."[179]

More practically, the formulae for successful implementation are quite different from each other. Pillar One is proposed to be implemented by a multilateral instrument. Therefore, even if consensus is reached, each country will likely need to amend its local laws to adhere to Pillar One. Making these changes within existing political and legal systems will take time and may raise difficult issues of complexity and implementation, especially for developing countries with limited tax administration resources. Moreover, Pillar One requires all countries to give up on existing DSTs, and, as noted above, it may be politically onerous to persuade countries to abandon an established, prevalent tax.[180] The United States, on the other hand, is unlikely to adopt Pillar One unless all countries abandon the DSTs.

Although the multilateral solution to Pillar One orchestrated by the OECD is not promising, there are in fact alternatives to Pillar One. The United Nations offers another multilateral solution for taxing the digital economy in Article 12B of the U.N. Model Tax Convention. Large market jurisdictions from which most of the profits are derived can implement a unilateral measure to deal with the tax challenges relating to Pillar One – namely, tax nexus and profit allocation. With its fractional apportionment proposal, India has shown that a large market jurisdiction has the requisite data to singlehandedly adopt this alternative measure. DSTs or other digital levies, such as a data excise tax discussed *infra*-Section 5.4.4, are viable unilateral alternatives to Pillar One.

Pillar Two, on the other hand, can be implemented by domestic legislation alone – at least the GLoBE rule, which is the main part of Pillar Two. It is a much better condition for initial implementation than Pillar One. Still, further international cooperation is required to make Pillar Two truly effective and successful, because if a country unilaterally adopts a minimum tax that is too high, it risks driving multinationals to establish their headquarters in other residence countries that do not have such a minimum tax. That is why the United States, when it adopted GILTI unilaterally in the TCJA of 2017, applied a very low tax rate (10.5 percent) which is much too low as a minimum tax.[181] Moreover, over 90 percent of

[179] U.S. Department of the Treasury, *supra* note 36, at 7.
[180] *See* Avi-Yonah et al., *supra* note 4, section I.A.
[181] 28 U.S.C. § 250 (2017).

large multinationals are headquartered in the G20, so only a relatively small number of countries need to agree to implement an effective minimum tax.

In short, Pillar Two, compared to Pillar One, is a low-hanging fruit to combat the international tax challenges in the digital era. But Pillar Two still requires international cooperation, which can be obtained by the forthcoming global deal. In contrast, Pillar One faces copious obstacles that are unlikely to be resolved by the forthcoming global deal and subsequent implementation process.

However, there are alternatives worth considering.

For these reasons, we contend that the two pillars should be separated. The United States seemed in the past to push the repeal of DSTs not only as a condition of US support for Pillar One, but also as a condition for Pillar Two, essentially making the two pillars indivisible.[182] However, risking Pillar Two to salvage Pillar One is unwise. The United States in the future should proceed with negotiations to adopt Pillar Two even if Pillar One fails.

5.4.3 *Avoid a Trade War*

The United States is the loudest voice against DSTs, claiming that DSTs violate international law because they are designed specifically to target US companies.[183] The United States has signaled several times that it is willing to start a global trade war to protect US multinationals from discriminatory DSTs. However, will starting a global trade war accomplish the US goal or protect US multinationals from DSTs? This section provides a case study about a 2019 dispute between the United States and France. It concludes that some of the USTR's claims are flawed and that a trade war should be avoided.

5.4.3.1 The US Trade Representative's Investigation

When the United States believes a foreign country has engaged in discriminatory or objectionable trade practices that disadvantage US companies, its first course of action is to begin an investigation under section 301 of the Trade Act of 1974.[184] Section 301 essentially grants the United States the authority to engage in a trade war with countries that have discriminatory policies.[185] Alternatively, the United States can file a complaint with the World Trade Organization (WTO) and utilize the WTO's forum to settle trade disputes with foreign governments.[186]

182 U.S. Department of the Treasury, *supra* note 36, at 7.

183 *See* Ruth Mason & Leopoldo Parada, *Company Size Matters*, 2019 BRIT. TAX REV. 610, 646–49 (2019); Ruth Mason & Leopoldo Parada, *Digital Battlefront in the Tax Wars*, 92 TAX NOTES INT'L 1183, 1193–96 (2018).

184 19 U.S.C. §§ 2411–2420 (2018).

185 *Id.* § 2411.

186 *Dispute Settlement*, World Trade Organization (Aug. 2, 2021), https://www.wto.org/english/tratop_e/dispu_e/dispu_e.htm [https://perma.cc/J26D-4CDK].

One contentious US move against foreign DSTs began in 2019, against France. The USTR initiated its investigation of France's DST under section 301 in July 2019, focusing on the discriminatory and unreasonable elements of the tax policy,[187] and determined that France's DST was "unreasonable or discriminatory" and "particularly burdensome for U.S. companies."[188] Based on this finding, the USTR initially proposed a 100 percent tariff on a variety of French products, including luxury goods and sparkling wine in December 2019,[189] with an import trade value of $2.4 billion.[190] After subsequent public comments and hearings, the USTR concluded that appropriate action was a 25 percent tariff on goods with a trade value of $1.3 billion.[191] This amount was intended to be "comparable, though somewhat lower," than France's "expected collections of approximately $450 million in [DST] taxes from U.S. companies for activities during 2020."[192] However, the USTR immediately suspended the tariffs until January 6, 2021, "to allow additional time for bilateral and multilateral discussions [on the global tax deal] that could lead to a satisfactory resolution."[193] Six days after the suspension expired, the USTR determined "that the imposition of duties on the current effective date of January 6, 2021, no longer is appropriate."[194] Thus, the retaliatory tariff for the DST was suspended indefinitely, retroactive to its effective date.[195] The timeline of this investigation is summarized in Figure 5.3.

In addition to the France case, the USTR imposed tariffs on certain goods from Austria, India, Italy, Spain, Turkey, and the United Kingdom in June 2021, arguing that the DSTs adopted by those countries discriminate against US digital companies.[196] However, the USTR terminated the investigations against Brazil, the Czech Republic, the EU, and Indonesia in March 2021, as these four jurisdictions have not yet adopted or implemented DSTs.[197]

[187] Initiation of a Section 301 Investigation of France's Digital Services Tax, 84 Fed. Reg., 34042, 34043 (July 16, 2019).

[188] Notice of Determination and Request for Comments Concerning Action Pursuant to Section 301: France's Digital Services Tax, 84 Fed. Reg., 66956, 66957 (Dec. 6, 2019).

[189] *Id.*

[190] *Id.*

[191] Notice of Action in the Section 301 Investigation of France's Digital Services Tax, 85 Fed. Reg., 43292, 43293 (July 16, 2020).

[192] *Id.*

[193] *Id.*

[194] Notice of Modification of Section 301 Action: Investigation of France's Digital Services Tax, 86 Fed. Reg., 2479, 2479 (Jan. 12, 2021).

[195] *Id.* at 2479–80.

[196] *USTR Announces, and Immediately Suspends, Tariffs in Section 301 Digital Services Taxes Investigations*, Off. of the U.S. Trade Representative (June 2, 2021), https://ustr.gov/about-us/policy-offices/press-office/press-releases/2021/june/ustr-announces-and-immediately-suspends-tariffs-section-301-digital-services-taxes-investigations [https://perma.cc/CHC3-9AVW].

[197] Termination of Section 301 Digital Services Tax Investigations of Brazil, the Czech Republic, the European Union, and Indonesia, 86 Fed. Reg., 16,828 (Mar. 31, 2021).

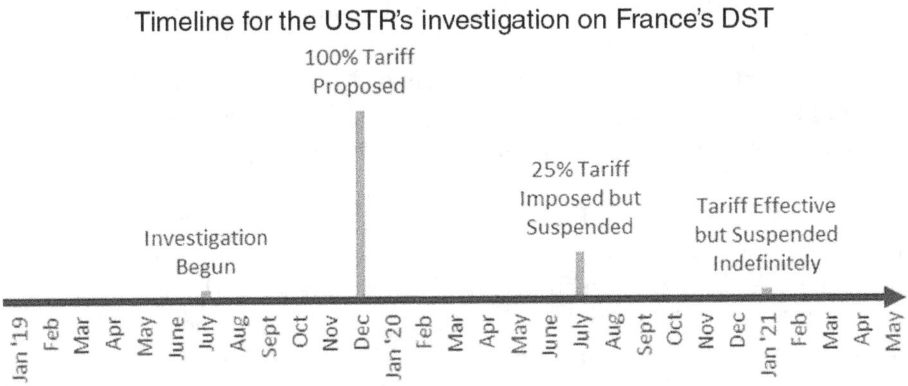

FIGURE 5.3 Timeline for US DST investigation

5.4.3.2 Is There Real Discrimination against American Tech Giants?

On December 2, 2019, the USTR released an investigative report on France's DST (the USTR Report). The report concluded that the French DST is both intentionally and effectually discriminatory.[198] This subsection explores in greater detail the USTR's conclusions on the French DST and examines the accuracy of the conclusions drawn.

Discrimination can be found in two different ways: (1) "where there is an intent to discriminate" and (2) "where the effect of the measure is discriminatory."[199] Intent discrimination "may be found in the expressed views of the legislators or regulators to put in place the measure or in the overall motive of the government in putting in place the measure, as gleaned from the wordings of the measure itself."[200] Effect discrimination "looks at whether the measure has a discriminatory effect or impact."[201]

It is generally well accepted that for a DST to be found discriminatory, there must be strong evidence of discriminatory effect, not just intentional discrimination.[202] Ruth Mason of the University of Virginia and Leopoldo Parada explain that "establishing discriminatory intent is not a necessary component of every fundamental-freedoms case" but "may be relevant . . . in cases involving facially neutral rules that

[198] Robert E. Lighthizer, Off. of the U.S. Trade Representative, Report on France's Digital Services Tax 76–77 (2019) [hereinafter USTR Report].
[199] *See* Ogbu Okanga, *Testing for Consistency: Certain Digital Tax Measures and WTO Non-discrimination*, 55 J. World Trade 101, 108 (2021).
[200] *Id.*
[201] *Id.*
[202] *See* Young Ran (Christine) Kim, *Will Digital Services Taxes Start a Global Trade War?*, *in* Thinker, Teacher, Traveler, Reimagining International Tax, Essays in Honor of H. David Rosenbloom 287 (Georg Kofler et al. eds., 2021).

have a discriminatory impact."[203] A finding of discriminatory intent may be used to "trigger impact analysis" or may even be used to "lower the quantum impact required to establish nationality discrimination."[204] Therefore, a discrimination claim against a DST must include evidence of a discriminatory impact and can be strengthened with evidence of intent to discriminate.

INTENT DISCRIMINATION The USTR Report found intent discrimination in public statements made by French leaders.[205] For example, (1) "French officials repeatedly referred to the French DST, and the EU proposal on which it was based, as the 'GAFA tax,' which stands for Google, Apple, Facebook, and Amazon, or the 'GAFAM tax,' which also includes Microsoft"; and (2) "French officials have expressed that the DST should cover the U.S. 'digital giants' and not French and European companies, in order to make the latter group more competitive against the former."[206]

Read together, these statements by French officials paint the picture that France purposefully designed their DST to discriminate against US companies. However, an alternative interpretation posits that France simply is tired of digital companies not paying their fair share of taxes to the appropriate sovereigns. From France's standpoint, digital companies have avoided existing corporate tax rules because current tax laws do not account for the absence of physical presence based on these companies' digital nature.[207] As proof that digital companies are avoiding current corporate taxation rules, the European Commission announced that "on average digital companies pay an effective tax rate of just 9.5%, whilst traditional enterprises pay an effective rate of 23.2%."[208]

Although France may have used American companies as scapegoats, the French statements indicate a desire to address a broader problem with the DST. Namely, that digital companies be made to pay their fair share of taxes and to prevent them from manipulating existing corporate income tax rules because of their digital nature. Thus, while the USTR Report finds intent discrimination, there is a plausible alternative argument for France.

EFFECT DISCRIMINATION It is presently unclear whether the United States or France will win the argument pertaining to intent discrimination. However, as discussed above, pervasive discriminatory intent alone is insufficient "to build a

[203] Ruth Mason & Leopoldo Parada, *The Legality of Digital Taxes in Europe*, 40 VA. TAX REV. 18, 18–19 (2020).

[204] *Id.*

[205] USTR REPORT, *supra* note 197, at 31–35.

[206] *Id.*

[207] Venetia Argyropoulou, *Digital Tax, Making Enterprises Pay Their "Fair" Share?* (TILEC Discussion Paper No. DP 2019-007, 2019), https://papers.ssrn.com/sol3/papers.cfm?abstract_id=3383389.

[208] *Id.*

successful tax discrimination case in international tribunals."[209] There must also be evidence of discriminatory impact.[210] This section examines two notable reasons the USTR Report uses to claim effective discrimination resulting from France's DST: (1) selective bias and (2) revenue thresholds.

Selective Bias The United States argues that France's DST is discriminatory because of the selection of the services it encompasses. The DST covers two types of services where US companies are very competitive: (a) internet advertising and (b) digital interfaces. Meanwhile, it excludes areas where French and other European companies are successful.[211]

Internet Advertising Sector France characterizes internet advertising under its DST by three conditions: (1) services marketed to advertisers or their agents; (2) advertising messages placed on a digital interface; and (3) messages targeted based on users' data.[212]

The USTR Report found that "U.S.-based company groups are highly successful in the internet advertising sector in France, and the French DST does not apply to other related sectors like traditional advertising, where French companies are more successful."[213] As evidence, the USTR Report notes that eight of the nine groups of internet advertising companies expected to be covered by France's DST are US-based, while none are French-based companies.[214] Thus, the USTR concluded that "the evidence on the record . . . suggests that the DST's focus on targeted Internet advertising reflects, and achieves, French policymakers' desire to focus the DST on U.S. companies and not French companies."[215] In summary, France is discriminating against US companies by choosing to only tax internet advertising, while ignoring traditional advertising.[216] However, the USTR's analysis is flawed in its assumption regarding the exclusion of traditional advertising companies. The purpose of enacting a digital services tax is to make sure digital companies are paying their fair share of taxes. There is no evidence that traditional advertising companies can similarly manipulate existing corporate income tax rules. Traditional advertising companies are not exclusively digital in nature, which is the key component digital companies rely on to avoid paying market country corporate income taxes. Conversely, US-based traditional advertising companies that are successful in France would have a physical presence in France and would have already paid

209 Kim, *supra* note 201, at 20.1.1.1.
210 *Id.*
211 USTR Report, *supra* note 197, at 35.
212 Ernst & Young, France Issues Comprehensive Draft Guidance on Digital Services Tax (2020).
213 USTR Report, *supra* note 197, at 35.
214 *Id.*
215 *Id.* at 37.
216 *Id.* at 31–35.

their fair share of French taxes. Additional tax rules would not be needed. The USTR's claim of discrimination is not convincing because it ignores the origin of the problems. A better analysis would be determining whether French internet advertising companies are taking advantage of physical presence corporate income taxation rules, and, if so, whether those French companies are being excluded from the tax. Or more broadly, if there are non-US internet advertising companies taking advantage of French corporate income tax laws, and they are excluded from the DST, there is a stronger argument for discrimination against US companies. The USTR Report states that "[t]here are French companies that provide Internet advertising services" and cites the French Interactive Advertising Bureau to illustrate the fact that these companies exist.[217] A recent article published by *The Manifest* provides the "Top 20 Digital Marketing Companies in France,"[218] Criteo is a large, successful, French internet advertising company. The companies on the list illustrate that French internet advertising companies also have the potential to take advantage of corporate income taxation rules due to their digital nature, just like GAFA.

Digital Interfaces France's DST only applies to digital platforms or marketplaces where users can connect with other users for social purposes or to buy and sell goods or services between themselves. It does not apply to "digital interface" providers (i.e., a company operating an online marketplace whereby they sell their own product online in addition to their physical store, such as Walmart or Target).[219] The USTR claims that this "distinction has the effect of excluding French companies from the scope of the DST while covering their U.S.-based competitors." The USTR Report lists several French companies they claim are successful in e-commerce and should be subject the DST, including Carrefour, Le Redoute, Cdiscount, Fnac, Vente-Privee, Auchan, and Showroomprive, but are not covered because of this distinction. In fact, on the digital interfaces side, twelve of the twenty-one company groups that will be subject to the French DST are US-based; not one French company group is expected to be covered by the tax.[220] The USTR Report noted that "U.S. companies do not dominate the French market" in the digital interfaces space and so while there was an opportunity to include French companies who use a digital interface, France purposefully defined "digital interface services" in a way to exclude French companies and discriminate against US companies. Thus, the USTR believes that France's definition of digital services is effectually discriminatory against US companies.[221]

[217] *Id.* at 36.

[218] *List of the Best France Online Marketing Agencies*, MANIFEST (Apr. 2022), https://themanifest.com/fr/digital-marketing/agencies [https://perma.cc/GG4J-9CB5].

[219] USTR REPORT, *supra* note 197, at 14, 38.

[220] *Id.* at 38.

[221] *Id.*

The USTR Report also notes that the French DST and EU DST proposals carve out types of digital interfaces where European or French companies are particularly successful, such as online music sales.[222] When the EU DST proposal carved out "digital content," commentators suggested that this was to avoid covering the Swedish music streaming giant Spotify. France also carved out "digital content," allowing them to avoid taxing Spotify and the French company Deezer. However,

> France eliminated the "digital content" carve-out as applied to apps, where two U.S. companies (Apple and Google) are the dominant sellers globally.[223] Therefore, this aspect of the French DST seems discriminatory toward U.S. companies.

However, one pitfall in the USTR's analysis is that many of the French companies described in the USTR Report are primarily traditional retailers and are not digital platform companies. These traditional retailers may have online components for selling products carried in-store, but they are not operating a digital interface in the way that Google, Amazon, Facebook, and Apple are. As noted earlier, the problem DSTs are attempting to solve arises through these companies' ability to engage in profit shifting activities and tax nexus avoidance in foreign countries based on the absence of physical presence. The French companies mentioned in the USTR Report already have tax nexus with France because they are physically located within the country. Because there is no tax nexus issue, France reasonably excluded these types of companies from their DST.

Revenue Thresholds The USTR argues that the revenue thresholds of France's DST are effectively discriminatory because "the revenue thresholds focus the DST on U.S.-based companies and exclude many non-U.S.-based companies that supply the covered services in France."[224]

France's DST only applies to companies that earn annual revenues of €750 million globally and €25 million in France from supplying the covered services.[225] The rationale for such high revenue thresholds in a DST is seemingly "to target tech giants that enjoy monopoly power and yet do not pay enough tax in the market countries."[226] Therefore, the USTR claims that the high revenue thresholds effectively discriminate against US companies by excluding French companies from DST liability while subjecting US companies to the tax.[227]

A possible counter to this argument is that the threshold requirements are not selectively targeting US companies, as any country's digital company above the threshold is subject to the tax. In terms of effect discrimination, however, there is

[222] *Id.* at 39–40.
[223] *Id.*
[224] *Id.* at 41.
[225] *Id.*
[226] *See* Kim, *supra* note 201, at 20.3.1.1.3.
[227] USTR Report, *supra* note 197, at 41; Kim, *supra* note 201, at 20.3.1.1.2.

a good argument to be made that France was aware that setting high thresholds would limit the effect of its DST to prominent American digital companies.

The USTR notes that there are non-US-based companies that supply covered targeted advertising services.[228] Most of the corporate members of the French Interactive Advertising Bureau are French.[229] Additionally, there are many traditional French advertising companies that also provide internet advertising services as part of their business, such as Publicis and Havas.[230] However, neither business meets both of France's DST revenue thresholds.[231]

The USTR Report concludes that because of the revenue thresholds "twelve of the twenty-one company groups expected to be covered by the DST with respect to 'digital interface' services are U.S.-based" and no French companies are expected to be covered.[232] The USTR Report provides examples of French companies that supply digital interface services in the French market,[233] yet despite their substantial revenues, are excluded from the DST.

As an initial observation, it is doubtful that the purpose of the DST is to target French companies that provide some internet advertising services as non-primary parts of their business. These companies already have tax nexus with France and the USTR has provided no evidence that these businesses are able to avoid their fair share of tax compared to digital companies. Therefore, the USTR's claim that the French DST is effectively discriminatory is weakened by the fact that French companies providing internet advertising services cannot avoid taxes like other digital companies, since tax nexus is already established by their physical presence in France.

For example, the USTR Report states that Orange S.A., a French multinational telecommunications company, should, and would, be subject to the DST if it were not for the revenue thresholds.[234] However, Orange S.A. provides telecommunication services similar to the US companies Verizon and AT&T. Its internet advertising services performed are programmatic targeted internet advertising services similar to those offered by Verizon and AT&T in the United States in the form of commercials and ads. These telecommunication companies are not providing the same type of internet platform services like Google offers and are therefore less likely to engage in profit shifting activities.

However, some examples provided by the USTR provide a strong argument in favor of discrimination. For example, the Report listed SoLocal Group, a group of digital advertising companies that works with over 700,000 advertisers to reach

[228] USTR Report, *supra* note 197, at 41.
[229] *Id.*
[230] *Id.* at 42–43.
[231] *Id.*
[232] *Id.* at 44.
[233] *Id.*
[234] *Id.* at 42.

individuals across Europe.[235] SoLocal Group's business is more in line with the internet advertising the DST attempts to tax because their digital nature allows them to provide services in foreign countries without physical presence, which creates opportunities for profit shifting. In 2017, SoLocal Group recorded €755.8 million in total revenue, including €635.8 million in Internet revenues. SoLocal Group escapes DST because their Internet revenues were less than the French threshold of €750 million required to subject them to the tax. The USTR may further investigate why France set the revenue threshold at €750 million, although France is expected to respond that it merely followed the global trend – that is, most DSTs either currently in effect or in consideration offer similar amounts as global revenue thresholds.[236] Nonetheless, this point is more effective than the case of Orange S.A.

In short, despite some merit, it is necessary to note the USTR Report's biases and exaggerations to reach the conclusion that France's DST is discriminatory.

5.4.3.3 The Case against Retaliatory Tariffs

Retaliatory tariffs will likely harm the United States without having a deterring effect. This section examines a case where tariffs were imposed on French sparkling wine to retaliate against France's proposed DST and demonstrates that such retaliatory tariffs have neither caused financial harm to the French wine industry nor pressured France to discard its DST.

Economists consistently indicate that international free trade and the elimination of protectionist measures benefit every nation involved and that tariffs are inefficient and harmful to economies.[237] Economist Kimberly Clausing of UCLA provides four reasons that tariffs "add insult to injury" for American workers.[238] Her four reasons are: (1) tariffs act as regressive taxes on consumption, (2) tariffs and trade wars wreak havoc on US labor markets by raising costs for American companies, (3) trading partners often retaliate when tariffs are raised on their imports, and (4) trade wars harm the global economy resulting in weakened alliances.[239] In addition to economists supporting free trade, Clausing argues that open economic policies are in the best interest of American workers.[240]

The four reasons against tariffs manifest in DST tariffs as well. To illustrate, consider the US importers of French sparkling wine affected by the retaliatory DST tariffs. The US sparkling wine importers are chosen by the USTR as "sacrificial companies" to protect GAFA (Google, Apple, Facebook, and Amazon), or

[235] *Id.*

[236] *See* Kim, *supra* note 201, at 20.3.1.1.3.

[237] *See, e.g.*, Matthew Nolte, *Causes and Casualties of History's Largest Trade War*, 38 Ariz. J. Int'l & Comp. L. 81, 84 (2021).

[238] Clausing, *supra* note 12, at 115.

[239] *Id.* at 115–16.

[240] *Id.* at 110.

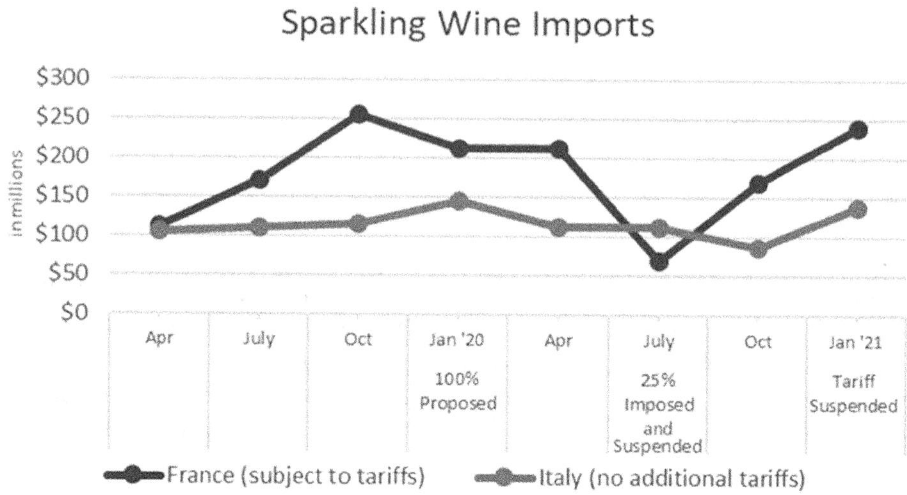

FIGURE 5.4 Impact of tariffs

"protected companies" arguably harmed by foreign nation discrimination. Theoretically, importers of French sparkling wine would suffer no economic impact because tariffs related to France's DST were immediately suspended. However, Figure 5.4 shows the increased imports prior to an anticipated tariff and decreased imports coinciding with the actual tariff, compared to the constant quantity of import of Italian sparkling wine where no additional duties were threatened. Figure 5.5 confirms this observation and shows that a 25 percent tariff proposal can result in a 70 percent reduction in import, meaning reduced profits.

In addition, wine that an importer continues to purchase suddenly costs 25 percent more than it had before the tariff. If the importer absorbs some of that cost, profit margins are reduced. If the importer passes along the increased cost, that impacts companies downstream in the value chain. It may take time for the tariff incidence to reach its ultimate destination, the consumer. However, given a stable consumer price index for alcoholic beverages throughout the period shown in Figure 5.6, it is reasonable to conclude that the DST tariff creates negative effects for sacrificial companies that will ripple throughout the supply chain.

Another critical question is whether the tariff has its intended effect on the foreign country – in this case, France. Again, the implied objective of retaliatory tariffs is to create an adverse financial effect on the foreign nation's market significant enough to induce the country to eliminate its discriminatory trade practices. However, DST tariffs neither caused discernable financial harm to the French wine industry nor has France abandoned its DST. First, Figure 5.7 is Eurostat's consumer price index for wine in Europe by country of origin. One might expect that intended consequences of DST tariffs would result in a decrease in US import from targeted countries, such as France, Spain, and the United Kingdom (as opposed to Italy and Portugal, which

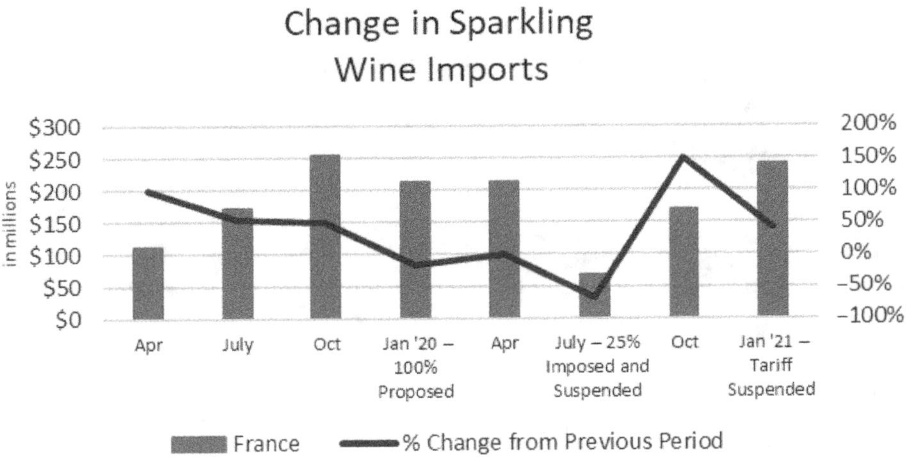

FIGURE 5.5 Impact of high tariffs

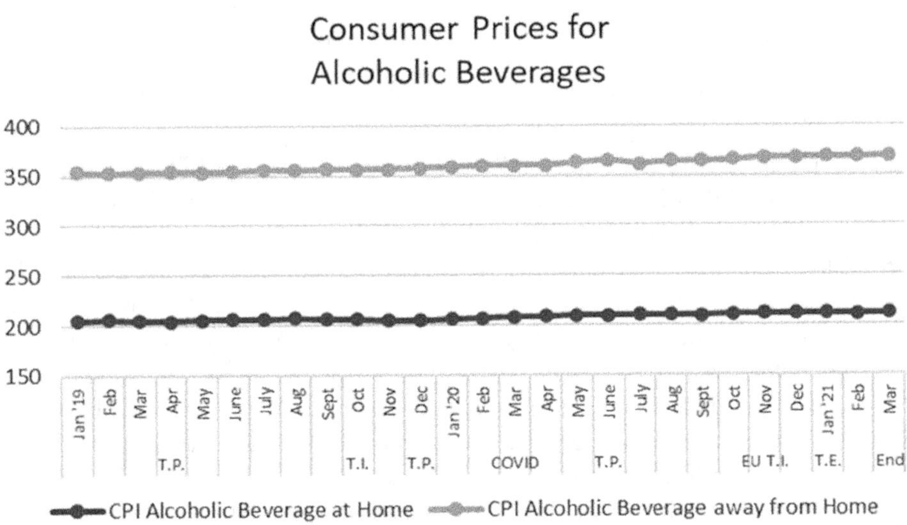

FIGURE 5.6 Impact of DST tariff

were not targeted), and thus a decrease in prices of the targeted wines in the months after October 2019, and again after January 2021, when tariffs were implemented. However, despite the decrease in US imports of wines from the targeted countries like France, there is no corresponding decrease in pricing in the home country. This means that countries like France were able to sell their wines in other markets.

Second, DST tariffs did not effectively motivate France to abandon its DST. The underlying issue of how to collect tax revenues from companies that provide value within France but do not meet physical presence requirements continues. Hence, as

FIGURE 5.7 Consumer price index for wine

the USTR acknowledges, France intends to continue with its DST. Not only was France's DST still in effect in 2021, but several other countries considered DSTs of their own. Ultimately, retaliatory tariffs failed to eliminate France's DST, and they failed to discourage other countries from enacting similar measures. Perhaps in recognition of its ineffectiveness in halting DSTs, the United States postponed the retaliatory tariff in July 2020,[241] before permanently suspending it in January 2021.[242]

As such, the tariffs failed to achieve the primary stated objective of causing foreign countries to eliminate their objectionable trade practices. The most favorable view is that the tariff encouraged foreign countries to consider changes to their practices and to continue discussions with the United States to achieve better solutions. However, the option to negotiate modified or improved agreements with foreign nations is a statutory action available to the USTR even without tariffs.[243] In the worst case, the tariffs can be seen as an aggressive, noncooperative act that may encourage a non-productive trade war and exacerbate the harmful effects of the tariff itself.

Even when additional objectives are considered, such as "pressuring affected countries into broader negotiations,"[244] the lack of economic impact on those

[241] Notice of Action in the Section 301, *supra* note 190.

[242] Notice of Modification of Section 301 Action, *supra* note 193.

[243] 19 U.S.C. § 2411(c) (2018).

[244] CONG. RSCH. SERV., RL45529, TRUMP ADMINISTRATION TARIFF ACTIONS: FREQUENTLY ASKED QUESTIONS 2 (2019).

foreign countries calls the effectiveness into question. Perhaps it is not the actual economic impact of tariffs, but the threat of the tariffs and the prospect of an escalating trade war, that serves as the pressure. Furthermore, additional negative impacts from tariffs may arise when countries retaliate with their own tariffs, such as impacting unrelated industries.[245] For example, then President Trump's steel and aluminum tariffs resulted in retaliatory Chinese tariffs against exported American goods, specifically soybeans.[246] This retaliatory measure affected a US industry that is otherwise removed from both the steel and aluminum industries. To combat this industry-shifting burden created by tariffs, Trump offered to cease future tariffs on automobiles and automobile parts in exchange for the EU Commissioner's agreement to lower their own retaliatory tariffs and expand imports of liquefied natural gas and soybeans.[247]

In brief, although the USTR claims of discrimination may justify starting a trade war, some of their claims are flawed. Hence, before taking trade-war actions, policymakers must consider the potential radiating effects. Retaliatory actions may have a far-reaching impact beyond initial concerns of sacrificing the value of free trade and may expand into a multiparty trade war. Throughout the course of a trade war, the harm falls on US consumers. When the trade war escalates, US consumers as well as small- and medium-sized businesses – sacrificial companies – will suffer from higher prices due to tariffs on imported goods and services. From an electoral perspective, it is unlikely that American consumers will be sympathetic to policymakers starting a trade war to protect tech giants.

5.4.4 *Alternatives to Pillar One*

Previous sections demonstrated the limitations of current digital tax reform proposals and advised guidelines for a future US reaction. This section provides normative proposals for digital taxation, first offering policy criteria and then developing multilateral and unilateral alternatives to Pillar One.

5.4.4.1 Criteria for Digital Taxation Policy

To solve the problems identified by this chapter, a proposal for digital taxation must meet three goals. First, a policy proposal should overcome the outdated physical presence nexus rule and fairly allocate appropriate tax revenue to market countries.

245 Csongor István Nagy, *World Trade, Imperial Fantasies and Protectionism: Can You Really Have Your Cake and Eat It Too?*, 26 Ind. J. Glob. Legal Stud. 87, 96 (2019) ("Retaliatory measures may target an industry other than the protected sector.").

246 Jacob Ely, *The "National Security" of Nations: President Trump's Pretextual Tariff Rationale and How to Overcome It*, 3 Int'l Comp. Pol'y & Ethics L. Rev. 241, 257 (2019).

247 *Id.*

Furthermore, the proposal should be free from any indicia that can be viewed as discriminating against companies based on nationality. Finally, the proposal needs to be administrable by tax authorities and taxpayers alike. A simple, targeted approach may in fact work better and more efficiently than an ambitious, comprehensive approach which inevitably invites political compromises.

The traditional criteria for evaluating tax policy are equity (or fairness), economic efficiency, and administrability (or simplicity).[248] What criteria, if any, for sound digital tax policy can be derived from them? After we discuss the traditional criteria, we will look at the policy rationales stated in the Pillar One Blueprint for additional criteria.

A proposal for the fair reallocation of tax revenue seems to implicate the *equity* prong. However, economists tend to explain this issue under the *efficiency* prong, because proposals to reallocate taxing rights to markets address taxpayers' incentives to shift profits and avoid taxes. In fact, fairness in the context of digital taxation has at least two dimensions – fairness among the countries that receive the tax revenue and fairness among the taxpayers who bear the economic burden of the tax. Evaluating fairness among taxpayers thus requires identifying the incidence of such a tax.[249] A group of scholars at Oxford University argues that the incidence of such tax depends on the conditions in each market where multinationals operate, and, as such, that identifying the tax incidence is "almost impossible."[250] Thus, instead of fairness, they emphasize economic efficiency and ease of administration in assessing digital tax proposals. It is also argued that taxation of business profit generally cannot be assessed in terms of fairness. Businesses adjust their behavior in response to taxation. Taxation affects the prices of goods and services sold, as well as the prices of inputs used, including employee wages. Where the burden falls on the income, distribution is difficult to determine. Without identifying its incidence, we cannot assess its progressivity or regressivity.[251]

Economic efficiency and administrability have inconsistent implications for digital tax policy. To maximize the profits allocation to market countries, the scope of the new digital tax proposal should be as broad as possible. However, where scope is defined by sector, the administrability prong suggests limiting the number of sectors – fewer complex revenue sourcing rules have to be designed and implemented. To prevent companies from reclassifying their activities to avoid market taxation, tax authorities will need to police the boundary between activities that are

[248] For an early statement of the traditional criteria, *see* Adam Smith, An Inquiry into the Nature and Causes of the Wealth of Nations (1776). For a comprehensive discussion of tax policy criteria, *see* Michael J. Graetz et al., Federal Income Taxation Principles and Policies 28–32 (8th ed., 2018); Allison Christians, Introduction to Tax Policy Theory (2018).

[249] *See, e.g.*, Richard Collier et al., *Comparing Proposals to Tax Some Profit in the Market Country*, World Tax J. 405, 415 (2021).

[250] *Id.*

[251] *See* Michael P. Devereux et al., Taxing Profit in a Digital Economy 34–37 (1st ed. 2021).

within and without scope.[252] Defining scope by a very high threshold amount, as the Statement does, "offers unambiguous administrative advantages."[253] This can make the proposal simple, but it may be less precise and too generalizing.

Under the principle of economic efficiency, a tax should be neutral. It should not distort economic outcomes. This has implications for the definition of "market" countries. In the context of digital taxation, efficiency requires minimizing distortion to the location choices of multinationals. To do so, the location of the tax base should be determined by immobile factors.[254] Indirect purchasers or users will not move in response to the multinational's new tax liability. Therefore, the "market" should be defined to include the location of indirect purchasers or users, as opposed to direct purchasers alone. However, defining the "market" as such will increase administrative costs. Revenue sourcing rules will be made even more complex by the need to look through sets of transactions for indirect purchasers or users.

Let us now connect the discussion above to the policy rationale of the Pillar One Blueprint. The Blueprint provides the foundation for an agreement "that would adhere to the concept of net taxation of income, avoid double taxation and be as simple and administrable as possible."[255] Should the new tax be on a net basis, specifically residual profit? Residual profit is similar to economic rent, although not equivalent, and thus, a net basis tax targeting residual profit would be less distortionary. However, tax on a *gross basis* is easier to collect. Since it does not take costs into account, revenue is easier to identify. While net basis taxation is more efficient, gross basis taxation is easier to administer with less opportunity to manipulate revenue sourcing rules.[256] Although that tips the scale slightly, the choice between net and gross basis taxation is not clear enough to declare one a criterion of "digital tax" policy. The prevention of double taxation (and of double non-taxation) is the purpose of the tax treaty network. Thus, any digital tax proposal should have a mechanism to eliminate double taxation.

The next two sections propose multilateral and unilateral alternatives to Pillar One and evaluate them using the criteria discussed in this section.

5.4.4.2 The UN Proposal as a Multilateral Alternative

Article 12B of the UN Model Tax Convention is the UN's response to the taxation of the digital economy. Approved in April 2021, Article 12B eliminates the physical presence requirement and expands the taxing rights of market countries to income from Automated Digital Services (ADS).[257] The scope of Article 12B is limited to

[252] *See* Collier et al., *supra* note 248, at 424.
[253] *Id.*
[254] *See* Devereux et al., *supra* note 250, at 34–37.
[255] OECD, Pillar One Blueprint, *supra* note 31, at 8.
[256] Collier et al., *supra* note 248, at 425.
[257] U.N. Proposal, *supra* note 7, ¶¶ 1, 2.

Automated Digital Services, defined as "any service provided on the internet or an electronic network requiring minimal human involvement from the service provider."[258] Note that this definition is substantially similar to the definition in the Pillar One Blueprint. Unlike the Pillar One Blueprint version, however, no minimum threshold is prescribed for revenue or profitability.

According to the Model Tax Convention, the country where income from Automated Digital Services arises may tax the income on a gross basis, possibly via a withholding tax, unless the income constitutes royalties or fees for technical services. Here, the source jurisdiction is the country from which payments for Automated Digital Services are made, either by a resident or by a person with a permanent establishment or fixed base which bears the payments. If the income from Automated Digital Services is attributable to a permanent establishment or fixed base in the source jurisdiction, it is excluded. Tax on gross income is capped at a rate to be negotiated between treaty partners.[259] The UN's Commentary to Article 12B suggests a modest rate of 3 or 4 percent.[260]

In addition, taxpayers may elect to be taxed on a net basis. This option provides relief when either: (i) the taxpayer's tax liability is lower than it would be under gross basis taxation subject to the withholding tax mechanism; or (ii) the taxpayer has a global business loss or a loss in the relevant business segment during a taxable year.

Article 12B has noteworthy merits and we believe it superior to Pillar One. It dispenses with the physical presence requirement for tax nexus and allocates more profits to market countries. It cannot be accused of discriminating against companies of certain nationalities. Article 12B's option of gross or net basis taxation is its most striking feature and may be its greatest strength. As discussed in the previous section, neither gross nor net basis taxation is a clear criterion of digital tax policy. However, Article 12B preserves the choice between the two, which may satisfy those who believe that income, not gross revenue, is the appropriate basis for corporate taxation. Article 12B is also simpler to administer than Pillar One. The withholding tax mechanism is a reliable and efficient method for collecting tax because taxpayers are not required to compute their net profits or file tax returns. Furthermore, because Article 12B builds on established foundations, it may be easier to introduce than Pillar One. For instance, Article 23 (methods for the elimination of double taxation) is already in place to deal with double taxation. A caveat for the United States is that it needs to offer a foreign tax credit against the US tax even though the tax paid to market countries is on a gross basis. However, Pillar One also has such foreign tax credit issues, if the new tax imposed by market countries is regulated by tax treaties.

Article 12B is technically a bilateral proposal. Because it is a part of the U.N. Model Tax Convention, it is supposed to be included in, and implemented by, a

[258] *Id.* ¶¶ 5, 20.
[259] *Id.* ¶ 2.
[260] *Id.* ¶ 28.

bilateral tax treaty between countries who want to model this approach. For the reasons adduced in this section, however, Article 12B may also serve as a proposal for a multilateral instrument, which would be a stronger model for a multilateral agreement than Pillar One's approach.

5.4.4.3 A Data Excise Tax as a Unilateral Alternative

This section proposes a unilateral alternative to Pillar One. After evaluating two data tax proposals – the New York Data Mining Tax and Omri Marian's Data Tax Proposal – and identifying the benefits and detriments of both, it proposes its own proposal, a data excise tax.

5.4.4.4 Existing Proposals

In a perfect storm of jurisdictional need for revenue and tech giants bursting at the seams with cash during an otherwise devastating time for businesses, various countries have enacted DSTs.

As part of the desire to harness the growth of the digital economy, not less than ten states in the United States are also enacting or proposing various types of DSTs, using these countries as models.[261] Maryland's Digital Advertising Tax, effective on January 1, 2022, is the frontrunner.[262] There is a novel Data Mining Tax by New York,[263] which provides insight into how to improve not only subnational DSTs but also international DSTs.

New York's Data Mining Tax is an excise tax on the collection of New York consumer data measured by the number of New York residents from whom data are collected.[264] The taxpayer is the commercial data collector, not the user. The rate structure of this tax is progressive: commercial data collectors who collect data from one to two million New York residents will pay $0.05 per resident per month.[265] At the far end of the progressive structure, the tax rate increases to $0.50 per New

[261] Andrew Appleby, *Subnational Digital Services Taxation*, 81 MD. L. REV. 1, 7–8 (2021); Darien Shanske & Young Ran (Christine) Kim, *Taxing Digital Platforms*, 98 NOTRE DAME L. REV., 19–20 (2022–23).

[262] HB 732, 2020 Leg., Reg. Sess. (Md. 2020); Timothy Vermeer, *State Tax Changes Effective January 1, 2022*, TAX FOUND. (Jan. 11, 2022), https://taxfoundation.org/publications/recent-state-tax-changes/ [https://perma.cc/63QZ-93D5].

[263] SB 4959, 2021 Leg., Reg. Sess. (N.Y. 2021) (introduced Feb. 19, 2021); AB 6199, 2021 Gen. Assemb., Reg. Sess. (N.Y. 2021) (introduced Mar. 10, 2021).

[264] Matt Hunsaker & Jeewon Kim Serrato, *NY Data Tax Bill Would Create Practical, Policy Hurdles*, 2021 LAW360 (Mar. 31, 2021), https://www.law360.com/articles/1370746/ny-data-tax-bill-would-create-practical-policy-hurdles.

[265] James Nani, *NY Proposal to Tax Data Collection Draws COST Objection*, 2021 LAW360 (Mar. 12, 2021), https://www.law360.com/tax-authority/articles/1364335/ny-proposal-to-tax-data-collection-draws-cost-objection [https://perma.cc/3VLL-P9GP].

York resident plus $2.25 million where commercial data collectors are collecting data from more than ten million New York residents each month.

This proposal has been praised for several aspects of its design. First, the tax is less discriminatory due to the application threshold being based on users rather than gross receipts.[266] Second, the conventional progressive rate structure eliminates severe "notch" or "cliff" effects. Taxpayers pay the same amount of tax based on how many users' data are collected within the taxable period, subjecting the largest collectors to a higher rate; but higher rates are only paid on each New York resident beyond the specified threshold. Third, because this tax directly taxes data collection, some commentators recommend this tax if jurisdictions want to impose a tax on the value associated with collecting and monetizing user data, whereas using digital advertising as a proxy for that value is ineffective.[267]

Despite the many positive features, there are a few drawbacks. First, given the tax's extreme effectiveness at raising revenue, businesses facing exorbitant tax bills may withdraw from jurisdictions or pass portions of the tax burden onto customers.[268] Furthermore, there are generally some reservations to excise taxes. As a result, the Council on State Taxation warned New York lawmakers that they are generally opposed to excise taxes on business inputs and that they believed subjecting commercial data collectors to this tax would result in double taxation.[269] Additionally, commentators argue that this tax would result in significant recordkeeping issues for commercial data collectors, citing concerns of double counting the same New York resident, the difficulty of determining New York resident status, and data anonymity issues.[270]

In the same vein, Omri Marian proposes a theoretical framework for a data tax like the proposed New York Data Mining Tax.[271] Marian's data tax is an excise tax with a broader tax base based on the *volume of data*, measured via gigabytes, rather than per resident.[272]

The crux of Marian's idea is as follows: "Data is the value, so it is being taxed as such. Not as a proxy for some other measurement of value."[273] He poses three principles for the data tax: (1) volume (not value) of raw data comprises the tax base; (2) all data uses are included in the tax base; and (3) the taxpayer is the user of the

[266] Appleby, *supra* note 260, at 22.
[267] *Id.* at 17; Karl A. Frieden & Stephanie T. Do, *State Adoption of European DSTs: Misguided and Unnecessary*, TAX NOTES (May 6, 2021), https://www.taxnotes.com/tax-notes-state/nexus/state-adoption-european-dsts-misguided-and-unnecessary/2021/05/10/59p2l[https://perma.cc/A27E-UAP2].
[268] Appleby, *supra* note 260, at 17–18.
[269] Nani, *supra* note 264.
[270] *Id.*
[271] Omri Marian, *Taxing Data*, 47 BYU L. REV. 511 (2022).
[272] *Id.* at 562.
[273] *Id.* at 569.

data.[274] In Marian's proposal both uploads and downloads are taxable and measurable.[275]

Marian argues that ascribing monetary value to data is an insurmountable and logically incoherent task, which is why the proposal attempts to avoid this by instead taxing its volume.[276] This is beneficial because "[a] tax on data volume has the benefit of being self-adjusting."[277]

Development in the legal system, including the tax system, is considered sluggish compared to the pace of technological development. However, taxing the raw commodity – in this case the data – will allow the tax to adjust to technological advances because the more advanced technology, the more data used, and, thus, the higher the tax.[278]

It is also worth noting Marian's justification for an excise tax as a data tax. Generally, excise taxes are criticized for being regressive. However, Marian argues that this data tax is progressive because it is a direct tax on data owners, arguably targeting the "data-rich" that are able to avoid income taxes, but not the "data-poor" who are unable to avoid them.[279] Marian also indicates that a direct data tax as an excise tax is efficient and easily administrable because the tax is collected where the data are collected, making the sourcing issue manageable. Moreover, measuring the volume of data is possible, as shown by cellphone companies.[280]

5.4.4.5 New Proposal

Inspired by the two proposals discussed above, this subpart proposes a direct data excise tax as an alternative unilateral measure to DSTs. The details of the EU's forthcoming digital levy are undetermined. But we believe that the proposed data tax would offer a good benchmark for the EU, resolving various policy concerns discussed throughout this chapter. Furthermore, the proposed data excise tax is helpful not only to foreign countries but also to the fifty states considering an improved subnational digital taxation mechanism.

The tax base of the proposed data excise tax is the *volume of collected data*, measured in gigabytes. It does not adopt the New York's Data Mining Tax's per capita measurement, which imposes the same amount of tax to commercial data collectors for the data of heavy users and that of light users, because each user counts only once regardless of the amount of data collected from those two users. That is

[274] *Id.* at 562.
[275] *Id.* at 563.
[276] *Id.* at 563.
[277] *Id.*
[278] *Id.* at 563.
[279] *Id.* at 565.
[280] *Id.* at 563–67.

neither efficient nor fair.[281] Also, this proposal is different from Marian's proposal in that it only taxes the volume of *collected* (or downloaded) data, and thus uploads are irrelevant.

To illustrate, consider the hypothetical example of William. William, who lives in the United Kingdom, wants to purchase a new car. William is particularly interested in a midsize luxury German sedan, and he begins the car-buying process by "googling" key words like "ten best sedans for 2021." Google shows search results, such as sedans by Toyota, Hyundai, Mercedes Benz E-Class, Audi A7, and BMW 5 Series. The search results include an advertisement of Mercedes-Benz E-Class. William skips Toyota and Hyundai, and only clicks Mercedes-Benz E-Class, Audi A7, and BMW 5 Series.

For Google, the data of "ten best sedans for 2021" collected from William are meaningful, because the algorithm processes that data associated with William's existing information, as well as with big data from other users, and can produce a tailored result. The information that William clicks only Mercedes-Benz E-Class, Audi A7, and BMW 5 Series is also substantial, because now Google has data of William's preference. Thus, Google is required to pay the proposed data excise tax on the collected (or downloaded) data from William – that is, "ten best sedans for 2021" and the user's click of Mercedes-Benz E-Class, Audi A7, and BMW 5 Series.

However, Google is not required to pay the proposed data excise tax on its uploaded search results, including the advertisement of the Mercedes-Benz E-Class. As a platform, Google serves two or more distinct groups of customers or users:[282] in this case, William for online search business, and Mercedes-Benz for online advertising business. Users on one side of the market (William) are charged little to nothing to participate, while the users on the other side (Mercedes-Benz) are charged all or most of the profits. Thus, when displaying the search results to William, Google may have earned income from Mercedes from its online advertisement business, but such income can be taxed under the existing income tax system. Tax reform is necessary to capture the other side of digital business: the exchange between Google and William. Because there is no cash flow between Google and William, it has been challenging for market countries (the United Kingdom) to collect tax from Google, which easily operates in the United Kingdom without physical presence. However, the proposed data excise tax provides tax revenue to market jurisdictions (the United Kingdom) where data providers (user William) are located. Thus, it fulfills the goal of revenue reallocation in favor of market countries.

[281] Steven A. Dean, *Tax Deregulation*, 86 N.Y.U. L. Rev. 387, 396–97 (2011); Neil Brooks, *Flattening the Claims of the Flat Taxers*, 21 Dalhousie L.J. 287, 307 (1998); Donna M. Byrne, *Locke, Property, and Progressive Taxes*, 78 Neb. L. Rev. 700, 733 (1999); Karl Manheim, *The Health Insurance Mandate – A Tax or a Taking*, 42 Hastings Const. L.Q. 323, 354 (2015).

[282] Carl Shapiro & Hal R. Varian, Information Rules: A Strategic Guide to the Network Economy 13 (1999).

It also overcomes the physical presence requirement in tax nexus because the tax will be imposed on data collectors regardless of their location, onshore or offshore.

Both the New York Data Mining Tax and Marian's proposal offer use of IP addresses to determine which (market) jurisdiction will tax the data collection. There has been opposition to use of IP addresses due to their susceptibility to manipulation. However, as Marian indicated, if someone does use a VPN, and these taxes are implemented on a wide scale, the data tax will be imposed on the VPN service provider as well.[283] In other words, it generates more revenue, instead of being vulnerable to loopholes.

Furthermore, we propose that the taxpayer be limited to *for-profit commercial data collectors*, like the taxpayer identified in the New York Data Tax. Differing from Marian's proposal, not all users of data would be part of the identifiable tax base. Safe harbor thresholds should be created to protect individual users and small businesses. The tax would be directed at businesses using and profiting from the data collected, not at those who offer the data for free. The proposed data excise tax is not measured in gross revenue or profits, and thus is an improvement compared to DSTs. DSTs have been criticized as a disguised income tax, resulting in double taxation – once by the existing income tax and again by DSTs as disguised income tax.[284] However, the tax base of the data excise tax we propose is the volume of collected data, which clearly distinguishes from income tax. Also, as an excise tax, the data excise tax would be easy to administer, and can be implemented independently or together with the multilateral alternative discussed in *supra*-Section 5.4.4.2. It may be very attractive to many governments seeking a practical solution regardless of the global one.

Joe Bankman, Alan Sykes of Stanford Law School, and Mitchell Kane of NYU imply that a well-designed excise tax would be a better tool to extract the profits of multinationals than a conventional income tax.[285] However, excise taxes are often criticized for being regressive.[286] Although Marian offers an excellent argument for the progressivity of a direct data tax, without empirical data it is not certain how progressive or regressive a data excise tax would be. To mitigate the regressivity issue, we recommend a progressive rate structure with graduated thresholds based on the number of gigabytes of data collected in each jurisdiction. The final point is whether the proposed data excise tax would be discriminatory against American tech giants. The proposal itself has nothing to do with the residence of businesses, and thus is facially neutral. However, given that American tech giants are

[283] Marian, *supra* note 270, at 51.

[284] Kim, *supra* note 38, at 166–67.

[285] Joseph Bankman et al., *Collecting the Rent: The Global Battle to Capture MNE Profits*, 72 Tax L. Rev. 197, 230–32 (2020).

[286] Marian, *supra* note 270, at 14; Joseph Pechman, Federal Tax Policy 199–200 (5th ed. 1987); Henry N. Butler & Jason S. Johnston, *Reforming State Consumer Protection Liability: An Economic Approach*, 2010 Colum. Bus. L. Rev. 1 (2010).

dominating the market, it is inevitable that majority of taxpayers of the proposed data excise tax would be American multinationals. Then, one might find that this proposal would be no less discriminatory than France's DST discussed above. Will the United States again use the card of discrimination, no matter how the reform proposal would be improved? We hope not, but if so, that discussion will be reserved for the authors' next project.

5.5 CONCLUSION

Despite the critiques in this chapter, the Statement for a global deal represents a remarkable step forward toward implementing an international tax regime fit for the twenty-first century. Pillar One eliminates, for Amount A, the obsolete physical presence requirement as well as the unworkable arm's-length standard for transfer pricing, and finally recognizes the crucial role of market jurisdictions in generating income. Pillar Two implements the single tax principle, meaning that corporate profits should be subject to a minimum tax and that if the country with the primary right to tax such income (source or residence) does not impose tax at the minimum level, the other country involved should tax it.

All of these are decisive breaks from the past, which have been suggested for twenty-five years but, until now, have gained little traction. We welcome the momentum for international tax reform. However, like most historical developments, the Inclusive Framework encompasses both revolution and evolution, and each building block has different prospects for success. Pillar Two has greater potential for success with global support. In contrast, Pillar One has sizable political and logistical challenges that will be difficult to overcome, in addition to the potential reluctance to repeal DSTs.

Considering these difficulties, we recommend separating the two pillars and pursuing Pillar Two during the global negotiation should Pillar One fail. Pillar One may have alternatives worth examining. This chapter focuses on the UN proposal and a data excise tax as such alternatives, but there may be others, such as a formulary apportionment in transfer pricing. Furthermore, starting a trade war to protect American tech giants is imprudent, because, during a trade war, US consumers and small- and medium-sized businesses will be the ones suffering. Given that American tech giants are dominating the global digital economy, it is conceivable that they will pay the largest tax bill, as their "fair share of tax," to market countries under any tax reform proposal.

6

The New Regime and the Global Tax, 2016–2023*

This chapter will discuss the promises and pitfalls of the new international tax regime, as embodied in Pillar Two of the Statement and incorporated into the Model Rules.[1] The Statement envisages this regime as built on two pillars. Pillar One is focused on expanding source country taxing rights on the income of large multinational enterprises. It targets digital companies such as Facebook or Google that can extract profits from a source jurisdiction without a physical presence.[2] We address Pillar One in the previous chapter; thus, we will not engage with it here.[3]

This chapter will discuss the circumstances that led to more than 130 jurisdictions around the world agreeing to implement the global minimum tax and the single tax principle of Pillar Two. The double-edged sword of globalization and tax competition created difficulties for many countries, as they were being increasingly squeezed by multinational enterprises to provide lower corporate tax rates and tax holidays as conditions for receiving foreign investment. While increased foreign direct investment (FDI) can create higher-paying job opportunities, economic growth, and the societal benefits of an increased tax base, these benefits are greatly diminished when the country needs to offer exceedingly low tax rates or tax holiday enticements to secure the FDI.[4] As tax competition has grown, global effective corporate tax rates have continued to be cut, creating a "race-to-the-bottom" where the tax rate needed

* This chapter originates from a previous work by authors, but is significantly updated. Reuven S. Avi-Yonah & Young Ran (Christine) Kim, *Tax Harmony: The Promise and Pitfalls of The Global Minimum Tax*, 43 Michigan J. Int'l L. 505 (2022).

1 https://www.oecd-ilibrary.org/taxation/tax-challenges-arising-from-digitalisation-of-the-economy-global-anti-base-erosion-model-rules-pillar-two_782bac33-en.

2 *See* Reuven S. Avi-Yonah et al., A *New Framework for Digital Taxation*, 63 Harv. Int'l L.J. 401 (2022).

3 *See id.*

4 *Options for Low Income Countries' Effective and Efficient Use of Tax Incentives for Investment*, Int'l Monetary Fund [IMF] (2015), http://www.imf.org/external/np/g20/pdf/101515.pdf.

to attract foreign investment is so low that there is almost no net benefit to the society securing the foreign capital.

Countries can address this problem by closing off their trade borders or by making cutbacks to their social safety net.[5] However, the better solution is to limit tax competition.[6] Pillar Two aims to address the issue of "race-to-the-bottom" tax competition and achieve tax harmonization through the adoption of a global minimum tax. Multinational enterprises that meet the €750 million revenue threshold – regardless of which jurisdiction they are headquartered in or operate from – will be subject to a global minimum tax. But the way this new regime works is quite complex because multinational enterprises' income involves at least two countries – the source country where income is generated, and the residence country where investors are located.

As an example, consider that Orange, a hypothetical US multinational enterprise, has a subsidiary corporation in Ireland.[7] The Irish subsidiary's income from its trade or business is considered active income, and Ireland (the source country) has primary jurisdiction to tax that income under the benefits principle.[8] Ideally, Ireland will tax the income at a substantive tax rate. However, with the large negotiating power of massive multinational enterprises, source countries do not always tax them at substantive rates. Under Pillar Two's global minimum tax, if the Irish subsidiary's income is taxed below the agreed minimum tax rate of 15 percent in Ireland (the source country), then the parent entity in the United States (the residence country) is required to include such undertaxed income in its US tax base and pay the difference in additional taxes to the United States. If the United States (the residence country) has not enacted Pillar Two's income inclusion rule as a corrective measure, then the Irish subsidiary's tax deduction in Ireland (the source country) would be denied, or an equivalent adjustment would be made to the extent that the low-tax income of the Irish subsidiary is not subject to minimum tax under an income inclusion rule.

As illustrated in the example, the mechanics of Pillar Two can be quite complicated. However, the objective of Pillar Two is clear: to implement the goal of the single tax principle (that is, "full taxation") in international tax, thereby solving the problems created by the tax competition prevalent in the twentieth century.[9] The single tax principle requires multinational enterprises' income to be subject to

[5] *See infra* Section 6.1.

[6] *See id.*

[7] *See, e.g.*, Simon Bowers, *Apple's Cash Mountain, How It Avoids Tax, and the Irish Link*, The Irish Times (Nov. 6, 2017), http://www.irishtimes.com/business/apple-s-cash-mountain-how-it-avoids-tax-and-the-irish-link-1.3281734.

[8] *See infra* Section 6.2.1; Reuven S. Avi-Yonah, *The Structure of International Taxation: A Proposal for Simplification*, 74 Tex. L. Rev. 1301, 1305 (1996).

[9] For a discussion of the single tax principle, *see, e.g., infra* Section 6.2.1; Reuven S. Avi-Yonah, *Who Invented the Single Tax Principle? An Essay on the History of US Treaty Policy*, 59 N.Y.L. Sch. L. Rev. 305 (2015) [hereinafter, Avi-Yonah, *Single Tax Principle*]. For full taxation, *see*

taxation only once. By doing so, it prevents both double taxation and double non-taxation. However, there are nuances to the single tax principle. First, the country (residence or source country) that can exercise primary tax jurisdiction is determined based on whether income is active or passive according to the benefits principle. With active income, the source country has primary tax jurisdiction, and the residence country has secondary jurisdiction. If taxation by the source country is substantial, the residence country will yield its secondary taxing right by allowing a foreign tax credit to prevent double taxation.[10] On the other hand, if the first taxation is nominal (below the minimum rate), it is not considered to have satisfied the imposition of a "single tax," and thus corrective rules by the secondary tax jurisdiction should apply to prevent double non-taxation. Thus, the single tax principle suggests that all income of multinationals must be taxed once at a substantive tax rate. Hence, Ruth Mason refers to this principle as "full taxation."[11]

The single tax principle was first conceived of in the early twentieth century as the basis for the foreign tax credit. The United States and other countries began to practically implement the principle in the 1960s and 1970s. However, until recently, it had not been fully integrated into international tax because of fierce tax competition and many unilateral tax policies that are inconsistent with the single tax principle. Many scholars did not believe that reasonable tax harmony could be achieved through the single tax principle, and thus, it had been somewhat controversial. Nonetheless, the OECD BEPS 1.0 Project in the 2010s aspired to achieve the single tax principle through global tax harmonization. Perhaps because of lingering doubts about its feasibility, the project achieved limited success.[12]

The passage of the US Tax Cuts and Jobs Act (TCJA) of 2017 played a crucial role in establishing the feasibility of the single tax principle. The TCJA adopted two new innovative breakthrough tax mechanisms: the Global Intangible Low Tax Income (GILTI) rule for residence taxation and the Base Erosion Anti-Abuse Tax (BEAT) rule for source taxation.[13] These two rules showed how the single tax principle can be achieved unilaterally to combat base erosion and profit shifting by US multinational enterprises. The success of the TCJA also demonstrated conceptually that there are ways to stop tax competition if the Group of Twenty (G20) countries implement the single tax principle fully with proper corrective measures.[14]

Building upon those previous efforts, Pillar Two implements the single tax principle globally for the first time by introducing a global minimum effective tax

Ruth Mason, *The Transformation of International Tax*, 114 Am. J. Int'l L. 353 (2020) [hereinafter, *Transformation*].

[10] *See, e.g.*, I.R.C. § 901.

[11] *Transformation*, *supra* note 9, at 22, 25.

[12] *See, e.g.*, Mindy Herzfeld, *The Case against BEPS: Lessons for Tax Coordination*, 21 Fla. Tax Rev. 1 (2017).

[13] I.R.C. §§ 951A, 59A. *See infra* Section 6.2.3.

[14] *See* Lilian V. Faulhaber, *Taxing Tech: The Future of Digital Taxation*, 39 Va. Tax Rev. 145, 175 (2019) [hereinafter, *Taxing Tech*].

rate of 15 percent, and various corrective measures, such as the Qualified Domestic Minimum Top-up Tax (QDMTT) for source taxation, the Income Inclusion Rule (IIR) for residence taxation, and the Undertaxed Profits Rule (UTPR) (denial of deduction or making an equivalent adjustment) as a backstop, and Subject to Tax Rule (STTR) to further enhance source taxation. The IIR and UTPR called together GLoBE Rules. Basically, a QDMTT applies first and allows jurisdictions where constituent entities are located to impose a top-up tax up to 15 percent effective tax rate. The IIR allows jurisdictions where (ultimate) parent entities are located to impose top-up tax up to 15 percent effective tax rate on low-taxed constituent entities (subsidiaries and branches) in other jurisdictions. The QDMTT thus applies first, and in case there are still any low-taxed constituent entities in the MNE group, for example, their jurisdictions do not have a QDMTT in place, the IIR applies. In cases where there are still low-taxed constituent entities with excess profits that were not subject to either a QDMTT or an IIR, the UTPR applies to constituent entities according to a formula. Unlike Pillar One, which requires changing more than 3,000 tax treaties with the participation of over 130 source jurisdictions, Pillar Two can supposedly generally be implemented unilaterally through domestic legislation with no changes to existing tax treaties, with the minor exception of the STTR. More importantly, Pillar Two only requires cooperation by the G20, which is home to over 90 percent of the world's largest MNEs, because it offers strong corrective measures exercised by residence countries. Pillar Two is therefore more likely to be implemented than Pillar One. Also, the two pillars deal with different problems – Pillar One with physical presence and source taxation and Pillar Two with a global minimum tax and residence taxation – and can conceptually be separated from each other.

The benefits that Pillar Two is expected to bring to the world are significant. At a global minimum tax rate of 15 percent, approximately $220 billion in additional global tax revenues will be generated each year. The various corrective measures imposed on both source and residence countries would reduce MNEs' motivation to engage in base erosion and profit shifting, because they would be paying a substantial "single tax" no matter where they are located, or where their profits are attributed.

Despite its promise, there are still some concerns about Pillar Two. The 15 percent global minimum tax rate is relatively low compared to the average G20 corporate tax rate of about 27 percent.[15] The substance carve-outs in the Statement also raise concerns that Pillar Two may still allow a certain level of tax competition. This chapter will describe Pillar Two of the new international tax regime and analyze its

[15] BEPS Monitoring Group Comments on the Model Rules for a Global Anti-Base-Erosion Minimum Corporate Tax, 105 *Tax Notes Int'l* 1421 (Mar. 21, 2022); Elke Asen, *Corporate Tax Rates around the World*, 2020, Tax Found. (Dec. 9, 2020), http://taxfoundation.org/publications/corporate-tax-rates-around-the-world/.

theoretic underpinnings.[16] Section 6.1 defines the tax competition problem Pillar Two was designed to address. Section 6.2 presents the existing efforts to resolve tax competition. It discusses the historical origins and development of the single tax principle and explains the TCJA's crucial role in leading to the fruition of Pillar Two. Section 6.3 analyzes Pillar Two as a new solution to tax competition. It highlights four rules that Pillar Two comprises (the QDMTT, IIR, UTPR, and STTR) and introduces the implementation plans by the OECD/G20 and the United States in the Inflation Reduction Act (IRA). Section 6.4 addresses the contribution, benefits, and potential challenges of Pillar Two. It concludes by reflecting on how, in retrospect, Pillar Two fits in with the two principles underlying the century-old regime, namely the benefits principle and the single tax principle.

6.1 TAX COMPETITION REVIEWED

The current age of globalization has made countries face the trilemma of (1) balancing economic openness for FDI-driven job creation and economic growth, (2) avoiding tax competition and preserving tax revenue, and (3) securing a social safety net.[17] First, globalization has allowed many countries to utilize FDI to create more and better-paying jobs for their citizens,[18] to generate investment in their economic infrastructure, and to introduce technologies that allow for modernization.[19] The economic growth of Asian countries, such as Singapore, Hong Kong, South Korea, and Taiwan, is believed to have been primarily initiated by the influx of FDI in the 1950s.[20] These countries' economies have since grown and flourished while the economies of other nations who were similarly developing in the 1950s have stalled. Many would attribute such contrast to these Asian countries' ability and success in attracting FDI.[21]

[16] *See, e.g.*, Jinyan Li, *The Pillar 2 Undertaxed Payments Rule Departs from International Consensus and Tax Treaties*, 105 Tax Notes Int'l 1401 (Mar. 21, 2022); Chris William Sanchirico, A *Game-Theoretic Analysis of Global Minimum Tax Design* (U. of Pa., Inst. for L. & Econ. Rsch. Paper No. 22-19, 2022), www.ssrn.com; Wei Cui, *New Puzzles in International Tax Agreements*, 75 Tax L. Rev. 201 (2021–22).

[17] On the importance of curbing tax competition to maintain democracy and the social safety net under globalization, *see* Reuven S. Avi-Yonah, *Globalization, Tax Competition, and the Fiscal Crisis of the Welfare State*, 113 Harv. L. Rev. 1573 (2000) [hereinafter, *Tax Competition*]; Reuven S. Avi-Yonah, Globalization, Tax Competition and the Fiscal Crisis of the Welfare State: A Twentieth Anniversary Retrospective, *in* Thinker, Teacher, Traveler: Reimagining International Tax, Essays in Honor of H. David Rosenbloom 39 (Georg Kofler et al. eds., 2021).

[18] OECD, OECD Benchmark Definition of Foreign Direct Investment 17 (4th ed. 2008), http://www.oecd.org/daf/inv/investment-policy/2090148.pdf.

[19] *See* Yoram Y. Margalioth, *Tax Competition, Foreign Direct Investments and Growth: Using the Tax System to Promote Developing Countries*, 23 Va. Tax Rev. 161 (2003).

[20] *See id.* at 163.

[21] *Id.* For different uses of tax incentives for FDI across countries, *see* IMF, *supra* note 4.

Second, a country that opens its economy to FDI faces the risks that come with a dependency on foreign capital that may be diverted elsewhere. These risks come from competition from peer countries vying to attract foreign capital to their economy. The epitome of such rivalry is "tax competition," which has been prevalent since the twentieth century.[22] Many developing countries who want to invite FDI to their soil offer a low tax rate to foreign investors, such as overall low corporate tax rates, or tax holidays where foreign investors are exempt from taxation for a predetermined period. Such tax competition is harmful to developing countries, which depend on corporate taxes to a much greater extent than developed countries.[23] On average, corporate tax accounts for approximately 24 percent of a developing country's tax revenue, and only around 8 percent of a developed country's tax revenue.[24] This problem has worsened as developed countries like Ireland have also begun engaging in tax competition, putting even more downward pressure on corporate tax rates. Ireland's current corporate tax rate of 12.5 percent is much lower than the OECD's average corporate tax rate of 23.51 percent.[25] To compete, developing countries may have to drop their rates even lower. Tax competition creates an incentive to continue to lower tax rates or offer other tax incentives to attract more FDI, potentially running these tax rates down to the point where jurisdictions may receive little to no net revenue benefit from the FDI. This "race-to-the-bottom" issue may not be apparent if one only compares statutory tax rates by looking at countries' published tax rate(s) for corporate income, but if one looks at the rate foreign corporations are paying – the effective tax rates – it is evident that poorer countries' effective tax rates were basically cut in half from 1996 to 2007.[26]

Third, a country also needs to maintain an adequate social safety net and various welfare programs to protect its low-income population from poverty and hardship. In the United States, the earned income tax credit, child tax credits, and a cash transfer program called Temporary Assistance for Needy Families (TANF) are examples of this safety net.[27] In Europe, these safety nets can encompass all health care costs, education, and housing. Such large safety nets require significant tax revenue, but countries reducing their corporate tax rates or offering tax holidays in

[22] *See, e.g.*, David Elkins, *The Merits of Tax Competition in a Globalized Economy*, 91 Ind. L.J. 3 (2016).

[23] *See* Ivan O. Ozai, *Tax Competition and the Ethics of Burden Sharing*, 42 Fordham Int'l L. J. 61, 68 (2018).

[24] *See* Avi Nov, *The "Bidding War" to Attract Foreign Direct Investment: The Need for a Global Solution*, 25 Va. Tax Rev. 835 (2006); Richard Bird, *The Personal Income Tax*, PREM Notes: Tax Policy No. 137 (June 2001) at 1, EconPapers – RePEc; *Revenue Statistics 2021: Initial Impact of COVID-19 on OECD Tax Revenues*, OECD (2021), http://www.oecd-ilibrary.org/sites/6e87f932-en/index.html?itemId = /content/publication/6e87f932-en.

[25] Asen, *supra* note 15.

[26] *See* Laura Abramovsky et al., *Corporate Tax in Developing Countries: Current Trends and Design Issues*, 35 Fiscal Stud. 4 (2014).

[27] *See* Earned I.R.C. § 32(a) (Earned Income Tax Credit); I.R.C. § 24(a) (Child Tax Credits); 42 U.S.C. §§601–19 (Temporary Assistance for Needy Families).

order to retain foreign investors will find maintaining a robust social safety net much more difficult with a revenue stream that is vulnerable to such downward fluctuations.[28]

Therefore, only two sides of the trilemma can be addressed simultaneously. If a country is economically open, it must choose between (1) attracting FDI, which requires tax competition and cuts to the social safety net, and (2) losing FDI by foregoing tax competition and maintaining the social safety net. If tax competition is inevitable in a globalized economy, a country may then either (1) close its economy, preserve its tax revenue, and forego the benefits of globalization; or (2) open its economy, endure tax competition, and subject the social safety net to potential volatility and cuts, even though it serves as a crucial buffer against the downsides of globalization. In fact, many European countries have reduced social safety net programs following the financial crisis in 2008. The United States retreated from economic openness during the Trump administration. However, neither approach has been praised as a reasonable solution to the trilemma because they are each destructive, requiring some fraction of the economy to sacrifice or be worse off.

Hence, the best solution to this trilemma is finding a way to productively limit tax competition. Stopping destructive tax competition that races to the bottom is a constructive way to solve the trilemma, and every country involved would benefit. The problem, however, is that source countries hosting FDI cannot curb tax competition unilaterally. If a country declares that it will not engage in tax competition by offering tax incentives, such as tax holidays, to MNEs, then these enterprises will invest elsewhere. For example, when the Philippines declined to give a tax exemption and $15 million in tax incentives to General Motors, the FDI was diverted to Thailand.[29] The fundamental problem is that modern MNEs are exceedingly mobile. They can be in any country with adequate infrastructure and an educated workforce. The geographic location of the investment does not matter since intellectual property can be moved at no cost from one location to another. The need of manufacturing facilities to be regularly updated or retrofitted for new processes or innovations also serves to make moving to new locations less cumbersome.

A common practice of MNEs is to assemble a list of countries that are acceptable in terms of infrastructure and an educated workforce. The MNE then approaches the government of each country and asks what it would receive by way of tax breaks if it invested in the country. If confronted by a refusal to compromise on taxes, the MNE threatens to go elsewhere, and few politicians can resist the pressure of losing the favorable headlines that accompany job creation by a major MNE.[30]

[28] *See, e.g.*, IMF, *supra* note 4, at 3.

[29] Gabriella Stern & Rebecca Blumenstein, *GM May Locate Major Plant in Thailand, Not Philippines*, Wall St. J. (May 16, 1996), http://www.wsj.com/articles/SB832194544528469500.

[30] *See* Avi-Yonah, *Tax Competition*, *supra* note 17, at 1645–46.

For example, Intel in the 1990s conducted an auction for its new source country, pitting Ireland against Israel, and was able to obtain over $1 billion in tax concessions from both countries.[31] More recently, Amazon conducted an auction among US localities to bid to become the locations of its second headquarters, which ended up in the vicinity of Washington DC, an area not lacking in development.[32]

The problem of tax competition is most acute in developing countries because they depend more on corporate tax revenues than richer countries. The percentage of total revenues from corporate tax in the OECD member states is around 7–8 percent, but in developing countries it is closer to 24 percent.[33] Recognizing the negative impact of tax competition on the global economy, the OECD issued the Harmful Tax Competition Report in 1998 to address the problem.[34] However, the problem remained unaddressed, perhaps because it was unrealistic to expect that developed countries would craft a solution to a problem that more seriously affects developing countries.

Nevertheless, the harm from tax competition is not limited to developing countries. Even the OECD member states suffer from the decline in corporate tax revenues resulting from tax competition because they cannot raise other taxes, which are already quite high.[35] Instead, most OECD members had to implement austerity measures that cut the social safety net in the wake of the financial crisis of 2008, even though they understood the importance of the social safety net for their citizens. For instance, Greece, one of the European Union (EU) members hardest hit by the financial crisis, was faced with either dramatically raising taxes or drastically curtailing public health spending, and chose to cut spending, which resulted in understaffed and underfunded hospitals and higher copays that drastically impacted vulnerable groups.[36] Similarly, the Netherlands' financial shortfalls necessitated a move to privatize insurance companies, while Sweden switched many hospitals and primary health care services over to the private sector to cut costs.[37] These cuts of the social safety net were what led to the first BEPS project of the OECD in 2013–15.[38] This BEPS 1.0 project was designed to limit tax competition by

[31] *Id.*

[32] *See* Reuven S. Avi-Yonah et al., *Federalizing Tax Justice*, 53 IND. L. REV. 479 (2020).

[33] *Revenue Statistics Brochure Initial Impact of COVID-19 on OECD Tax Revenues*, OECD (2021), http://www.oecd.org/tax/tax-policy/revenue-statistics-highlights-brochure.pdf.

[34] *Harmful Tax Competition: An Emerging Issue*, OECD (1998), http://www.oecd.org/ctp/harmful/1904176.pdf.

[35] *Revenue Statistics Brochure*, supra note 33, at 9.

[36] *See* Elisavet Athanasia Alexiadou, *Health Care Reforms and the Challenge of Inequality from a Human Rights Lens: Lessons from Europe*, 17 IND. HEALTH L. REV. 63 (2020).

[37] *Id.* at 74.

[38] *See* Reuven S. Avi-Yonah, *The Great Recession and the International Tax Regime*, KLUWER INT'L TAX BLOG (Apr. 23, 2019), http://kluwertaxblog.com/2019/04/23/the-great-recession-and-the-international-tax-regime.

introducing various measures to prevent tax base erosion and MNEs shifting profits to low-tax jurisdictions.[39]

A major question regarding potential solutions to curbing tax competition is whether they only address artificial profit shifting to low-tax jurisdictions, such as tax havens, or also target real investment shopping around the world. The OECD's Harmful Tax Competition report from 1998 focused on artificial profit shifting to low-tax jurisdictions, as did the BEPS 1.0 project, which was based on the concept of "value creation."[40] Pillar One of the global tax deal also focuses on artificial profit shifting. Pillar Two, on the other hand, addresses both artificial profit shifting and real investment shifting, although the latter is limited only by the substance carve-out described in Sections 6.3 and 6.4.

6.2 EXISTING SOLUTIONS TO TAX COMPETITION

Destructive tax competition would disappear if the international tax regime achieved tax harmony. The difficult part is how to achieve this harmony. Having a uniform tax system across the globe would be the simplest solution, but it is not realistic when each sovereign country has the ability and right to develop its own tax system. Consequently, an international tax regime should offer a principle and framework that can systematically prevent tax competition if countries agree to participate. This section introduces the single tax principle that we endorse and examines the existing efforts to combat tax competition prior to the Statement and Pillar Two.

6.2.1 *The Single Tax Principle, 1918–2015*

The best solution to the problems created by tax competition is the single tax principle, which requires that all income of MNEs be subject to taxation once.[41] However, there is nuance to the single tax principle. If the effective tax rate for single taxation was nominal, then it would be an empty solution to resolve tax competition. Thus, to make this principle effective, the single tax principle accompanies a practical principle – that is, that all income of MNEs be taxed once at a substantive tax rate, such as the average G20 tax rate (currently around 26.96 percent).[42] If this proposition is not met, corrective rules would need to apply to accomplish the result that MNEs' income be taxed at a substantive rate.

39 *See* Itai Grinberg, *The New International Tax Diplomacy*, 104 GEO. L.J. 1137 (2016); *Transformation*, *supra* note 9, at 354.

40 *See* Reuven S. Avi-Yonah, *The OECD Harmful Tax Competition Report: A Retrospective after a Decade*, 34 BROOK. J. INT'L L. 783 (2009).

41 *See* Avi-Yonah, *Single Tax Principle*, *supra* note 9.

42 *See generally* Asen, *supra* note 15.

The income of MNEs' cross-border transactions involves more than one country. Thus, the next issue stemming from the single tax principle is which country should have primary jurisdiction to tax such income. The international tax regime answers this question with the benefits principle. The benefits principle was originally developed in 1923,[43] under which: (1) active income from trade or business is primarily assigned to the source country's tax jurisdiction (with the residence country having secondary jurisdiction), and (2) passive income, such as dividends, interest, and royalties, is primarily assigned to the residence country's tax jurisdiction (with the source country having secondary jurisdiction).[44] MNEs' corporate income from their trade or business is considered active income and, thus, is primarily assigned to source countries where such trade or business is conducted, and income is generated. Because of the primacy of source taxation for active income under the benefits principle, residence countries of MNEs that have secondary tax jurisdiction over such income should grant a foreign tax credit for source taxes.[45] However, the journey toward achieving the single tax principle encountered challenges. Globalization in the late twentieth century resulted in increased tax competition among source countries, which are mostly developing countries with strong needs to lure FDI. Hence, source-based taxation with a substantive tax rate was difficult to sustain. Furthermore, there are too many source countries to be able to effectively cooperate to curb tax competition.[46]

The single tax principle solves tax competition among source countries by requiring a secondary tax jurisdiction to enforce the single tax principle at a substantive tax rate if source-based taxation is nominal. Such nominal source taxation should not count as fully taxed "once" for the purposes of the single tax principle. Ruth Mason (a Professor of Law and Taxation at the University of Virginia School of Law) refers to this concept as "full taxation."[47] Under the benefits principle, residence countries have secondary tax jurisdiction. If residence countries exercise the secondary tax jurisdiction at a substantial tax rate, the single tax principle can still be accomplished. This is relatively straightforward to accomplish compared to an effort to curb source country tax competition, because over 90 percent of the world's largest multinationals are residents of the G20.[48]

[43] Thomas S. Adams, Interstate and International Double Taxation, Lectures on Taxation 101 (Roswell Magill ed., 1932).

[44] *Id.*

[45] *See* Mitchell A. Kane, *Strategy and Cooperation in National Response to International Tax Arbitrage*, 53 Emory L.J. 89 (2004); *see also* I.R.C. §§ 901, 903.

[46] *See* Reuven S. Avi-Yonah & Haiyan Xu, *Evaluating BEPS: A Reconsideration of the Benefits Principle and Proposal for UN Oversight*, 6 Harv. Bus. L. Rev. 185 (2016).

[47] *Transformation*, *supra* note 9, at 22, 25.

[48] *Role of the* G20, European Comm'n, http://ec.europa.eu/info/food-farming-fisheries/farming/international-cooperation/international-organisations/g20_en (last accessed Jan. 18, 2025); Emmanuel Saez & Gabriel Zucman, *A Wealth Taxation on Corporations' Stock*, G20 Insights (2021), http://www.g20-insights.org/policy_briefs/a-wealth-tax-on-corporations-stock/

More importantly, if all residence countries exercise "full taxation" power on MNEs' global income, it would eliminate the problem of MNEs shopping source countries by removing the incentive to do so.[49] If an MNE's residence country is going to ensure that the MNE pays its full income tax regardless of the country or tax haven where they claim to have "earned" the income, there will be no economic benefit for MNEs to source country shop.

6.2.1.1 The Origins of the Single Tax Principle

The origins of the single tax principle can be traced back to the adoption of the US foreign tax credit in 1918.[50] Double taxation occurs in international tax when a source country and residence country levy tax on the same declared income.[51] Many countries enter income tax treaties to avoid such double taxation. Under such tax treaties, source countries offer reduced withholding tax rates for aliens' income from domestic sources, whereas residence countries offer tax exemption or credit to foreign-source income.[52] Thomas Adams, the US Treasury adviser who introduced the credit, stated that he rejected the exemption system used by most European countries because it led to double non-taxation.[53]

The same formulation can be found in the commentary to the first model tax treaty, issued under the auspices of the League of Nations in 1927, which states as follows:

> It is highly desirable that States should come to an agreement with a view to ensuring that a taxpayer shall not be taxed on the same income by several different countries, and it seems equally desirable that such international cooperation should prevent certain incomes from escaping taxation altogether. The most elementary and undisputed principles of fiscal justice, therefore, required that the experts should devise a scheme whereby all incomes would be taxed once and only once.[54]

American tax policy began to change in the 1960s under the guidance of Stanley Surrey, the first Assistant Secretary for Tax Policy and the true intellectual father of the single tax principle. Surrey had publicly advocated for the single tax principle in 1957 when he testified in the US Senate against a proposed US–Pakistan tax treaty

("Corporations headquartered in the G20 represent over 90% of global corporate equity market value.").

49 *See* Reuven S. Avi-Yonah, *Hanging Together: A Multilateral Approach to Taxing Multinationals*, 5 MICH. BUS. & ENTREPRENEURIAL L. REV. 137 (2016).

50 *See id.*

51 *See* Klaus Vogel, *Double Tax Treaties and Their Interpretation*, 4 BERKELEY J. INT'L L. 4 (1986).

52 *See* Charles H. Gustafson ET AL., TAXATION OF INTERNATIONAL TRANSACTIONS: MATERIALS, TEXT, AND PROBLEMS 63 (4th ed. 2011).

53 ADAMS, *supra* note 43, at 101, 112–13.

54 *Reports Presented by the Comm. of Technical Experts on Double Taxation and Tax Evasion*, League of Nations Doc. C.216M.85 1927 II (1927).

that provided for double non-taxation.[55] The treaty was not ratified. Surrey proposed imposing US taxation in full on all Controlled Foreign Companies (CFCs)[56] of US MNEs. Although Subpart F enacted in 1962 only applied the tax in situations where the income was likely to escape source taxation,[57] Surrey achieved his main aim of generally imposing the single tax principle on US MNEs. Surrey also incorporated the single tax principle into US tax treaties (for example, the US–Luxembourg tax treaty)[58] by making it clear that US withholding taxes would not be reduced unless the income was subject to tax in the residence jurisdiction.[59] This provision was also included in the first US Model Tax Treaty of 1981.[60]

In the same year, however, the United States succumbed to the pressures of globalization and the need to attract foreign investment by enacting the portfolio interest exemption, which abolished the US withholding tax on portfolio interest regardless of whether it was taxed at the source.[61] The rule violated the single tax principle, but also led to massive capital flight into the United States. It is one of the first globalization examples of US tax competition.[62] Furthermore, in the 1990s, Congress began weakening Subpart F by adopting exceptions, such as for active banking and insurance, even though the income was mobile and not taxed at the source.[63]

The erosion of the single tax principle culminated with the establishment in 1997 of the "check the box" rule, which led to the complete undermining of Subpart F, especially after it was codified in 2006.[64] The "check the box" rule enables US MNEs to shift income from both the United States and high-tax foreign countries to tax havens without triggering Subpart F.[65] The result of this erosion and violation of the single tax principle was that, by 2017, US MNEs had amassed more than $3 trillion of income in low-tax foreign jurisdictions.[66]

55 Joseph J. Thorndike, *Stanley Surrey Knew a Thing or Two About Loopholes*, Tax Analysts Art. Archive Online (Feb. 7, 2013), http://www.taxhistory.org/thp/readings.nsf/ArtWeb/05B6E5635C931F6F85257B160048DD4D?OpenDocument.

56 I.R.C. §§ 957(a), 951, 952.

57 I.R.C. §§ 951–65.

58 Income and Capital Tax Treaty, Lux.–U.S., Article XVI, Dec. 18, 1962, http://www.irs.gov/pub/irs-trty/luxem.pdf.

59 This is the origin of the Subject to Tax Rule (STTR) in Pillar Two, discussed *infra* Section 6.3.1.2.

60 Avi-Yonah, *Single Tax Principle*, *supra* note 9; Reuven S. Avi-Yonah & Gianluca Mazzoni, *Stanley Surrey, the 1981 US Model, and the Single Tax Principle*, 49 Intertax 729 (2021).

61 I.R.C. § 871(h)(3); *see* Marilyn Franson, *Repeal of the Thirty Percent Withholding Tax on Portfolio Interest Paid to Foreign Investors*, 6 Nw. J. Int'l L. & Bus. 3 (1984).

62 Reuven S. Avi-Yonah, *What Goes around Comes around: Why the USA Is Responsible for Capital Flight (and What It Can Do about It)*, 13 Haifa L. Rev. 321 (2019).

63 David R. Sicular, *The New Look-Through Rule: W(h)ither Subpart F?* taxanalysts (Apr. 23, 2007), http://www.paulweiss.com/media/104725/SubPartF04-May-07.pdf.

64 Treas. Reg. § 301.7701-2; *see also* Sicular, *supra* note 63.

65 *Id.*

66 Richard Phillips et al., *Offshore Shell Games 2017*, Inst. on Tax'n & Econ. Pol'y (Oct. 17, 2017), http://itep.org/offshoreshellgames2017.

Due to the increasingly intense and competitive nature of tax competition between countries over the past twenty-five years, the first author has advocated for the single tax principle as a solution to tax competition since 1997.[67] Income from cross-border transactions should be subject to onetime taxation. However, taxing cross-border income just once also means care should be taken that it should not be undertaxed. The first author has argued that the appropriate rate of tax for purposes of the single tax principle would be determined by the second principle of international taxation: the benefits principle. That means the active income should be taxed at least at the source tax rate (which tends to be lower than the residence rate), but at no more than the residence rate.

As Section 6.3 demonstrates, the underlying idea behind Pillar Two can be traced back to the concept of the single tax principle.[68] Specifically, Pillar Two offers various measures by which residual taxation by the residence (or source) jurisdiction should occur when the tax imposed by the source (or residence) jurisdiction falls below a specified level – that is, the global minimum tax rate. This embodies the idea of corrective measures to prevent under taxation as argued by the first author of this chapter in support of the single tax principle.[69]

6.2.1.2 Academic Debate

Scholars and commentators have engaged in a long debate on whether tax harmony or achieving the single tax principle would be possible in the real world. H. David Rosenbloom of New York University, in his famous Tillinghast Lecture[70] in 1998,

[67] Reuven S. Avi-Yonah, *International Taxation of Electronic Commerce*, 52 TAX L. REV. 507 (1997) [hereinafter, *Electronic Commerce*]. Avi-Yonah later developed a different normative argument for the single tax principle, basing it for corporate taxation on the need to curb the power of the largest multinationals. *See* Reuven S. Avi-Yonah, *Corporations, Society and the State: A Defense of the Corporate Tax*, 90 VA. L. REV. 1193, 1202 (2004); Reuven S. Avi-Yonah, *A New Corporate Tax*, 167 TAX NOTES FED. 653, 654 (2020).

[68] This similarity has been noted by other scholars. *See, e.g.*, Elizabeth Gil García, *The Single Tax Principle: Fiction or Reality in a Non-Comprehensive International Tax Regime?* 11 WORLD TAX J. 497 (2019); *Transformation, supra* note 9, at 353; Leopoldo Parada, *Full Taxation: The Single Tax Emperor's New Clothes*, 24 FLA. TAX REV. 729 (2021); Wolfgang Schoen, Is There Finally an International Tax System? *in* THINKER, TEACHER, TRAVELER: REIMAGINING INTERNATIONAL TAX, ESSAYS IN HONOR OF H. DAVID ROSENBLOOM 475 (Georg Kofler et al. eds., IBFD 2021).

[69] *Electronic Commerce, supra* note 67, at 517.

[70] H. David Rosenbloom, *The David R. Tillinghast Lecture International Tax Arbitrage and the "International Tax System"*, 53 TAX L. REV. 137, 137 (2000) [hereinafter, *Arbitrage*]; Reuven S. Avi-Yonah, *Commentary on Rosenbloom*, 53 TAX L. REV. 167, 167 (2000); Michael J. Graetz, *Taxing International Income – Inadequate Principles, Outdated Concepts, and Unsatisfactory Policy*, 54 TAX L. REV. 261, 335 (2001); DANIEL SHAVIRO, FIXING US INTERNATIONAL TAXATION 2 (2014), http://web.law.columbia.edu/sites/default/files/microsites/law-theory-workshop/files/DShaviro.pdf; Julie Roin, *Taxation without Coordination*, 31 J. LEGAL STUD. S61, S61 (2002); *see* Kane, *supra* note 45, at 92; Yariv Brauner, *An International Tax Regime in Crystallization*, 56 TAX L. REV. 259, 262–63 (2003). For a summary of the academic debate, *see* Ruth Mason & Pascal Saint-Amans, Has Cross-Border Arbitrage Met Its Match?, *in* THINKER, TEACHER,

characterized international tax arbitrage as "the deliberate exploitation of differences in national tax systems."[71] To Rosenbloom, international tax harmony was an unachievable ideal, whereas tax competition and the resulting arbitrage was an inevitable by-product of independent tax policymaking by sovereign states. Thus, preventing mismatches in tax policy "is not and should not be a first-rank policy objective of the United States."[72] Rosenbloom also identified line-drawing problems related to distinguishing impermissible arbitrage from permissible tax planning. Rosenbloom considered "international income" and the "international tax system" to be imaginary, rejected the single tax principle, and, thus, argued that there was no principled objection to arbitrage.[73]

Academics, including the first author of this chapter, responded to Rosenbloom's critique by clarifying the policy concerns raised by international tax competition and tax arbitrage and further detailing the efficiencies and benefits of the single tax principle.[74] Adam Rosenzweig[75] and Diane Ring[76] argued that international tax competition and the resulting arbitrage raised equity concerns because not everyone could benefit from it. Daniel Shaviro, Mitchell Kane, Ring, and Rosenzweig highlighted the efficiency concerns, arguing that tax competition and the resulting arbitrage could cause various behavioral responses of taxpayers, such as distorting the choice of location for investment.[77]

Some commentators were concerned about the interaction effect that could arise from US tax policy responses to arbitrage. Shaviro pointed out that a unilateral response may cause retaliation by other countries.[78] Kane developed a model involving zero-sum tax competition among states seeking to attract capital and argued that a state might exploit the ambiguity of mismatching tax rules to win this competition without instigating retaliatory responses.[79] Omri Marian's study of the LuxLeaks rulings demonstrated how the country Luxembourg was able to exploit

Traveler: Reimagining International Tax, Essays in Honor of H. David Rosenbloom (Georg Kofler et al. eds., IBFD 2021), *reprinted in* 41 Va. Tax Rev. 1, 10–11 (2021).

71 *Arbitrage*, *supra* note 70, at 166.

72 H. David Rosenbloom, *Cross-Border Arbitrage: The Good, the Bad, and the Ugly*, 85 Taxes 115, 116 (2007).

73 *Id.* at 115.

74 Avi-Yonah, *supra* note 70, at 170–71.

75 Adam H. Rosenzweig, *Harnessing the Costs of International Tax Arbitrage*, 26 Va. Tax Rev. 555, 564–65 (2007).

76 *See* Diane M. Ring, *One Nation among Many: Policy Implications of Cross-Border Tax Arbitrage*, 44 B.C. L. Rev. 79, 125–28 (2002).

77 Daniel Shaviro, *Money on the Table?: Responding to Cross-Border Tax Arbitrage*, 3 Chi. J. Int'l L. 317, 323–25 (2002); Kane, *supra* note 45, at 114; Ring, *supra* note 76, at 126–27; Rosenzweig, *supra* note 75, at 564–65.

78 Shaviro, *supra* note 77, at 327.

79 Kane, *supra* note 45, at 142.

the mismatches/arbitrages of tax rules in such a way as to gain a significant economic advantage over its neighboring states without attracting notice.[80]

Rosenbloom also pushed back on the notion that tax competition and arbitrage was a threat to revenue. He argued that if the taxpayer complies with each national tax regime, no one country has cause to complain about revenue loss.[81] Kane and Rosenbloom rejected the conception of hypothetical, collective income, or revenue that could have been available had tax competition not existed.[82] However, the over 140 member jurisdictions of the BEPS Inclusive Framework who signed on to the Statement and Pillar Two clearly disagree.[83]

On a more direct challenge to the single tax principle, scholars have raised concerns about what it means to tax only once.[84] Shaviro suggests that being taxed twice at low rates (for example, 2 percent and 2 percent) need not necessarily be worse than being taxed once (for example, 5 percent).[85] He further argues that the single tax principle would be hard to operationalize despite higher levels of international cooperation because it is "challenging to coordinate distinctive tax systems across multiple complex dimensions" and, worse, countries have little interest in harmonizing their tax rules.[86]

Nevertheless, recent developments, such as 137 Inclusive Framework (IF) member jurisdictions agreeing to the two-pillar solution – including the global minimum tax in the Statement – indicate that international interest in tax harmony is not as outlandish as some scholars suggest.[87] But the global tax deal in the Statement was not built in a day. The next subpart further explains the global reaction toward the single tax principle and tax harmony prior to the creation of Pillar Two.

6.2.2 *Global Efforts Begin in the Late 2000s*

The recent international struggle in combatting tax competition is well known among those in the field of international taxation. The first promising step toward the single tax principle occurred in the context of tax information transparency.

80 *See* Omri Marian, *The State Administration of International Tax Avoidance*, 7 HARV. BUS. L. REV. 1, 27–28 (2017).

81 Avi-Yonah, *supra* note 70, at 167.

82 Mason & Saint-Amans, *supra* note 70, at 5; *see* Kane, *supra* note 45, at 115.

83 OECD, *Hybrid Mismatch Arrangements: Tax Policy and Compliance Issues* 11 (2012), http://www.oecd.org/ctp/exchange-of-tax-information/hybrid-mismatch-arrangements-tax-policy-and-compliance-issues.pdf.

84 John Bentil, *Situating the International Tax System within Public International Law*, 49 GEO. J. INT'L L. 1219, 1251–52 (2018); *see also* Daniel Shaviro, *The Two Faces of the Single Tax Principle*, 41 BROOK. J. INT'L L. 1293, 1294 (2016).

85 Shaviro, *supra* note 84, at 1294.

86 Daniel Shaviro, *The Crossroads versus the Seesaw: Getting a "Fix" on Recent International Tax Policy Developments*, 69 TAX L. REV. 1, 3–4 (2015).

87 *See* Bentil, *supra* note 84, at 1251–52; Shaviro, *supra* note 86, at 330.

Following the 2008 financial crisis, the Foreign Account Tax Compliance Act of 2010 (FATCA) was enacted in the United States.[88] FATCA was designed to stop the practice of US residents pretending to be foreigners to escape from US taxation.[89] This practice enabled double non-taxation of income hidden in offshore accounts, where such assets were rarely detected because of bank secrecy.[90] Thus, FATCA required foreign financial institutions, such as Swiss banks, to report accounts held by US residents and citizens to the US government.[91] If foreign financial institutions do not comply, they are subject to tax penalties and criminal charges. FATCA's major success directly led to the development of the Common Reporting Standard at the global level, which linked over 100 foreign jurisdictions in a system where they could automatically exchange tax information with each other.[92] The enhanced transparency in tax information among countries can help achieve the single tax principle because it prevents double non-taxation of passive investment income earned by individuals. It is still not perfect (as evidenced by the recent leaks, such as the Pandora Papers),[93] but it is a significant step forward to full implementation of the single tax principle.

Second, in recent years, many countries have been more willing to cooperate and harmonize substantive tax rules to resolve tax competition.[94] In Europe, the 2008 financial crisis led to massive austerity, which in turn put pressure on politicians to raise concerns that MNEs (especially US MNEs) were not paying their fair share of tax to Europe as a source jurisdiction.[95] Some countries, such as the United Kingdom and France, realized that traditional international tax rules with a physical presence requirement did not allow them to tax Big Tech, even though those companies collected and profited from the user data of their citizens.[96] Thus, they adopted digital services taxes (DSTs).[97] This move caused heated debate around the world, leading the OECD to launch BEPS Project 1.0 to try to update the

[88] *See, e.g.*, Michael S. Kirsch, *Revisiting the Tax Treatment of Citizens Abroad: Reconciling Principle and Practice*, 16 Fla. Tax Rev. 117, 122 (2014).

[89] *See* Young Ran (Christine) Kim, *Considering "Citizenship Taxation": In Defense of FATCA*, 20 Fla. Tax Rev. 335, 359–62 (2017).

[90] *Id.*

[91] I.R.C. §§ 1471, 1472, 1473, 1474.

[92] *See id.*

[93] *See The Pandora Papers: An ICIJ Investigation*, Int'l Consortium Indep. Journalists http://www.icij.org/investigations/pandora-papers/ (last accessed Mar. 11, 2022).

[94] *See* OECD, *Inclusive Framework on Base Erosion and Profit Shifting*, http://www.oecd.org/tax/beps/ (last accessed Mar. 11, 2022).

[95] *See* Schreuer Rappepert & Singer Tankersley, *Europe's Planned Digital Tax Heightens Tensions with US*, N.Y. Times (Mar. 19, 2018), at 1–2, http://www.nytimes.com/2018/03/19/us/politics/europe-digital-tax-trade.html.

[96] *Id.* at 3–4.

[97] *See, e.g.*, Young Ran (Christine) Kim, *Digital Services Tax: A Cross-border Variation of the Consumption Tax Debate*, 72 Ala. L. Rev. 131, 136 (2020).

international tax regime that overlooked undertaxation of the digital economy and to prevent trade wars over individually enacted DSTs.[98]

Through these efforts, countries realized that a complete harmonization of substantive tax law was unlikely to be fully successful as a comprehensive solution to tax competition because individual states would be reluctant to defer to another states' underlying tax rules or agree to implement a common set of rules for harmonization that may not match their tax objectives.[99] An alternative to harmonization that states have pursued recently are conditional rules.[100] Mason explains these conditional rules as "fiscal fail-safe" measures to guarantee full taxation and implement the single tax principle.[101] In other words, the conditional or secondary rules attempt to ensure that cross-border income does not escape tax by identifying "conditions under which, if one country does not tax, another country fills the tax void."[102] These conditional rules emerged in the BEPS Project 1.0, such as in Action 3 for expanding the CFC regimes[103] and Action 2 for anti-hybrid rules.[104] The BEPS Project 2.0 Pillar Two for a global minimum tax is also built on these conditional, fiscal fail-safe rules as demonstrated in Section 3.1.[105] Although not extensively harmonious because of various carve-outs and specific exceptions that various countries demanded, the examples reflect a new willingness to cooperatively coordinate efforts to address international tax arbitrage in a more comprehensive way.

On reflection, BEPS Project 1.0 included some significant steps toward tax harmony and the single tax principle. BEPS Project 1.0 is contrary to Rosenbloom's preferred solution for tax competition and arbitrage, which is doing nothing, because he did not believe there was a problem to solve. However, while this project advanced the single tax principle, most of its actions have been recommendations, not requirements, and for the most part its recommendations went unimplemented throughout the world. However, the EU did adopt various action items of BEPS Project 1.0 through its own directives, such as the Anti-Tax Avoidance Directive (ATAD).[106] But such a regional approach is limited in its ability to advance the single tax principle because of the need for global harmonization.

98 OECD, *supra* note 94.

99 *See, e.g.*, Yariv Brauner, *Treaties in the Aftermath of BEPS*, 41 Brook. J. Int'l L. 974, 976–77 (2016).

100 *See Transformation*, *supra* note 9, at 378–79.

101 *Id.* at 374–75.

102 *Id.* at 381.

103 OECD, *Designing Effective Controlled Foreign Company Rules, Action 3 – 2015 Final Report* 12, OECD/G20 Base Erosion and Profit Shifting Project (2015), http://dx.doi.org/10.1787/9789264241152-en.

104 OECD, *Neutralising the Effects of Hybrid Mismatch Arrangements, Action 2 – 2015 Final Report* 49–50, OECD/G20 Base Erosion and Profit Shifting Project (2015), http://dx.doi.org/10.1787/9789264241138-en.

105 *See infra* Section 6.3.1.

106 Reuven S. Avi-Yonah & Gianluca Mazzoni, *BEPS, ATAP and the New Tax Dialogue: A Transatlantic Competition?* 46 Intertax 885, 885 (2018).

BEPS Project 1.0 was disappointing because it did not fully implement the single tax principle on any meaningful scale or update the international tax regime for the twenty-first century.[107]

The shortcomings of BEPS Project 1.0 were addressed in BEPS Project 2.0. The new project developed a plan for international taxation that addressed the most pressing concerns in the plan's two pillars. However, the impetus of the plan did not come from the EU or any other multilateral agreement – it was a direct result of the passage of the TCJA. The next subsection discusses the important provisions of the TCJA that inspired BEPS Project 2.0.

6.2.3 *The TCJA as Constructive Unilateralism*

The United States has a long history of unilaterally adopting tax policies that are later enacted by many other countries around the world. This risk-taking on the part of the United States is considered by many to be internationally constructive because it allows other jurisdictions to evaluate the effectiveness of a tax policy before implementation.[108] Most notably, the United States has led the way with the Foreign Tax Credit, CFCs, and the two international tax rules in the TCJA–GILTI and BEAT, discussed in more detail below.[109]

Passage of the TCJA was not primarily motivated by a desire to implement the single tax principle. Instead, the US government wanted to bring back and tax the nearly $3 trillion of offshore corporate profits of the US MNEs.[110] Before the TCJA, US parent companies with foreign subsidiaries were generally not taxed on the earnings of their subsidiaries until the earnings were distributed to them (or repatriated to the United States).[111] If the foreign corporation did not distribute earnings back to the United States, US parents could indefinitely defer paying US taxes at the 35 percent rate on this foreign income. As a result, US MNEs, such as Apple, could incorporate a subsidiary in tax havens or low-tax jurisdictions like Ireland (where the corporate tax rate is 12.5 percent) and allocate as much taxable income as possible to these low-tax jurisdictions to minimize US corporate income tax.[112] Between 2005 and 2017, US MNEs had accumulated $2.6 trillion of low-taxed foreign income offshore that had never been subject to the 35 percent corporate income

[107] Reuven S. Avi-Yonah, *Full Circle: The Single Tax Principle, BEPS, and the New US Model*, 1 Global Tax'n 12, 12 (2016).

[108] Reuven S. Avi-Yonah, *Constructive Dialogue: BEPA and the TCJA* 2 (U. Mich. Pub. L. Rsch. Paper No. 665, 2020), http://papers.ssrn.com/sol3/papers.cfm?abstract_id = 3544065.).

[109] *Id.* at 2, 4, 16.

[110] Reuven S. Avi-Yonah, *The International Provisions of the TCJA: A Preliminary Summary and Assessment* (U. Mich. Pub. L. Rsch. Paper No. 605, 2017), http://papers.ssrn.com/sol3/papers.cfm?abstract_id = 3193278.

[111] *Id.*

[112] Padraic Halpin, *Ireland Collects Disputed Apple Taxes in Full ahead of Appeal*, Reuters (Sept. 18, 2018, 8:55 AM), http://reut.rs/38wQSLQ.

tax rate.[113] Thus, one of the primary goals of the TCJA was to remove potential tax benefits from offshoring income, thus returning the $2.6 trillion in capital to the United States for taxation and deterring such profit-shifting activity in the future.[114]

At the same time, other corporations whose businesses are more focused on the domestic market, such as Walmart, lobbied to reduce the 35 percent corporate tax rate, while owners of pass-through entities (like then-President Trump) pushed for a reduction of the tax rate on partnerships.[115]

The result was the TCJA. The TCJA implemented a participation exemption for dividends from CFCs, cut the corporate tax rate from 35 percent to 21 percent,[116] and cut the partnership and other pass-through tax rate from 37 percent to 29.6 percent.[117]

However, to pay for all these tax cuts within the confines of Budget Reconciliation, the Republican members of Congress decided to apply the single tax principle to US MNEs to stop their base erosion and profit-shifting strategies that have harmed US revenue.[118]

Three important provisions of the TCJA represented steps toward the single tax principle. First is the one-time mandatory "repatriation tax" (sometimes referred to "transition tax"). A significant tax rate (between 8 and 15 percent) was imposed on the past accumulated offshore profits of US MNEs.[119] It was imposed only one time, and it did not matter whether those offshore profits were repatriated to the United States.[120] Those profits were parked in low-tax jurisdictions, resulting in nominal source taxation. They were not subject to residence taxation by the United States because the pre-TCJA tax law allowed the US MNEs to defer taxation until the profits were repatriated. Hence, the new temporary repatriation tax in the TCJA implemented the single tax principle because these profits were previously subject to double non-taxation through the "check the box" policy.

Second, the GILTI rule imposed a tax on certain foreign subsidiaries' income from intangible assets.[121] Although the TCJA lowered the top corporate income tax rate from 35 percent to a flat 21 percent, the US corporate tax rate still exceeds the

[113] *Key Elements of the U.S. Tax System*, TAX POL'Y CTR., http://www.taxpolicycenter.org/briefing-book/what-tcja-repatriation-tax-and-how-does-it-work (last accessed May 2020).

[114] *See* Avi-Yonah, *supra* note 110.

[115] *See* John Ydstie, *How Trump's Corporate Tax Cut Is Playing Out for Wal-Mart*, NPR (Jan. 13, 2018, 5:47 PM), http://www.npr.org/2018/01/13/577900650/how-trump-s-corporate-tax-cut-is-playing-out-with-wal-mart; *see also* Reuven S. Avi-Yonah, *How Terrible Is the New Tax Law? Reflections on TRA17* (U. Mich. Pub. L. Rsch. Paper No. 586, 2018), http://papers.ssrn.com/sol3/papers.cfm?abstract_id=3095830.

[116] I.R.C. § 11.

[117] *Id.* § 199A.

[118] *See* Avi-Yonah, *supra* note 110, at 5–6.

[119] I.R.C. § 965.

[120] *See* Reuven S. Avi-Yonah, *The International Provisions of the TCJA: Six Results after Six Months* (U. Mich. Pub. L. Rsch. Paper No. 621, 2018), http://papers.ssrn.com/sol3/papers.cfm?abstract_id=3242008.

[121] *See id.*

rate in many countries.[122] Thus, situating ownership of a profitable patent, for example, in a foreign subsidiary in a lower rate or no-tax jurisdiction instead of in the United States, still could produce a substantial tax savings for an MNE. GILTI aims to prevent such profit shifting from easily movable intangible assets by imposing the US tax as residence taxation on foreign-source income from intangibles.[123] GILTI is foreign income earned by US shareholders of CFCs from intangible assets, such as copyrights, trademarks, and patents. It is calculated as the total active income earned by a CFC that exceeds 10 percent of the firm's depreciable tangible property (known as the Qualified Business Asset Investment, or QBAI). The resulting US shareholders who own 10 percent or more of a CFC are liable for the tax on its GILTI, which generally applies at a rate between 10.5 percent and 13.125 percent.[124] GILTI is perhaps the most successful and influential achievement of the single tax principle contained within the TCJA. Income subject to the GILTI rule would be subject to little to no tax in source and otherwise not be subject to US residence taxation. The exclusion for offshore tangible assets returns (the QBAI exemption) may tarnish the purpose of GILTI, but it is unlikely to be a major drawback because the largest US MNEs had few tangible assets offshore.

Finally, the BEAT provision addressed the problem of base erosion by foreign MNEs.[125] Suppose that a US corporation pays deductible payments, such as interest and royalties, to a related foreign entity. From the foreign entity's perspective, such interest and royalties are US source income. But suppose further that the foreign entity is not subject to US withholding tax for various reasons, such as tax treaty benefits and statutory tax exemptions. This is a classic example of multinationals escaping source-based taxation (in this case, US taxation) by accumulating large amounts of deductible payments offshore. Neither the US corporation nor the foreign recipient pays tax to the source country. To avoid such base-erosion payment, the BEAT reverses deductions and imposes an alternative minimum tax set at 10 percent (12.5 percent from 2026) on the modified tax base of the US corporation.[126] The BEAT was enacted despite potentially violating the nondiscrimination provision of all US tax treaties because the rule applies to the case of "US subsidiary–foreign parent" but not the case of "US subsidiary–US parent." Nonetheless, BEAT effectively denies deductions in source countries for payments that are unlikely to be subject to residence-based taxation. BEAT achieves the single tax principle by strengthening source-based taxation.

The TCJA, albeit begrudgingly, moved the United States toward the single tax principle and combating tax competition. The global result was remarkably

[122] *Id.*

[123] *Id.*; Reuven S. Avi-Yonah, *The Baby and the Bathwater: Reflections on the TCJA's International Provisions*, 101 TAX NOTES INT'L 599 (Feb. 1, 2021).

[124] I.R.C. § 951A.

[125] *Id.* § 59A.

[126] *Id.*

constructive, as the TCJA demonstrated a means to feasibly achieve reasonable tax harmonization. Inspired by the international tax provisions of the TCJA, the G20 and the OECD launched BEPS Project 2.0 in 2017, using GILTI and BEAT as the models for its Pillar Two proposal. While Pillar One of the Statement focuses on updating outdated rules in source-based taxation,[127] Pillar Two is more directly on point for implementing the single tax principle through a combination of rules strengthening residence-based taxation (for example, the IIR) and source-based taxation (UTPR and STTR). The benchmark of "substantial tax" counted "once" for single tax purposes is set at 15 percent, the global minimum tax. Section 6.3 will discuss Pillar Two in greater detail .

6.3 A NEW SOLUTION: PILLAR TWO AND GLOBAL MINIMUM TAX

The Statement presents Pillar Two and the global minimum tax as a new solution to tax competition. Together with Pillar One, the entire framework in the Statement represents a revolution in international taxation by offering many solutions, such as eliminating the obsolete permanent establishment requirement for Amount A in Pillar One and proposing a 15 percent global minimum tax in Pillar Two. All of these are decisive breaks from the past and have been suggested for twenty-five years but have gained little traction until now.[128] Thus, the Statement encompasses both revolution and evolution.

This section focuses on Pillar Two. Pillar Two is a new solution to tax competition. It is aimed at systematically preventing the race to the bottom and eliminating incentives for both states and MNEs to engage in tax competition. However, this novel solution builds upon past efforts. We argue that Pillar Two has finally embodied the single tax principle which states that all income of MNEs ought to be taxed *once* at a *substantive effective tax rate*. If this proposition is not met, corrective rules apply to accomplish the result. This section explains the details of Pillar Two and the relevant implementation rules, such as the Inflation Reduction Act of the United States. The rules are very technical and complex. Evaluating these rules through the lens of the single tax principle – that all income must be taxed once substantially – will help readers understand the rules intuitively if the technicalities overwhelm.

6.3.1 *Unpacking Pillar Two*

Pillar Two consists of: (1) optional domestic minimum taxation, (2) two interlocking domestic rules requiring income inclusion (for residence countries [IIR] and denial

[127] *See* Avi-Yonah et al., *supra* note 2.

[128] Reuven S. Avi-Yonah, *The New International Tax Framework: Evolution or Revolution?*, 25 Am. Soc'y Int'l L. 11 (2021), http://www.asil.org/insights/volume/25/issue/11.

of deduction or an equivalent adjustment for source countries [UTPR], together referred to as the Global anti-Base Erosion [GLoBE] Rules), and (3) a treaty-based subject-to-tax rule (STTR).

6.3.1.1 Domestic Rules: Global Anti-Base Erosion Rules

GLoBE Rules have two components: income inclusion (IIR) and denial of deduction or an equivalent adjustment (UTPR). MNEs that meet the €750 million revenue threshold determined under the Model Rules (similarly to the BEPS Action 13 on country-by-country reporting) are subject to a global minimum tax regardless of the jurisdiction where they are headquartered or operating. Also, the Statement makes it clear that the US GILTI regime will co-exist with the GLoBE rules,[129] which was later confirmed by the February 2023 Administrative Guidance to Pillar Two.

First, the IIR requires the residence countries of multinational corporations to impose top-up tax[130] on an ultimate parent entity (UPE) at a minimum rate of 15 percent if the source country where a subsidiary operates imposes tax below such minimum rate on the subsidiary's income. The 15 percent global minimum tax rate is an effective rate, not a nominal rate. The IIR allocates top-up tax based on a top-down approach.[131] With the single tax principle in mind, this rule acts as a corrective measure that allows residence countries to tax if source taxation is not substantial enough to count "once."

Second, if a residence country does not impose this minimum tax, the subsidiary's deduction for payment to the parent entity would be denied or an equivalent adjustment would be required as per the UTPR to the extent that the low-tax income of a subsidiary is not subject to tax under an IIR.[132] This represents an additional corrective measure to guarantee substantial source taxation if residence countries do not cooperate.

To illustrate, suppose that a subsidiary in the source country earns $100 of income and the source country imposes tax at 10 percent, which is below the 15 percent global minimum tax rate. Then, the residence country of the parent entity includes the $100 in the parent's income and imposes tax at a rate that is equal to the difference between the 15 percent of global minimum rate and the said 10 percent tax rate. Suppose further that the subsidiary pays the $100 to the parent in a deductible form, such as a royalty. If the residence country does not have the IIR, the subsidiary's deduction for the $100 royalty payment will be denied. Pascal Saint-

[129] *Id.* at 5.

[130] David Lawder & Leigh Thomas, *Explainer: What Is a Global Minimum Tax and How Could It Affect Companies, Countries?* Reuters (Apr. 14, 2021, 8:50 AM), http://www.reuters.com/business/what-is-global-minimum-tax-how-could-it-affect-companies-countries-2021-04-14.

[131] *Id.*

[132] *Id.* at 3.

Amans, the former director of the OECD's Center for Tax Policy and Administration, explains that the UTPR is intended as an insurance policy against countries that refuse to implement Pillar Two.[133] If companies move to noncooperating jurisdictions in hope of gaining a tax advantage, the effect would be fully neutralized. However, certain MNEs will not be subject to the undertaxed profits rule (UTPR) for the first five years after meeting the €750 million ($866 million) revenue threshold if their foreign tangible assets do not exceed €50 million ($57.7 million) and they operate in no more than five foreign countries.

During the Pillar Two negotiations, the Inclusive Framework added another rule to Pillar Two, a qualified domestic minimum top-up tax (QDMTT). This top-up tax enables jurisdictions to tax their low-taxed constituent entities before an IIR or a UTPR would apply. Otherwise, residence countries would have right to tax all low-taxed constituent entities in source countries first, which would lead to shifting tax revenue from source countries (often developing countries) to residence countries (often developed countries). Therefore, any QDMTT applies first and then the QDMTT is credited toward any IIR or UTPR paid by an MNE group. Ideally, the QDMTT calculated under laws of a source jurisdiction and the QDMTT credit should equal top-up tax due calculated under an IIR or a UTPR under laws of respective jurisdictions. To avoid these issues, a QDMTT may be granted a safe harbor status if a QDMTT complies with stricter safe harbor requirements under the July Administrative Guidance. If a QDMTT is granted the safe harbor status, then excess profits of low-taxed constituent entities located in a jurisdiction with a QDMTT safe harbor status is exempt from taxation under an IIR or a UTPR.

There are important carve-outs to the GLoBE rules. First, the substance-based carve-out of income from the Pillar Two rules will exempt, in the first year, 8 percent of the carrying value of tangible assets and 10 percent of payroll. These percentages will decline by 0.2 percent each year for the next five years, and by 0.4 percent (for tangible assets) and 0.8 percent (for payroll) each year for the subsequent five years, after which the exemption will be 5 percent of both tangible assets and payroll. Second, a de minimis carve-out will exclude profits from countries where the MNE has less than €10 million ($11.6 million) in revenue and less than €1 million in profits. These substantial carve-outs harm the spirit of the single tax principle, and *infra* Section 6.4.2.2 discusses their pitfalls.

6.3.1.2 Treaty-Based Rule: Subject to Tax Rule (STTR)

The STTR is a standalone treaty rule whose origin can be traced back to Stanley Surrey's US tax treaty policy in the 1960s, discussed in Section 6.2.1. It specifically

[133] Alex Parker, *How the Global Tax Agreement Could Backfire for Biden*, LAW360 (Oct. 18, 2021), http://www.law360.com/tax-authority/articles/1431269/how-the-global-tax-agreement-could-backfire-for-biden.

targets intercompany payments that exploit treaties to shift profits to low-tax jurisdictions.[134] Therefore, this rule applies to certain categories of deductible payments that present a greater risk of base erosion, such as interest and royalties.[135] There were negotiations by the Inclusive Framework regarding the minimum rate for STTR, between 7.5 percent and 9 percent;[136] however, the Statement stipulates that the minimum rate will be 9 percent.

For example, suppose that a subsidiary in the source country pays a royalty to a parent company of $100, and the parent's $100 royalty income is subject to a nominal tax rate of 1 percent below the minimum rate (9 percent) in the residence country. Then, the source country is allowed to impose withholding tax on the royalty payment at a rate that is equal to the difference between the minimum rate provided for under the STTR (9 percent) and the said nominal tax rate (1 percent).[137]

6.3.1.3 Model Rules

The Statement provides, "[P]illar Two should be brought into law in 2022, to be effective in 2023, with the UTPR coming into effect in 2024."[138] The OECD/Inclusive Framework will present Model Rules for Pillar Two to define the scope and mechanics of the GLoBE rules and provide a template for domestic legislation to implement the GLoBE regime. The OECD/Inclusive Framework will also provide model treaty provisions to give effect to the STTR by mid-2022.[139] At the end of 2022, the OECD expects to have an implementation framework to facilitate the coordinated implementation of the GLoBE rules.[140]

In December 2021, the OECD/Inclusive Framework released Model Rules for Pillar Two, consisting of ten chapters that explained the GLoBE regime in detail.[141] In addition to this seventy-page document, the OECD/Inclusive Framework

[134] OECD, *Tax Challenges Arising from Digitalisation – Report on Pillar Two Blueprint: Inclusive Framework on BEPS*, OECD/G20 Base Erosion and Profit Shifting Project 150, ¶ 566 (2020), http://doi.org/10.1787/abb4c3d1-en [hereinafter, Pillar Two Blueprint].

[135] *Id.* at 150, ¶ 568.

[136] OECD, *Statement on a Two-Pillar Solution to Address the Tax Challenges Arising from the Digitalisation of the Economy* 5, OECD/G20 Base Erosion and Profit Shifting Project (July 1, 2021), http://www.oecd.org/tax/beps/statement-on-a-two-pillar-solution-to-address-the-tax-challenges-arising-from-the-digitalisation-of-the-economy-july-2021.pdf [hereinafter July Statement].

[137] Pillar Two Blueprint, *supra* note 134, at 165, ¶ 650.

[138] July Statement, *supra* note 136, at 5.

[139] OECD, *Global Anti-Base Erosion Model Rules (Pillar Two), Frequently Asked Questions* 6 (Dec. 2021), www.oecd.com (last accessed Jan. 18, 2025).

[140] *Id.*

[141] OECD, *Tax Challenges Arising from the Digitalisation of the Economy – Global Anti-Base Erosion Model Rules (Pillar Two)* (Dec. 2021), http://www.oecd.org/tax/beps/tax-challenges-arising-from-the-digitalisation-of-theeconomy-global-anti-base-erosion-model-rules-pillar-two.htm [hereinafter, *Model Rules*].

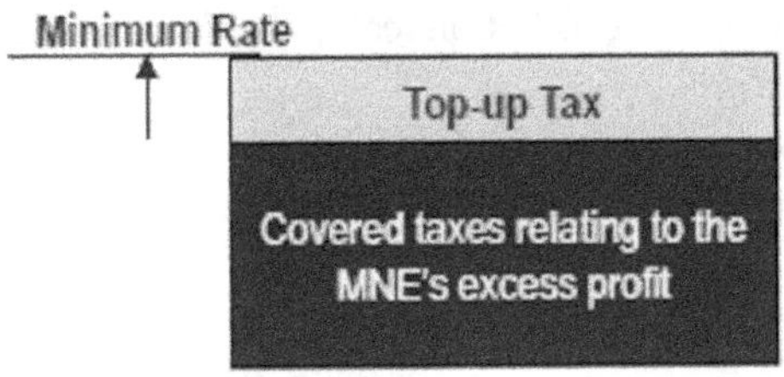

FIGURE 6.1 Top-up tax explained
Sources: OECD, *The Pillar Two Rules in a Nutshell*; OECD, *Overview of the Key Operating Provisions of the GloBE Rules* (referred to as "fact sheets" in the file name assigned by the OECD), at 1.

distributed Commentary to the Model Rules (Pillar Two) later in March 2022, which is about 230 pages long. There are also multiple supplements issued by the OECD/Inclusive Framework,[142] but the authors found the six-page fact sheets most helpful for many readers.[143]

First, the Model Rules explain what "top-up tax" means in Pillar Two. As Figure 6.1 shows, top-up tax first assumes a minimum tax amount relating to the MNE's excess profit calculated at the minimum tax rate of 15 percent. If certain covered taxes – not all, but certain respectable taxes – paid by constituent entities of the MNE do not reach the minimum tax amount, the GLoBE Rules will impose an additional tax to fill the deficient tax amount. So, the top-up tax seems to describe the tax rules that pull the top of the tax liability amount up to a certain minimum level. To determine top-up tax liability for an MNE, the Model Rules offer five steps:[144]

- Step 1: An MNE Group determines whether it is within the scope of the GLoBE rules. If so, it identifies the location of each Constituent Entity within the MNE Group.
- Step 2: Determine income of each constituent entity. This so-called GLoBE Income of a constituent entity is the income used for preparing a consolidated financial statement of the ultimate parent entity.[145]
- Step 3: Determine taxes attributable to income determined in Step 2. (Covered Taxes)
- Step 4: Calculate the effective tax rate of all Constituent Entities located in the same jurisdiction. If an MNE is subject to an effective tax rate

[142] *See, e.g.*, OECD, *The Pillar Two Rules in a Nutshell* (Dec. 2021), http://www.oecd.org/tax/beps/pillar-two-model-rules-in-a-nutshell.pdf; OECD, *Overview of the Key Operating Provisions of the GloBE Rules* (Dec. 2021), http://www.oecd.org/tax/beps/pillar-two-GloBE-rules-fact-sheets.pdf (referred to as "fact sheets" in the file name assigned by the OECD).

[143] *Id.*, Overview.

[144] *Id.*

[145] *Model Rules*, *supra* note 141, at 15, Article 3.1.

below 15 percent in any jurisdiction, calculate the top-up tax with respect to that low-tax jurisdiction.

- Step 5: Impose top-up tax under QDMTT in the source country, IIR in the residence country, or UTPR in the source country in accordance with the agreed rule order.[146]

The initial and overwhelming responses are that the Model Rules are so complex that they need to be simplified.[147] For example, Step 4 requires MNEs to calculate their effective tax rate in each jurisdiction where they do business. It is a novel compliance challenge that requires MNEs to prepare new information systems.[148] The OECD/Inclusive Framework also acknowledges the challenges, so the Model Rules promise to develop safe harbors that let MNEs avoid full calculations of top-up tax in certain circumstances.[149] However, the Model Rules Commentary did not include the details on safe harbors, so the OECD/Inclusive Framework used administrative guidance to set rules that govern safe harbors.

6.3.2 *The US Implementation through the Inflation Reduction Act (IRA)*

The United States planned to implement Pillar Two by international tax provisions of the Build Back Better (BBB) Bill.[150] However, this initiative reached only a partial fruition in the form of the IRA, but ultimately did not align the United States with Pillar Two. This subsection discusses the enacted changes in the IRA, and how they fit in with the new international tax regime, especially Pillar Two.

6.3.2.1 Corporate Alternative Minimum Tax (CAMT)

A domestic tax provision in the IRA that is also relevant to the single tax principle in the new international tax regime is the new book-based alternative minimum tax (AMT) for corporations, set at 15 percent.[151] The AMT was designed to reduce a taxpayer's ability to avoid taxes by using certain deductions and other tax benefit

146 Jinyan Li makes a noteworthy observation on the Model Rules' revised approach on the UTPR. *See* Li, *supra* note 16.

147 *See, e.g.*, Isabel Gottlieb, *Companies Eager to See Details on Minimum Tax Simplifications*, BLOOMBERG TAX (Mar. 23, 2022), http://news.bloombergtax.com/daily-tax-report-international/companies-eager-to-see-details-on-minimum-tax-simplifications; Allison Christians, Full Professor, H. Heward Stikeman Chair in Tax Law, McGill University Faculty of Law, Oral Presentation "Let the GILTI GloBE Games Begin" at the 4th Annual UCI Law – A. Lavar Taylor Tax Symposium (Mar. 21, 2022); *BEPS Monitoring Group Comments*, *supra* note 15, at 1427.

148 Gottlieb, *supra* note 147.

149 *Model Rules*, *supra* note 141, at 47, Article 8.2.

150 H.R. 5376, 117th Cong. (2021) [hereinafter Build Back Better (BBB) Act].

151 *Id.*, H.R. 5376, § 138101(a).

items.[152] The TCJA had repealed the AMT for corporations, but the IRA reintroduced it.[153] The new rule applies to MNEs with an average revenue of over $1 billion over a three-taxable-year period.[154] The modified corporate AMT rule applies to both US MNEs and foreign MNEs whose US revenue exceeds $100 million over three years.[155] Thus, it is an important backstop to the BEAT as well as GILTI by offering another minimum tax rate. It is also consistent with both the IIR for residence country and the UTPR for source country.[156] Even though the AMT is a 15 percent tax rate minimum tax, it still does not comply with Pillar ZTwo as a QDMTT and therefore will probably be considered as a covered tax under Pillar Two. Certain mechanics of the corporate AMT in relation to Pillar Two might also need an IF administrative guidance.

6.3.2.2 Global Intangible Low Tax Income (GILTI)

The BBB Bill was supposed to amend the GILTI to make it closer to Pillar Two GLoBE Rules because the GILTI rule looks similar to the IIR, which is reminiscent of CFC rules, but contains several differences from the QIIR. First, the GILTI tax rate of 10.5 percent[157] does not correspond to the minimum effective tax rate under Pillar Two. Therefore, it is necessary to raise the GILTI rate to at least 15 percent[158] (15.8 percent with foreign tax credits). Luckily, this might happen automatically in 2026 to 16.406 percent effective tax rate. Second, the GILTI has 10 percent exemption ratio of income from tangible assets (net deemed tangible income return),[159] which also needs to be amended, ideally to correspond to the substance-based income exclusion under Pillar Two. Third, the GILTI rule applies on worldwide basis while Pillar Two accounts for jurisdictional blending; that is, GILTI would have to have a country-by-country basis.[160] Last, GILTI tax base would have to be the same as the IIR's base.

152 Internal Revenue Serv., *Topic No. 556 Alternative Minimum Tax*, http://www.irs.gov/taxtopics/tc556 (last accessed Jan. 21, 2022).
153 BBB Act, H.R. 5376, § 138101.
154 *Id.*, H.R. 5376, § 138101(a)(2), at 1733.
155 *Id.*, H.R. 5376, § 138101(a)(2), at 1733.
156 *See infra* Section 6.3.1.1.
157 Daniel Bunn, *Piling on the GILTI Verdicts*, Tax Found. (July 15, 2021), http://taxfoundation.org/biden-gilti-proposal/ ("Half of GILTI is taxed at the U.S. corporate rate of 21 percent, which means the basic rate on GILTI is 10.5 percent.")
158 BBB Act, H.R. 5347, § 138131(a)(3) (2021).
159 I.R.C. § 951A(b)(2)(A).
160 BBB Act, *supra* note 158, § 138124(a); Daniel Bunn, *GILTI by Country Is Not as Simple as It Seems*, Tax Found. (May 18, 2021), http://taxfoundation.org/gilti-by-country/. For game theoretic model analysis comparing a global average regime and a country-by-country regime, *see* Sanchirico, *supra* note 16.

Besides those five changes to GILTI to make it closer to the QIIR, another question arises regarding providing tax credits under GILTI for Pillar Two top-up taxes paid in other jurisdictions. Hence, it is also important that the GILTI foreign tax credit limit is raised from 80 percent to 95 percent[161] or even 100 percent because that means that source country taxes that meet the global minimum tax rate will be almost fully creditable against residence taxation. This change shows another important element of the single tax principle, because if a source tax is substantial enough to satisfy the global minimum tax rate, it counts as taxing "once" and thus residence taxation yields to source to guarantee a "single" tax on such income. Nevertheless, such amendment might also hurt the United States from the tax revenue perspective.

We would have preferred the global minimum tax rate in Pillar Two and the GILTI rate in general to be higher than 15 percent – for example, 21 percent – because 21 percent is the current corporate income tax rate of the United States[162] and is closer to the average nominal corporate tax rate of the G20 countries (26.96 percent).[163] Furthermore, we would have preferred to eliminate the exemption for offshore tangible assets because there is no reason to limit the corrective measures initiated by the residence country, such as GILTI, to income from offshore intangible assets. Nonetheless, the GILTI provisions in the BBB Bill represented a reasonable compromise position to realize the single tax principle.

Some Democrats in the US House of Representatives, such as Congressmen Tom O'Halleran, Henry Cuellar, and Lou Correa, expressed concern that the changes to GILTI in the BBB Bill could have reduced the competitiveness of US MNEs.[164] Their concern is primarily that the US government has moved too quickly by instituting these rules before the rest of the world and creating what they argue are new rules, specifically, the country-by-country regime.[165] These Congressmen posit that the "new rules in the [Ways and Means Committee's] draft would allow other countries to take advantage of our rules, and harm U.S. companies. If we wait, it will allow Congress the opportunity to adjust the implementation of the policy based on how G20 countries write their own GILTI regimes."[166]

[161] BBB Act, *supra* note 158, § 138127(a).
[162] I.R.C. § 11.
[163] Asen, *supra* note 15.
[164] *Lawmakers Recommend Caution on GILTI Changes*, Tax Notes (Oct. 8, 2021), http://www.taxnotes.com/tax-notes-today-international/global-intangible-low-taxed-income-gilti/lawmakers-recommend-caution-gilti-changes/2021/10/20/7bcn7?highlight=headquartered%20G20.
[165] *Id.*
[166] *Id.*

Reservations expressed by members of Congress lend support to the notion that achieving a global tax deal is complicated by domestic political implications in the United States.

The changes to be done to GILTI are nonetheless still pending because the BBB Bill was not enacted and the IRA does not deal with the GILTI regime. The can has thus been kicked down the road by the IF by implementing the transitional UTPR Safe Harbor and the temporary administrative guidance dealing with the allocation of taxes arising under Blended CFC Tax Regimes. This should hopefully allow the United States enough time to make the necessary changes to the GILTI regime.[167]

6.4 PROMISES AND PITFALLS OF THE GLOBAL MINIMUM TAX

The two pillars in the Statement have different goals. Pillar One is a reform intended to strengthen source-based taxation. It is the most effective way to eliminate profit shifting and tax competition given the location of customers. Pillar Two would significantly reduce MNEs' incentives to change their place of residence or the location of their headquarters to exploit tax competition by source countries. However, it is important to note that although Pillar Two combines measures to strengthen both source taxation and residence taxation to implement the single tax principle, it also offers measures for effective residence-based taxation. This section discusses the promises and pitfalls of Pillar Two. First, we discuss the promise of global tax reform, specifically, raising additional revenue and reducing profit shifting. Second, we explore the various challenges facing Pillar Two, notably, concerns of developing countries, various carve-outs, and the logistical puzzle of implementation.

6.4.1 *Promise of the New International Tax Regime*

Many policymakers who participated in the global tax deal hail the Statement as a long-waited international tax reform and an important step in combating tax competition, tax base erosion, and profit shifting. Mathias Cormann, OECD Secretary-General, said that "the deal would make the international corporate tax system 'fairer and work better'."[168] We believe that Pillar Two would generate substantial revenue and lead to behavioral changes in both countries and taxpayers to engage in less tax competition. In short, Pillar Two is the modern embodiment of the single tax principle.

[167] The Trump administration expressed its opposition to pillar 2 and threatened retaliation against any country that adopts the UTPR, but it is unclear whether this will have an impact.

[168] Chris Giles et al., 136 *Nations Agree to Biggest Corporate Tax Deal in a Century*, FIN. TIMES (Oct. 8, 2021), http://www.ft.com/content/5dc4e2d5-d7bd-4000-bf94-088f17e21936.

6.4.1.1 Additional Revenue

Pillar Two, with its global minimum corporate income tax of 15 percent, is expected to generate approximately $220 billion in additional global tax revenues each year.[169] While the primary revenue effects of Pillar One will be the reallocation of profits (about $100 billion) to source countries annually,[170] Pillar Two is a true revenue generator. Hence, from a global perspective, the global tax reform will benefit the world via revenue generation.[171] The IMF, representing an additional fifty-one countries, also backs the plan, indicating broader global support outside the Inclusive Framework.[172] The additional revenue generated by Pillar Two may be used to recover national economies from the pandemic or to support sustainable tax policies relating to environmental, social, and corporate governance (ESG).[173]

6.4.1.2 Reducing Profit Shifting and Tax Competition: A Realization of the Single Tax Principle

Pillar Two mandates a 15 percent global minimum tax, compelling the global community to stop tax competition and the race to the bottom. As a result, Pillar Two is expected to reduce profit shifting by MNEs. If enough large economies agree to implement Pillar Two, there will be no incentive for companies to move their businesses to low-tax jurisdictions. US Treasury Secretary Janet L. Yellen, who negotiated the deal, praised Pillar Two as ending the race to the bottom on corporate taxation rates.[174]

169 OECD, *Two-Pillar Solution to Address the Tax Challenges Arising from the Digitilisation of the Economy* 5, OECD/G20 Base Erosion and Profit Shifting Project (Oct. 2021), http://www.oecd.org/tax/beps/brochure-two-pillar-solution-to-address-the-tax-challenges-arising-from-the-digitalisation-of-the-economy-october-2021.pdf.

170 OECD, *130 Countries and Jurisdictions Join Bold New Framework for International Tax Reform* (July 1, 2021), http://www.oecd.org/newsroom/130-countries-and-jurisdictions-join-bold-new-framework-for-international-tax-reform.htm.

171 William Horobin, *Global Tax Overhaul Endorsed by 130 Nations as Deal Gets Closer*, Bloomberg (July 1, 2021, 9:57 AM), http://www.bloomberg.com/news/articles/2021-07-01/global-tax-overhaul-endorsed-by-130-nations-as-deal-gets-closer.

172 Eric Martin, *IMF Sees Room to Simplify Global Tax Deal to Boost Participation*, Bloomberg (July 10, 2021), http://www.bloomberg.com/news/articles/2021-07-10/imf-sees-room-to-simplify-global-tax-deal-to-boost-participation.

173 Stephen Cooper, *House Sends Biden's $1.75T Budget Plan to Senate*, Law360 (Nov. 19, 2021), http://www.law360.com/tax-authority/federal/articles/1442179.

174 David J. Lynch, *Global Minimum Tax Effort Moves Forward as Ireland and Hungary Join Pact*, Wash. Post (Oct. 8, 2021), http://www.washingtonpost.com/us-policy/2021/10/08/minimum-corporate-tax-oecd-biden.

Therefore, Pillar Two resolves the traditional economics debate between advocates of capital export neutrality (CEN) and supporters of capital import/ownership neutrality (CIN/CON),[175] because this debate rests on the assumption that corporate tax rates cannot be harmonized and thus companies have different incentives for choice of location under each theory.[176] However, if corporate tax rates are harmonized, as expected in Pillar Two, then CEN, CIN, and CON can be achieved simultaneously.[177]

Importantly, Pillar Two eliminates the main critique that has bedeviled the US attempts to raise taxes on its MNEs since the 1960s. The argument that the unilateral adoption of higher rates of corporate tax on MNEs' foreign source income puts US MNEs at a competitive disadvantage vis-à-vis MNEs from other countries is often used.[178] This argument has never been persuasive because, both in the 1960s and today, US MNEs dominate their competition.[179] But it had political appeal, leading to the TCJA reducing the corporate tax rate to 21 percent.[180] However, such competitive rhetoric would disappear as a concern if all the G20 MNEs, which comprise over 90 percent of all MNEs, were subject to the same minimum tax rate. An important aspect of Pillar Two that is not addressed in the Statement but is essential for successful implementation is the prevention of MNEs from leaving the G20 and thereby escaping the IIR of residence country (although perhaps not the UTPR/STTR). In most EU countries this is unlikely because of their corporate exit taxes.[181] But the United States and the United Kingdom do not have such taxes, making corporate exodus a viable concern.[182]

[175] *See* Mihir A. Desai & James R. Hines Jr., *Evaluating International Tax Reform*, 56 Nat'l Tax J. 487 (2003); Michael J. Graetz, *David R. Tillinghast Lecture Taxing International Income: Inadequate Principles, Outdated Concepts, and Unsatisfactory Policies*, 54 Tax L. Rev. 261, 270–77 (2001); Daniel Shaviro, *The David R. Tillinghast Lecture – The Rising Tax-Electivity of U.S. Corporate Residence*, 64 Tax L. Rev. 377, 386–87 (2010).

[176] Desai & Hines, *supra* note 174; Graetz, *supra* note 174; Shaviro, *supra* note 174.

[177] Reuven S. Avi-Yonah, *Is It Time to Coordinate Corporate Tax Rates? A Note on Horst* (U. Mich. Pub. L. & Legal Theory Rsch. Ser., Paper No. 382, 2014), http://ssrn.com/abstract=2389959 or http://dx.doi.org/10.2139/ssrn.2389959.

[178] Daniel Bunn, *U.S. Cross-Border Tax Reform and the Cautionary Tale of GILTI*, Tax Found. (Feb. 17, 2021), http://taxfoundation.org/gilti-us-cross-border-tax-reform/#Key.

[179] Reuven S. Avi-Yonah & Nicola Sartori, *Symposium on International Taxation and Competitiveness: Introduction and Overview*, 65 Tax L. Rev 313, 319 (2012); *see also Biggest Companies in the World* 2022, FinanceCharts, http://www.financecharts.com/screener/biggest (last accessed Mar. 29, 2022) (indicating the top ten companies are from the United States).

[180] I.R.C. § 11.

[181] Sebastian Dueñas & Daniel Bunn, *Tax Avoidance Rules Increase the Compliance Burden in EU Member Countries*, Tax Found. (Mar. 28, 2019), http://taxfoundation.org/eu-tax-avoidance-rules-increase-tax-compliance-burden (indicating that seventeen of twenty-eight EU countries have exit taxes).

[182] Reuven S. Avi-Yonah, *For Haven's Sake: Reflections on Inversion Transactions*, 95 Tax Notes 1793 (June 17, 2002).

Furthermore, the United States has a different definition of corporate residency from the rest of the world: A business incorporated in the United States is a US tax resident regardless of its domiciliary or place of management,[183] whereas other countries, to a broad extent, use both the place of incorporation and place of management tests.[184] Such mismatches of corporate residence rules may aggravate the concern that, even if Pillar Two firmly established the single tax principle in the G20, another form of tax competition among non-G20 countries may emerge for hosting migrating companies.

6.4.2 *Potential Challenges*

So far, Pillar Two has received overall positive responses from the media and commentators. However, there have also been criticisms about the specifics of the agreement. Common criticisms are that Pillar Two does not go far enough to ensure MNEs are taxed fairly, that various carve-outs and exceptions make the agreement unbalanced, and that it is unclear what would happen to Pillar Two in the implementation stage. This subsection discusses these challenges and offers possible responses.

6.4.2.1 Priority to Residence-Based Taxation and Developing Countries' Concerns

It is true that Pillar Two is quite complex and possibly flawed since it accords primacy to the country of residence by giving priority to IIR for residence taxation over UTPR and STTR for source taxation. Thus, the source country's tax will only be applicable if the residence country chooses not to tax.

The precedence of the IIR over the UTPR/STTR in Pillar Two has also led to critiques of Pillar Two – namely that it is not reflective of the concerns of developing countries that largely consist of source countries. For example, the Tax Justice Network and Oxfam criticized the global minimum tax for unfairly providing advantages to the world's wealthier countries.[185] Specifically, they argue that the imposition of residence-based tax on MNEs under the IIR will make it impossible

[183] *See* David R. Tillinghast, *A Matter of Definition: Foreign and Domestic Taxpayers*, 2 Int'l Tax & Bus. L. 239, 252–53 (1984).

[184] Christos Theophilou, *Insight: Corporate Residence Post-BEPS and Global Mobility*, Bloomberg Tax (June 10, 2020, 3:00 AM), http://news.bloombergtax.com/daily-tax-report-international/insight-corporate-residence-post-beps-and-global-mobility.

[185] Hamish Boland-Rudder & Spencer Woodman, *136 Countries Agree to Global Minimum Tax for Corporations in "Historic" OECD Deal*, Int'l Consortium Investigative Journalism (Oct. 8, 2021), http://www.icij.org/investigations/paradise-papers/136-countries-agree-to-global-minimum-tax-for-corporations-in-historic-oecd-deal.

for developing countries to attract FDI by granting tax concessions, and that the UTPR and STTR are meaningless if all the income of MNEs is already subject to the minimum tax rate of 15 percent under the IIR.[186] Despite lofty goals of ending tax havens and tax competition, the critiques highlight sizable incentives for profit shifting that remain due to exemptions and loopholes that the global tax deal was supposed to curtail.[187]

This critique is only partially valid, however. The first criticism about the ability to attract FDI assumes that developing countries wish to grant tax concessions to MNEs based on a cost/benefit analysis. This is not true. Most empirical studies suggest that the main reason to allow tax concessions, tax holidays, and tax competition is the threat of the MNEs going elsewhere. If that is the case, developing countries would benefit from the IIR because it neutralizes the MNE's ability to conduct such an auction by subjecting it to the minimum tax wherever it goes. It is true that if the UTPR/STTR for source taxation were given primacy over the IIR for residence taxation then developing countries might gain more revenue. However, it is not clear that in the absence of the IIR, developing countries would be able to impose taxes under the UTPR/STTR because, without the IIR for residence taxation, the MNE could threaten to go elsewhere.[188] In other words, the IIR neutralizes the behavioral incentives of multinational taxpayers to engage in location shopping and the UTTR/STTR neutralizes the incentive of source countries to engage in tax competition.

In addition, foreign tax credits will be available under the IIR just like they are (with limitations) under GILTI. This means that, in practice, developing countries can impose source taxation on MNEs' FDI, and those MNEs will not suffer because these taxes will be credited against the residence taxation imposed by the IIR.

Finally, the substance carve-outs will enable developing countries to engage in some level of tax competition for real investment. Large developing countries are also expected to gain significant additional revenue from Pillar One. For all these reasons, we believe that the critique that Pillar Two disadvantages developing countries is exaggerated.[189]

Nonetheless, there might be an alternative to Pillar Two that implements the single tax principle more effectively with fewer concerns to developing countries. That is, Pillar Two may be tweaked to ensure that countries can tax MNEs on both

[186] *Id.*

[187] *Id.*

[188] Reuven S. Avi-Yonah, *Bridging the North–South Divide: International Redistribution and Tax Competition*, 26 Mich. J. Int'l L. 371 (2004).

[189] *See* Cui, *supra* note 16.

inbound and outbound investments. This could be done by applying a substance-based test using a fractional apportionment method in transfer pricing. This method would allocate MNEs' profits that have not been effectively taxed among all countries in which an MNE has a taxable presence. Once profits of MNEs are allocated among relevant countries based on the substance-based test, each country would impose taxes on such profits according to their own respective tax rates. This alternative would not require the application of the complex IIR and UTPR, and instead rely on fractional apportionment based on assets, personnel, and sales revenue (by locations of customers or users). While the GLoBE rules impose a top-up tax only in the country of residence, this alternative would allow all affected countries, either as residence or as source, to impose tax based on their respective shares of the undertaxed profits.

6.4.2.2 Various Carve-Outs

During the negotiation of Pillar Two in mid-2021, there were nine countries that opposed it.[190] These countries included several in Europe, namely, Hungary, Ireland, and Estonia. Although they account for just 4 percent of the EU's economic output, they were able to deal a significant blow to the prospects of the OECD's tax plan.[191] Tax directives in the EU require the unanimous consent of all twenty-seven member states, effectively giving a single EU member veto power over the agreement.[192]

Statements made by officials in each country emphasized that Ireland, Hungary, and Estonia did not present a united front or adhere to a common core principle.[193] Ireland supported Pillar One but demanded that the 15 percent global minimum tax

[190] Cliff Taylor & Ellen O'Riordan, *Ireland One of 9 Countries to Hold Out on Signing OECD Global Tax Deal*, Irish Times (July 1, 2021, 5:08 PM), http://www.irishtimes.com/business/economy/ireland-one-of-9-countries-to-hold-out-on-signing-oecd-global-tax-deal-1.4609129; *see also* Jorge Liboreiro, *Ireland, Hungary and Estonia Opt out of OECD Tax Deal and Cast Shadow over EU's Unified Position*, Euronews (Aug. 26, 2021), http://www.euronews.com/2021/07/02/ireland-hungary-and-estonia-opt-out-of-oecd-tax-deal-and-cast-shadow-over-eu-s-unified-pos.

[191] Zoltan Simon & Peter Flanagan, *European Trio Cast Dissatisfied Shadow over Global Tax Accord*, Bloomberg (July 2, 2021), http://www.bloomberg.com/news/articles/2021-07-02/europe-s-new-awkward-squad-casts-shadow-over-global-tax-deal.

[192] Christopher Condon, *G-20 Finance Chiefs Back Tax Deal and Vow to Clear Hurdles*, Bloomberg (July 10, 2021), http://www.bloomberg.com/news/articles/2021-07-10/yellen-optimistic-congress-will-back-part-of-global-tax-deal. *Cf.* Faulhaber, *supra* note 14.

[193] Stephanie Soong Johnston & Sarah Paez, *Ireland, Estonia to Join OECD Global Tax Reform Deal*, Tax Notes (Oct. 11, 2021), http://www.taxnotes.com/tax-notes-international/base-erosion-and-profit-shifting-beps/ireland-estonia-join-oecd-global-tax-reform-deal/2021/10/11/7bbn3?highlight=opposition%20to%20OECD%20g.

rate be lower because its corporate tax rate is 12.5 percent.[194] Hungary had issues with the plan's industry carve-outs.[195] Finally, Estonia simply wanted to preserve its unique tax system.[196]

Eventually, the EU holdout did not occur. A total of 137 countries, including Ireland, Hungary, and Estonia, agreed to the global tax deal, including Pillar Two. For example, Ireland agreed to end its 12.5 percent corporate tax rate and join the deal at the last minute, "with assurances sought and received from the EU that it would not seek to increase the tax rate further down the line."[197] "Hungary secured a longer transition period for the 'substance-based carve out,' allowing it to offer a lower rate of tax for tangible investments in its jurisdiction – such as automotive plants – for ten years."[198] China also succeeded in having a clause inserted that would limit the effect of the global minimum tax on companies who are starting to expand internationally – because of concerns that its growing domestic companies would be clipped by the measures.[199]

Commentators argue that these carve-outs and exemptions failed the original ambition of the global tax deal. Instead of leveling the playing field, the watered-down measures mean that only a "sliver of the profits" of MNEs will become taxable, while incentives to shift profits remain sizable.[200] Alex Cobham, CEO of the Tax Justice Network, commented in a statement that "[i]t's no wonder that Ireland and other havens have embraced the deal, especially after obtaining various concessions."[201] Civil society organization Oxfam also criticized that the global deal panders to tax havens and multinational corporations, with exemptions and loopholes that meant the new measures have "practically no teeth" and will offer no revenue help to the world's poorest countries.[202] We also disfavor these carve-outs.

194 Liz Alderman, *Ireland's Days as a Tax Haven May Be Ending, but Not without a Fight*, N.Y. Times (July 12, 2021), http://www.nytimes.com/2021/07/08/business/ireland-minimum-corporate-tax.html.

195 Elodie Lamer, *Growing Unease in EU over Global Tax Deal's Next Steps*, Tax Notes (July 12, 2021), http://www.taxnotes.com/tax-notes-today-international/corporate-taxation/growing-unease-eu-over-global-tax-deals-next-steps/2021/07/12/76rz4?highlight=OECD.

196 Todd Buell, *Estonian Official Airs Country's Objections to Global Minimum Tax*, Law360 (July 16, 2021), http://www.law360.com/tax-authority/international/articles/1403781/estonian-official-airs-country-s-objections-to-global-minimum-tax. *See also* Kyle Pomerleau, *The Key Component of the Estonia's Competitive Tax System*, Tax Found. (Oct. 6, 2015), http://taxfoundation.org/key-component-estonia-s-competitive-tax-system.

197 Lisa O'Carroll, *Ireland Ends 12.5% Tax Rate in OECD Global Pact*, The Guardian (Oct. 7, 2021), http://www.theguardian.com/world/2021/oct/07/ireland-poised-to-drop-125-tax-rate-in-oecd-global-pact.

198 Giles et al., *supra* note 167.

199 *Id.*

200 Boland-Rudder & Woodman, *supra* note 184.

201 Alex Cobham, *OECD Tax Deal Fails to Deliver*, Tax Just. Network (Oct. 8, 2021), http://taxjustice.net/press/oecd-tax-deal-fails-to-deliver.

202 Press Release, OXFAM Int'l, *OECD Tax Deal Is a Mockery of Fairness: Oxfam* (Oct. 8, 2021), http://www.oxfam.org/en/press-releases/oecd-tax-deal-mockery-fairness-oxfam.

Some level of compromise is inevitable to achieve a global tax deal and bring more than 140 jurisdictions to the negotiation table. However, the purpose of seeking a global deal for Pillar Two is to accomplish tax harmony to end tax competition. These carve-outs clearly violate the single tax principle by offering various methods for certain countries to continue tax competition, especially among source countries. What is worse, the carve-outs disturb tax harmony, weakening the effectiveness of Pillar Two measures among countries that are fully committed to the single tax principle.

6.4.2.3 Logistical Puzzle

There is an additional concern about whether the global tax deal consisting of Pillars One and Two could be implemented, especially in the United States. But this did not happen and the Trump administration opposes the global tax deal.[203] The goal was for countries to sign a multilateral convention during 2024, although most practitioners viewed this timeline as highly unlikely. Political realities in the United States illustrate the complexities of implementing the global tax agreement.[204] The Biden administration had a thin majority in the Senate and none in the House of Representatives. And after 2025, the Republicans control both houses, so it is very doubtful that the G20/OECD international tax plan will be passed by the US Congress in a single bill, increasing the difficulty of ratification in the US Senate.[205] Considering that the United States is important to have on board to ensure the effective implementation of both pillars, the successful implementation of the global tax deal is an open question.

Pillar One will alter US treaties with other countries and, therefore, will need to be implemented through a multilateral treaty approved by two-thirds of the US Senate.[206] However, even if there is a Democratic majority in the Senate, getting Republican senators to support a treaty measure that many view as penalizing US companies may be a nonstarter in the current economic and political climate.[207] The senior Republicans on the tax-writing Senate Finance and House Ways and Means committees already expressed opposition to Pillar One.[208] Furthermore, in a

[203] Aime Williams, *G7 Tax Deal Faces Opposition in US Congress*, FIN. TIMES (June 9, 2021), http://www.ft.com/content/6c98b271-bd13-4517-81bb-6ef7f1798085

[204] James-Paul Galligan et al., *OECD Tax Deal: When Does It Become Law?*, JDSUPRA (Oct. 18, 2021), http://www.jdsupra.com/legalnews/oecd-tax-deal-when-does-it-become-law-3448977.

[205] Stephanie Soong Johnston, *The End Is Nigh: An Update on the OECD Tax Reform Plan*, FORBES (Oct. 19, 2021), http://www.forbes.com/sites/taxnotes/2021/10/19/the-end-is-nigh-an-update-on-the-oecd-tax-reform-plan/?sh = 353cdb891634.

[206] Lilian Faulhaber, *Will the OECD Plan Fix International Taxation?*, LAW360 (July 7, 2021), http://www.law360.com/articles/1400693.

[207] Mindy Herzfeld, *Pushing Pillar 1 Past Congress*, TAX NOTES (July 19, 2021), http://www.taxnotes.com/tax-notes-today-federal/fundamental-tax-system-structure/pushing-pillar-1-past-congress/2021/07/19/76vyv?highlight = base%20erosion.

[208] Lynch, *supra* note 173.

joint statement, Senator Mike Crapo (R-Idaho) and Congressman Kevin Brady (R-Texas) criticized the Biden administration for pursuing the global tax deal agreement before Congress has acted on the administration's proposed changes to US tax law, such as GILTI, calling into question how quickly lawmakers may act on needed change.[209] They also mentioned in a joint statement that "as other countries delay implementation and secure side agreements and carve-outs to protect their own companies, U.S. businesses will be hit by tax increases ultimately borne by American workers, savers and consumers."[210] Hence, Senate approval of Pillar One in any form will almost certainly require the inclusion of a ban on all current and future DSTs, including the proposed EU digital levy.[211] Pillar Two, on the other hand, is viewed by the OECD/Inclusive Framework as compatible with existing tax treaties and can likely be implemented with changes to domestic tax legislation.[212] Unlike Pillar One, Pillar Two can be implemented without any changes in existing tax treaties as far as the IIR is concerned, as evidenced by the United States unilaterally adopting GILTI.[213] UTPR and STTR may require changes in tax treaties, but they are of secondary importance because they work conditionally. Since treaties are hard to change in the United States because of Senate ratification, this is an important advantage of Pillar Two over Pillar One. We also anticipate that a lot of countries will be implementing Pillar Two by domestic legislation, given the strong interest in its development and the fact that it helps countries protect their tax base by embodying a modern single tax principle.

Hence, the United States enacting domestic legislation to implement Pillar Two is the key to solving the logistical puzzle for the overall success of the global tax reform plan as well as the modern single tax principle. To make it possible, the two pillars could be severed. The objective of both the OECD and the United States seems to be to adopt both Pillars One and Two as a package deal.[214] Both address the tax challenges in the digitalized economy and combat the base erosion and profit

[209] Letter from Senator Mike Crapo, Ranking Member, Comm. on Fin. & Congressman Kevin Brady, Ranking Member, Comm. on Ways and Means, to Senator Ron Wyden, Chairman, Comm. on Fin. and Congressman Richard Neal, Chairman, Comm. on Ways and Means (Sept. 2, 2021).

[210] *Brady, Crapo: Biden Global Tax Deal Puts Politics over Progress, Surrenders Fate of U.S. Economy to Foreign Competitors*, U.S. SENATE COMM. ON FIN. (Oct. 8, 2021), http://www.finance.senate.gov/ranking-members-news/brady-crapo-biden-global-tax-deal-puts-politics-over-progress-surrenders-fate-of-us-economy-to-foreign-competitors.

[211] Stephanie Soong Johnston, *Crapo and Brady Urge Yellen to Push for Immediate End to DSTs*, TAX NOTES (July 12, 2021), http://www.taxnotes.com/tax-notes-federal/digital-economy/crapo-and-brady-urge-yellen-push-immediate-end-dsts/2021/07/12/76rtc?highlight=OECD.

[212] *Taxing Tech, supra* note 14.

[213] I.R.C. § 951A; *see also* Bunn, *supra* note 177 (indicating that the United States adopted GILTI as an anti-base erosion rule).

[214] U.S. Dep't of the Treasury, *Presentation by the United States to the Steering Group of the Inclusive Framework Meeting* (2021), http://www.politico.com/f/?id=00000178-b389-d098-a97a-f79960510001 (slide seven).

shifting by MNEs. However, Pillars One and Two are conceptually separate from each other – Pillar One modernizes source-based taxation, whereas Pillar Two embodies the single tax principle by reinforcing residence-based taxation. There is no logical reason to treat the two pillars as "linked by more than just politics," as the United States argues.[215]

Furthermore, Pillar Two can be implemented by the G20 even if Pillar One collapses because some countries refuse to abolish DSTs. In other words, Pillar Two does not need universal implementation by all IF member states because it is a measure that a country can implement to protect its own tax base, irrespective of what other countries do. Hence, it is less critical, although not desirable, if a low-tax jurisdiction does not implement Pillar Two, because the domestic legislation resulting from Pillar Two will allow the residence country to essentially tax back the income that has not been taxed in the low-tax jurisdiction. Moreover, over 90 percent of large MNEs are headquartered in the G20,[216] so only a relatively small number of countries need to agree to implement an effective global minimum tax. However, Pillar Two still requires international cooperation among the G20 countries to adopt the harmonized domestic legislation that is essential to stopping tax competition, base erosion, and profit shifting. Thus, the United States should cooperate with the G20 countries to enact Pillar Two even if Pillar One fails. Risking Pillar Two to salvage Pillar One is unwise and regrettable because Pillar Two would be the first global tax harmony in substantive tax law guided by the single tax principle.

6.5 CONCLUSION

The roots of the new international tax regime as embodied in the Statement can be traced to the benefits principle and the single tax principle, both of which stem from the origins of the international tax regime a century ago. The benefits principle was the compromise between the claims of residence and source jurisdictions reached by the four economists in 1923, while the single tax principle can be traced to Thomas Adams in 1918 and the League of Nations experts in 1927.

Nevertheless, the new international tax regime envisaged in the two pillars in the Statement is revolutionary. Pillar One (if implemented) will partially remove the two main obstacles to taxing modern MNEs operating in the digital economy, namely, the physical presence requirement and the arm's-length standard. Pillar Two will fully implement the single tax principle on a global level for the first time through strengthening both source and residence taxation with various secondary corrective measures. It will raise significant revenue for the participating countries, stop tax competition, and reduce base erosion and profit shifting. However, the

215 *Id.*

216 Saez & Zucman, *supra* note 48.

proposed global minimum tax rate of 15 percent would be lower than the average G20 corporate tax rate, and substance carve-outs would maintain some double non-taxation. Additionally, it may disproportionately harm developing countries more than developed countries.

Overall, Pillar Two promises to finally break the back of tax competition by implementing the single tax principle harmoniously. This should enable both developed and developing countries to maintain free trade and globalization while also retaining and strengthening the social safety net from the added revenues extracted from the world's largest corporations. We should all hope that in the face of the pressures of de-globalization and rising nationalism, the new international tax regime seeking tax harmony will survive and enable all countries to overcome tax competition and maintain a robust social safety net for their citizens.

7

The Future of the New Regime

In the previous chapters of this book, we discussed the past, which is immutable (even though its interpretation varies). In this chapter we will speculate about the future, ever mindful of the admonition of Rabbi Yohanan Ben Zakkai, the leader of the Jewish community in Palestine, after the destruction of the temple in 70 CE, who said that "from the day the temple was destroyed, prophecy was taken from prophets and given to fools and babies."[1]

On November 16, 2022, the leaders of the G20 declared:

> We are committed to the swift implementation of the OECD/G20 two-pillar international tax package. We welcome the progress on Pillar One... We call on the OECD/G20 Inclusive Framework on Base Erosion and Profit Shifting (BEPS) to finalize Pillar One, including remaining issues and by signing the Multilateral Convention *in the first half of* 2023. (Emphasis added.)

This declaration is remarkable in its optimism, because at this point it seems highly unlikely that Pillar One can come into effect anytime in 2023 (Pillar Two, on the other hand, is progressing because it does not depend on a multilateral tax convention [MTC]), despite the Inclusive Framework's Progress Report from September 2023.[2] But the rush is understandable because after January 1, 2025, many new countries may enact and/or implement DSTs.

In what follows, we will discuss the likely prospects of the two pillars. Fundamentally, Pillar One seems destined to fail, while Pillar Two is being implemented by a critical mass of countries.

[1] Babylonian Talmud Baba Batra 12:2.

[2] https://www.oecd.org/tax/beps/oecd-g20-inclusive-framework-on-beps-progress-report-september-2022-september-2023.pdf.

7.1 PILLAR ONE

Pillar One[3] is unlikely to succeed for three reasons. First, it requires an MTC to be implemented because Amount A requires overriding Articles 5 (Permanent Establishment, PE), 7 (Business Profits) and 9 (Associated Enterprises) of every tax treaty to abolish the PE and Arm's Length Principle (ALP) limits enshrined therein. Negotiating an MTC is hard, especially when over 100 countries are involved and there are fundamental disagreements among them. While many countries may sign a Pillar One MTC in 2024, ratification is much harder.

Second, because Pillar One (despite its October 2021 expansion) is still aimed primarily at taxing the US digital giants (Big Tech), it is hard to envisage it being implemented without the United States. But despite the support of the Biden administration, the Republicans are adamantly opposed, and so is the Trump administration. Hence, an MTC implementing Pillar One cannot be ratified by the Senate (which requires sixty-seven votes) or enacted as a Congressional Executive Agreement (which requires passage in the Republican-controlled House).

Third, Pillar One is premised on all the countries that have adopted DSTs ultimately repealing them. But DSTs are popular politically and, in some cases (e.g., the UK), brought in significant revenue. The only reason countries agreed to suspend DSTs was US pressure, and now that the United States cannot ratify an MTC, there is no reason for those countries not to implement their DSTs as scheduled in January 2024.

What will happen then? This section first discusses what options countries have to tax Big Tech without Pillar One, and then addresses the US response. But since the future is unknowable, the section also discusses the alternative of what may happen if Pillar One does come into force without the United States (like many other multilateral treaties including recently the Multilateral Convention to Implement Tax Treaty Related Measures to Prevent BEPS [BEPS MLI] and the MAATM/CRS).

7.1.1 *If Pillar One Fails*

7.1.1.1 Taxing Big Tech without Pillar One

The cause of Pillar One was that following the financial crisis of 2008–10 it became politically untenable in the EU and elsewhere not to impose tax on Big Tech, who were deriving billions of profits from market jurisdictions but not paying any tax because of the PE limit in the treaties. The UK was a pioneer in enacting the Diverted Profits Tax (DPT) in 2015, followed in 2016 by Australia with the

[3] This section is built upon a previous piece written by the first author. Reuven S. Avi-Yonah, *After Pillar One*, 2023(3) Brit. Tax Rev. 1 (2023).

Multinational Anti-Tax Avoidance Law (MAAL) and India with the Equalization Levy (which is like a DST). France was the first country to enact an explicit DST in 2019, followed by over thirty other countries. However, Pillar One, as agreed upon in October 2021 and extended subsequently, requires suspension of the DSTs until June 2024. Canada has adopted a new DST after that date, and other countries are expected to follow.

Countries have three options to tax Big Tech if Pillar One collapses: DSTs, withholding taxes, and income taxes.

DSTS DSTs are gross-based taxes on the provision of digital services into a market jurisdiction and the use of data from a market jurisdiction to sell advertising. They are aimed at taxing Big Tech on profits derived from consumers or users in the market jurisdiction without being subject to corporate income taxes.

If Pillar One collapses or is not ratified early enough, the existing DSTs will automatically come into force in 2024, and it is likely that many more countries will enact DSTs. DSTs generally have low rates (below 5 percent), are politically popular, and have significant revenue generating potential (the UK DST brought in more revenue than expected before it was suspended).[4]

WITHHOLDING TAXES IN THE UN MODEL The UN has adopted Article 12B (digital services) in its model tax convention, which imposes a withholding tax (at a rate to be negotiated bilaterally) on the provision of digital services (including user data). If Pillar One collapses, various countries may negotiate treaties that include Article 12B.

INCOME TAXES There are several ways in which countries can apply net-based income taxes to Big Tech despite the PE and ALP limits of the treaties.

DPTs First, countries can adopt a DPT like the UK. The DPT was intended primarily to address structures like Google's Double Irish Dutch Sandwich, which is contained in the guidance published by HMRC as example 3.[5]

The DPT has been criticized as in substance contradicting the UK tax treaties, which require an actual PE. HMRC has defended it as a new tax that is not subject to the treaties, but this issue is unlikely to arise because UK treaties are not "self-executing" and have not been applied to the DPT by legislation. This means that a UK taxpayer cannot challenge the DPT as inconsistent with a UK tax treaty.

[4] *See* National Audit Office, Report, *Investigation into the Digital Services Tax, HR Revenue & Customs* (Nov. 23, 2022), https://www.nao.org.uk/wp-content/uploads/2022/11/Investigation-into-the-digital-services-tax.pdf.

[5] HMRC, Diverted Profits Tax: Interim Guidance (Mar. 2015), 37.

Anti-Abuse Rules Countries may also adopt anti-abuse rules in their corporate income tax, like the Australian MAAL. The MAAL was designed to "prevent foreign corporations from using complex, contrived and artificial schemes that enable them to have substantial sales activities in Australia but pay little or no tax anywhere."[6] Unlike the DPT, this is not a new tax, but an amendment to Australia's General Anti-Avoidance Rule (GAAR) (section 177DA, part IVA of the Income Tax Assessment Act 1936 [ITAA]). The Australian MAAL became effective on January 1, 2016, and applies to enterprises with annual income over AUD 1 billion.

New Australian MAAL applies if a nonresident of Australia sells goods or services to an unrelated Australian resident, income from such sales is not attributable to a PE, and activities are undertaken by an Australian associate of the provider in connection with the sale. Under these circumstances, if it is reasonable to conclude that the scheme is designed to avoid income attributable to a PE and tax reduction was a principal purpose, the Australian Tax Office (ATO) is free to disregard the arrangement. Like the DPT, this rule was likewise designed to address structures like the "Double Irish Dutch Sandwich."[7]

The MAAL has been defended as consistent with Australia's tax treaties because it is an anti-avoidance rule, and the PE limit should not apply when the business profits are not taxed by the country of residence.[8] In addition, in Australia, treaty overrides are possible, so a treaty-based challenge to the MAAL is unlikely.

Fractional Apportionment Before Pillar One was agreed to, India proposed to tax MNEs operating in India using a fractional apportionment method based on their profits derived from sales into India without regard to the PE and ALP limitations.[9] It differs from other formulary apportionment methods since it limits itself to India-related information; it does not require consolidating profits from all tax jurisdictions. The proposed method relies primarily on information relating to Indian operations and adopts a three-factor formula (based on the Common Consolidated Corporate Tax Base [CCCTB]), according equal weight to sales, employees (manpower and wages), and tangible assets. In addition, the proposal suggests a formula for calculating the profits derived from India, which relies on the nonresident's revenue derived from India and its global operational profit margin. The proposal also offers a solution to tax the digital economy; it allows user participation to count as the fourth factor in the fractional apportionment method;

6 AU, Exposure Draft Explanatory Material, para. 1.10.

7 *Id.*, para. 1-40 and examples 1.14, 1.15.

8 Michael Butler & Marianna Danby, *Draft Legislation Released for Anti-Google Tax*, 22 INT'L TRANSFER PRICING J. 349 (Nov. 2015);Douglas Fone, *The Diverted Profits Tax*, 16 TRANSFER PRICING INT'L J. 24 (2015); David Richardson, *Corporate Tax Avoidance: Submission*, The Australia Institute, Submission 62 (Feb. 2015).

9 *See* Reuven S. Avi-Yonah & Ajitesh Kir, *India's New Profit Attribution Proposal and the Arm's-Length Standard*, 93 TAX NOTES INT'L 1183 (June 17, 2019).

the relative weight of the user participation may range from 10 to 20 percent depending on the user intensity of the business enterprise concerned. The proposal does not rely on either the PE limit or the ALS.[10]

This proposal could be adopted by some countries unilaterally if Pillar One collapses. It is clearly inconsistent with the tax treaties but can be adopted by countries that can override treaties, which includes the UK and countries that derive their laws from the UK legal system (Australia, Canada, India, New Zealand, etc.) as well as some European countries (Austria, Germany). Even in the case of EU countries that cannot override treaties (e.g., Italy), an EU directive can override treaties (but must be adopted unanimously).

7.1.1.2 The US Response

DSTS In the case of DSTs, the US response is well known: to impose trade sanctions on the implementing countries. In addition, Itai Grinberg (formerly the Deputy Assistant Secretary of Tax Policy for multilateral tax negotiations, i.e., the main US BEPS negotiator in the Biden administration) has in the past advocated using section 891 of the Internal Revenue Code to impose retaliatory taxes on corporations from countries imposing DSTs because they are discriminatory. The Trump administration has threatened to use both tariffs and section 891 to retaliate against DSTs and the UTPR, which it views as extraterritorial and discriminatory.[11]

In our opinion, DSTs are not discriminatory because their purpose is to tax large MNEs who are able to derive profits from a market jurisdiction without having a PE, and the fact that all of these MNEs (Big Tech) are US-based is irrelevant since the DST would also apply, for example, to Alibaba or Tencent if they went global. But the United States disagrees and therefore may retaliate even to DSTs like the Canadian one that also applies to Canadian companies (because the revenue threshold includes all income, not just income from digital services).[12]

But is the US response important? We do not think so, because applying section 891 seems improbable – it has never been applied – and the trade sanctions are minimal compared to other trade disputes (e.g., on subsidies to Boeing and Airbus and potentially on the US subsidies to EVs manufactured domestically and on FDII). Even though DSTs were the stated reason for Pillar One, DSTs are far less important than other reactions to Big Tech, and even the affected corporations may not care too much because the rates are low and the incidence may be shifted to consumers or advertisers (after all, Big Tech are quasi-monopolists). DSTs are really a VAT add-on, and the fuss about them is a classic example of much ado about very little.

10 *See also* UN Model Article 12B(3), which includes a similar proposal.

11 *See* Mindy Herzfeld, *News Analysis: What Is a Reciprocal Tax?*, 107 Tax Notes 462 (Mar. 6, 2017).

12 Wei Cui, *The Canadian Digital Services Tax, in* International Tax at the Crossroads (C. Elliffee ed., 2024).

WITHHOLDING TAXES IN THE UN MODEL The United States will presumably never agree to incorporate Article 12B of the UN Model in any of its future tax treaties. That does not matter to other countries that may include the article, but it means that Article 12B is unlikely to apply to Big Tech, who are presumably able to avoid it by operating from jurisdictions that have not agreed to it (including the United States). Article 12B is a good alternative to Pillar One, but if Pillar One collapses, it will not achieve the same purpose – that is, taxing Big Tech.

INCOME TAXES In 2021, the United States adopted new final foreign tax credit (FTC) regulations. Treas. Reg. § 1.901-2(b)(5) imposes a new attribution requirement to obtain the FTC as follows (emphases added):[13]

> (5) ***Attribution requirement.*** A foreign tax satisfies the attribution requirement if the amount of gross receipts and costs that are included in the base of the foreign tax are determined based on rules described in paragraph (b)(5)(i) of this section (with respect to a separate levy imposed on nonresidents of the foreign country)...
>
> (i) ***Tax on nonresidents.*** The gross receipts and costs attributable to each of the items of income of nonresidents of a foreign country that is included in the base of the foreign tax must satisfy the requirements of paragraph (b)(5)(i)(A), (B), or (C) of this section.
>
> (A) ***Income attribution based on activities.*** The gross receipts and costs that are included in the base of the foreign tax are limited to gross receipts and costs that are attributable, under reasonable principles, to the nonresident's activities within the foreign country imposing the foreign tax (including the nonresident's functions, assets, and risks located in the foreign country). For purposes of the preceding sentence, attribution of gross receipts under reasonable principles includes rules similar to those for determining effectively connected income under section 864(c) *but does not include rules that take into account as a significant factor the mere location of customers, users, or any other similar destination-based criterion, or the mere location of persons from whom the nonresident makes purchases in the foreign country.* In addition, for purposes of the first sentence of this paragraph (b)(5)(i)(A), *reasonable principles do not include rules that deem the existence of a trade or business or permanent establishment based on the activities of another person* (other than an agent or other person acting on behalf of the nonresident or a pass-through entity of which the nonresident is an owner), *or that attribute gross receipts or costs to a nonresident based upon the activities of another person* (other than an agent or other person acting on behalf of the nonresident or a pass-through entity of which the nonresident is an owner) ...

DSTs are already not creditable because they are not income taxes. The attribution requirement will further deny FTCs to withholding taxes under Article 12B of the

[13] This regulation was suspended by the Biden administration and its future is unclear.

UN Model (although they are unlikely to be imposed on Big Tech) and will also deny FTC to taxes like the DPT, the MAAL, and taxes imposed under fractional apportionment, because they are all "extraterritorial" under the above regulation and ignore the PE and ALP limits.

This is the most significant US response because it could create a lot of double taxation if many other countries adopt income tax solutions. The question is whether it is tenable. In this case of US FTC regulations, Big Tech will complain about the denial of FTC. And because this is just a regulation with no basis in the Code or in Supreme Court precedent, one can imagine a future administration reversing course or Congress overriding it. A court may also declare that it is void because, for example, Treasury ignored adverse comments during the now essential notice and comment period, like the Tax Court reviewed opinion in *Altera*.

7.1.1.3 Conclusion

The OECD maintains that if Pillar One is not adopted the ITR would collapse. But to us that seems unlikely. Among the potential US responses, the response to DSTs is unimportant and irrelevant to the ITR; any withholding taxes under Article 12B of the UN Model will not result in double taxation under the FTC regulation because they are unlikely to apply to Big Tech; and the denial of FTC to DPTs, MAALs, and fractional apportionment is not very likely to survive.

In addition, Pillar Two is likely to be implemented, and it will assure that all large MNEs will pay a tax at 15 percent of book profits with some exceptions for substantive investment and refundable credits that are unlikely to benefit Big Tech internationally. This tax will apply to Big Tech, who are already subject to the new US corporate alternative minimum tax. It is still somewhat unclear how the revenue from Pillar Two will be divided because of the convoluted ordering rules and country and taxpayer responses, but source jurisdictions where Big Tech are operating could get some of it via the UTPR and/or QDMTT. That would not apply to pure market jurisdictions since the PE and ALS limits remain under Pillar Two. But in many cases, market jurisdictions would still get some revenue from Pillar Two (because they will have a subsidiary or a PE in the taxing jurisdiction), and the DSTs will alleviate the political pressure to tax Big Tech more heavily under traditional income tax measures.

Finally, it may not be disastrous if the OECD domination of the ITR would end. The OECD is very unrepresentative, and the Inclusive Framework is a fig leaf for OECD/G20 domination of the BEPS process. If OECD domination ends, the obvious alternative is the UN. The EU and other rich countries (except the United States) may then be persuaded to shift adequate resources to the UN so that it can resume the role of the League of Nations in developing the ITR.[14]

[14] *See* Philip Baker, *The Reform of the Institutional Structure of International Taxation, in* International Tax at the Crossroads (C. Elliffe ed., 2024).

7.1.2 If Pillar One Succeeds without the United States

While it seems highly unlikely that a Pillar One MTC can be concluded, it is not impossible to imagine that the OECD will eventually succeed in negotiating a Pillar One MTC and getting enough countries to ratify it that it will come into force. As was the case for Pillar Two, the key question will be whether the EU (or at least its G20 members) will ratify Pillar One, since that will encourage other large market economies like China to go ahead.

What will happen then? A recent economic study by Mona Barake and Elvin Le Pouhaër has attempted to quantify who are the winners and losers from the adoption of Pillar One based on publicly available financial statements from in scope MNEs.[15] First, Mona Barake and Elvin Le Pouhaër estimated the revenues from Amount A based on the sample of Covered Groups consisting of sixty-nine MNEs. The Covered Groups are headquartered in thirteen different countries, primarily with developed economies. Based on the UNCTAD classification, seven of these Covered Groups are considered Automated Digital Services (ADS) and include companies such as Alphabet Inc, Meta Platforms Inc, Microsoft Corporation, Oracle Corp, SAP SE, and Tencent Holdings Limited. Hence, it is not surprising that Amount A only applies to some of the largest and most profitable MNEs in the world, which are almost all found in developed economies, such as the United States, China, and the EU.

Barake and Le Pouhaër find that the estimated profits from corporations fulfilling the requirements of Amount A were €94.4 billion. Michael Devereux and Martin Simmler had previously researched this issue and they estimated profits of $87 billion.[16] While slightly off, both studies independently came to similar potential estimates for Amount A. Moreover, in the OECD's 2023 Economic Impact Assessment, the total Amount A profits for 2020 are estimated at $113.5 billion (around €100 billion at 2020 average exchange rate).[17] While all three studies come to slightly different estimates, they can give us a good, rough estimate of the potential Amount A profits and allow us to analyze the potential tax consequences of proposed reforms.

Barake and Le Pouhaër further offer revenue estimates. Prior to the elimination of double taxation, taxes on reallocated profits at market jurisdictions' statutory corporate income tax rates will likely bring in €24 billion in tax revenue. Once double taxation has been eliminated and gross losses are estimated using market jurisdictions' effective tax rates, the taxes should still bring in an estimated €15 billion in tax revenue. This amount is on the higher end of the OECD 2023 Economic Impact

[15] Mona Barake & Elvin Le Pouhaër, *Tax Revenue from Pillar One Amount A: Country-by-Country Estimates* (EU Tax Observatory, HALSHS Working Paper 04039288, 2023).

[16] Michael Devereux & Martin Simmler, *Who Will Pay Amount A?*, EconPol Pol'y Brief 36 (July 2021).

[17] OECD, Economic Impact Assessment of the Two-Pillar Solution (2023).

Assessment for the year 2020, which estimated a range between \$6 billion and \$23 billion (€5.3 and €20.2 billion). The United States, China, and Germany are the top three countries that would collect the most revenues, around 74 percent of total net gains, while the EU as a whole would see around €2.6 billion in revenue.

There will also be prospective losses after the elimination of double taxation. Countries classified as tax havens would bear the brunt of Amount A, giving away rights to tax an estimated €62 billion, around 66 percent of total Obligations to Eliminate Double Taxation (OEDT). Tax havens would also become net losers of around €1.2 billion in tax revenue. The €2.4 billion of gross revenue loss for tax havens are much lower than their €62 billion allocated to OEDT. This is because the effective tax rates in tax havens are usually low. The net losses faced by tax havens would constitute double their gross gains. Applying the OEDT to the EU and the OECD would see their gains shrink by 20 and 18 percent. This is because the burden of the OEDT falls primarily on jurisdictions where Covered Groups have their highest returns on depreciation and payroll.

Developed countries would collect more than 77 percent of the net revenues, with the G7 countries alone collecting 71 percent of the total net revenues of Amount A. The developing countries would collect almost all of the remaining 23 percent, with China collecting the majority. The remaining developing countries (Argentina, Brazil, Korea, Malaysia, Mexico, Russia, and Turkey) would all take over €100 million. Unfortunately, the least developed countries would bring in almost no revenue from Amount A, representing 0.15 percent of total tax revenue.

It is also interesting to compare the estimated revenue losses and gains of Pillar One and those of DSTs. Barake and Le Pouhaër expect that Amount A would bring almost the same level of revenues as a digital tax for France, the UK, Poland, and Italy. In contrast, Spain, Hungary, and India would be better off with digital tax than with Amount A because they have negative net gains. In addition, the European Commission estimated that member states could generate revenues of €5 billion a year with DSTs at a rate of 3 percent, while Amount A would generate only half of such, around €2.5 billion.

Finally, Barake and Le Pouhaër assume that the United States will ratify Pillar One and estimate the overall global net gains from Pillar One Amount A as €15.6 billion, among which the United States is expected to be the biggest gainer – €7.6 billion. However, as we expressed our skepticism, it is almost impossible to imagine the United States ratifying it given the current economic and political circumstances. If, as expected, the United States does not ratify it, then total global net revenue gained from amount A will drop from €15.6 billion to €8 billion.[18]

Furthermore, barring Spain, Hungary, and India, most countries do not lose from substituting Pillar One for their existing DSTs. The main big losers are the tax havens but that does not matter because Pillar One can be implemented without their

[18] Even this low number is too high if Pillar Two is adopted first.

cooperation (and they have in any case already agreed to it in principle, so it is harder for them to object).

In sum, if the rest of the world adopted Pillar One without the United States, revenue losing countries like Spain, Hungary, and India may maintain their existing DSTs. Since DSTs apply almost exclusively to the US digital giants, only the United States will care, and while it may impose trade sanctions on these countries, the amounts involved are small (€23 million for India, €20 million for Hungary, and €250–750 million for an expected Spanish DST[19]), and the effect on trade likely to be negligible.

Presumably, the United States will maintain its existing regulation denying the FTC to both DSTs and to Pillar One Amount A taxes.[20] This regulation is not based on the text of the Code or on any Supreme Court decision, so the US courts may strike it down if (as is likely) it is challenged by affected US MNEs.

But even if it is not, the resulting maximum double taxation burden according to Barake and Le Pouhaër is only €8 billion for all sixty-nine covered MNEs. Even assuming the extreme and unlikely case that this is all borne by US MNEs (who are only 45 percent of all covered MNEs) and results in €16 billion in tax (€8 billion to other countries and another €8 billion to the United States as a result of the denial of the FTC[21]), the total amount is quite small compared to their profits.[22] For comparison, the net profits in 2022 of the four US digital giants included in the analysis above were Alphabet ($257.64 billion), Meta ($23.2 billion), Microsoft ($198.27 billion), and Oracle ($6.7 billion). And this does not include non-ADS US Big Tech like Amazon ($33 billion profit in 2021) and Apple ($167 billion profit in 2022). We have advocated a much higher US corporate tax rate for US MNEs making over $10 billion per year because these mostly represent economic rents of monopolies. Even assuming that they cannot shift the tax to their consumers or advertisers, they can afford it.[23]

7.2 PILLAR TWO

Unlike Pillar One, Pillar Two[24] is rapidly advancing. Legislation implementing Pillar Two has been proposed in Australia, Belgium, Canada, Denmark, France,

19 Both Spain and Hungary will not be able to maintain DSTs if the EU adopts Pillar One.

20 Treas. Reg. 1.901-2(b)(5).

21 Although presumably even a tax denied the credit will remain deductible, the actual US tax cost will be lower.

22 The actual amount will be smaller since Pillar Two will be adopted first.

23 We have advocated a much higher US tax rate for US MNEs making over $10 billion per year because these mostly represent economic rents of monopolies. *See e.g.*, Reuven S. Avi-Yonah, *A New Corporate Tax* (July 27, 2020), 197 TAX NOTES FED. 653 (July 27, 2020).

24 This section draws heavily from a previous piece written by the first author. Reuven S. Avi-Yonah, *Pillar Two and the Credits*, 49 INT'L TAX J. 65 (Nov.–Dec. 2023). This article is reprinted with the publisher's permission from the *International Tax Journal*, a bimonthly journal published by WOLTERS KLUWER. Copying or distribution without the publisher's permission is prohibited.

Germany, the Netherlands, Switzerland, and the UK. Most importantly, in December 2022 the EU unanimously adopted a directive requiring all twenty-seven member states to implement Pillar Two by the end of 2024. Even in the United States, Pillar Two was within one vote in the Senate to being implemented, and it is not inconceivable that the United States will implement it if the Democrats again control both houses of Congress and the presidency.

One of the most important questions regarding Pillar Two is how it will affect countries that have not yet adopted it, such as China and the United States, as well as developing countries. The main issue is Pillar Two's impact of domestic tax incentives like tax holidays, accelerated depreciation, and tax credits, all of which can be affected by either the IIR or the UTPR if a country has not adopted a QDMTT.

7.2.1 *China*

In the case of China, Mindy Herzfeld has argued that

> The chorus of approval around countries that are adopting the Pillar Two global minimum tax obscures the silence from the world's second largest economy. China has made no comment about its plans to adopt the global anti-base erosion (GLoBE) rules, nor has it made any statement about joining the Pillar One agreement. Any statements it has made suggest that it remains skeptical about the benefits of the agreements, and that it won't sign on unless it is convinced otherwise. But whether China signs on or not, its role in the process is critical.[25]

Professor Herzfeld focuses on the two largest Chinese multinational enterprises – Tencent and Alibaba – and on Apple, a US MNE with massive operations in China. She argues that the Chinese tech giants benefit tremendously from their parent entity being incorporated in the Cayman Islands due to their ability to shift income from China to the Cayman Islands. As for Apple, it benefits from low tax rates in China derived from various tax incentive programs. All these tax benefits, Professor Herzfeld argues, are at risk due to Pillar Two. As one of the most important economies in the world, China's response to this risk is very important.

Professor Herzfeld concludes by stating that

> It's hard to characterize a minimum tax deal as global if the world's second largest economy declines to join it. And yet that's just what advocates of Pillar Two have done: They have touted the GLoBE regime while failing to acknowledge the consequences of large emerging markets rejecting it. Staying outside the regime may create a competitive advantage for Chinese companies, leading to an unlevel playing field that disquiets lawmakers from the United States and other countries.

[25] Mindy Herzfeld, *International Tax Stability? The China Factor*, 110 Tax Notes Int'l 979 (May 22, 2023).

> There may be value in multilateral agreements that don't include China – the WTO produced benefits for member countries even before China's accession. But China's uncertain role in a supposedly global minimum tax regime warrants far greater discussion on the risks it poses to non-Chinese companies, the U.S. government, and the U.S. public. It's difficult to envision a regime that can offer any effective stability emerging from such murky origins.

While we agree that China has important potential concerns, we have several reservations about Professor Herzfeld's analysis.

First, since the United States is unlikely to join Pillar Two any time soon, we do not believe it is a necessity for China to participate. If Pillar Two can be effective without the world's largest economy, then it can also be effective without the second largest one. The whole point of Pillar Two is that it does not require *any* specific economy to participate in it to function.

Second, Professor Herzfeld writes that

> *China's adoption of GLOBE could also permit other countries to tax the profits generated in China by Chinese-headquartered companies that now benefit from Chinese tax incentives, or that are being shifted to the Caymans.* The amount of UTPR revenue a country can collect is not limited to the total revenue generated in its jurisdiction, so in theory all the top-up tax on the low-taxed profits of companies like Tencent and Alibaba could be collected by other countries, even though those countries contribute only a small share of the companies' overall profits. [Emphasis added.]

To the extent Chinese MNEs operate in other countries, this may be the case, but crucially it does *not* depend on whether China adopts the GLoBE rules. A country in which a Chinese MNE has a subsidiary or a branch can apply the rule commonly known as the UTPR, formerly the undertaxed profits or undertaxed payments rule, to the income of that subsidiary or branch if the global effective tax rate of that MNE is below 15 percent. China's adoption or non-adoption of Pillar Two will not matter. This is precisely the reason why there is concern in the United States about the UTPR applying to US MNEs, even though the United States has not adopted Pillar Two.

As a practical matter, neither of Professor Herzfeld's Chinese examples (Tencent and Alibaba) does significant business outside of China, so the Pillar Two rules will not affect these companies regardless of what China does because another country can only apply the UTPR to them if they have subsidiaries or permanent establishments in that country. The only other country that could affect them is the Cayman Islands, but we suspect the Cayman Islands will find a way to avoid Pillar Two as it avoided the BEPS 1.0 initiative. This presumably explains why the Chinese are indifferent to Pillar Two. China seems to accept Tencent and Alibaba using the Cayman Islands to underpay their taxes to China, which is similar to how the United States handled US MNEs before the Tax Cuts and Jobs Act – that is, supporting its national champions by undertaxing them in practice while taxing them in theory.

The Chinese attitude could change if other countries start taxing foreign MNEs like Apple on their China operations via the UTPR. At that point, China may consider switching to refundable credits for its incentive programs for the Apples of the world.

7.2.2 *The United States*

The United States is unlikely to adopt Pillar Two. Therefore, it is important to understand how Pillar Two will impact US MNEs without the US adoption of Pillar Two.

American critics of Pillar Two and the UTPR have focused on the potential impact of the top-up tax on green credits created in the Inflation Reduction Act (IRA) and on credits to encourage domestic chip manufacturing in the CHIPS Act of 2022. These critics argue that the ability of Congress to effectively implement policy goals is undermined because the UTPR, when applied to other parts of US MNEs, will undercut or eliminate the benefit of the tax credits. This, critics argue, is an unacceptable interference with Congress's ability to tax US corporations on US source income in any way it chooses.

In general, it is true that the UTPR can apply to US source income of US MNEs if the effective tax rate (ETR) on such income falls below the minimum rate of 15 percent. For example, since the FDII rate is currently 13.125 percent, the UTPR could result in an increased tax liability for such income until 2026, when the FDII rate is scheduled to increase to 16.406 percent. This calculation assumes that the current US corporate alternative minimum tax (CAMT) will not itself raise the rate of FDII eligible export income to 15 percent (on a financial income base, like the UTPR base). Due to the CAMT, it is entirely likely that the US MNEs that benefit from FDII will only rarely be affected by the UTPR.

However, the main risk posed by Pillar Two to the US tax system is if the IRA green credits or the CHIPS credits reduce the ETR, they could result in an added UTPR tax liability because they are excluded from the CAMT. To prevent the CAMT from adversely affecting some incentives created by the CHIPS Act and the IRA, the statute explicitly protects credits treated as "direct payments" (i.e., refundable) from the reach of the new tax. In addition, the IRA credits are transferrable. While Congress did not directly address how the CAMT affects transferred credits, the Treasury Department and the IRS provided interim guidance on the interaction of the corporate AMT and the credit monetization regimes in section 6 of Notice 2023-7, 2023-3 IRB 390. The notice provides that the same level of protection that the statute explicitly affords to taxpayers electing direct pay also applies to taxpayers electing transferability.

It thus becomes important to determine the extent to which the green credits of the IRA and the CHIPS credits reduce the ETR for UTPR purposes.

7.2.2.1 Qualified Refundable Tax Credits (QRTC)

The OECD Blueprint for Pillar Two distinguishes between refundable and nonrefundable credits. Nonrefundable credits are treated as negative taxes and reduce the numerator (top line) of the ETR calculation, while qualified refundable tax credits (QRTCs) are treated as income and increase the denominator (bottom line). The OECD Blueprint for Pillar Two explains this distinction as follows:

> 235. It is a matter of judgement to determine the most appropriate accounting treatment for an ITC based on a qualitative analysis of the legal requirements that must be met in order to generate the credit rather than a quantitative assessment of the economic outcomes for how a particular ITC is realised in practice. An ITC that is determined or limited by reference to an entity's income tax liability or provided in the form of an income tax deduction is likely to be accounted for under IAS 12 (Income Taxes) and recorded in the financial accounts as a reduction in current tax expense. If the realisation of the ITC is not dependent on the amount of taxable profit or on any past or future income tax liability generated by an entity, then it is likely to be accounted for under IAS 20 (Government Grants) and recorded in the financial accounts as other income.
>
> 236. Therefore, it is expected that generally under IFRS and equivalent accounting standards any "refundable" ITCs would be treated as income, whereas any nonrefundable ITCs would be treated as a reduction in a tax liability. The term "refundable" is understood in a broad sense and covers ITCs that may become payable as cash or available as cash equivalents, including being available to be used to discharge liabilities other than a covered tax liability. The rationale, from an accounting perspective, for treating refundable tax credits in the same way as grants is that, similar to grants, the taxpayer's entitlement to a refundable tax credit is not tied to its income or tax liability, and so in terms of economic substance grants and refundable tax credits are equivalent.
>
> 237. IFRS may treat a credit as "refundable" even if it is eligible to be refunded only after a number of years or where the taxpayer has the option to offset the credit against a non-CIT liability, such as a payroll tax or VAT liability. Most importantly, IFRS generally takes an "all-in" approach to refundability by which if a credit has some feature of potential refundability (e.g. the credit is required to be carried forward and only the unused / excess portion of the credit is refundable after a certain number of years), the entire amount of the credit is treated as income even if in practice the credit is used to offset a CIT liability, and thus may never actually be refunded.

The OECD then adopts a rule as follows:

> **Treatment of government grants and tax credits under the GloBE**
>
> **General rule**
>
> The treatment of government grants and tax credits will be based on the financial accounting rules with safeguards for refundable tax credits to address risk areas:

(a) Where a refundable tax credit meets certain conditions, i.e. a "qualified refundable tax credit", the entire amount of the credit is treated as income (in line with the financial accounting treatment for refundable tax credits).
(b) Where a refundable tax credit does not meet the conditions, i.e. a "non-qualified refundable tax credit", the entire amount of the credit is treated as reducing a covered tax liability.
(c) For non-refundable tax credits, the entire amount of the credit is treated as reducing a covered tax liability (in line with the financial accounting treatment for non-refundable tax credits).
(d) For all government grants, the entire amount of the grant is treated as income (in line with the financial accounting treatment for government grants).

Conditions for a "qualified refundable tax credit" under the GloBE:

In order to be treated as a "qualified refundable tax credit" under the GloBE, the tax credit regime must be designed in a way so that a credit becomes refundable within 4 years from when it is first provided. Where the tax credit regime under the laws of a jurisdiction provides for partial refundability such that only a fixed percentage or portion of the credit is refundable, in order for the refundable portion of the credit to be treated as a qualified refundable tax credit, it must become refundable within 4 years from when it is first provided.

In general, the green credits of the IRA include two relevant features – direct pay and transferability – while CHIPS credits include direct pay but not transferability.

Direct pay refers to the ability of certain entities either to use their credits to offset tax liability (e.g., for estimated taxes) or, if they do not have any, to receive a cash payment from the federal government. In the United States, tax-exempt entities, states and their political subdivisions, tribal governments, Alaska Native Corporations, the Tennessee Valley Authority, and cooperative corporations that furnish electric energy to rural areas can elect to be treated as having made a direct payment in lieu of certain tax credits for energy property and electricity from renewable resources. Other taxpayers can make this election for some, but not all, of the applicable credits.

With an applicable credit, an "applicable entity" can elect to be treated as making a payment equal to the credit against their federal income tax for the tax year for which the credit was determined. Taxpayers that are not one of the "applicable entities" can make the election but only for three specific credits. The election must be made at a time and in a manner provided by the Treasury Secretary. Importantly, payments more than the total tax liability of the taxpayer can be refunded to the applicable entities, allowing the credits to be received as "direct pay."

How do these provisions interact with the UTPR rules? In the case of direct pay credits, it is clear that they should qualify as QRTCs for UTPR purposes to those entities eligible to receive refunds, and therefore should not reduce the ETR of the entity. The term "refundable" is interpreted in a broad sense and covers Investment Tax Credits (ITCs) that may become payable as cash or as cash equivalents, including the option to be used to discharge liabilities other than a covered tax liability.

Direct pay credits under the IRA and CHIPS are typically refundable in cash (for nontaxable entities) within four years and, therefore, qualify as QRTCs for GLoBE purposes. They can still affect the calculation because they are treated as income, but they do not directly trigger top-up tax liability.

7.2.2.2 Transferable Credits

Transferability refers to the ability of taxpayers that are ineligible for direct payment election to elect to transfer part or all of certain tax credits for energy property and electricity from renewable resources to an unrelated taxpayer. If the transferee pays the transferor for a credit, the payment must be in cash, must not be included in the transferor's gross income, and must not be deductible by the payer.

The impact of the UTPR on transferable credits is less clear than its impact on direct pay credits. However, to the extent that the credits are transferred from a taxpayer that cannot benefit from direct pay to a taxpayer that can, the transferability provisions should be effective in transforming the credits into QRTCs. This is because they are refundable to the taxpayer that claims them and the benefit accrues to the transferor through the cash payment.

The green credits in the IRA are either refundable directly, in which case they clearly qualify as QRTCs, or are transferable, in which case they still should qualify as QRTCs because the taxpayer that transfers them receives the funds indirectly from the government through the transferee.

For these reasons, the UTPR will significantly interfere with the transferable green credits, since the impact of including them in income on the calculation is much smaller than if they were treated as nonrefundable.

7.2.2.3 Qualified Flow through Tax Benefits (QFTB)

The OECD administrative guidance released in 2023 elaborated on qualified flow through tax benefits (QFTBs) which are relevant to the application of UTPR to common partnership structures designed to enable taxable investors to benefit from tax credits.

The administrative guidance provides as follows:

> **Treatment of tax credits derived through a Tax Transparent Entity**
>
> 57.3 The direct or indirect owner of an Ownership Interest in a Tax Transparent Entity shall treat any tax credits that flow through the Tax Transparent Entity in

accordance with the ordinary requirements of the GloBE Rules based on the character of the credit received. For example, in the case of a Qualified Refundable Tax Credit (QRTC), the amount of the credit that flows through a Tax Transparent Entity to an owner shall be treated as income in the owner's GloBE Income or Loss. On the other hand, a non-QRTC or a non-refundable tax credit that flows through a Tax Transparent Entity to the owner shall not be treated as GloBE Income but rather as a reduction to Adjusted Covered Taxes of the owner (unless such credit is a Qualified Flow-through Tax Benefit as described further below).

Treatment of Qualified Flow-through Tax Benefits of Qualified Ownership Interests

57.4 An owner that is subject to an Equity Investment Inclusion Election shall apply the treatment described in paragraphs 57.5 through 57.7 to Qualified Flow-through Tax Benefits that flow through a Qualified Ownership Interest...

57.5 Qualified Flow-through Tax Benefits will be allowed as a positive amount in the Adjusted Covered Taxes of the direct owner of a Qualified Ownership Interest or an indirect owner of such an interest through a chain of Tax Transparent Entities that are not Constituent Entities of the MNE Group of a Qualified Ownership Interest to the extent the Qualified Flow-through Tax Benefit was treated for financial accounting purposes as reducing tax expense. A Qualified Flow-through Tax Benefit is any amount described in paragraph 57.6(a) or (b) (other than a Qualified Refundable Tax Credit) that flows through a Qualified Ownership Interest to the extent it reduces the owner's investment in the Qualified Ownership Interest pursuant to paragraph 57.6.

57.6 An owner's investment in a Qualified Ownership Interest is treated as being reduced by receipts with respect to the Qualified Ownership Interest of any of the following types:

(a) The amount of tax credits that have flowed through to the owner;
(b) The amount of any tax-deductible losses that have flowed through to the owner multiplied by the statutory tax rate applicable to the owner;
(c) The amount of any distributions (including a return of capital) to the owner; and
(d) The amount of proceeds from a sale of all or part of the Qualified Ownership Interest.

This rule shall in no circumstances cause the owner's investment to be less than zero, and accordingly no amount shall be treated as reducing the investment to the extent it would reduce the investment below zero.

57.7 Any of the items described in paragraphs 57.6(a) through (d) that flow through or are received in respect of the Qualified Ownership Interest after the owner's investment has been reduced to zero pursuant to paragraph 57.6 shall be treated as a negative amount in the owner's Adjusted Covered Taxes. However, an item described in paragraph 57.6(c) or (d) or a Qualified Refundable Tax Credit, shall be treated as a negative amount in the owner's Adjusted Covered Taxes only to the extent of the amount of any Qualified Flow-through Tax Benefits that flowed

> through the Qualified Ownership Interest and that were treated as a positive amount in the owner's Adjusted Covered Taxes.
>
> 57.8 A Qualified Ownership Interest is an Ownership Interest in a Tax Transparent Entity where the assets, liabilities, income, expenses, and cash flows of the Tax Transparent Entity are not consolidated on a line-by-line basis in the Consolidated Financial Statements of the MNE Group and the total return with respect to that Ownership Interest (including distributions and benefits of tax losses and Qualified Refundable Tax Credits derived through the Tax Transparent Entity, but excluding tax credits other than Qualified Refundable Tax Credits) is expected to be less than the total amount invested by the owner of the Ownership Interest such that a portion of the investment will be returned in the form of tax credits other than Qualified Refundable Tax Credits. The determination of the expected total return is made at the time the investment is entered into and is based on facts and circumstances, including the terms of the investment.

The way this rule works is that in the case of a QFTB, the credits are regarded as reducing the ETR, but the payment made by the investor is treated as a payment of tax, so only the profit of the investor reduces the ETR.

As a result, the tax equity investment arrangements commonly used in the United States for renewable energy credits and for low-income housing credits may qualify as QFTBs. For example, if a utility cannot use an income tax credit for investment in a wind power station, a partnership may be created to acquire the asset. And under the terms of the partnership agreement, the utility receives the pretax income and the investor benefits from the credits. In these cases, the tax credit is an essential component of the expected return on the equity investment. The special rule does not, however, provide a complete exclusion for credits derived through equity-method investments and is not applicable to transferrable credits that are monetized outside of tax equity investment arrangements.

Nevertheless, the special rule for QFTBs is beneficial to US tax credits because many of them can be used through tax equity investment arrangements, and when they are used, the tax credits will only reduce the ETR to the extent of the profit made by the outside investor, which is significantly less than the full amount of the credit.

7.2.2.4 Conclusion

The main US critique leveled against the UTPR, accusing it of limiting Congress's ability to impose US taxes on the US income of US MNEs, is exaggerated. In the case of tax credits that are eligible for direct pay under the CHIPS act and the IRA, the credits should qualify as QRTCs and therefore do not reduce the ETR for the top-up tax calculation. In the case of transferable credits under the IRA, a strong argument can be made that they should be treated as QRTCs as well. This is because the effect of transferability on the transferor is the receipt of a cash payment from the government indirectly through the transferee. In the case of credits structured as part of a tax equity investment arrangement, the credits should qualify as QFTBs and only the profit of the investor affects the top-up tax calculation.

7.2.3 *Where Should the Line Be Drawn?*

The fact that the US IRA and CHIPS credits are likely to qualify as QRTCs under Pillar Two does not mean that this *should* be the case. Why should refundability be the dividing line?

To answer this question, it is worthwhile to take a step back and ask what the purpose of corporate tax is. A common belief is that corporate tax is a way for governments to tax the wealthy through their ownership of corporations. Pillar Two has sometimes been justified as part of President Biden's "foreign policy for the middle class" as Pillar Two preserves the corporate tax base from being eroded by tax competition. In this view the corporate tax is important in reducing inequality and strengthening the middle class because it falls at least in part on wealthy shareholders.

There are four issues with this argument. First wealthy US shareholders should be paying tax at a 37 percent rate, not 15 percent, and on all their investments, not just in their stockholdings of large MNEs. Taxing Bezos, Musk, or Zuckerberg at 15 percent going forward does very little to tax the billions of unrealized gains they have already accumulated (gains with which they can borrow money against, as Musk did when he bought Twitter).

Second, it is not clear that the corporate tax falls primarily on shareholders. In the case of large MNEs subject to Pillar Two, they are frequently monopolies or quasi-monopolies and may be able to shift the burden of the corporate tax to employees or customers.

Third, many shareholders are far from rich. They are precisely the middle class investing through tax-exempt pension funds, and a corporate tax may reduce the benefit of the tax deferral that encourages them to save for retirement. Other investors are frequently tax-exempt institutions like universities. If we believe in the rationale for granting them the exemption, then we should not be taxing them indirectly either.

Finally, there is a much better way to tax the rich. Proposed by both Senate Finance Committee Chair Ron Wyden (D-OR) and the Biden administration, a current tax on the unrealized appreciation of stock would more effectively target the wealthy. Furthermore, taxing billionaires on publicly traded stock poses no liquidity or valuation concerns, a common criticism of taxing unrealized gains.

Nonetheless, while taxing the rich is not one of them, there are two good reasons for the corporate tax.

First, most of the profit of the largest MNEs is economic rents derived from their quasi-monopoly status, and taxing them on their rents is a good supplement to antitrust enforcement. Such taxation of rents is efficient and will not cause the

MNEs to change their behavior, except perhaps to discourage anticompetitive acquisitions of their rivals. In fact, we have argued that for a country like the United States, home to many of the largest MNEs, the corporate tax should be progressive with much higher rates at the top.[26]

Second, the corporate tax is a good instrument to regulate corporate behavior. Corporations, especially the largest MNEs targeted by Pillar Two, are very important economic actors, and the government should be able to incentivize them to, for example, engage in clean energy, chip manufacturing, or affordable housing. Having a robust corporate tax enables the government to grant tax breaks for positive externality producing activities. From this perspective, ensuring that large MNEs pay 15 percent everywhere enables the government to reduce their tax at least from 21 percent to 15 percent on activities it deems worthy.

There is still the important question of in which cases should Pillar Two allow for reductions below 15 percent. This is what happens with QRTCs, QFTBs, or the Substance-Based Income Exclusion (SBIE).

The theoretical answer can be derived from the above analysis. Tax incentives, like tax holidays, special economic zones, and patent boxes, are designed to attract investment from other countries and therefore undermine the corporate tax base of those countries. It is those types of incentives that just relate to the geographic location of income producing activities (*spatial tax expenditures*) that are the proper target of Pillar Two and should not be allowed to reduce the 15 percent minimum rate. They just shift the corporate tax base to another country and therefore neither increase taxation of rents nor address market failures.

On the other hand, tax incentives to address market failures (*market failure tax expenditures*) such as green energy credits, chip manufacturing credits, low-income housing credits, and research and development credits should be acceptable, because their main purpose is not to draw investment that will happen anyway in some other location (and therefore the tax reduction is a windfall to the MNE and a cost to other countries) but rather encourage or create investment that would not have happened at all but for the credit.

But what has refundability of credits got to do with the rationales above?

Ideally, it would be better to investigate the purpose of each tax expenditure and establish whether it has a legitimate link to a market failure. But that would be very difficult to administer. Instead, drawing the line at refundability can be a reasonable proxy for this division.

Tax holidays, special tax zones, and patent boxes involve a reduction of the tax rate, frequently to zero. The same applies to expensing and accelerated depreciation, both of which reduce the effective tax rate. They are typically not refundable but just involve the government refraining from collecting tax revenue.

[26] *See, e.g.*, Avi-Yonah, *supra* note 22.

In theory such spatial tax expenditures could be made refundable. But most developing countries that engage in this type of harmful tax competition cannot afford refundability, because it requires a cash outlay. Rich democracies can afford refundability, but they suffer from political constraints against doling out cash handouts to large MNEs that do not apply to less visible tax expenditures. China may be an exception because it is both rich and non-democratic, but even China has not recently chosen to directly subsidize foreign MNEs (as opposed to its domestic EV, solar panel, and chip manufacturers).

On the other hand, the market failure tax credits are frequently refundable. As we have seen, it is even true in the United States since both the IRA and the CHIPS credits are refundable and other credits are typically QFTBs. The major exception in the United States is research and experimentation (R&E), which traditionally has involved expensing and is not refundable. But it could, and should, be made refundable, as discussed below.

Thus, we believe the line drawn by Pillar Two is defensible. What is not defensible is the SBIE, because that involves spatial tax competition for tangible investment (depreciation) and jobs (payroll), and it should never have been carved out of Pillar Two (or GILTI for that matter). It only makes matters worse that it can be satisfied by a single highly paid manager driving a Porsche.

Nevertheless, refundability has its limitations as a proxy for the distinction between spatial tax expenditures and market failure expenditures. The refundability criterion relies on a lack of resources, so it is biased against poorer countries; it also relies on political visibility, so it is biased against democracies. Rich nondemocratic countries benefit because they can afford refundable credits and do not have to worry about the potential impact on upcoming elections.

It would be better if the OECD were explicit and clear about the line it is drawing, saying that the relevant distinction is between spatial and market failure tax expenditures. This would clearly leave some expenditures like tax holidays on the wrong side of the line, and it would clearly leave green credits on the right side of the line.

Just like any line drawing exercise in tax law (including refundability), countries could try to manipulate this line. But that is precisely what the peer review process in the Inclusive Framework (IF) is designed to do: to enable any one of the 140 member countries to investigate suspicious tax expenditures in another member country and report them to the IF so that it can decide. Peer review worked well in the WTO to detect violations of trade agreements (e.g., on export subsidies, where peer review forced small countries to give up on tax holidays that were in fact all about exports). Peer review can work in this case as well, but only if it has a good criterion to work with, and the line between spatial and market failure tax expenditures seems to us a better line than refundability.

7.2.4 US Applications

As we have already seen, Pillar Two would treat the IRA and CHIP credits as QRTCs while treating many other market failure–oriented credits as QFTBs. These credits would not significantly reduce the ETR for Pillar Two purposes.

But what about other US tax incentives? The main ones are (R&E) and foreign derived intangible income (FDII). In both cases, the UTPR could neutralize US tax benefits under current law, even though the CAMT is likely to reduce the frequency of such an impact from the UTPR.

FDII is an export subsidy that grants corporations that export goods, services, or intangibles from the United States at a reduced tax rate of 13.125 percent. The UTPR could result in the effective rate on FDII income being raised to 15 percent instead of 13.125 percent (but only until 2026, when the FDII rate increases to 16.406 percent). This is exactly the type of effect Pillar Two is supposed to have. FDII is a blatant form of a spatial tax incentive designed to incentivize US and foreign MNEs to shift export income to the United States. It is not necessary for MNEs to make any real US investment, since all that is needed is to shift intangibles used to produce foreign income. As such, it is a violation of the WTO rule against export subsidies, but no country can sue the United States in the WTO because the United States has deliberately sabotaged the WTO dispute resolution mechanism. Thus, imposing UTPR on FDII income is perfectly justified by the need to establish a level playing field. Furthermore, it is consistent with the intentions of Congress, as evidenced by the scheduled rise of the FDII rate above 15 percent in 2026 and by the adoption of the CAMT.

R&E, on the other hand, is a market failure tax expenditure because it attempts to generate positive externalities. Currently, R&E is a deduction, which must be amortized (under the TCJA) rather than expensed (as was the case before TCJA). Congress is considering reinstating the R&E expensing provision, but that can reduce the ETR and make MNEs subject to the UTPR.

Instead, Congress should turn R&E into a credit refundable over four years, which is a more effective way of subsidizing R&E but does not result in a lower ETR under the UTPR rules. A refundable credit for R&E is more effective than expensing because it is available to genuinely innovative start-ups that have losses, rather than limited to hugely profitable corporations, where expensing can eliminate US tax liability without producing anything new. Congress has already approved direct pay credits on a bipartisan basis in the CHIPS Act. And it can do so again, especially if the cost is mitigated by the four-year provision and by allowing an R&E credit against payroll tax liabilities, which is also permitted under Pillar Two.

It can be argued that Congress could also substitute a refundable credit for FDII, and the same can be said for other patent boxes abroad with which FDII competes. The revenue cost of R&E and FDII over the 2023–32 budget window is about the same ($111 billion each). But in both cases the cash outlay would be quite visible, and it would be much easier for members of Congress to justify an R&E refundable credit that goes primarily to activities the public supports (e.g., inventing new drugs) and that are frequently done by small start-ups rather than a refundable credit that goes primarily to the biggest MNEs. The main benefits of FDII go to US MNEs bringing back intangibles which they shifted offshore before 2017, and it is much harder to justify a tax break for that given that no jobs are created by this action. Finally, the benefit of FDII compared to a 15 percent rate disappears in 2026 (and perhaps earlier because of the CAMT), while the benefits of a refundable R&E credit could be made permanent.

7.2.5 *Conclusion*

The fundamental logic behind Pillar Two is to create a level playing field. From a US perspective, by enacting the CAMT, Congress decided in 2022 that the effective tax rate of US MNEs should not be below 15 percent. The world made the same decision for all large MNEs with Pillar Two. Even if the United States never adopts Pillar Two, it benefits from it because US MNEs will be less incentivized to shift profits out of the United States if their ETR is 15 percent both within and outside the United States (as opposed to 21 percent within and 10.5 percent outside as under US law before the CAMT and Pillar Two). The global application of Pillar Two means that no US MNE will be put at a competitive disadvantage by having competitors subject to an ETR lower than 15 percent regardless of whether the United States adopts Pillar Two.

Given these goals, it makes sense to distinguish between those tax expenditures that should be allowed to reduce the ETR below 15 percent and those that should not. Tax expenditures that are designed to attract mobile business like FDII should be discouraged, but tax expenditures designed to address market failures should be encouraged. Although we would prefer to see the OECD directly investigate the rationale behind each tax expenditure through the Pillar Two peer review process, refundability is a reasonable proxy for such distinction.

8

Evolution or Revolution?

In *L'ancien Regime et la Revolution* (1856), Alexis de Tocqueville[1] argued that the major innovations of the French Revolution were prefigured in developments during the old regime, so that the revolution was less of a sharp departure from the ancien régime than previously thought. This chapter will make a similar argument for the current revolution in international tax contained in the two pillars of BEPS 2.0. Specifically, we will argue that Pillar One derives from efforts to redefine the source of active income considering the digital revolution, which builds on US states' use of sales factors since the 1930s as a source of corporate income. Pillar Two implements the single tax principle, which can be traced back to the first model treaty from 1927. Both ideas were already articulated and developed in the first author's own early writing on international taxation from the 1990s, when the internet was in its infancy.

8.1 THE 1923 REPORT AND BEPS 2.0

The four economists' Report on Double Taxation in 1923 (the Report) was the basis of the old international tax regime (ITR).[2] While the ITR that was based on the Report of 1923 is outdated, the ITR has been revolutionized in the past decade. On the surface the changes brought about by the BEPS project seem radical enough to consider them an "international tax revolution." But we will argue that the principles developed in the Report are still influential to the modern ITR.

The Report originated with a request by the International Chamber of Commerce to the newly established League of Nations to study the problem of double taxation. The sharp increase of income tax rates during World War I and the fear that tariff barriers and a retreat from globalization would restrict cross-border investment had led to concerns surrounding the issue of double taxation.

1 Alexis de Tocqueville, L'Ancien Régime et la Révolution (7th ed. 1866).

2 *League of Nations Report on Double Taxation Submitted to the Financial Committee by Professors Bruins, Einaudi, Seligman, and Sir Josiah Stamp*, League of Nations Doc. E.F.S. 73 F. 19 (1923).

In 1921 the Financial Committee of the League asked four economists to study the issue: Prof. Bruins from the Commercial University in Rotterdam, Prof. Einaudi from Turin University, Prof. Seligman from Columbia University, and Sir Josiah Stamp from London University. Out of the four, only Prof. Einaudi represented a capital importing country, and he did not participate in the actual meetings of the committee. The inclusion of Prof. Seligman is remarkable as although the United States never joined the League, an American was necessary because the United States was already the world's largest economy and a pioneer in relieving double taxation through the foreign tax credit, which it had unilaterally adopted in 1919.

The committee met in Geneva in March 1923 and issued the Report in April. The report was based on Stamp's initial draft but after it had been revised; it primarily reflected the views of Prof. Seligman, the group's lone American. The report contains numerous passages drawing on examples from US states, which only Prof. Seligman would be deeply familiar with, as well as drawing from his own books and ideas.

The Report is divided into three parts. Section 8.1 is an economic analysis of the consequences of international double taxation. Its main conclusion is that double taxation impacts existing cross-border investments and deters new cross-border investment. Therefore, double taxation should be avoided as much as possible. Section 8.1 also argues that in most cases the burden of double taxation is shifted to the residents of the source country because the investor will insist on receiving the world market return on the investment.

Section 8.2 discusses the general principles which govern international tax jurisdiction. It argues that the proper basis for income taxation is not an exchange of taxes for benefits managed by the taxing government, but rather progressive taxation based on one's ability to pay. Section 8.2 also develops the concept of economic (rather than political) allegiance as the justification for tax and the right of both domicile (residence) and origin (source) countries to impose a tax.

Section 8.3 applies these principles to the avoidance of double taxation. It develops four methods to avoid double taxation. First, the credit method, under which the source country imposes tax and the residence country grants a foreign tax credit. Second, the exemption method, under which the source country refrains from taxing the income of nonresidents. Third, the formulary method, under which the tax is divided by an agreed upon formula between residence and source jurisdictions. Finally, the classification and assignment method, under which income is divided into various categories and then assigned to either source or residence countries based on the income's classification.

Section 8.3 then sets out the practical application of these methods. The credit method is rejected as overly generous to source countries. The Report expresses a preference to the exemption method but has doubts as to whether it will be acceptable to the source countries. The Report supports the formulary method, but it also points out that this method requires agreement between the respective jurisdictions. Finally, the Report settles on classification and assignment method as the most likely method to be applied in practice. In addition, in the portion dealing with source taxation, the Report suggests that income derived from real estate and from business activities (active income) be taxed at source while income from investments (passive income) be taxed at residence. This part of the Report had the most immediate effect on the international tax regime, because it was incorporated into the work of the technical experts who drafted the first model treaty in 1927.

There are significant questions as to whether the Report should continue to have relevance today despite the radical changes the ITR has undergone since the 2008 financial crisis. Even under the new BEPS 2.0, the base structures of tax treaties will remain the same. The classification and assignment scheme used by many of these treaties is derived directly from the Report. While on the surface the Report's modern impact may seem to be limited to the classification and assignment scheme, that view dramatically underestimates the modern relevance and impact of the report on both Pillar One and Pillar Two of the new ITR.

8.1.1 *The Report and Pillar One*

Pillar One applies a formulary method to allocate a portion of the residual profits of large multinationals (Amount A) to the market jurisdiction. The main innovation in Pillar One is to recognize the right of the market jurisdiction to a portion of the profits from an entity that sells goods or provides services in that market jurisdiction. To do so, Pillar One overrules the two main limitations on source taxation of active income included in the tax treaties, namely the permanent establishment (PE) threshold and the arm's length standard (ALS). Neither of these limitations appears in the Report. The PE threshold is derived from nineteenth-century tax treaties but was not considered generally binding until later, while the ALS was developed by Mitchell Carroll (the protégé of Seligman's main rival Thomas Adams) in the 1930s.

The four economists who wrote the Report would, presumably, have approved of Pillar One. Pillar One has drawn direct inspiration from the Report in its application of the formulary method for allocation. The general idea of formulary allocation by consensus is the third method they approved of to prevent double taxation.

In addition, they agreed that the market jurisdiction has the right to tax the income derived from sales into the market. The Report states that one of the bases of economic allegiance is the establishment and protection of the market, which confers benefits on the taxpayer:

> The same is true of the benefits connected with the consumption side of faculty, where there is room even for a consideration of the cost to the government in providing a proper environment which renders the consumption of wealth possible or agreeable.

The Report also argues that the market jurisdiction is essential to the production of wealth:

> By *production of wealth* we mean all the stages which are involved up to the point of wealth coming to fruition, that is, all the stages up to the point when the physical production has reached a complete economic destination and can be acquired as wealth. The oranges upon the trees in California are not acquired wealth until they are picked, and not even at that stage until they are packed, and not even at that stage until they are transported to the place where demand exists and until they are put where the consumer can use them. These stages, up to the point where wealth reaches fruition, may be shared in by different territorial authorities. (Emphasis added)

The Report is also clear that all the countries that contribute to the production of income are essential and therefore should share in the tax imposed upon it:

> It may be said that no one of these four elements can be omitted without ruining the efforts of the other three and spoiling the whole apparatus for the production of wealth. These have no relation whatever to the place where the final owner enjoys his income from the labours of the four elements. The four of them are thus in different measures related to the origin of the wealth, that is, its production as a physical product.

The Report also recognizes that failure in selling goods or services can render all the efforts of previous stages of production irrelevant:

> It may well be that productive operations up to a certain point have been well and profitably conducted and that the whole of the excellent results to this point are thrown away by bad selling.

Thus, Pillar One reflects the ideas in the Report in two ways. First, by dividing up Amount A between the source and residence jurisdictions by a formula. Second, by acknowledging the right of the market jurisdiction to some of the tax upon the income derived from selling goods or services in that market.

We may have some indication of the origin of these elements in the Report. As the reference to California suggests, this section was likely first drafted by Prof. Seligman. By 1923, over twenty US states used formulary apportionment to divide the corporate income tax base among themselves, and many of them (seventeen out of the twenty-nine who used formulary apportionment in 1929) used a sales factor as either one of the factors of the formula or even as the exclusive factor. We would therefore suggest that US state practice influenced the Report (just like it influenced the adoption of the ALS in the 1930s, since Carroll explicitly discussed and rejected it in his report to the League on the allocation of income between related parties).

8.1.2 *The Report and Pillar Two*

The major contribution of Pillar Two is acceptance of the single tax principle (STP), which states that cross-border income should not be subject to either double taxation or double non-taxation. As Chapter 6 explained, the single tax principle is also referred to as "full taxation," as it suggests that all income must be taxed once at a substantive tax rate. This principle is implemented through an agreement on a minimum global corporate tax rate and the various practical steps to be adopted by residence jurisdictions (IIR) or source jurisdictions (UTPR and QDMTT) to enforce it in practice.

The focus of the Report was the prevention of double taxation. What is remarkable is that the Report is also based on the assumption that all cross-border income should always be *fully* taxed, and therefore it implicitly adopts the STP. This can be seen clearly in that the Report barely mentions the most common method to prevent double taxation in 1923, namely, that the residence county should exempt foreign source income. This exemption method (to be distinguished from what the Report calls exemption, namely the abolition of source country taxes) was the practice of most European countries when the Report was written, but the Report explicitly does not include it among the methods, it discusses to prevent double taxation.

The reason for this omission is that the Report is based on Seligman's fervent advocacy for ability to pay taxation (rather than benefits-based taxation which would have justified a territorial regime). The Report states that as far as income taxation is concerned:

> *The ideal solution is that the individual's whole faculty should be taxed, but that it should be taxed only once, and that the liability should be divided among the tax districts according to his relative interests in each.* The individual has certain economic interests in the place of his permanent residence or domicile, as well as in the place or places where his property is situated or from which his income is derived. (Emphasis added.)

This preference for ability to pay taxation underlies the US global system under which the income tax is imposed on "all income from whatever source derived." If ability to pay is the foundational criterion for income taxation, then methods like exemption by the residence country must be rejected because they lead to double non-taxation whenever the source country does not tax, and the Report endorses full residence taxation and the abolition of source taxation as its preferred method for preventing double taxation.

This insistence on preventing double taxation by methods which do not lead to double non-taxation can be seen throughout the Report. Consider, for example, the four methods advocated for the relief of double taxation. The first method is what we would call the credit method, as adopted by the United States under the leadership of Seligman's rival Thomas Adams:

> (1) A country might deduct from the tax due from its residents any tax paid by them on their income from abroad (analogous to the United States practice in the case of its own citizens). This throws the whole burden of increased taxation in debtor countries upon the creditor country, and is opposed to the general practice observed by foreign Governments when issuing their loans. If this course were followed, Governments need no longer make provision for making the loans free of tax to non-resident investors, knowing that it will fall upon the exchequer of the creditor country. It is to be doubted whether such creditor countries as the United States, Great Britain and the Netherlands, having regard to their interests abroad, would ever agree permanently to put their exchequers at the mercy of all the unknown increases of taxation of foreign Governments. This may be called *the method of deduction for income from abroad*. (Emphasis added.)

The Report rejects this method, presumably because Seligman, Bruins, and Stamp did not favor it due to the revenue impact on residence countries (note the reference to their countries), but it also accepts it as a valid method of full ability to pay taxation.

The second method in the Report involves the source countries giving up tax jurisdiction, so all income is taxable in full by the residence country:

> (2) The extreme converse, *viz.*: that the country of origin should exempt all non-residents from taxation imposed on income drawn from sources within its borders, recognises the theoretical fact that the country wanting the money cannot successfully "tax the foreigner"; it can only shut him out. It would have the effect of increasing the flow of capital from abroad and the development of less-favoured regions. This may be called *the method of exemption for income going abroad*. (Emphasis added.)

This is the method favored by the Report as most consistent with ability to pay, and it clearly envisages full taxation by the residence country. However, the Report acknowledges that source countries are unlikely to fully give up on their right to tax foreigners, however economically ill-advised such a course of action may be:

> A survey of the whole field of recent taxation shows how completely the Governments are dominated by the desire to tax the foreigner. It seems to be clearly instinctive in laying down general principles to treat "origin" as of *first* importance, and residence as of "secondary" importance; *i.e.*, if the origin and source of income are within a country's borders, it is assumed that country has the *prime* right of taxation on that income, although it goes to some person abroad. There are a few modifications, but this is the *main* instinctive principle. From this follows the consequence that, when double taxation is involved, Governments would be prepared to give up residence rather than origin as establishing the prime right. (Emphases added.)

This is the only reference in the Report to the possibility of a pure exemption system (i.e., exemption by the residence jurisdiction), and it is unequivocally repudiated because it leads to double non-taxation and is based on outdated benefit-based notions of taxing rights that should over time be eliminated.

The third method the Report approves of is division by formula:

> (3) It may be possible by convention to divide specific taxes so that a portion should be borne by the country of origin and the remainder by the country of residence.... This is an attempt to recognise both principles and to spread the burden upon the two Governments. It would leave in an unsatisfactory position issues of State loans, and is open to many of the objections, though not to the same extent, as those raised to the first proposal. This may be called *the method of division of the tax*. (Emphasis added.)

This method also envisages *full taxation* because the tax revenue is divided between the taxing jurisdictions. In fact, the Report emphasizes that this method should never be used in a way that reduces tax below what it would be if there was only domestic income (e.g., if the source rate is below the residence rate). This result is achieved by not applying the agreed-upon formula to the tax base but rather to the revenues from the tax, so that the rate is assumed to be the same in both countries:

> *Now it is of the essence of this method that the resident shall not gain by the relief in double taxation, that is, shall not be in a better position than he would be if his income were all derived in the country where he resides*. Relief is desired only to the extent of the excess over such a sum; and therefore the essence of method 3 is that the country of residence should give relief by a definite amount that has been levied in the country of origin, with, if it is desired, a maximum for that relief equal to one-half of the rate of tax levied by the country of residence. (Emphasis added.)

Finally, there is the fourth method, which proved to be the most influential:

> (4) By convention it might be determined to attach origin taxation specifically and wholly to particular classes of investments or embodiments of wealth, such as rents of land and of houses and mortgages on real property, but to exempt the non-resident in respect of income derived from business securities. The country of residence would allow the whole of the foreign tax as a deduction from its income tax on the resident in respect of such sources of income, *but would charge other sources in full. The country of origin would retain its specific origin taxes in full.* It would be necessary to give the country of residence complete power of charging all sources except for certain specified exemptions, so that the scope of its liability to remit the tax would be easily determined, and the investor, from his total income-tax demands, would be able to deduct certain specified taxes on any real property he might have. It might be desirable to impose some limit upon the power of the country of origin to levy in future specially heavy specific origin taxes, which would unduly deplete the exchequer of the country of residence. This may be called *the method of classification and assignment of sources*. (Emphases added.)

Here too is the emphasis on *full taxation*, in this case by either the county of residence or the county of source depending on the type of income involved.

The problem with this method, as adopted in the treaties, is that unlike the other three (but like the rejected exemption by the residence country method), it gives the source jurisdiction the exclusive right to tax certain types of income. So, to the extent it does not do so, the principle of taxation based on ability to pay is violated. That is presumably one reason why the Report prefers for both methods 3 and 4 to have full taxation by the residence country and then a sharing of the proceeds with the source country, rather than exclusive taxation by the source country.

To sum up, the Report implicitly endorses the idea of *full taxation* (i.e., the STP) and explicitly rejects the most common method of preventing double taxation prevalent at the time, namely, the exemption of foreign source income by the residence jurisdiction. In this way, it is consistent with Pillar Two as well as with the original statement of the STP in the preamble to the 1927 model.

***

As we reach the centennial of the Report, its continuing influence can be seen despite the radical changes in the ITR in the past decade. Specifically, the Report is congruent with Pillar One in its acceptance of formulas as a valid method of allocating income among taxing jurisdictions and in its acceptance of the right of the market jurisdiction to tax income from sales into it. The Report is congruent with Pillar Two in its insistence on full taxation of cross-border income. In this general sense, it can truly be said about the ITR that "plus ca change, plus c'est la meme chose (the more it changes, the more it is the same thing)."

8.2 THE ORIGINS OF PILLAR ONE

The main conceptual innovation in Pillar One is Amount A, which is to be taxable in the market jurisdiction regardless of the PE threshold and the ALS. This idea is derived from the use of the sales factor by US states to allocate corporate income as part of formulary apportionment. All US states that tax corporate income use a sales factor with no requirement for physical presence, and many of them use a sales factor exclusively (i.e., tax all corporate income based on sales).

In 1993, the first author first proposed applying this method to international taxation. The first author further developed this idea in a more extensive fashion in 1996. In 1997, the first author incorporated it into the first extensive article on how to tax "electronic commerce," i.e., internet-based digital activities.[3]

Below is the excerpt:

> The PE threshold, as Jeffrey Owens points out, may have represented an acceptable compromise when it was first crafted because it was created when a

3 Reuven S. Avi-Yonah, *International Taxation of Electronic Commerce*, 52 TAX L. REV. 507 (1997).

> physical presence was necessary to conduct significant business operations in a jurisdiction. Solicitation through the mail, or through independent agents, was certainly possible, but it had obvious drawbacks: Technology only allowed for slow and intermittent communications between businesses and customers. However, electronic commerce fundamentally changed the business landscape. Interactivity, speed, and electronic payment meant that commerce was possible on a much grander scale without any physical presence in the consumer's jurisdiction.
>
> If the goal is to tax income from electronic commerce in a way that preserves the underlying rationale of the PE rule and the benefits principle, a different type of threshold is required – one that is not linked to physical presence. This threshold could be a de minimis amount of sales in the jurisdiction, as suggested by Walter Hellerstein and others in the state tax context. For example, the rule could be that if a seller in electronic commerce has gross sales of $1 million or less from a given tax jurisdiction, it would not be subject to taxation at source and instead subject to taxation in the market jurisdiction. The same rule also could be used to define a US trade or business in the context of electronic commerce (in fact, it would be highly advisable to have a uniform definition of these two terms, as is the norm in many other countries). The figure chosen should be high enough to exclude most small businesses as the growth of electronic commerce has enabled many small businesses to sell internationally, and the burden of compliance with various countries' tax laws could be too much for them to bear. In addition, the threshold should be high enough to ensure that, in most cases, the income derived from the jurisdiction would exceed the costs of complying with its tax laws to avoid driving businesses out of jurisdictions.
>
> Our recommendation is for a gross sales threshold, rather than a net income threshold. We recommend this approach primarily for administrability reasons. A net figure would require a tax administration to know the taxpayer's income from sales into a jurisdiction, which it may not have the information to determine, while the gross amount can be determined from the records of other parties (the customers). For the same reason, a threshold based on a percentage of total sales worldwide raises its own set of administrability challenges since it requires knowledge available only to the taxpayer.

This is like the way Amount A is defined for purposes of Pillar One, except that it envisages that all the income of the multinational would be taxed in this way, without regard to the PE threshold or the ALS. In later work, the first author proposed limiting the sales-based amount to excess returns and keeping the ALS for normal returns, similarly to Pillar One.

8.3 THE ORIGINS OF PILLAR TWO

Pillar Two is based on what the first author called in 1997 the "Single Tax Principle." The single tax principle can be traced all the way to the adoption of the foreign tax credit by the United States in 1918 and the development of the first model tax treaty by the League of Nations in 1927. Chapter 6 and the first author's previous work on electronic commerce described the historical evolution of the single tax principle from its origins with the development of the foreign tax credit, through the tax treaties developed by Stanley Surrey in the 1960s, and ultimately to Pillar Two.

Below is the excerpt of the first author's previous work:

> International income taxation involves two basic questions: First, what is the appropriate level of taxation that should be levied on income from cross-border transactions? And, second, how are the resulting revenues to be divided among taxing jurisdictions?
>
> The answer to the first question is the single tax principle. Income from cross-border transactions should be subject to tax only once. However, taxing cross-border income once also means that it should not be undertaxed or (at the extreme) be subject to no tax at all.
>
> The appropriate rate of tax in line with the single tax principle is determined by the second principle of international taxation, the benefits principle. The benefits principle assigns the primary right to tax active business income to source jurisdictions and the primary right to tax passive income to residence jurisdictions. Therefore, the rate of tax for purposes of the single tax principle is generally the source rate for active business income and the residence rate for passive income. However, when the primary jurisdiction abandons their responsibility and refrains from taxation, residual taxation by other (residence or source) jurisdictions is possible and may be necessary to prevent under taxation. Such residual taxation means that all income from cross-border transactions should be taxed at least at the source rate, which tends to be lower than the residence rate, but at no more than the residence rate.
>
> As an initial matter, the normative basis for the single tax principle assumes that most countries would like to maintain both a personal income tax and a corporate income tax. In fact, most countries have maintained and continue to maintain their existing personal and corporate income taxes.
>
> Given a preference for imposing both a personal and a corporate income tax on domestically derived income of individuals and corporations, it becomes relatively easy to establish why the single tax principle is justified as a goal of the ITR. From a theoretical perspective, if income derived from cross-border transactions is taxed more heavily than domestic income, the added tax burden creates an inefficient incentive to invest domestically. This will move capital and resources away from more efficient transactions to adjust to the new tax burden. This proposition is widely accepted and underlies the effort, which by now is about a century old, to prevent or alleviate international double taxation.
>
> The opposite is also true: If income from cross-border transactions is taxed less heavily than domestic income, this creates an inefficient incentive to invest internationally rather than at home. The deadweight loss created by undertaxation is the same as that from overtaxation.

> In addition, there is also a strong equity argument against undertaxation of cross-border income. Undertaxation of cross-border income violates both horizontal and vertical equity when compared to higher tax rates imposed on domestic source income and on domestic labor income. In this case, the argument that equity violations tend to turn into efficiency issues does not hold, because labor is less mobile than capital and wage earners typically do not have the ability to transform their domestic wages into foreign source income.
>
> On a practical level, the single tax principle can be justified because double taxation leads to tax rates that can be extremely high and stifle international investment. Zero taxation, on the other hand, offers an opportunity to avoid domestic taxation by investing abroad, and therefore threatens to erode the national tax base. T. S. Adams, the architect of the foreign tax credit and a major influence in shaping the ITR, recognized both issues in the 1920s. In justifying the foreign tax credit, Adams wrote "the state which with a fine regard for the rights of the taxpayer takes pains to relieve double taxation, may fairly take measures to ensure that the person or property pays at least one tax." Contrary to an exemption system, Adams's credit operated to eliminate double taxation by both source and residence jurisdictions but preserved residual residence-based jurisdiction to maintain the single tax principle.
>
> The practical justification for the single tax principle can be seen most easily if one imagines a world with only two countries, A and B, and only two companies, X (a resident of A) and Y (a resident of B). If both A and B tax the foreign-source income of their residents and domestic source income of foreigners, and neither gives relief from double taxation, then both X and Y would minimize their taxes by only deriving domestic source income (since any foreign tax would be an added burden). The result would be adequate revenues collected by both A and B, but no cross-border trade or investment. On the other hand, suppose both A and B exempted from tax both foreign source income and domestic source income of foreigners (a not inconceivable proposition in many developing countries, which tax residents territorially and grant tax holidays to foreign investors to attract foreign capital). In that case, the way for both X and Y to minimize their taxes would be to derive their entire income from cross-border transactions. The result would be adequate cross-border trade, but no revenues for A or B. In a world where international trade and investment are important but taxes (unlike tariffs) cannot be reduced to zero, the single tax principle is the best solution to this dilemma.

The underlying idea of Pillar Two can be traced back to the concept of the single tax principle. Specifically, Pillar Two envisages residual taxation by the residence (or source) jurisdiction when the tax imposed by the source (or residence) jurisdiction falls below a specified minimum level. This is the same idea as the one the first author developed in 1997: "When the primary jurisdiction refrains from taxation, however, residual taxation by other (residence or source) jurisdictions is possible and may be necessary to prevent under taxation."

8.4 CONCLUSION: A NEW CHAPTER OF THE INTERNATIONAL TAXATION

The current revolution in international taxation, as reflected in BEPS 2.0 Pillars One and Two, is less revolutionary than many have argued. Specifically, the main innovation of Pillar One builds on the US state sales–based apportionment, which dates back to the 1930s and which we have argued should be applied to international taxation. Pillar Two is based on the single tax principle, which dates to the origins of the ITR in the 1920s and which the first author articulated and developed since the 1990s. Thus, just as Tocqueville argued about the French Revolution, the revolution in international taxation builds on elements that existed in the old regime it seeks to replace.

Although the new ITR is less revolutionary built upon existing elements, there are new elements worth appreciating. The last section of this book will examine those new elements. The first is the new dynamics in the trilemma – open economy (globalization), tax competition, and social safety net. The minimum tax and Pillar Two are pursued to end the tax competition. If Pillar Two is successful and becomes effective, can we get rid of the tax competition in the trilemma and conclude that one of the major problems of the ITR is now resolved? One may think that, at least in theory, the answer is positive. But it would also be naïve to stop worrying about the flawed ITR. For example, Wei Cui explains that the existing narrative of the ITR emphasizes the mobility of capital as a source of tax competition, but he further argues that such narrative justifying Pillar Two lacks strong empirical evidence.[4] There might be good explanations, other than tax competition, of why countries offer tax holidays and reduce tax rates. Also, there are other important aspects of the ITR – such as (i) exemption or credit methods for relieving double taxation for outbound investments and (ii) inbound tax rules that resemble optimal tariffs and other instruments for taxing location-specific rent. Cui asserts that because of such prevailing narratives blaming tax competition as the major problem of the ITR, we might have overlooked more important ways where countries cooperate, or fail to cooperate, to address other important aspects of the ITR. The authors still believe that tax competition is one of the major problems of the old ITR and the new ITR has a good chance to overcome it by adopting the STP. However, Cui's argument points out that we have not made enough efforts to revisit other problems that will be discussed later in this section. In addition, implementing the 15 percent global minimum tax is not a simple task at all. Due to the complexity of the rules and many substantial carve-outs, we may end up having a global minimum tax that is far from perfect. It may be time to explore other sources of problems in international tax, such as disguised export subsidies, check-the-box rules, and transfer pricing rules.

[4] Wei Cui, *The Mirage of Mobile Capital* (May 7, 2023).

The second new element is the ITR's update to address the tax challenges in the digital economy. The global deal attempted to deal with the new challenges in the digital economy by adopting Pillar One, but many commentators, including the authors, do not expect that Pillar One would be successful. The United States will not join the multilateral convention to implement Pillar One, and the individual agreement that the United States made with several countries to pause the DSTs will likely expire. Then the DSTs unilaterally implemented by countries are likely to prevail. DSTs may be a solution to update the revenue allocation rules in the digital economy by allowing market countries to collect more revenue. Nonetheless, it is far from a systemic solution for the ITR. To be more specific, Pillar One aims to update two rules of the ITR – physical presence requirement and revenue allocation rules. DSTs may solve the second problem by allocating more revenue to market countries. However, DSTs are local and consumption tax, and the international income tax still needs to eliminate the physical presence requirement.

The third new element is the different dynamics in revenue competition. In the old ITR, the tax revenue was allocated between source and residence countries based on the BP. However, there is now a third competing jurisdiction – market countries – consisting of both developing and developed countries. The old ITR gives preferences to residence countries in revenue allocation, which harms global equity because many residence countries are developed countries. Many commentators and developing countries argued and proposed that source taxation should be strengthened, but there was not much success. However, the emergence of market jurisdictions changed such dynamics because market countries consist of both developing and developed countries. Consider the tension between the United States and Europe with respect to taxing US Big Tech.[5] European countries challenged the residence-based tax rules and the resulting revenue allocation for taxing US multinationals because they are market countries in this context. When European countries landed on the losing side, a strong momentum was created to revisit the revenue allocation rule. The United States and Europe confronted each other when several European countries enacted DSTs. Then they temporarily reunited to pause DSTs and instead pursue Pillar One, because Pillar One may reward European countries with more revenue for taxing US Big Tech but still preserve residence taxation in other sectors. But such temporary reunite may end if the United States does not join the multilateral convention to implement Pillar One. The departing interest between the United States and Europe may create interesting new dynamics to change the revenue allocation rules in the new ITR.

The fourth new element is the strengthening of multilateral cooperation in international tax matters. But the level of success varies between procedural and substantive matters: We can observe more success in cooperation in the former than the latter. The success in multilateral cooperation in procedural matters is explained

[5] Ruth Mason, *The Transformation of International Tax*, 114 AM. J. INT'L L. 353, 394 (2020).

in Chapter 3. The AEOI, CRS, and CbC reporting significantly enhanced transparency in tax administration. On the other hand, there is only half-success in substantive matters, such as hybrid mismatches and digital economy, as demonstrated in Chapter 4. This makes sense in a way that enhanced transparency is a necessary condition to most of the substance-related reforms. But also, where we lack information, the reforms are not fully enforceable. For example, hybrid mismatches rules under BEPS 1.0 Action 2 are neither commended in practice nor effectively curb the aggressive tax planning in place. CFC rules under BEPS 1.0 Action 3 have similar problems. BEPS 2.0 Pillars One and Two attempt to deal with substantive matters again, but it is uncertain how successful they will be. The road to cooperation is something we should continue to deliberate in the new ITR.

The fifth new element is the shift from bilateralism to the dynamics between multilateralism and unilateralism. The old ITR was based on bilateralism. Hundreds of bilateral tax treaties were the major source of international tax rules. The new ITR emerged with multilateral cooperation to enhance transparency in tax administration. Such multilateralism continues in BEPS 2.0. Rebecca Kysar explains that multilateralism was first popular among trade agreements, but that seems out of reach now and instead "tax multilateralism" is ascendant.[6] However, despite recent attempts at achieving true multilateralism, we are doubtful about its prospects. The AEOI and CRS achieved the momentum when the United States enacted FATCA. The authors described this phenomenon as "constructive unilateralism." Also, the MLI is a mechanism for changing bilateral treaties, rather than a multilateral convention, and important countries like the United States have not joined. Pillar One requires a true multilateral convention, but the United States will not join, and neither will many countries that wish to keep their unilateral DSTs. In these circumstances, we doubt that a multilateral convention can be enacted, because it was designed primarily to tax US multinationals and eliminate DSTs. In addition, many recommendations of BEPS 1.0 and Pillar Two are implemented by domestic legislation of individual countries, which cannot be considered multilateralism. Perhaps "coordinated unilateralism" suggested by Ruth Mason would be a better term to describe such implementation of agreed-upon standards via domestic law.[7] Hence, it would be more accurate that we are experiencing the new dynamics between multilateralism and unilateralism.

A difficult question on the dynamics between multilateralism and unilateralism is whether the former is better than the latter. Intuitively and ideally, multilateralism would be better than unilateralism. Consider the prisoner's dilemma. Multilateralism would bring an optimal result if successful. But the reality is far from ideal. In the second-best world, unilateralism might happen more often, and

[6] Rebecca M. Kysar, *The Global Tax Deal and the New International Economic Order* (2023) (on file with the authors).

[7] Mason, *supra* note 5, at 374.

sometimes it is effective as shown in the success in FATCA/IGAs. Also, Pillar Two is more promising than Pillar One because its implementation depends not on the MIL but on unilateral measures (i.e., domestic legislation). This might posit a provocative question of whether effective unilateralism would be better than ineffective multilateralism. We believe that this is an important question and should not be dismissed in the new ITR. Morally speaking, this question is less problematic than a popular question in political science comparing effective authoritarianism and ineffective democracy, because international taxation presupposes tax sovereignty of individual countries that justifies unilateralism. We cannot answer for sure that one is better than another. Rather, the answer may depend on what's going on in international tax when we ask that question. When tax competition prevailed, the world would have been better off with multilateral efforts like Pillar Two. When the outcome of BEPS 1.0 was not satisfactory, many countries thought that they would be better off by relying on unilateral measures, like DSTs. When DSTs became prevalent, the opposing countries wanted to seek Pillar One, a multilateral effort. This answer may not be satisfactory because it is only descriptive and ex post. We may never be able to offer a normative answer. But it is worth noting that it does not make sense to pursue multilateralism for the sake of multilateralism.

The last, but not least, new element of the new ITR is the emphasis on the equity issues. The old ITR was developed by the League of Nations in the era of imperialism, and there was little room to protect the interest of developing countries. Later in the twentieth century, the international tax discussion was led by the OECD, also known as the "Rich Countries' Club." The new ITR attempts to strengthen the source-based taxation as shown in the QDMTT of Pillar Two and market jurisdiction's interest as shown in Pillar One. The OECD/G20 expanded the participating countries by creating the Inclusive Framework, and so over 140 countries signed on to the global tax deal. Nonetheless, developing countries criticize the current effort as not enough. The Africa Group issued a strong call for all countries to sit down as equals and negotiate a fair, effective, and truly global tax deal. As a result, in November 2023, the UN General Assembly voted 125–48 for the resolution to create a framework convention for a more inclusive discussion on international taxation. Nine countries abstained. The vote contributes to a debate about which forum between the OECD and the UN is better suited to conduct the work on international tax cooperation. Developed countries are adamant that discussions on international taxation should remain at the OECD and that developing countries do have a say in the OECD's Inclusive Framework. It is too early to reach a verdict on which forum we endorse. However, the hostile comment by developed countries toward the UN's movement would be improper given the insufficient efforts and results toward equity in the old ITR. Regardless of which forum countries would resort to eventually in the new ITR, there might be some wisdom for the purposes of effective negotiation. The forum would need an impartial secretariat and inclusive voting system – ideally consensus. Also, the pace of negotiations should be reasonable. In fact, the pace of negotiations in BEPS 2.0 was too quick, and there was not great communication between politicians and technical experts. Also, the negotiated reforms should avoid complex rules and strive for administrative simplicity. Complex rules not only bar the effective implementation but also curb the participation of developing countries suffering from lack of resources.

In conclusion, the new ITR is less revolutionary than many expect. But there are many new elements so that we cannot treat the new ITR as a mere evolution. The two principles that the old ITR was based on were transformed: The STP survived in the changed form of Pillar Two, and the BP survived but has shown many limitations and will go through more changes. Additional new elements of the ITR, such as the emphasis of equity issue and adaptation to the digital economy, may not be enough to make the new ITR fully adapt to the twenty-first-century political economy. But as in every evolution or revolution, those are the vestiges that the ITR has struggled to adapt to amid the changing conditions. This book records such historical moments that open a new chapter of the ITR.

The new ITR has been challenged by the United States under the Trump administration. On his first day in office president Trump signed executive orders threatening retaliatory taxes and tariffs against countries adopting DSTs and the UTPR. It remains to be seen what the impact of such actions by the United States might be, but at least Pillar Two is likely to survive, as are elements of Pillar One. The new ITR is here, and no single country is likely to be able to repeal it.

Index

For EU product safety concerns, contact us at Calle de José Abascal, 56–1°, 28003 Madrid, Spain or eugpsr@cambridge.org.

www.ingramcontent.com/pod-product-compliance
Lightning Source LLC
LaVergne TN
LVHW011811200926
848484LV00005B/1142

* 9 7 8 1 0 0 9 3 3 1 8 4 5 *